ON LAW AND REASON

LAW AND PHILOSOPHY LIBRARY

Managing Editors

VOLUME 8

ALEKSANDER PECZENIK

Lund University, Sweden

ON LAW AND REASON

KLUWER ACADEMIC PUBLISHERS

DORDRECHT / BOSTON / LONDON

Library of Congress Cataloging in Publication Data

Peczenik, Aleksander.
    [Rätten och förnuftet. English]
    On law and reason / Aleksander Peczenik.
        p.   cm. -- (Law and philosophy library)
    Rev. translation of: Rätten och förnuftet.
    Includes bibliographical references.
    ISBN 0-7923-0444-6
    1. Law--Methodology.   2. Law--Philosophy.   I. Title.   II. Series.
    K212.P43513   1989
    340'.1--dc20   89-37808

ISBN 0-7923-0444-6

Published by Kluwer Academic Publishers,
P.O. Box 17, 3300 AA Dordrecht, The Netherlands.

Kluwer Academic Publishers incorporates
the publishing programmes of
D. Reidel, Martinus Nijhoff, Dr W. Junk and MTP Press.

Sold and distributed in the U.S.A. and Canada
by Kluwer Academic Publishers,
101 Philip Drive, Norwell, MA 02061, U.S.A.

In all other countries, sold and distributed
by Kluwer Academic Publishers Group,
P.O. Box 322, 3300 AH Dordrecht, The Netherlands.

printed on acid free paper

Printed in the Netherlands

Preface

This is an outline of a coherence theory of law. Its basic ideas are: reasonable support and weighing of reasons. All the rest is a commentary.

I am most grateful to many colleagues for extensive discussions and criticism concerning various ideas presented in this book, in particular to Aulis Aarnio, Robert Alexy and Horacio Spector. Others to whom I am indebted for comments are more numerous than it would be possible to mention here. I will do no more than to record my gratitude to the readers of the publisher whose penetrating remarks helped me to reorganise the manuscript.

A Scandinavian reader must be informed that the present book constitutes a modified version of my Swedish work <u>Rätten och förnuftet</u>. However, the content has been radically changed. I hope that the alterations make the main point of the work clearer. Especially, the key sections 2.3, 2.4, 3.2.4, 5.4, 5.8 and Chapter 4 are entirely new.

The book contains extensive examples of legal reasoning and reports of various moral and legal theories. Though relevant, this material could make it difficult for the reader to focus attention on the main line of argument. To avoid this, a smaller printing-type size has been chosen for such a background information.

Lund, 18 May, 1989

Aleksander Peczenik

CONTENTS

INTRODUCTION

In his book "Juridikens metodproblem" (Methodological Problems in Law), Aleksander Peczenik describes the concept of "neorealism" with the help of six criteria: (1) research in jurisprudence should utilise varied disciplines in law, philosophy and the social sciences; (2) these varied and multifaceted disciplines can and must be utilised particularly effectively in an analysis of the fundamental legal concepts (for example "valid law"); (3) the analysis should be deliberately neutral in respect to philosophical conflicts; (4) this type of analysis should be adapted to numerous examples of the use of concepts in law; (5) the author uses such an analysis as the point of departure for a description of established rules of legal interpretation and calls this "practical jurisprudence"; and (6) the analysis can also be used in a comparison between legal research and the established scientific disciplines.

The author calls jurisprudence that meets the conditions described above "juristic theory of law". It is "juristic", since it is based on legal research, and it is "theory" because it is more general and analytical than ordinary legal research. "Neorealism" is another term for this juristic theory of law. However, Peczenik does not approve of the view of Legal Realism which demands that legal research must avoid all loose and "metaphysical" concepts. It is the task of neorealism to specify what is valuable in legal research and alive in legal practice. Neorealism is constructive and not, as classical Legal Realism, destructive.

Since over ten years, Aleksander Peczenik has modified his theories in many ways. Yet, the basic attitude is the same as in the beginning of the 1970s. Also today, Aleksander Peczenik can be characterised as a neorealist. In the following, I shall seek to provide a general description of the legal, jurisprudential and philosophical background which renders Peczenik´s neorealism understandable from another point of view than that he himself uses. My perspective is to a large extent that of a collaborator, as I have had the privilege to work together with Peczenik for almost fifteen years. This fact has both advantages and disadvantages for the present introduction. The advantage is that it makes it possible to "see" through Peczenik´s conceptual apparatus, which is both technical and complex. Because

of this, it is easier than it might otherwise have been
to understand the sound basic ideas which colour his
entire theoretical system. On the other hand, it is
precisely this closeness as a collaborator that is a
source of weakness. The introduction can, in this sense,
become subjectively coloured.

2. The purpose of this introduction is the following.
First, I shall briefly define the concept of legal
dogmatics and then I shall use this definition to analyse
certain basic elements in the very complicated phenomenon
known as legal interpretation. This will lead us to
fundamental problems concerning legal **truth** and in legal
knowledge. It is not possible to understand neorealism
without entering into these cornerstones of Peczenik´s
world of ideas.

3. In the ordinary legal usage, the term "legal
research" refers to at least four different types of
scientific activity. We can distinguish between the
history of law, the sociology of law, comparative
jurisprudence and legal dogmatics. Of these, the last two
are close relatives. The difference lies in the object of
the activity: comparative law describes, analyses and
explains legal norms in force in other countries, while
legal dogmatics concentrates on a particular legal order.
Sociology of law has a special position in the family of
legal disciplines. It is not particularly interested in
the interpretation of legal norms in force; instead, it
concentrates on certain **regularities** in legal society,
for example in respect of the behaviour of people, or the
effects legal norms have in society. Sociology of law
uses special research methods (empirical, statistical
etc.). This means that there is a clear line of
demarcation between legal dogmatics and sociology of law.
On the other hand, sociology of law is closely related to
history of law. The latter uses, in many respects, the
same methods as does the former: it describes, analyses
and explains historical material in the same way as does
the sociology of law - or at least it can do so. The
difference between the two disciplines lies in the object
of inquiry. History of law is interested in the past,
while the sociology of law focuses on the present
society.

From the point of view of our analysis, the difference
between sociology of law and legal dogmatics is central.
Legal dogmatics is a typical interpretative discipline.
It uses facts provided by sociology of law, but the
interpretation itself has a non-empirical nature.
According to normal usage, legal dogmatics has two

functions: to interpret and to systematise legal norms. In Peczenik´s book, systematisation is dealt with only as an implicit condition for legal interpretation.

On the other hand, legal dogmatics is legal dogmatics precisely due to the fact that it interprets and systematises legal norms. Legal dogmatics has this specific role in the division of labour in society. No other discipline offers practical legal life the same information. It is not, for example, the function of sociology of law. Systematisation in different areas (family law, other civil law, criminal law, and so on) is a necessary tool for all legal interpretation. As I shall argue later on, systematisation is the theoretical aspect of legal dogmatics. Systematisation plays the same role in legal dogmatics as the theoretical social sciences in sociology. From this point of view, legal interpretation is the practical aspect of legal dogmatics, and it is primarily directed towards practical goals. Interpretation can be compared to empirical research in the social sciences.

Theory and practice work together in all fields of science. Theoretical structure, by necessity, influences practice. Theoretical concepts, theories and so on are tools of the scientist. Just as the carpenter needs his hammer, saw and nails, the scientist needs his scientific tools. This is also the case in legal dogmatics. For this reason, interplay between interpretation and systematisation is inherent in all serious descriptions of legal dogmatics. Consequently, systematisation is implicit in everything Peczenik said about interpretation. At the end of this introduction, I shall attempt to explain certain aspects of this question.

4. The concept of "interpretation" has many senses. In the following, I use this concept to refer to a process where one must **choose** between different alternative meanings. Many factors can determine such a choice. They are all derived from everyday language, which is the medium used by the legislator. Language is open, vague, ambiguous and so on, and there are gaps and inner inconsistencies in law. To take an example, ambiguity lends richness to language and makes it possible for us to adapt ourselves to different circumstances. On the other hand, ambiguity is a very common origin of interpretation.

Schematically, the point of departure of interpretation can be described, as follows. Firstly, a statutory provision can have many possible interpretations. It is the task of the person interpreting the law to choose

between them. Secondly, it may be unclear which of
several provisions should be applied to a problematic
case. This can be called the problem of qualification.
In legal dogmatics, the first case is more common, as the
point of departure is often an ambiguous text of law. In
judicial practice, the situation is typically closer to
the second case. For example in a criminal case, the
problem can be to choose between different ways of
describing the act, and thus between different penal
provisions. Despite the differences, the nature of legal
thought is the same in both cases. It is only the point
of departure that distinguishes the two: a legal text or
a concrete case.

5.   Certain   fundamental   questions   of   legal
interpretation can best be illustrated if one analyses
the activity of the judge. It is a part of the role of
the judge within the legal machinery to exercise the
power to make decisions in all cases brought before him.
This power has a necessary link with the coercion which
is typical of law. Indeed, the law has been often defined
as   a   coercive   order.   As   a   counterweight   to   his
decision-making power, the judge has the obligation to
decide all cases that are brought to the court. The judge
must make a decision, even if he is not aware of the
proper content of the law. And, as a consequence of the
nature of everyday language, it is not possible for the
judge to know immediately which solution is the lawful
one. In such situations citizens in general and the
litigants in particular naturally expect a solution that
fulfils the demands for **legal certainty**. What, then, does
legal certainty mean?

The reformer Olaus Petri provides certain indications
in his judicial rules of 1540 which, even today, are an
important measure in the Nordic concept of law. Olaus
Petri took up arms against **arbitrariness**. According to
him, arbitrary judicial activity did not serve the
people. The meaning of "arbitrariness" was left open in
his work. However, on the basis of an overall analysis of
the judicial rules, it is possible to say that
arbitrariness is the same thing as random elements in
judicial activity. According to modern usage, this means
that the judicial decision must be predictable; indeed,
predictability is one of the fundamental conditions for
human activity. If judicial decisions are unpredictable,
it is impossible for citizens to make predictions related
to their own future activity.

On the other hand, the avoidance of arbitrariness is
not the only condition for legal certainty. In the Nordic

legal culture, legal certainty also contains certain
material demands. Already Olaus Petri referred to "the
good and benefit of the common people" when he talked
about avoiding arbitrariness. In Finish philosophy of
law, Otto Brusiin has emphasised this side of the
problem. Briefly, the material demands can be described
in the following manner.

Let us assume that we are a party of a legal dispute.
What - apart of predictability - are our fundamental
expectations regarding the court? Presumably, the
majority of citizens in a democratic society would answer
that they assume that the decision shall be both lawful
and acceptable. The judge must make his decision in
accordance with the law in force and, at the same time,
take into consideration the values that are generally
accepted in society. Thus, the concept of legal certainty
involves two central elements, law and values or, in
order to use everyday language, law and morality. This is
particularly typical for the so-called welfare state.
Aleksander Peczenik has grasped this point. For him, the
connection between the legal and the moral is the central
problem. The concept of legal certainty ties this
connection with certain elementary and fundamental
phenomena in society. The "alliance" between law and
morality thus has deep roots in the legal culture. For
this reason, analysis of the background of legal
interpretation is always, in a way, a culture analysis.

6. How can a judge fulfil his duty to base his
decisions on uncertain information and, at the same time,
achieve maximal legal certainty? We have already observed
that the judge must choose between different alternative
interpretations of the law. However, it is not enough
that he simply chooses and then announces the judgment. A
justification must also be given for the judgment. Why?
Even a few decades ago, all Western European countries
were in many ways and to varying degrees authoritarian.
Citizens blindly relied on authority, the church, the
court system, the administrative machinery and so on.
Especially after the Second World War, this faith in
authority decreased. There are many clear signs of this
development. Certain sociological studies in the United
States and the OECD countries note that, among other
things, only a minority of citizens have confidence in
the administrative authorities. The same trend applies to
the courts even though they continue to enjoy more
confidence than other institutions in society. As Gunnar
Bergholtz has noted, the demand for justification of
decisions thus has its roots in the development of

society. Authority on its own is no longer sufficient.
Every institution, the courts included, must repeatedly
regain the confidence of citizens, and this can only be
done by giving justification for decisions. Reasons must
be given for decisions, and citizens trust the reasons,
not the decision alone. Thus it is not surprising that
theory of law all over the world is today interested in
legal interpretation and argumentation. These background
factors also explain the basic components of Aleksander
Peczenik´s line of thought. The target of his analysis is
always the process of justification.

7.   Justification   can   be   examined   in   different
perspectives.   One   can   describe   the   process   of
interpretation. Doing this, theorists are interested in
the so-called "context of discovery", that is, the way in
which the decision came about. The other possibility is
to   explain   why   certain   interpretation   has   been
formulated. The explanation can be either causal or
teleological. In the latter case, one attempts at making
interpretation and interpretative process understandable.
For   example,   one   might   refer   to   certain   goals   that
necessarily   bring   about   a   certain   type   of   decision.
Aleksander   Peczenik   has   chosen   a   third   perspective,
common   in   the   international   discussion,   a   perspective
which can be called the "context of justification".

The problem of justification is complex. Legal theory
can be interested in the **factual** structure or process of
justification, typical for a court or legal dogmatics. To
this extent, one might speak about the description of
justification. There are considerable problems involved
in this. The greatest is that the factual justification
varies from one legal system to another. On the other
hand,   it   is   possible   that   a   judicial   decision   is
explicitly justified in one way even though it has been
based on other grounds, not openly stated. However, it is
not a task of legal theory to describe the justification
of court decisions. Such a description belongs more to
the   sociology   of   law   than   to   legal   theory.   In   all
sciences, the role of theory is to construct **models** to be
used in practical activity. Everyday scientific work can
then more or less fulfil the demands of the model, and
theory   has   described   the   ideal   which   serves   as   the
measure for what is (good) science. The same applies to
legal theory as a theory of legal dogmatics or judicial
activity. Aleksander Peczenik´s work is a typical attempt
to construct a model for judicial interpretation.

The model is not arbitrary. As we could note in
connection with the analysis of the concept of legal

certainty, this model of interpretation has deep roots in Western European culture. It corresponds to the most important expectations that people in our cultural circle have. Georg Henrik von Wright has said that such a model cannot be proven. It can only be more or less adequate. If a model as a theoretical construct violates common usage of language, framework of behaviour or implicit expectations, it cannot work in our culture.

8. There are two levels in Peczenik's model. He distinguishes between two different types of justification, (1) contextually sufficient justification and (2) deep justification, in other words justification of justification. The former describes what legal interpretation is. The latter states how we can justify the evaluation of legal interpretation as reasonable and beneficial for legal society. In contextually sufficient justification, we come across the concepts of "jump" and "transformation" which occupy a key position in Aleksander Peczenik's thinking. It would be quite justified to say that these concepts are the most contested of his constructs. The doctrine of transformation has been much discussed in international philosophy of law. There are many serious misunderstandings regarding this concept. In order to give the reader a better possibility of proper understanding this doctrine, I shall deliberately simplify it.

Let us assume an interpretative situation in which A, who is interpreting a law, has reached a result, R, supported by a certain justification, J. The problem is how R **follows** from J. Is there a bridge that connects the justification with the result? In legal interpretation, justification is based on sources of law, such as statutes, precedents, legislative materials etc. How is it possible to reach a certain interpretation with the help of sources of law? In this connection, Jerzy Wróblewski has written about two types of justification, **internal** and **external**. Both belong to contextually sufficient justification.

Wróblewski describes internal justification schematically:

$$
\begin{array}{l}
S1 \ldots Sn \\
I1 \ldots In \\
\underline{V1 \ldots Vn} \\
R
\end{array}
$$

In this diagram, S stands for the sources of law,
including the interpreted statute, together with relevant
factual circumstances; I stands for rules and principles
of legal interpretation; V stands for valuations and R
stands for the juristic conclusion. Wróblewski´s diagram
provides   the   following   information.   Internal
justification is guided by rules. Its result is a
deductive consequence of the justification. On the other
hand, legal interpretation often requires valuation. This
is necessary, e.g., because the sources of law must be
placed in a certain order of priority. Moreover, the
person interpreting the law may be forced to rely upon
analogy. In other cases he must rely on moral grounds,
and so on. In this way, valuations are to be found in the
justificatory material.

It is always possible to reconstruct (ex post facto)
the internal justification as a logically correct
inference, where the conclusion follows from a certain
legal norm, the factual material, certain rules of legal
interpretation and a valuation. The problem remains,
however, why the premises have been stated precisely in
the actual way. Here we meet external justification, that
is, justification of the choice of premises. One can
argue that the really difficult problem of legal
interpretation concerns the external justification. Let
us recall legal certainty. The central demand of legal
certainty is not fulfilled if the premises are selected
arbitrarily.

The internal and the external justification jointly
elucidate the concept of transformation. In our example,
internal and external justification resulted in the
transformation from the interpreted statute to the
juristic conclusion, R. Let us ask why A, in interpreting
the statute, utilises a specific legal norm as his first
premise. The legal norm need not match the wording of the
statute. However, it is possible to refer to another
source of law, for example to the travaux préparatoires
or a precedent: in this way a new inference can be
constructed; the first premise in the first inference is
the conclusion of the second inference. This means that
the first premise is justified by referring to a new
source of law. In this way we get a chain of inferences
that finally create acceptable external justification.
The transformation has become justified.

The concept of "transformation" is only a practical way
of describing certain key questions in legal
interpretation. The central problem is whether legal
interpretation is a purely deductive operation, or rather

a puzzle in which various deductive inferences fit together in a reasonable, though not deductive way. Here we come to the key questions in Peczenik´s work: coherence. All justification is a concrete whole. In this respect, justification is comparable to a puzzle where the different pieces find their proper place in the moment when one obtains a general view of the outlines of the figure. The difference between an ordinary puzzle and legal justification lies in the fact that the former has a predetermined picture while the latter is more problematic: it is impossible to demonstrate which picture is the correct one. The ultimate measure is whether or not the legal justification as a whole is accepted in legal society. The core of legal truth is to be found in this relativism.

9. The doctrine of transformation has also another dimension. Legal dogmatics interprets and the courts apply <u>valid</u> legal norms, that is the law in force. In everyday practice, there is no need to ask whether or not a legal norm is valid. The lawyers take for granted that it is. It would be even more strange to ask about the content of the concept of legal validity; only law theorists are interested in this question. On the other hand, it is the purpose of legal theory to construct a coherent total picture of the legal order. For this reason, the problem of the law in force is an important one for theorists.

Hans Kelsen´s ideas about the structure of the legal order as a pyramid of norms provides a useful point of departure. According to Kelsen, a "lower" norm is (formally) valid if is it has been created on the basis of a higher norm; e.g., a law is in force if the Parliament has followed the Constitution when passing it. This relationship is thus not a logical one: a law is not a deductive conclusion of the Constitution. All legal norms can, in this way, be located in a norm pyramid, the top of which consists of the Constitution. The formal validity of norms can easily by examined by checking whether or not they belong to the pyramid. One central question, however, remains unanswered. How can the legal order be distinguished from other pyramids of norms? Are there any criteria that would make it possible for us to identify a legal order as a legal order, when compared for example with a pyramid of rules used by the Mafia? From the point of departure of legal theory, the question can also be formulated, as follows: How can the Constitution be justified? Hans Kelsen answered this question by assuming the so-called **basic norm**: the

Constitution must be followed. Kelsen presented different versions of the content of the basic norm and its philosophical and logical status. Regardless of these variations, the basic norm is the "top" of the pyramid of legal norms. We must assume such a basic norm. Without this assumption, the chain of validity shall continue ad infinitum. All of this is acceptable. On the other hand, one can ask how an <u>assumed</u> basic norm can justify an order as a **legal** one. Why must we follow the Constitution?

Aleksander Peczenik has an answer to this question. The core of the answer lies in the fact that the law must "follow" in some way from certain non-legal social phenomena, that is, from social facts and valuations. The latter are transformed to the law. This can occur through the construction of a justifying basic norm: "If certain social facts F and social values V exist, then the basic norm must be followed." A system of rules can be a legal order only if it covers a certain territory, applies to all citizens, claims a monopoly of force, and so on.

As H.L.A. Hart has pointed out, a legal order must also have a minimum value content. We are not inclined to accept, e.g., Hitler's or Pol Pot's system of rules as true legal systems. The reason is that these systems violate what, for us, are vital basic values. For example, we hold that a Pol Pot cannot guarantee his citizens the legal certainty that is a requirement of a true legal order. For this reason, Peczenik deems it necessary to include valuations (V) in the justifying basic norm.

At this stage, someone may ask whether the justifying basic norm must, in turn, be justified, and so on ad infinitum. Peczenik has answered that this is not necessary, and has referred to Neil MacCormick's ideas about so-called "underpinning reasons". These are necessary and fundamental conditions of identification of a system of rules as a legal order. For example, if we are willing to accept total chaos in society, it does not matter whether or not there are legal norms. The concept of "chaos" includes by definition that people in this case do not care about legal certainty. But if a society wants to avoid chaos, it must accept the justifying basic norm. Avoidance of chaos is thus an "underpinning reason" that breaks the chain of justification.

Here we come face to face another key problem in Peczenik's presentation. This "underpinning reason" is a moral reason. It is moral - at least <u>prima facie</u> - to avoid chaos. In this way, Peczenik formulates his statement: what is _prima facie_ legal is also _prima facie_ moral.

The transformation of non-legal phenomena to law is not an exception from the famous principle according to which it is impossible to derive norms from facts. This principle has been called "Hume´s guillotine": the gap between what is and what should be cannot be bridged. The doctrine of transformation cannot be understood to say that the normative order is derived from a factual background. The constitution is not justified directly by facts, but instead by a justifying basic **norm**, and this norm refers to facts and _values_. However, this does not mean that the concept "justifying basic norms" is unproblematic. There are good reasons to discuss, e.g., the role of values in this construction. A critic could say that Peczenik mixes law and morality together, which results in ambiguity of the concept of law. For such a critic, legal validity is a purely legal concept, as it is in Hans Kelsen´s pure theory of law. This discussion touches upon fundamental questions in law and morality. Aleksander Peczenik has answered these eternal questions in a well-formulated manner. The undeniable benefit of the doctrine of transformation lies in its clarity and emphasis of morality. In our times, one does not always recall that already Olaus Petri regarded morality as an integral part of law. Aleksander Peczenik continues this old Nordic tradition of thought in a modern form.

10. Let us return to the contextually sufficient justification in the law. As we were able to note, there are no clear criteria deciding when the chain of external justification in the law can be cut off. This means that we do not **know** if our justification is right or not. Yet, it has been quite common in legal theory to argue that there is always one right solution to all problems of legal interpretation. In later years, the most famous doctrine of the one right answer has been associated with Ronald Dworkin. Dworkin represents a weak version of this doctrine: he claims that there is always one right solution, but not that it is always found. An ideal judge ("Hercules J" in Dworkin´s terminology), who fulfils the highest standards of impartiality, has full information and knows all the rules of interpretation, can find this one right solution.

Aleksander Peczenik criticises such theoretical models. Throughout his entire long career in legal science, Peczenik has sought to formulate a legal theory that, without fundamental or practical weaknesses, would recognise that a legal norm can be interpreted in more

than one way. To this end he has developed the concept of
"deep justification" by asking under what circumstances
legal interpretation can be justified. This question,
again, concerns the place of valuations in the
interpretative process.

Peczenik has the same point of departure as Wróblewski.
In many ways, valuations are built in into legal
justification. But why does this insight justify a
criticism of the doctrine of the one right solution? The
reason is a simple one. If we accept the theory of
objective values, then Dworkin´s line of thought is
acceptable. In such a case, Hercules J is capable of
discovering these values. He can possess **knowledge** about
objective values. Peczenik, however, is a value
relativist. He denies that there are objective values. To
be sure, he writes about "good-making facts", but these
merely tell us what is prima-facie valuable. A
definitive, all-things-considered, value cannot be
derived from empirical facts. Different valuations can
compete in society, and it is impossible to demonstrate
that any one of these is false.

Since values are an integral part of legal
interpretation, and often play a key role in
interpretative activity, it is natural to reject the
doctrine of the one right solution. A certain
interpretation I1 can be based on certain valuations,
whole another interpretation can be based on another set
of valuations. In such cases legal "truth" is relative in
respect of the background valuations. Does this mean
that, ultimately, legal interpretation is arbitrary? Are
there as many interpretations as there are interpreters
of the law?

11. Before we discuss this problem, it is necessary to
define our terms more precisely. The difference between
various interpretations can in practice often be
explained by factors other than valuations. The person
interpreting the law can have insufficient knowledge
about sources of law, and he may perhaps be careless in
his use of interpretative rules. It may also happen that
his terminology is unclear, vague or ambiguous. But such
random elements have been eliminated from Peczenik´s
model, since the person interpreting the law is assumed
to be **reasonable**. On the other hand, it is important to
emphasise the difference between feelings and valuations.
The former are not open to discussion. Feelings can be
compared to tinted glasses. They form prejudices that
hamper a reasonable discussion. On the other hand, a
feature typical for valuations is that they can be based

on reasons, within certain limits. This feature is characteristic of both instrumental and so-called basic or intrinsic values.

An instrumental value is involved when, for example, one says that "this is a good axe". The property of being good is a feature of the axe. It is instrumental when it is possible to use the axe as a tool for achieving a goal. Statements that connect this property with the axe express an instrumental valuation. It is always possible to ask "why?", or in other words to study what reasons justify the statement referring to the goodness of the axe. The answer refers to the result that can be achieved with the help of the axe.

A basic value, such as equality, is something else. It is not a mere instrument for achieving something "external". Instead, it is a goal in itself. Despite this, a basic value can be justified. One can ask "why?" and receive certain reasons for the valuation. However, somewhere there is a limit that cannot be passed. The chain of justification must be cut off: something is good because it **IS** good. Here we find the core of value relativism. Many incompatible chains of justification are possible. One can assume more than one justified perspective.

12. We have always assumed that the person interpreting the law and his adverse party - the person posing the legal question - are behaving as reasonable people. If we do not accept this assumption, we cannot avoid arbitrariness, and thus we cannot achieve legal certainty. Law **and reason** is therefore a well chosen title for a book that deals with models for legal justification.

Let us, e. g., assume an enactment L1 for which five different **semantic** (linguistically possible) alternative interpretations can be presented. On the basis of the sources of law and the rules of legal interpretation three of the semantic possibilities (I1 - I3) can preliminarily be eliminated. Thus, the legal material leaves open the final choice between I4 and I5. Legally, the sources of law justify both alternatives. In this situation, the final interpretation will be based (at least in part) on valuations, in other words on a certain assumed priority order among sources of law. Rationality is involved both when the legally "impossible" alternatives (I1 - I3) are eliminated and when the final choice is made between the remaining interpretations. If the activity of the person interpreting the law had not fulfilled the general criteria of rationality, we would not be willing to accept the interpretation as **legal**. Why not? The reason is simple. The legal interpretation must guarantee predictable results and a non-rational decision is not predictable.

A great deal of Aleksander Peczenik´s work thus consists of an analysis of the concept of rationality. Peczenik has reformulated and modified the criteria of rationality that Robert Alexy originally established in his monumental work, "Theorie der juristischen Argumentation" (1978). Peczenik defines rationality with the help of certain general principles and such concepts as "support" and "coherence". Rationality is bound by criteria and principles of coherence, for example the principle demanding generality of justification. At the same time, this does **not** imply that Peczenik would accept a rationalist doctrine of natural law. He does not suggest that a reasonable person can always discover the objective values. Rationality guarantees that interpretative activity is reasonable, but it permits the two reasonable to evaluate differently.

Law, morality and reason are thus combined. The connection is not a result of arbitrary definitions, assumed by law theorists. It is based on our concepts, _inter alia_ on everything that we deem legal in our Western legal culture. Not only law and morality, but also the concept of "reason" are cultural phenomena. They assume that certain moral and rational demands are fulfilled in legal interpretation.

On the other hand, Peczenik does not intend to argue that people **are** reasonable or that, as a result of certain development, they will **become** reasonable. People try to be reasonable and make mistakes. Rationality is an **ideal** that can be realised more or less. Despite this, human culture needs such a measure, among other things in order to know what is just and what is not, and to identify the optimal framework for action. To be sure, the demand for rationality changes along with the development of society. We do not think today in the same way as did the inhabitants of the Roman Empire 2000 years ago, even though we have inherited the Roman tradition. In particular, we cannot demonstrate that reason is an integral (necessary) element of the definition of man or that we are rational due to our nature. But it is the case that our language and our concepts are constructed so that we expect that judges shall behave in a rational manner. In this sense, the concept of rationality is a necessary element of our culture.

13. Different valuations are not the only source of
differences in legal interpretation. If we disregard
insufficient knowledge about the sources of law and
linguistic usage, there still remains a fundamental basis
for differences in interpretation. Different
interpretations can be based on different theoretical
concepts. Here we meet the second function of legal
dogmatics, the **systematisation** of legal norms.

Concepts are used in all human thinking. One of the
most important goals of scientific activity is to
construct concepts. The same is true of legal dogmatics.
Theoretical concepts and theories are tools of
presentation of scientific results. They are also
instruments for **thinking** about the objects of experience.
Let us say, for example, that in front of us there is an
object that we call a "chair". Nothing is a chair without
the concept of "chair". We analyse and systematise a
certain complex of facts with the help of this concept.
For us, the world as it is **because** we use such analytical
tools. The concept of "resistance" in the study of
electricity is another good example. Without the concept,
it is not possible for us to identify such a phenomenon.
All that we can do is to note the results of certain
measurements our instruments give us. These are then
interpreted with the help of the concept of "resistance".
Thus, the concept is a scientific tool for capturing and
making sense of reality.

In the legal field, concepts and constructions of
concepts have a similar position. In civil law, we speak
about the invalidity of an agreement. During the 1950s,
the Finish analytical school developed this concept in a
very detailed manner. The view was formulated that the
invalidity could be either (a) absolute or relative,
depending on which group of persons was in question
(contra omnes or inter partes), (b) final or subject to
correction through, e.g., acceptance of the agreement,
(c) to be stated ex officio or only on the basis of a
complaint, a claim and so on. The point was that one
could not ask in general whether or not an agreement was
valid; instead, one had to ask **in what sense** an agreement
could be called invalid. In this way, we find an
increasing number of ways of asking questions, and more
sophisticated questions provide better possibilities of
analysing the legal situation. The dichotomy between
valid and invalid is too schematic in complicated legal
conflicts, even if it is sufficient in typical cases.

This means that our knowledge of law depends on our
concepts. Formation of concepts normally requires

systematisation of phenomena. As we have already noted,
there is a necessary connection between systematisation
and interpretation. Legal interpretation is impossible
without the formation of concepts, while practical
systematisation must often be corrected by
interpretation. This is the case when interpretation
needs more precise concepts than those that can be
provided by the prevailing theory. There is thus an
interplay between interpretation and systematisation.
This interplay ultimately and finally produces the
coherence that is so important for Peczenik´s model of
thinking.

14. This is a particularly important phenomenon when we
try to understand the growth and progress of legal
dogmatics. If one asks whether legal dogmatics has made
any progress over the past 100 years, the answer can be
formulated only with reference to the change of the legal
concepts. A progress of legal dogmatics would not be
possible without conceptual change. Peczenik´s theory of
coherence provides some criteria for evaluation of
conceptual changes. On the other hand, two persons
interpreting the law may highly fulfil all the demands of
rationality and coherence, and yet reach different
results, due to the fact that they use different
concepts. It is thus possible for person A, interpreting
the law, to deem an agreement to be null and void, and
for person B to deny this. The reason for the
disagreement can be that, for B, "null and void" refers
only to invalidity that is absolute, final and <u>ex
officio</u>, while A understands this concept as covering
some other types of invalidity as well.

When Aleksander Peczenik analyses the legal paradigm,
the law as a cultural phenomenon, and the demands of
coherence, he deals with these basis problems. He has
succeeded in his book in combining the analysis of legal
interpretation with the most central philosophical, moral
and cultural problems of our time. For this reason,
Peczenik´s present work is one of the most important
contributions to the Nordic theory of law.

Aulis Aarnio

CHAPTER 1
THE DILEMMA OF LEGAL REASONING:
MORAL EVALUATION OR DESCRIPTION OF THE LAW?

1.1. A THEORY OF LEGAL REASONING

This is a book in legal theory. Its purpose is to justify
the legal method.
   There are many different types of legal research. Such
disciplines as history of law, sociology of law, law and
economics, philosophy of law etc. apply, first of all, a
historical, sociological, economical, philosophical or
another non-legal method. Another type of legal research,
occupying the central position in commentaries and
textbooks of law etc., implements a specific legal
method, that is, the systematic, analytically-evaluative
exposition of the substance of private law, criminal law,
public law etc. Although such an exposition may also
contain some historical, sociological and other points,
its core consists in interpretation and systematisation
of (valid) legal norms. More precisely, it consists in a
description of the literal sense of statutes, precedents
etc., intertwined with many moral and other substantive
reasons. One may call this kind of exposition of the law
"analytical study of law", "doctrinal study of law", etc.
In the Continental Europe, one usually calls it "legal
dogmatics". The standard German word is **Rechtsdogmatik**.

The word "legal science", frequently used in many European
countries, is ambiguous. It may refer to the legal dogmatics, pure
or containing some elements of legal sociology, history etc. It may
also refer to any kind of legal research.

The specific legal method constitutes not only the core
of the "legal dogmatics" but also characterises the
legal, inter alia judicial, decision-making. Of course,
there are also some differences. For example, compared
with judicial method, legal dogmatics lacks the decision
component; it is more abstract and less bound to a
"given" case; it deals with many examples of real and

imaginary cases. The most profound difference consists in
the fact that legal dogmatics often claims to be more
rational than legal practice, that is, more oriented
towards general theses, supported by extensive arguments.
The similarities are, however, far deeper than the
differences.

The central part of jurisprudence, on the other hand,
has another object of research and another method. It
constitutes a "metadiscipline", similar to theory of
science (cf. Peczenik 1974, 9 ff.). It is not a part of
legal dogmatics but a theory about legal dogmatics and
legal decision-making. It thus does not interpret legal
norms but includes a theory of their legal
interpretation. Consequently, it has a specific method,
closely related to philosophy.

This part of jurisprudence contains the following.

1) A description of the legal method. One attempts at
describing systematically and extensively
- the goals of such legal practices as statutory
interpretation, interpretation of precedents,
justification of judicial decisions etc.;
- particular legal reasons, e.g. statutory analogy, and
argumentum e contrario;
- various legal methods, such as literal, teleological
and historical interpretation etc.

2) An analysis of fundamental legal concepts such as
"valid law". One describes the concepts and their
relations, proposes a precise reconstruction of vague
concepts, etc.

3) An evaluation and justification of these goals,
reasons, methods, concepts and conclusions based on them.
One tries to answer such questions as, Is statutory
analogy a valid reasoning?, Is the concept "valid law"
theoretically meaningful and practically useful?, Does
legal reasoning render true knowledge of the law?, etc.

4) Philosophical considerations, necessary for the
evaluation. To answer, e.g., the question, Is statutory
analogy a valid reasoning?, one must, inter alia, deal
with such problems as, What does validity of legal
reasons consist in?, What is the relation between valid
reasons and truth?, and so on.

5) History of legal philosophy.

1.2. LEGAL DECISION-MAKING AND EVALUATIONS

1.2.1. Introduction. Subsumption in Clear and Hard Cases

A legal solution of the case under consideration must fit the law. One may present the solution as a logical consequence of a set of premises, containing a statutory provision, precedent etc. together with other relevant norms, value statements and the description of the facts of the case. Establishment of this logical relation is called "subsumption" (cf. Alexy 1989, 221 ff. and 1980, 192; Aarnio, Alexy and Peczenik 1981, 154 n. 66).

In "easy" cases, the decision follows from a legal rule, a description of the facts of the case and perhaps some other premises which are easy to prove.

Assume, e.g., that John parks his car without paying the required charge. A carpark attendant comes and John is fined 150 kronor. The following subsumption justifies the attendant's decision:

Premise 1 (a rule)	If a carpark attendant finds a car at a place where charge is required and the charge is not paid, he shall impose a fine 150 kronor on the driver
Premise 2	The carpark attendant Svensson found John's car at a place where charge was required and the charge was not paid

----

Conclusion	The carpark attendant Svensson shall impose a fine 150 kronor on John

A "hard" case, on the other hand, "presents a moral dilemma, or at least a difficult moral determination" (Morawetz 1980, 90). The decision does not follow from a legal rule and a description of the facts (cf. Dworkin 1977, 81). However, it follows from an expanded set of premises containing, inter alia, a value statement, a norm or another statement the decision-maker assumes but cannot easily prove. Suppose, e.g., that John threatened a cashier of a bank with a pistol and thus got some money. Later, the pistol turned out to be a toy. The Supreme Court decided (in the case NJA 1956 C 187) that such an act was a robbery. (A corresponding change of the statute followed soon). The decision presupposes a subsumption, containing the following components:

Premise 1 (Ch. 8   Whoever steals through violence or
Sec. 5 of the Swedish   threat constituting acute danger...
Criminal Code at the   is to be sentenced for robbery...
moment of decision)

Premise 2   John got some money through a threat
                             that the victim (wrongly) interpreted as
                             an acute danger

Conclusion   John is to be sentenced for robbery

The conclusion does not follow from premises 1 and 2. To
obtain logical correctness one must add a premise. The
following inference is thus correct.

Premise 1   Whoever steals through violence or threat
(see above)   constituting acute danger... is to be
                        sentenced for robbery...

Premise 2   John got some money through a threat that the
                        victim (wrongly) interpreted an acute danger

Premise 3   A threat that the victim (wrongly) interprets as
                        an acute danger is to be judged in the same way as
                        a threat actually constituting such a danger
----

Conclusion   John is to be sentenced for robbery

Premise 3 is a norm, endorsed by the court. Its
justification consists, _inter alia_, of the following
reasons. A value judgment: An apparent threat is not
better than an actual one. A prediction of consequences:
A milder decision would increase the number of such
crimes. It would also create expectation that the pistol
used to threat the victim is a mere toy. This would
encourage the victims to disregard threats and thus risk
their lives. Another value judgment: This risk is
unacceptable. Of course, the value judgment involved
could be elaborated much more. Was it, e.g., not
sufficient to regard such cases as gross larceny? One
must consider the fact that, in Sweden, the maximal
punishment for the latter crime is the same as for
robbery. On the other hand, one may pay attention to the
fact that the ordinary victim of such a crime perceives
the situation as nothing less but a robbery. And so on.

1.2.2. Interpretative Problems - Ambiguity, Vagueness and Value-Openess

A lawyer must make value judgments, *inter alia* in order to make a choice between different interpretations of a statute, a precedent, another source of the law, a contract etc. This possibility of choice is a result of vagueness and ambiguity of the law. One may also speak about "open texture" (Hart 1961, 121 ff.) and "fuzziness" of the law (Peczenik and Wróblewski, 24 ff).

A decision does not follow from a vague or ambiguous legal norm. It follows, however, from an expanded set of premises, containing such a norm together with some reasonable premises, *inter alia* value statements.

Vagueness consists in the fact that the meaning of a word allows for borderline cases. For example, Sec. 36 of the Swedish Contracts Act stipulates that "undue" contractual conditions may be disregarded. Obviously, the borderline between due and undue conditions is not sharp.

The vague words, occurring in the law, are often value-open (cf. Alexy 1980, 190 ff. and Koch 1977, 41 ff. See also Moore 1981, 167 ff.). One must, e.g., employ evaluations in order to make a precise interpretation of the expression "undue contractual condition".

One can thus state the following.

1) This term has a practical meaning. By calling a contractual condition "undue", one expresses or encourages a disapproval of this condition.

2) This term has also a theoretical meaning, related to some facts which constitute criteria indicating that a particular contractual condition is "undue".

Suppose, for example, that an unexperienced businessman enters into a contract with a big company, dominating the market. According to the contract, the company may unilaterally decide whether future disputes are to be decided by a general court or arbitration. A dispute occurs. The businessman sues the company before a general court but the company claims that the case shall be referred to arbitration. Is the arbitration clause "undue"? A reason for this conclusion may be that it deprives the weaker party of the possibility to have his right examined (cf. NJA 1979 p. 666). This example elucidates the fact that the sentence "the contractual condition C is undue" has a connection with some theoretical (fact-describing, "value-free") propositions. Inter alia, it follows from the proposition "the contractual condition C deprives the weaker party of the possibility to have his right examined by an impartial court" together with some reasonable value statements.

The following (logically correct) inference elucidates a part of the theoretical meaning of the expression "undue contractual condition":

Premise 1 (a theoretical proposition?)	The contractual condition C deprives the weaker party of the possibility to have his right examined by an impartial court
Premise 2 (a reasonable value statement)	If the contractual condition C deprives the weaker party of the possibility to have his right examined by an impartial court, then the contractual condition C is undue

---

Conclusion   The contractual condition C is undue

3) The theoretical meaning of the term "undue contractual condition" is vague. It is not clear, _inter alia_, what the expression "deprives the weaker party of the possibility to have his right examined by an impartial court" exactly means. For example, what kinds of arbitration deserve the name "impartial"? How much weaker the "weaker" party must be? What circumstances constitute a "deprivation"?; and so on. Neither is it clear what other facts make the contractual condition undue.

4) One thus must weigh and balance various considerations, in order to decide in a concrete case whether the contractual condition is or is not undue.

One may distinguish between a contextual and a lexical vagueness, the first in a particular context, the second determined by general rules of language (cf. Evers 1970, 16.). For example, the word "forest" is lexically vague (How many trees do constitute a forest?). But in a given context, it may be entirely clear that a given area is a forest, for example, if a map indicates it as such. The value-open term "undue contractual condition" is doubtless lexically vague. It would be contextually precise if one could _prove_ in any particular case whether the condition is "due" or undue.

Can one prove value statements, such as "If the contractual condition C deprives the weaker party of the possibility to have his right examined by an impartial court, then the contractual condition C is undue"? There are reasons against this possibility. Vagueness may be caused by historical peculiarities, such as old age of the statute in question, its foreign origin etc. A statute can also have a number of different goals; some

requiring preciseness, some not. One goal can be, e.g.,
to guide judicial practice, another to influence conduct
of private persons. While the former often demands as
great preciseness as possible, the latter does not. A
vague but persuasive expression can have greater
influence than a precise but "technical". Another reason
against the possibility of proving value statements is
more philosophical. The conclusion is plausible that one
can only prove a provisional, prima-facie, value
statement, such as "If the contractual condition C
deprives the weaker party of the possibility to have his
right examined by an impartial court, then a reason
exists for concluding that the contractual condition C is
undue". On the other hand, the answer to the question
whether a condition definitively is or is not "undue"
depends on an act of weighing and balancing. Rightness of
this act is not demonstrable (see section 2.4.6 infra).

Ambiguity consists in the fact that a word has more
than one meaning. Consider the following case,
constituting a simplified version of the Swedish decision
NJA 1950 p. 650. A person injured by a car lost his
working capacity and, in consequence of it, a part of his
income. A little later, it was discovered that he had
suffered from a gastric ulcer that would have made him
incapable to work, even if he had not been injured. The
Municipal Court held the driver liable in torts, since
the car accident had been a sufficient cause of the
incapacity. The Court of Appeals reduced the compensation
to 50%. Three different standpoints were represented in
the Supreme Court. With support of some procedural rules,
the Court did not hold the driver liable for the part of
the loss for which the ulcer alone had been a sufficient
cause. The reason for this decision was that the car
accident had not been a necessary cause of the loss. The
main question was thus whether one is liable in torts for
an action constituting a sufficient but not necessary
cause of a loss. The answer to this question does not
follow from the wording of the Swedish Liability for
Damages Act (Ch. 2 Sec. 1), which stipulates that one
intentionally or negligently causing a personal injury or
a property damage should compensate the victim therefor.
The word "to cause" is ambiguous, that is, it has two
meanings, (1) to do something that is a necessary
condition for the result, and (2) to do something that is
a sufficient condition for the result, regardless whether
it also is a necessary condition of it.

Ambiguous words, occurring in the law, are often
value-open. For example, one must employ evaluations in

order to make a choice in the case under consideration
between interpreting the word "to cause" as related to a
necessary condition or as related to a sufficient
condition.

One may distinguish between a contextual and a lexical ambiguity,
the first in a particular context, the second determined by general
rules of language; e.g., the word "house" is lexically ambiguous,
since it means, inter alia, both a building and a family (e.g., the
House of Windsor), but contextually unambiguous in such sentences as
"I live in a red house".

Value-openness is a special case of both ambiguity and
vagueness. Such value-open words as "good", "evil",
"just", "unjust", "courageous", "cowardly", "generous",
"stingy", "undue" etc. have the following properties.
   1) They have a practical meaning, related to feelings,
attitudes, action etc.
   2) The have also a theoretical meaning, related to some
facts.
   3) Their theoretical meaning is lexically vague or
ambiguous.
   4) In a particular case, one needs weighing and
balancing of several considerations in order to determine
whether the word in question refers to this case.

1.2.3. Gaps in the Law

Legal reasoning in some hard cases also involves value statements
necessary to fill up the so-called gaps in law. Such a gap can occur
in the literal sense of the established law, such as a a statute, or
in the set of norms one obtains by interpreting the established law
in the light of traditional legal methods. Let me discuss here only
the former kind of gaps. The latter will be dealt with in section
5.4.6 infra. (One may also speak about gaps in the set of legal
reasons. Cf. Raz 1979, 53 ff.).
   A gap means that (1) the established law does not regulate a given
case (an insufficiency gap); (2) the established law regulates the
case in a logically inconsistent way (an inconsistency gap); (3) the
established law regulates the case in a vague or ambiguous manner
(an indeterminacy gap); or (4) the established law regulates the
case in a morally unacceptable way (an axiological gap; cf.
Wróblewski 1959, 299 ff.; Opalek and Wróblewski 1969, 108 ff.).
   1. Insufficiency gaps result, inter alia, from the fact that the
literal text of the statute does not regulate a given case.

Achourrón and Bulygin 1971, 15 ff. have formulated the following
classical example. Assume that a statute stipulates that (1) the
restitution of legal estate is obligatory, if the transferee is in
good faith, the transfer is made with consideration and the
transferor is in bad faith; and (2) the restitution of legal estate
is obligatory if the transfer is made without consideration. Assume
now that the transferor is in good faith and the transfer is made
with consideration but the transferee is in bad faith. Is the
restitution of legal estate obligatory? The norm does not answer the
question. A gap occurs.

One can establish such gaps in an objective, "value-free" manner
but to fill them up, one must complete the statute with an
additional norm, such as the following one: An action is permitted,
if it is not explicitly forbidden by the law (cf. a more precise
formulation in section 7.4 infra). Such a norm may be established in
a statute or another source of the law. If it is not, then filling
up of the gap demands that one makes a value judgment.

The "genuine gaps" are a special case of insufficiency gaps. A
legal norm stipulates, e.g., that one can demand compensation in a
given situation but leaves it open who has to pay the compensation.
Another example is this. A (higher) norm stipulates that a certain
norm should be enacted or a certain legal action performed (e.g.,
appointment of an official). However, such a norm can be enacted, or
such an action performed, only if the law states precisely who may
do it and how it may be done. The gap consists in the fact that the
law leaves these questions open. (I omit here several possible
distinctions. Cf. Opalek and Wróblewski 1969, 109; Larenz 1983, 356
ff.; Kelsen 1960, 254; Zittelmann 1903, 27 ff.).

For example, the Polish constitution contained a provision that
judges shall be elected, but no legal norms stated precisely by whom
and how. No established legal norm helps one to fill up such a gap.

2. Gaps may also result from logical inconsistency of legal norms
(cf. Ziembinski 1966, 227). One norm may, e.g., forbid and another
permit the same action. For example, the Danish constitution
contained both a provision that the first chamber of the parliament
must not have more than 78 members, and another, implying that there
must be 79 members. One can establish such gaps in an objective,
"value-free", manner but to fill them up, one must complete the
statute with a collision-norm, stipulating, e.g., what follows: A
less general legal rule must be interpreted as an exception from a
more general one, incompatible with it. Such norms are established
within the legal tradition. But they may be vague. In some cases,
e.g., one cannot tell which norm is more general (cf. section 7.6
infra). Filling up the gap requires then a value judgment.

3. Indeterminacy gaps result from vagueness or ambiguity of the
established legal norms (cf., e.g., Schweitzer 1959, 64-76;
Alchourrón and Bulygin 1971, 33 ff.). It is doubtful whether they
deserve the name "gap" at all. Certainly, a distinction is often
drawn between filling indeterminacy gaps and ordinary interpretation
of statutes. The distinction is, however, obscure. In any case, one
can establish the fact that a statute is vague or ambiguous in a
"value-free" manner. On the other hand, to remove vagueness or

ambiguity, one needs an expanded set of premises, containing some reasonable value statements. Cf. Section 1.2.2 supra.

4. Finally, axiological gaps occur when the established law regulates a given case in a morally unacceptable way (cf., e.g., Alchourrón and Bulygin 1971, 94 ff.). A typical gap of this kind exists when the law lacks a norm it ought to contain from the moral point of view. Or, the law contains a norm it ought not to contain.

Of course, one cannot establish axiological gaps in a "value-free" manner. To fill them up, one must rely upon moral value judgments.

In brief, one can establish some gaps in the law in an objective, "value-free" manner. To establish other gaps, one needs an expanded set of premises, containing some reasonable value statements. Some gaps may be filled up, some not. To fill up the former, one must make some (moral) value judgments.

1.2.4. Evidence of Facts

Value judgments may also have a role to play in connection with evidence of facts which are relevant for the case. Suppose that Peter plays poker with strangers and loses much money. A witness says that one of the players manipulated the cards. The other party objects and claims that the witness is not reliable, since he is a close friend of Peter. Besides, it turns out that one of the players, under one night's game, three times showed four kings. A statistician estimates probability of this as one of billion. Is this evidence sufficient to condemn the winners for cheating?

One must thus answer several questions of fact. Has the statistician counted correctly? Is the witness really a close friend of Peter? Does friendship make it probable that he lies? Only the first question can be answered in an exact way. The second and the third require a vague, perhaps intuitive, estimation of probability.

Another important question is "probability - of what?". One has a choice between two methods. Assume that a witness says he saw that X happened. The "theme-of-proof method" estimates probability that X happened. The "value-of-proof method", on the other hand, estimates probability that X caused the observation the witness made and reported. It thus pays attention only to the cases in which the witness actually saw X, not merely guessed that X happened.

Complex questions concern also chains of "evidentiary facts", contrary evidence etc. Cf. Koch and Rüssman 1982, 272 ff.; Stening 1975 and Ekelöf 1982, 7 ff.

One must also answer some moral value questions, e.g. Ought the judge to base his decision on a statistical probability? To answer such value questions, the court may to some extent rely on some established norms of evidence, supported by precedents and other sources of the law. It must, however, make genuine (moral) value judgments, too.

1.2.5. Choice of a Legal Norm

Moreover, value judgments may affect the choice of one of
many legal norms, applicable to the case to be decided
(cf. Frändberg 1984, 84 ff.). In other words, one must
make a choice of one of many possible subsumptions. One
thus selects the norm from which - together with the
appropriate additional premises - it follows logically
what kind of decision is legally possible in this case.
Let us suppose that A repeatedly hits B with malicious
pleasure but at the same time intends not to inflict any
bodily injury on his victim, not wanting to leave
evidence of his action. Despite A´s "caution", however, B
sustains severe concussion. One can subsume A´s action
under three provisions of the Swedish Criminal Code: Ch.
3 Sec. 5 assault and battery); Ch. 3 Sec. 6 (gross
assault and battery) and Ch.3 Sec.8 (the causing of
bodily injury or illness). A has deliberately "caused
another person pain" (cf. Sec. 5 and 6) and had also
"through lack of care inflicted grievous bodily harm on
another person" (cf. Sec. 8). The choice between these
alternatives involves value judgments. For evaluative
reasons, one must regard A´s action as gross assault and
battery (Sec. 6), not as assault and battery simpliciter
(Sec. 5). Moreover, one must not qualify A´s action as
the causing of bodily injury (Sec. 8). The commentary to
the Code states, what follows: "The scale of penalties
for gross assault and battery has such a high maximum
that the penalty for assault and battery can be permitted
to consume the penalty for causing bodily injury."
(Beckman et al., 106. Cf. the case SvJT 1966 rf. 57).
   The problem of choice of the applicable legal norm
arises not only in penal law but also in other parts of
the legal system, inter alia in international private law
("the choice of the applicable statute"). Also in private
law of a particular state, one often must answer the
question which of many applicable statutory provisions is
to be implemented in the case at bar.
   The choice of the applicable legal norm requires value
judgments. How can one state precisely that the penalty
for assault and battery can be permitted to consume the
penalty for causing bodily injury? To answer such value
questions, the court may, to some extent, rely on
established norms, expressed in statutes, precedents,
commentaries and other sources of the law. It must,
however, make genuine (moral) value judgments, too.

1.2.6. Choice of a Legal Consequence

Having solved the problems of interpretation, evidence and choice of a legal norm, one must often choose a legal consequence (cf. Rödig 1973, 174 ff.; Wróblewski 1974, 44 ff.). For example, one sentences the person guilty of gross assault and battery to five years in prison; the law stipulates imprisonment between one and ten years.

Of course, the choice of a legal consequence requires value judgments. To some extent, the court may rely on some established norms, expressed in statutes etc. The Criminal Code stipulates, e.g., that when judging assault and battery as gross, the court must consider whether the accused endangered the victim's life, inflicted grievous bodily harm or serious illness, or otherwise showed particular ruthlessness. But the court must make a moral judgment to decide whether the act in question was "particularly ruthless".

The choice of a legal consequence is important not only in criminal but also in civil cases. For example, Sec. 36 of the Swedish Contracts Act stipulates that "undue" contractual conditions may be modified or disregarded. Having established that the condition is "undue", the court must choose between these two alternatives. It may also face a choice between several possible modifications of the contractual condition. To make the choice, the court may consider the content of the contract, the situation at the time it was concluded, later facts and "other circumstances". Weighing and balancing of all this requires a value judgment.

1.2.7. Obsolete Laws and Desuetudo

In some cases, one must answer the question whether a certain statutory provision is valid or applicable at all. Suppose, e.g., that A produces sausages containing some controversial chemicals, and does not ask proper authorities for approval according to the law. B buys a sausage. A zealous prosecutor accuses the buyer on the bases of Ch.1 Sec. 10 of the Swedish Commercial Code of 1734. The provision stipulates, what follows: "The goods that stadens vräkare should behold and examine may not be taken by the buyer before that happened; or both buyer and seller are to be fined 10 dalers each" (cf. Strömholm 1988, 314 ff.). Is this old provision applicable to modern cases? Logically, it is possible. To be sure, no stadens vräkare exist any more. This old Swedish word, hardly comprehensible today, designated more or less a "municipal heaver". Yet, one can assume that present supervisory authorities correspond to them. Or is the provision obsolete, that is, so much out of date that the courts, although recognising its validity, may ignore it?

Or even more than that, does newer custom cause that the provision already lost its legal validity (the so-called desuetudo derogatoria) and thus must be ignored?

The process of in which a provision customarily loses its validity takes some time. At first, the courts are inclined to frequently "forget" the provision, without entirely precluding the legal possibility of its application in other cases. They would perhaps call it "half-valid", if the legal language permitted them to do so. Instead, one calls the provision "obsolete". Later, however, one may find that no reason any longer justifies such an uncertainty. The provision has definitively lost validity through desuetudo.

Questions of obsolescence and desuetudo require, of course, value judgments, although one may, to some extent, rely on certain established norms, expressed, e.g., in some precedents. The court must, however, make genuine value judgments, as well.

1.3. THE CONCEPT "LEGAL DECISION-MAKING"

A lawyer thus must make value judgments, inter alia in order to perform a subsumption (section 1.2.1.); to interpret a statute or another source of the law (Section 1.2.2.); to establish and fill up gaps in the law (Section 1.2.3.); to establish facts of the case (Section 1.2.4.); to choose the applicable norm (Section 1.2.5.); to choose a legal consequence (Section 1.2.6.) and to answer the question whether a statute is obsolete (Section 1.2.7.).

This role of values affects the very concept of "legal decision-making". A decision of a court or an authority deserves the name "legal", if the following conditions are fulfilled.

1. The decision is supported by a statute and/or another source of the law, such as precedent, legislative history, custom, juristic literature etc.

Instead of "legal decision-making", the Continental law theorists often speak about "application of law" (in German, Rechtsanwendung).

A legal dogmatist applies the law in a week sense. He does not make decisions but gives advices how to decide cases.

2. In "hard" cases, the decision is also supported by moral value statements.

3. One can reconstruct legal decision-making as a logically correct process of reasoning.

Keeping in mind these conditions, one may summarise our discussion in the following manner.

One may distinguish between the following operations, involved in legal decision-making: (1) interpretation in abstracto of a legal norm, (2) application of the norm to a particular case, and (3) choice of a legal consequence (cf. Peczenik 1974, 54 ff.; Agge 1969, 63).

1) Interpretation in abstracto. Interpretation in abstracto comprises two operations:

a) One interprets a statutory provision (e.g., concerning assault, Ch. 3 Sec. 5 of the Swedish Criminal Code), a precedent, an opinion included in legislative preparatory materials (travaux préparatoires) etc. according to its literal sense.

b) One interprets the statutory provision, the precedent, the opinion included in legislative preparatory materials etc. in the light of particular legal concepts, reasons and methods.

2) Application of the statutory provision, the precedent etc. to a particular case. It comprises five operations.

a) Consideration of other relevant norms and value statements, possibly modifying the sphere of application of the implemented legal norm, for instance stipulating some exceptions. To apply the provision concerning assault, one must thus consider the norm about intent (Ch. 1 Sec. 2 of the Criminal Code).

b) Establishment of the facts of the case.

c) Subsumption. One presents the solution of the case under consideration as a logical consequence of a set of premises, containing the statutory provision, precedent etc. together with other relevant norms, value statements and the description of the facts of the case.

d) The choice of one of many possible subsumptions. One thus decides to judge the case according to the provision concerning gross assault and battery (Ch. 3 Sec. 6 of the Criminal Code), not assault simpliciter (Sec. 5).

3) A choice of a legal consequence. For example, one sentences the person guilty of gross assault and battery to five years in prison; the law stipulates imprisonment between one and ten years.

In most cases of application of law, the decision-maker performs all of these operations, but not in a predetermined order. The operations influence one another (cf., e.g., Esser 1972, 82).

1.4. WHY DO THE LAWYERS NEED SPECIAL INTERPRETATION METHODS?

1.4.1. Expectation of Legal Certainty

Why should value judgments, based on weighing and balancing of various considerations, play such a great role in legal reasoning, particularly in legal interpretation? The answer is based on the fact that the interpretation and application of law is to some extent rational and, for that reason, promotes legal certainty in material sense, that is, the optimal compromise between predictability of legal decisions and their acceptability in view of other moral considerations.

The term "legal certainty" is a literal translation of the German word Rechtssicherheit. The English legal terminology has no corresponding word although, of course, the very phenomenon of legal certainty is as important in the Common Law systems as elsewhere. The best approximation is "the rule of law".

Terms such as "legal certainty", "legal security", "the rule of law" etc. are often used in a formal sense, as synonymous to "predictability of legal decisions". Among others, Opalek 1964, 497 ff. advocated a "formalist" terminology, identifying the rule of law with adherence of authorities to the law. Cf., e.g., Hayek 1944, 72 ff.; Oakeshott 1983, 119 ff.; Raz 1979, 210 ff.; Zippelius 1982, 157 ff. In Sweden, this terminology is shared, e.g., by Frändberg 1982, 41 ("legal security" as synonymous with "legal predictability") and Strömholm 1988, 394 (predictability and uniformity).

To be sure, this terminology constitutes a linguistically possible interpretation of vague words, such as "Rechtssicherheit", which in many European languages correspond to the expression "legal certainty". The formal sense of "legal certainty" may be adequate for some purposes, e.g., in criminal law. But in the present work, dedicated to the problem of legal method, the material sense is more appropriate, among other things because the formal one has the following strange consequences.

1) Jews under Hitler's rule could predict that they would be discriminated. Did they possess a high degree of "legal certainty"?

2) Assume for a moment that "legal certainty" is the same as "predictability of legal decisions", and nothing more pretentious. One must now state precisely what is the ground for predictions.

a) Is predictability based on valid legal rules? If so, then, ceteris paribus, the better the interpretation of the rules, the

higher the degree of legal certainty. But what is the yardstick of
goodness of interpretation? Ceteris paribus, the higher the degree
of **moral acceptability**, the better the interpretation. The use, if
not the content, of the concept of "legal certainty" in the formal
sense implies thus indirectly the material sense: "Predictability of
legal decisions" implies "predictability of legal decisions based on
legal rules"; the latter implies "predictability of legal decisions
based on morally acceptable interpretation of legal rules"; and this
implies "predictability and moral acceptability of legal decisions".
    b) Or, is it plausible to speak about legal certainty as
predictability contra legem, e.g., when legal decisions inconsistent
with the law are based on actual loyalty of officials towards the
ruling Party, the leader personally etc.? In this case, Soviet Union
under Stalin would be an example of a country possessing a fairly
high degree of legal certainty.
    In many works, I claimed that "in legal practice there is a
compromise between the principle of the strict observance of law and
the principle of justice", cf., e.g., Peczenik 1967, 138. This view
was influenced by Opalek and Zakrzewski 1958, 19 and 31-35. Later,
in a close cooperation with Aulis Aarnio, I changed the terminology
(though my views concerning the correct legal method remained
unchanged) and defined the "rule of law" (that is, legal certainty)
as the fact that "legal decisions are simultaneously predictable and
morally acceptable"; cf. Peczenik 1983, 78. Cf. Aarnio 1987, 3 ff.
    The present terminology constitutes a further refinement. It pays
attention to the fact that predictability is one of many moral
values. I thus interpret "legal certainty" in the material sense, as
the optimal compromise between predictability of legal decisions and
their acceptability in view of other moral considerations.
    This material sense of "legal certainty" should not be confused
with another, also called "material", in which "legal certainty" is
identified with any kind of protection the law provides individuals,
collectives and the state itself, e.g., against crimes. This use of
the term may be called "extended material one". It dominated the
Soviet legal theory and appeared in some Swedish contexts, too (cf.,
e.g., Report "Ekonomisk brottslighet i Sverige", SOU 1984:15). The
rationale of it is to play down protection of an individual against
abuse of public power and to advocate protection the state provides
against other risks. Though such protection is important, I find it
confusing to call it "legal certainty"; cf. Mattsson 1981, 459 ff.

In modern society, people expect in general that legal
decisions be highly predictable and, at the same time,
highly acceptable from the moral point of view. Ceteris
paribus, the higher the degree of such predictability,
the higher the chance of an individual to efficiently
plan his life. And, ceteris paribus, the higher the
degree of moral acceptability of legal decisions, the
higher the chance of one to make the life thus planned
satisfactory. A normal individual expects to be able to
plan a satisfactory life. I assume that such expectations

create responsibility; decision-makers thus have a <u>social responsibility</u> for legal certainty in the material sense. Predictability results from the fact that legal decisions are based on general norms. It is justifiable by the principle "the like should be treated alike".

In other words, people expect that the law consists of general norms. This expectation influenced the historical evolution of the concept of <u>Rechtsstaat</u>, inspired by codification of the law in 18th century's Prussia and philosophical influence of <u>Kant</u> and <u>Humboldt</u>, and fully developed by German lawyers of 19th century.

In some cases, however, the wording of the law collides with moral opinions of its interpreter. The like shall be treated alike but the text of the law establishes some criteria of likeness whereas the interpreter has reasons to prefer other criteria. An increased predictability, based on the wording of the law, can thus cause the fact that the decision in question pays a lesser attention to other moral considerations. On the other hand, an increased role of other moral considerations can result in a decreased predictability. A very exact legislation concerning, e.g., invalidity of undue contractual provisions, can thus, in some cases, result in injustice whereas a just general clause can make it difficult to predict legal decisions. In such cases, legal certainty means that one tries to find the best compromise between predictability and other moral considerations.

The expectation of legal certainty has the following consequences. Legal decisions should be based on legal norms (item 1 below). In some cases, an interpreter of the law must creatively correct these norms (item 2). Courts and authorities should not refuse to apply a legal norm, however unclear this norm may be (item 3).

1. Courts and authorities have thus a duty to support their decisions with legal norms.

Mattsson 1984, 374, demands also that, the range of normatively possible application of legal rules must be highly determined.

If no statutory provision applies to the case under consideration, one must support the decision with other authority reasons, such as precedents, legislative history, competent juristic literature etc.

This duty permeates the conceptual apparatus of the
lawyers. Many lawyers understand the concept of legal
reasoning in a way supporting the following thesis: If
decisions in a given kind of cases are made without any
support of authority reasons, these decisions are, by
definition, not legal.

2. On the other hand, courts and authorities must use
special interpretation methods to adapt legal norms to
moral requirements. This duty, too, affects the concepts.
One can understand the concept of legal reasoning in a
way supporting the following theses: If decisions in a
given kind of cases are made without attention to the
established juristic tradition of reasoning, they are, by
definition, not legal. If they are made without attention
to moral considerations, they are, by definition, not
legal, either.

3. Legal certainty implies, finally, that courts and
authorities must not refuse to make decisions. Refusal to
decide (denegatio iustitiae) is not morally acceptable,
since people expect access to justice. Denegatio
iustitiae is thus forbidden by written or customary law
of many countries. As an example, one can quote Sec. 4 of
the French Code Civile, stipulating criminal
responsibility of a judge who refuses to decide the case
because the law is silent, unclear or insufficient.

The demand that legal interpretation, e.g., statutory
interpretation, interpretation of precedents etc.
promotes legal certainty, that is, results in the fact
that legal decisions follow a reasonable compromise
between predictability and other moral considerations,
can be explained by two factors, practical character of
legal interpretation (item 1 below) and the connection of
legal interpretation with the use of official power (item
2).

1. Since legal interpretation affects important
decisions, it is natural that people expect that it not
only follows the wording of the law but also the demands
of morality.

Interpretation in general helps one (1) to obtain and communicate
knowledge (theoretical interpretation) and (2) to influence people
(practical interpretation). Theoretical interpretation occurs in
literary criticism, historical research and the work of translators,
actors, musicians etc. Practical interpretation characterises, first
of all the law, theology and political ideologies.

2. Practical importance of legal interpretation results from the fact that legal order is intimately connected with exercise of power. The lawyer interprets authoritative texts, created by power-exercising institutions. Moreover, the interpreter himself is a component of a power-exercising institution.

But why to use interpretation to adapt the law to moral demands? Is it not better to achieve the adaptation via change of legal statutes? The answer to this question must take into account the character of moral evaluations and professional skills of a judge.

1. The law-giver cannot predict in advance or acceptably regulate all cases that can occur in future practice. The evaluations to be done in legal practice, among other things concerning the question whether a decision of a given kind is just are easier to make in concrete cases, not in abstracto.

2. Historical evolution of the method of legal reasoning has adapted it to the purpose of weighing and balancing of the wording of the law and moral demands. The judge has a far greater practical experience in applying this method to concrete cases than any legislative agency can have.

This fact has recognised since antiquity. In Roman republic, the praetor could thus order the judge to assume the fiction that the demands of ius civile were fulfilled in the case under adjudication. The praetors, acting in a close contact with judicial practice, thus developed an entirely new legal system. A partly similar evolution took place in medieval England.

1.4.2. The Law and Democracy

In a democratic society, however, the moral component of the legal decision-making receives both an additional justification and a richer content.

The modern concept of democracy evolved historically, under influence of various moral and prudential considerations. Consequently, it is vague and value-open. When calling a social order or a state organisation democratic, one thus expresses a certain acceptance of it. Democracy is, in other words, a special case of a good organisation of society.

It is logically possible that even some undemocratic states and ways
to organise the society are good, but I disregard this problem.
   The point of the value-open concept of democracy consists in its
usefulness for an evaluative political debate. For other purposes,
one can stipulate various "value-free" definitions of democracy,
e.g., a "formal" definition identifying it with the majority rule
(cf., e.g., Heckscher, 54). The value-laden concept of democracy can
be called "material" (cf., e.g., Taxell 1987, 9 ff.).

For both historical and linguistic reasons, it is natural
to primarily apply the concept of democracy to the state,
the organisation of the society as a whole, as well as to
the public decision making. In a merely secondary sense,
one can also call other organisations and their decisions
democratic.   "Democratisation"   of   such   industrial
enterprises, universities etc. promotes values and causes
problems which are not identical with those connected
with democracy in the primary sense (cf. Taxell 1987,
42).
   The fact that the concept of democracy is value-open
does not mean, however, that it lacks a definite sense.
Democracy is the same as the power of the people. This is
the main idea of democracy.

According to Ross 1963, 92 ff., the concept of democracy as power of
the people is an ideal type. The facts can approximate it more or
less, depending on such things as the number of persons involved in
decision-making, effectiveness of their influence and extension of
the sphere submitted to the control of the people.

To be sure, the expression "the power of the people" is
vague. Nevertheless, a ("value-free") study of the
political language shows that it makes sense to proffer
some facts as reasons for the conclusion that a state or
a social order is democratic. These criteria of democracy
make the central idea of the power of the people clearer.
Inter alia, one may consider the following, partly
overlapping, criteria: 1) political representation of the
interests of the citizens, 2) majority rule, 3)
participation of citizens in politics, 4) freedom of
opinion, 5) some other human and political rights, 6)
legal certainty, 7) division of power and 8)
responsibility of those in power. Each criterion
corresponds to a different value, which can be realised
to a certain degree, more or less. It follows that there
are degrees of democracy (cf. Ross 1963, 92 ff.).

The main idea of democracy, the power of the people, is more or less intimately related to each criterion. It has thus a clear conceptual connection with the fact that those in power represent the interests of the citizens, follow the will of the majority and permit the citizens´ participation in politics. The connection with freedom of opinion, other basic rights, legal certainty, division of power and responsibility is less obvious. One may reasonably interpret the concept of democracy in two ways. According to one interpretation, enforcement of the rights, legal certainty, division of power etc. merely constitute a <u>causal</u> condition of democracy. According to another interpretation, they constitute a <u>conceptually</u> necessary condition of a fully developed democracy.

In any case, there is an analytic, conceptually necessary relation between basic rights and the well-known institution called in the Continental political philosophy <u>"Rechtsstaat"</u> (the state based on the law). Many reasons support the conclusion that legal validity of basic rights constitutes a conceptually necessary condition of a fully developed <u>Rechtsstaat</u> and, at the same time, when no <u>Rechtsstaat</u> at all exists, one cannot, for conceptual reasons, speak about the validity of basic rights.

Both the main idea of democracy and the criteria have a relatively general character. They are equally relevant, e.g., for the Swedish, West-German and North-American democracy. But the political language and hence the list of necessary conditions of democracy may change. Today, everybody regards the principle "one man one vote" as the consequence of the majority rule, and thus a precondition of democracy. Yet, some generations ago, women and persons less well off lacked the right to vote in the states generally considered as democratic. On the other hand, no single criterion is sufficient for democracy. One can perhaps hope to find some combinations of criteria jointly constituting such sufficient conditions. In practice, however, one faces great difficulties.

Assume, e.g., that a state fulfils to some extent all the mentioned criteria but the ruling party controls both trade unions and employers' associations, dominates all big companies, owns almost all newspapers etc. The opposition acts freely but has no chance to take over the political power. In such a situation, one can doubt whether the state is democratic. The question deserves a debate, in which one weighs the criteria the state in question fulfils and those - perhaps newly created - it does not fulfil.

The criteria of democracy are not only established in the
ordinary language but also morally justifiable. One also
needs moral considerations to state the criteria more
precisely and apply them to concrete societies. One can
give reasons both for and against the conclusion that a
given state, which to some extent fulfils some criteria
but sets aside others, is democratic. One must weigh and
balance those reasons. One may need an act of weighing
even when applying a single criterion; e.g., how great
respect for the basic human and political rights makes a
state democratic? How great importance of majority
decisions in a given society makes a state democratic,
even if it severely restricts human rights? An so on...

1) <u>Political Representation of Interests.</u> One of the most important
properties of democracy consists in the fact that those in power
protect common interests of citizens and weigh various particular
interests against each other (cf., e.g., Eikema Hommes, 31 ff.).

The moral judgments, permeating legal decision-making, must thus
have a connection with common interests of citizens. Other criteria
of democracy, first of all legal certainty, determine, however, some
limits for the role of the common interests. Equality before the law
(cf. Sections 2.5.2 and 4.1.4 infra about "universalisability")
excludes, at the same time, an adaptation of legal decision-making
to interests of particular social groups. On the other hand,
interests of the parties have a special position. Any citizen can be
involved in a legal dispute. His legal certainty is promoted by the
fact that he can rely upon the court's respect for his interests.

2) <u>Majority Rule.</u> Even an absolute monarch can pay attention to
the interests of the people. A democratic state, however, respects
not merely the interests but also the will of the citizens.

One can justify majority rule, <u>inter alia</u>, as follows.

a) It is an approximation of the calculus of human <u>preferences</u>,
often regarded as the core of morality. To decide what actions are
morally good, one must thus pay attention to both the number of
people having certain preferences and to the strength of the
preferences (cf. section 2.5.2 infra).

b) Furthermore, one can justify majority rule as promoting some
values people usually respect,e.g., <u>freedom</u> and <u>equality</u>. See also
Kelsen 1929, 3. Taxell 1987, 32 ff. mentions also <u>security</u>.

Majority rule thus presupposes that a general election is free and
approximates the egalitarian principle "one man one vote" (cf.,
e.g., Ch. 1 Sec. 1 par. 2 of <u>Regeringsformen</u>). On the other hand, it
does not imply either the citizens' equal ability to participate in
politics or their equal economic equality.

c) The third way to justify the majority rule is, what follows.
Political views compete with each other and it might be practically
impossible to prove which is the right one. A majority decision is
then a good means to achieve a <u>peaceful solution</u>. (According to
Kelsen 1929, 101, democracy thus is a consequence of value
relativism, though an objectivist can also be a democrat).

The relation between the majority rule and the political representation of interests raises difficult problems. It is not certain that the representatives actually protect the interests of the citizens. Their knowledge is limited, they must follow their party leaders and pay attention to other prudential reasons, etc. But the more their practice reflects the interests of the voters, the more democratic the state organisation is.

A total fulfilment of the majority rule implies that clear statutory provisions are interpreted literally, and that general clauses and other vague laws are interpreted according to the instructions the legislators give in the _travaux préparatoires_. In a democratic state, however, the majority rule ought not to entirely dominate the decision-making. Instead, one must find a harmony, a reasonable compromise between the wording of the law and moral considerations, _inter alia_ concerning rights, legal certainty and division of power. Several examples, _inter alia_ the history of the French revolution, show that unlimited power of a democratically elected legislative assembly does not prevent oppression.

3) _Participation_. Participation of citizens in politics is another criterion of democracy (cf., e.g., Anckar, 53 ff.). Democracy implies a kind of "amateur rule". It is also important that even the citizens who have no public duties exercise pressure on those in power, e.g., through public criticism. An organisation of courts, admitting both professional judges and lay judges, expresses a reasonable balance of the idea of participation and the professional lawyers' skill to perform rational legal reasoning.

4) _Freedom of opinion_. Democracy requires, conceptually or at least causally, a free formation of public opinion (cf., e.g., Ch. 1 Sec. 1 and Ch. 2 Sec. 12 par. 2 of the Swedish Constitution, _Regeringsformen_). The citizens must be free to express their views and to attempt at carrying out them in practice. Free formation of public opinion is related to rational debate about political and other practical questions. If citizens, instead, were manipulated by appeal to their emotions, the development of public opinion would only formally be free but, in fact, affected by the demagogues.

To facilitate free formation of opinion, legal decisions should be accompanied by comprehensible justification; cf. section 6.5. infra.

5) _Rights_. Besides, democracy requires (conceptually or causally) other rights. Democracy is no dictatorship of majority. There are many, more or less established, lists of rights. One can perhaps regard them as interpretations of such _basic values of democracy_ as freedom and equality. Let me merely mention freedom of opinion, freedom of the press, freedom of information, freedom of movement, freedom of assembly, freedom of demonstration, freedom of association, freedom of religion; right to life, protection of physical integrity, right to privacy, protection of family life, right of private property, protection of correspondence; freedom from inhuman or denigrating treatment, freedom from compulsory labour, freedom from discrimination, right to due process of law; and equality before the law (cf., e.g., Ch. 2 of the Swedish Constitution and the European Convention of Human Rights). I disregard here the complex problem of the so-called social and economic rights, such as right to employment, education etc.

Such lists vary in time and space. But a social order in which citizens have no rights at all is hardly democratic. Among many reasons of principle for the rights, let me mention the following: (1) Many governments tried to promote welfare at the expense of the rights and the result was always the same: decay of culture and economics. (2) Some rights are necessary to understand the point of such basic social practices as rational discourse. If, e.g., one denies other participants of a debate a right to be taken seriously, one cannot understand why a rational argument is better than bribery and other kinds of emotional manipulation (cf. Alexy 1986).

The point of legal decision-making is either to establish and enforce the rights of the parties, or at least to decide to what degree their interests should be protected. Collective goods and policies may be taken into account but never to such a degree that the rights are entirely ignored; cf. section 5.9.2 infra.

6) Legal Certainty. Democracy requires conceptually or at least causally legal certainty (section 1.4.1 supra). On the other hand, legal certainty presupposes a certain degree of respect for democratic values. Legal certainty thus means that legal decisions express a compromise between predictability and other moral considerations. The latter include the basic values of democracy.

Legal decisions should be loyal to the democratically elected legislature. The Swedish doctrine of the sources of law thus recommends that a person interpreting the law pays attention to the instructions the legislators give in the travaux préparatoires, even if these collide with his moral opinion. On the other hand, the great European tradition of legal certainty assumes that a judge must find a reasonable compromise between the wording of the law and moral considerations. The preparatory materials ought not to entirely dominate the decision-making.

7) Division of Power. A division of power promotes the legal certainty, the rights, the free majority decisions and the political representation of the interests of the electorate. A monopoly of power is always a threat to freedom of an individual. Not even the parliament should have the whole public power. Independent courts, relatively independent civil service, the division of power between the state and municipalities etc. thus constitute a causal, and perhaps also a conceptual, condition of democracy..

Though the Swedish constitution (Regeringsformen, Ch. 1 Sec. 4 and 6, etc.) in principle denies the division of power and regards the parliament as a supreme representative of the sovereign people, it emphasises independence of the courts and, to a lesser extent, state bureaucracy. No one, not even the parliament, may instruct the courts how to interpret the law in a concrete case (Ch. 11 Sec. 2).

But why to use judicial interpretation to adapt the law to moral demands? Is it not better to achieve the adaptation via continually changing legislation? Re this problem, cf. section 1.4.1 supra.

A relatively strong position of the courts is an important component of the system of division of power; e.g., a person affected by an administrative decision must be able to appeal to a court. General courts are perhaps most appropriate to decide in such cases, inter alia because of their long tradition of independence. Other reasons, such as professional skill, support establishment of special administrative courts. A special question concerns the courts' review of constitutionality of statutes. In Sweden, Ch. 11 sec. 14 of the Regeringsformen provides inter alia that, in the case under consideration, no court or authority may apply a regulation issued by the parliament or the government if it is obviously incompatible with the constitution. But one can wonder whether a special Administrative Tribunal would not be a better solution from the point of view of both independence and professional skill.

One can also argue for a strong position of various non-public organisations, such as parties, unions, enterprises etc., even if not all of them are organised according to the majority principle. (Cf. e.g., Eikema Hommes, 44; cf. Encyclopaedia of Philosophy, vol. 2, 340 re various theories of division of power).

8) Responsibility of Those in Power. Responsibility is another causal factor, promoting legal certainty, rights, free majority decisions and political representation of the interests of the electorate. One can even interpret the concept "democracy" in such a way that the division of power becomes conceptually necessary for democracy. Democracy presupposes responsibility of the government before the parliament (cf. Ch.1 Sec. 6 and Ch. 12 Sec. 1-5 of the Regeringsformen). Criminal responsibility of officials for abuse of power also promotes democracy (cf. Ch. 20 of the Swedish Criminal Code). An informal responsibility of the members of the parliament before the electorate is promoted by the fact that an unpopular representative risks not to be re-elected. Another kind consists of the fact that those in power are exposed to wide range of pressures (cf., e.g., Encyclopaedia of Philosophy, vol. 2, 339). However, responsibility of those in power before the electorate is efficient only if the citizens are well informed about the public decision making. The democratic law contains thus some provisions securing information (cf., e.g., Ch.2 Sec. 1 and 11 of the Regeringsformen).

As regards legal decisions, the following form of responsibility is of a peculiar importance. The decisions should be accompanied by clear and honest justification; cf. section 6.5. infra. This makes it possible for everybody to check their correctness.

Thus, democracy demands a legal decision making which harmonises respect for both the wording of the law and its preparatory materials and, on the other hand, moral rights and values, including freedom and equality. It also demands that the decisions are justified as clearly as possible. It does not demand a servile following of the text of the statutes or preparatory materials.

1.5. LEGAL KNOWLEDGE?

1.5.1. Introductory Remarks on Theoretical and Practical Statements

Peculiarities of the legal method affect the character of legal interpretatory statements. In order to understand this problem, let me draw, at first, some elementary distinctions.

Both the wording of the law and moral value judgments affect legal interpretation and legal reasoning in general. It is thus natural that any juristic text, e.g., a justification of a decision, an opinion supporting a legislative draft, or a scholarly work, contain not only law-describing propositions but also law-expressing norm- and value-statements. The former, sometimes called "spurious legal statements" report "value-freely" the content of statutes and other sources of law. When a lawyer utters a law-descriptive proposition, he certainly acts in a way similar to that of a scientist. The law-expressing statements, on the other hand, often called "genuine legal statements" do not describe but express norms and value judgments. They express an opinion that something ought to be done, is valuable etc. When a lawyer utters such a statement, his speech act is rather similar to a moral judgment or a legislative act.

Law-descriptive propositions are thus theoretical, whereas law-expressive statements are practical.

The most important function of a theoretical proposition is to give information. Its meaning is thus descriptive. A theoretical proposition is either true or false. Two main categories of theoretical propositions are empirical and analytical. Truth of empirical propositions, e.g., "Peter is older than John", depends on facts. Analytical propositions are true or false in all possible worlds", independently of facts. Their truth depends on concepts; e.g., the proposition "all bachelors are unmarried" is true due to the meaning of the words "all", "bachelor", "are" and "unmarried". It will stay true even if the number of married persons increased dramatically. A special case of analytical propositions are **logical propositions**, e.g., "if one is married than it is not so than one is not married", true or false due to the meaning of such logical words as "if... then", "either... or", "not", "all", "some" etc.

Two main categories of practical statements are value-statements and norm-statements. The main function of a value-statement is to express a value judgment, e.g. that something is beautiful, ugly, good or bad. The main function of a norm-statement is to express a norm and thus to influence people.

Already these distinctions, elementary and trivial, may be criticised. The borderline between different categories of statements may be fuzzy. For some purposes, it is better to speak about theoretical and practical (or non-theoretical) meaning, not statements. Cf. Evers 1970, 20 ff. But regardless all criticism, the fact remains that everybody, including the critics, can give unambiguous examples of empirical, analytical, normative and evaluative statements. I am assuming these distinctions as a working hypothesis, a point of departure of a further discussion.

1.5.2. Legal Interpretatory Statements

Keeping these distinctions in mind, one can ask the
question, What is the character of legal interpretatory
statements? Are they theoretical or practical? Let me
return to the quoted case NJA 1950 p. 650 (cf. Section
1.2.2 supra). The case concerns a choice between two
possible interpretations of Ch. 2 Sec. 1 of the Liability
for Damages Act , which states that one intentionally or
negligently causing a personal injury or a property
damage should compensate the victim therefor. One may
interpret the provision in two ways, as stipulating
liability for a person whose action was either (1) a
necessary condition for the result or (2) a sufficient
but perhaps not necessary condition for it.

Suppose that one chooses the interpretation 2, and
expresses the choice in the following interpretative
statement: "If a person's negligent action constitutes a
sufficient but not necessary condition for a damage, then
the person is not liable according to Ch. 2 Sec. 1 of the
Liability for Damages Act."

Since the interpretative statement expresses a choice
between admissible interpretations, one can regard it as
a _practical_ statement, either evaluative, proclaiming
that the interpretation 2 is right, or normative,
demanding that one ought to follow the provision thus
interpreted. On the other hand, the interpretative
statement claims to report the true sense of the legal
provision in question, that is, Ch. 2 Sec. 1 of the
Liability for Damages Act. From this point of view, it
appears to be a _theoretical_ proposition.

In fact, the interpretative statement follows from a
complex set of premises, some theoretical, some
practical, including, for example, what follows:

1) a theoretical proposition, m, about the meaning of
the interpreted provision;

2) theoretical propositions, p_1-p_n, e.g. about social
results of a certain interpretation of the provision;

3) theoretical propositions, r_1-r_n, about the sources
of law, e.g. precedents, relevant for the interpretation;

4) some theoretical propositions, s_1-s_n, about the
commonly accepted legal interpretation norms;

5) a "closing" practical statement, such as "if the
theoretical propositions m, p_1-p_n, r_1-r_n and s_1-s_n are
true; and if a person, intentionally or negligently, did
something that was a sufficient but not necessary
condition for the damage in question, then this person is

not liable according to Ch. 2 Sec. 1 of the Liability for
Damages Act.

Legal interpretative statements have thus both a
complex meaning and a complex justification.

Cf., e.g., Wedberg 1951, 252 ff.; Aarnio, Alexy and Peczenik 1981,
427 ff.; Peczenik 1983, 76 ff.; Aarnio 1987, 47 ff. and 180 ff.

1.5.3. The Main Problem: Knowledge, Truth And Rightness In Legal Reasoning

Complexity of meaning and justification of legal
interpretative statements is a reason for some
philosophical controversies concerning evaluation of
their correctness. Such an evaluation of goals, reasons,
methods, concepts and conclusions of legal reasoning is
the core of jurisprudence, cf. sec. 1.1 supra.

This is a normative question. Such questions belong to
the so-called context of justification. One must
distinguish it from such descriptive questions, asked in
the so-called context of discovery, as What factors did
cause a given outcome of a legal dispute?, What reasons
do the lawyers actually regard as convincing?, etc.

Justification of legal reasoning faces difficult
philosophical problems.

1) This form of reasoning presupposes apparently
incompatible theses.

a) When one performs legal reasoning and seriously
utters value judgments and norms, one assumes that these
are right. The statement "I am arguing for p although p
is not right" is strange. Even a liar hopes that others
will believe that what he says is right; otherwise, why
should he say it at all?

b) Yet, persons performing legal reasoning often admit
that incompatible value judgments and norms may be
possible and acceptable, without being absolutely right.
From this point of view, legal reasoning is similar to
practical advices. When Peter recommends holidays in Las
Palmas ("because the climate is warm and the night life
exciting") and John recommends holidays in Alaska
("because one can hunt and fish"), none of them needs to
assume that the other is wrong. One person may simply
think that the other has a different taste.

2) Legal reasoning constitutes a peculiar mixture of two different, ideally distinguishable, components. The first one is a description of the sources of the law, established evaluations, traditional legal reasoning norms etc. The second is a continual creation of value judgments that tell one whether to follow or not these sources, evaluations and norms. The first component is not enough. In section 1.5.2 supra, I have argued that both components affect the meaning and justification of legal interpretative statements. Let me give an additional example. Section 4 of the old Swedish Constitution (Regeringsformen), derogated as late as 1969, stipulated that "the King has the right to govern the realm alone". The actually applied norm was, instead, "The Government, responsible to the Parliament, has the executive power". Could one read the word "the King" as meaning "the Government responsible to the Parliament" and the words "the right to govern the realm alone" as meaning "the executive power"? Yet, legal reasoning is expected to be justified.

The main problem is what the word "justified" refers to in this context. Is legal reasoning justified if, and only if, it give us knowledge of the law? Is this knowledge the same as knowledge of statutes and other sources of the law?

The assumption that justified legal reasoning gives us a kind of knowledge leads to a serious problem. The following diagram illustrates this problem:

"own" norms and value judgments, endorsed or made by the person performing legal reasoning	AND	the sources of the law and established reasoning norms; value judgments established in the society	GIVE	knowledge of valid law or of juristic meaning of the sources of the law

This creates a puzzle. In what sense, if any, a legal interpretative statements can give us knowledge? To say that a theoretical proposition gives us knowledge is the same as to say that it is true. Can a legal interpretative statement then be true, even if regarded as a practical statement, and justifiable in some sense by a set of premises containing a norm or a value judgment? It is difficult to see how practical statements, ultimately based on one´s feelings (cf. section 2.4.5 infra), can give one true knowledge of the law. Or can a legal interpretative statement be justified in any other sense? One must thus choose one or more of the following ways to characterise legal reasoning:

1. Legal reasoning, deviating from the wording of the law, is <u>unjustifiable</u>, wrong, irrational etc. But this thesis is unacceptable, since it contradicts centuries of social practice. How was it possible that generations of lawyers let a wrong method to determine their work?

2. Legal reasoning is deeply justified and right, if it gives a <u>true knowledge</u>. One may hereby distinguish between two versions.

a) Legal reasoning is deeply justified and right, if it gives a true knowledge of the special juristic <u>meaning</u> of the sources of the law. This thesis has the advantage of reducing the problem of rightness to the well-known idea of truth. But again, how can a legal conclusion be true, even if it is justifiable by a norm or a value judgment? One must also explain why the same words and expressions have a special juristic meaning when occurring in the law and a different meaning when occurring elsewhere.

b) Legal reasoning is deeply justified and right, if it gives a true knowledge of the <u>real valid law</u>, not identical with the sources of the law. This thesis has the same advantage and disadvantage as 2a supra. Moreover, it is not clear what the "real valid law" is. Where does it exist, if not in the legal texts? If it is unwritten, what is the mode of existence of it?

3. Legal reasoning is deeply justified and right, though it <u>does not give one a true knowledge</u>. To be sure, it has support of some value judgments and norms, but these are continually created by the person interpreting the law. Legal reasoning thus <u>transforms</u> the established law into something else, that is, the <u>interpreted law</u>.

I will argue for the third way to characterise legal reasoning. But what does it mean that legal conclusions can be right (or correct) though not true? One needs a theory of rightness as distinct from truth.

One can also say that legal (interpretative) conclusions are true propositions about the interpreted law. But this leads to the following difficulty. The interpreted law is created exactly at the moment of interpretation. On the other hand, true propositions are true because they correspond to something <u>preexistent</u>. The discussed view thus implies the strange idea that interpretative conclusions are true, because they correspond to... themselves.

CHAPTER 2
RATIONALITY OF MORAL JUDGMENTS

2.1. COGNITIVISM AND NON-COGNITIVISM

At first, I must return to the preliminary question, Why not to assume that legal conclusions can be true, even if they are fully justifiable only by a set of premises containing a norm or a value judgment? Such an assumption implies another one, namely that norms or value judgments themselves possess truth values. This is, of course, the central problem of value theory. Let me thus make some observations, belonging to this area.

Different (meta-)theories of value statements compete with each other. One may classify them, as follows (cf., e.g., Moritz 1970, 9 ff.):

```
                    theories of value statements
         cognitivist                    non-cognitivist
naturalist          non-naturalist
```

Cognitivist theories identify value statements with some theoretical propositions, true or false. Naturalist theories regard value statements as theoretical propositions about "natural" properties of persons, states of affairs, objects, actions etc.

One can, e.g., define a morally good action, as follows.

1) If and only if an action, H, increases happiness of other people, then H is morally good.

2) If and only if an action, H, fits a certain calculus of human preferences, then H is morally good.

3) If and only if an action, H, promotes fulfilment of human talents, then H is morally good.

However, all naturalist theories face Moore´s famous "open question argument" (Moore 1959, 15 ff.; cf. Moritz 1970, 74 ff.). One can thus meaningfully ask such questions as "To be sure, H increases happiness, but is H good?", "To be sure, H fits the preferences, but is H good?" etc. The fact that such questions are meaningful shows that goodness is not identical with any naturalist property. If it were, such questions would be as

meaningless as the question "To be sure, John is a
bachelor but is he married?". The latter is meaningless
precisely because a bachelor is identical with a man who
never married. The former are meaningful, since to be
good is <u>not</u> the same as to increase happiness etc.

The failure of the naturalist theories makes it
understandable why the non-naturalist were created.
Non-naturalist (yet cognitivist) theories regard thus
value statements as theoretical propositions about
"non-natural" properties of persons, states of affairs,
objects, actions etc. One can, e.g., say that the
statement "an action, H, is morally good" means "H has
the property of goodness", not identical with any
"natural" property or a combination thereof. However, it
is difficult to state anything precise about this
property.

Certain philosophers have also assumed that people
possess a "sense of value" (analogous to sight, sense of
hearing etc.). One uses one's eyes to see that something
is red etc. Analogously, one uses the sense of value to
"see" that an action etc. possesses such a non-natural
value-property as goodness.

Theories of "the sense of values" are, however,
controversial. Value-properties are unique in this
respect that they only cause one single result, that is,
affect the sense of value, and thus cannot be confirmed
in any other way. If a person is "value-blind", that is,
lacking the sense of value, he cannot learn at all that
an action etc. is good. The situation is worse than in
the case of ordinary blindness. A blind person can use
physical instruments to learn what colours a thing has
but a value-blind one has no access to any
value-indicators. Any discussion between a value-blind
and a value-seeing person is thus impossible (cf. Moritz
1970, 35).

All cognitivist theories face also the following
difficulty. Value statements are reasons for action.
Suppose that Peter seriously claims that H is a morally
good action and that nothing incompatible with H is
better. It is then natural for Peter to have a
disposition both to approve of H and to perform H, if he
has an opportunity to do it. On the other hand, a pure
description of properties, either natural or other, does
not seem to be so intimately connected with action.

One may regard the <u>non-cognitivist</u> theories as a
reaction against the difficulties unsolved by the
cognitivist ones. The non-cognitivist theories regard
value statements as merely expressing (not describing!)

attitudes, feelings etc. One can, e.g., say that the statement "H is a good action" means "Hereby I am expressing my attitude: I like H". Value statements are emotional projections and have no truth value. They can no more be true than numbers healthy.

Among non-cognitivists, one must mention <u>Axel Hägerström</u>. His views were built up around the following theses (cf. Hägerström 1929, 111 ff.). All knowledge concerns things extant in time and space. Value statements lack truth values, since they "describe" something outside of time and space. The value "existing" in an object does not exist in any definite sense at all. Suppose that a person, A, gave bread to a poor man, B, and this was a good action. It is meaningless to attempt at stating precisely where the goodness does exist, it A's hand, in the bread, in B's mouth etc. Neither can values exist in a world outside time and space, since no such world can exist. The expression "the world outside time and space" is self-contradictory. Value statements are self-contradictory, too, apparently telling something about the objects but in fact only expressing feelings; cf. section 5.5 infra.

An important version of non-cognitivism, elaborated by Charles L. Stevenson (cf. 1944, 20 ff.) assumes that the value statement "this is good" has two functions. First, it expresses a combination of approval and exhortation: "I approve of x and I want you to do so as well". Second, it describes the the speaker's attitude .

However, one can also criticise the non-cognitivism.

1. Value statements, such as "H is good", are object oriented. The statement "H is good" is thus a statement about H. But a non-cognitivist claims that this statement only <u>apparently</u> tells something the action H but <u>in fact</u> only expresses feelings. The non-cognitivist assumes thus a corrective attitude as regards the ordinary language. It is not easy to tell what gives him sufficient reasons to do so.

2. Value statements can meaningfully be, and often actually are, supported by reasons. When Peter says that John is a good person, he may add, e.g., "... <u>because</u> John has a disposition to help people". Feelings, on the other hand, need no such support.

3. Non-cognitivists must deny that value statements, uttered by different persons, can be logically incompatible. No logical incompatibility exists between a description of the fact that Peter approves of H and a description of the fact that Paul disapproves of H. Yet, when Peter says "H is good" and Paul says "H is not good", these value statements seem to be incompatible.

4. Suppose that Peter approves of telling the truth and disapproves of causing unhappiness. If John tells Paul the truth and thus makes him unhappy, Peter experiences two different feelings, approval of the action of telling the truth and disapproval of causing happiness. In other words, he experiences "mixed feelings". It is perfectly possible to feel in this way. On the other hand, when morally evaluating the action of John, Peter cannot satisfy himself with a "mixed" judgment. He must make up his mind, that is, must weigh and balance the reasons for and against the conclusion that the action is good.

Moral statements have often a provisional, prima facie character. "Prima-facie" means, among other things, that other, overriding, reasons may justify the contrary conclusion. To tell the truth is thus a good action, unless it causes too much unhappiness, too much suppresses human talents etc.

Peter must thus tell in the concrete case whether the goodness of telling the truth outweighs the bad property of causing unhappiness.

5. Whoever utters a value statement, assumes that it is right (cf. Alexy 1989, 127 ff.).

Feelings, on the other hand, are neither right nor wrong, they simply are there.

The following story elucidates some of these difficulties. In many countries, pollution caused serious damage of the forest. Suppose that pollution is an inevitable result of industrial development, and the latter a necessary condition of high material standard of living. Suppose that a supporter of the high standard of living, A, discusses with an environmentalist, B. To be sure, they can have different beliefs concerning facts. A can, e.g., say that industrial output can increase without increasing pollution. B can claim that high standard of living is possible without industrial growth. But even if they agree about the facts, the discussion can continue. One must often decide what is better, growth of the standard of living or protection of clean air. The question does not concern either A´s or B´s feelings. These are clear. A likes the increased standard of living more than protection of environment, B likes the latter more than the former. The discussion concerns, instead, the question who is right. Is protection of environment in this case more important than the growth of living standard or is it not? The question is

practically important and both participants in the
discussion claim that it is soluble.

To be sure, a moderate non-cognitivist can regard the
discussion between A and B as mutual attempts to show the
opponent that he endorses incompatible value statements.
But so what? If one is a non-cognitivist, one must tell
that value statements merely express feelings and these
can be "mixed", see above. Moreover, if both A´s and B´s
different value systems are logically consistent, the
discussion must stop. If the non-cognitivists are right,
one cannot attempt at showing which system is better.

There exists an interesting analogy between non-cognitivism in moral
theory and scepticism in epistemology. A non-cognitivist argues that
no knowledge of values can exist. A sceptic gives philosophical
reasons for the conclusion that no knowledge at all is possible. The
objective reality is not accessible for human beings. Our knowledge
is based on observations but these are fallible, e.g., as a result
of optical illusions. If an evil demon all the time deceived all of
us, we could not know it. One cannot falsify scepticism, but in
order to live a normal life, one must ignore it.

2.2. PRACTICAL AND THEORETICAL MEANING OF PRACTICAL STATEMENTS

2.2.1. Practical Meaning

I will now present another theory, attempting at unifying
some cognitivist and non-cognitivist insights. The theory
deals only with moral statements, albeit one can perhaps
extend it to other kinds of practical statements.

A practical statement, i.e. a norm-expressive statement
or a value statement has, first of all, a practical
meaning.

Most elementary norm-expressive statements qualify a
human action as prescribed (obligatory), permitted, or
prohibited (forbidden). The statement "A should not park
his car here" thus qualifies A´s action of "parking the
car here" as prohibited (cf. section 4.4.2 infra). More
sophisticated norm-expressive statements will be
discussed in section 5.6.5 infra. From another point of
view, norm-expressive statements qualify a human action
as conforming to or violating the norm in question.

A value statement characterises an object as good, bad, beautiful, ugly, etc. It expresses a value judgment. Inter alia, it expresses or encourages approval or disapproval of an object. It is also a reason for action. Suppose that a person, A, seriously claims that H is a morally good action and that nothing incompatible with H is better. It is then natural for A to have a disposition to approve of H and to perform H, if an opportunity exists. If A has no such disposition, one may doubt whether the evaluative claim is serious. It would be strange to seriously claim that H is a morally good action and that nothing incompatible with H is better and yet to disapprove of H. It would also be strange not to perform H, given the opportunity.

The most important function of a norm-expressive statement is to affect people, that is, to bring about some actions and suppress other.

A norm-expressive statement is thus a reason for action. This is even clearer than in the case of moral value statements. Suppose that a person, A, seriously claims that H ought to be performed and that no overriding reasons tell against performing H. A has then a disposition both to wish that H is performed and to actually perform H, if an opportunity exists. It would be strange to seriously claim that H ought to be performed, to admit that no overriding reasons tell against performing H, and yet to wish that H is not performed. It would also be strange not to actually perform H, given the opportunity. In such a case, one would doubt whether the normative claim is serious.

2.2.2. More About Practical Meaning. Norms and the Will

An important question concerns the relation between a norm-expressive statement and the will. One must distinguish between four different things:

a) An utterance or an endorsement of a norm-expressive statement is often a causal result of the fact that an individual wants to achieve a certain goal and regards this norm as a means therefor. A will of a politician to achieve a goal can, e.g., cause his participation in a legislative process.

b) In some cases, however, one cannot identify an individual human being whose will the norm-expressive statement is supposed to express. A norm can be issued in the name of an institution, e.g., the parliament (cf. Olivecrona 1939, 32 ff. and 1971, 18 ff.).

c) An utterance or an endorsement of a norm-expressive statement often <u>causes</u> the fact that some people think of someone whose will corresponds to it. If something is obligatory, they think that "one" wishes it, if something is forbidden, they think that "one" does not wish it. So is the case, regardless of whether people can tell whose will they think about.

A norm-expressive statement, in particular a legal one, can thus express an <u>independent imperative</u>. Its meaning is such that one understands it as if it were a command, regardless of whether one can tell whose will it expresses. Neither is it necessary to know to whom it is addressed. A genuine command, on the other hand, exists only if a definite individual wants something and tells another one to do it (cf. Olivecrona 1939, 42 ff. and 1971, 128 ff.).

d) The <u>meaning</u> of a norm-expressive statement, e.g. imposing an obligation, is thus such that one cannot fully understand it, if one does not think about a will. This fact explains why many thinkers (wrongly) understood norms as meanings of acts of will (cf., e.g., Kelsen 1960, 4 ff.). Generally speaking, there is a link between the norm and an idea of the will of the person who follows this norm. The meaning of a norm includes a component which corresponds to the Latin word <u>"ut"</u> ("let it be that"; Opalek 1973, 222 and 1974, 49 ff.; cf. Hare 1952, 17 ff. on <u>neustic</u>). This component makes the norm "A ought to do H" a reason to perform the action H; and to perform an action presupposes an intention, that is, a will to act. But this is not the will of a person who enacted the norm but merely the will of a person who obeys it.

Cf. Harris 1979, 39: The idea that "(a)ll norms are meanings of acts of will (...) is acceptable provided it is understood as relating only to the logical category into which norms fall, not to any assumptions about actual willings."

Only as regards socially established norms, such as enacted statutes, one also assumes that there is another link, between the norm and a will of its creator. An obligatory action is the action that "one" wishes to be performed; but to understand the socially established norm, one does not need to have an exact idea of the person whose will it is supposed to express.

2.2.3. Theoretical Meaning of Practical Statements: Justifiability

Another important property of the meaning of most, if not all, practical statements is that they <u>may be justified</u>. Justifiability is an important component of <u>theoretical</u> meaning of practical statements (cf., e.g., Alexy 1989, 127; cf. Popper 1966, 384-5).

The following classification is conceivable:
  1) Some value statements are justifiable. One can support them with reasons. For instance, the following conversation makes sense: "-This picture is so beautiful! -Why? -Because it gives an impression of movement, and yet is so harmonious".
  2) Some (apparent?) "value statements" are perhaps not justifiable, as the following example indicates: "-This fish is so good! -Why? What a stupid question, I like it!".
  3) Some norm-expressive statements are justifiable. For instance, the following conversation is thinkable: "-Punishment ought to be stipulated for using drugs. -Why? -Because it would reduce the consumption of drugs. -But why ought one to reduce it? -Because using drugs is habit-forming and causes more pain than pleasure."
  4) Some commands and (apparent?) "norm-expressive statements" are perhaps not justifiable, as the following examples seem to indicate: "-Switch on the lamp! -Why? -What a stupid question, I told you, switch on the lamp!!". Or: "-All citizen of this country should worship the Leader! -Why? -What a stupid question, they should!!".
  Yet, one can regard the "unjustifiable" value statements and norm-expressive statements as justified by tacitly assumed authority reasons. One thus proffers the authority of the person who makes a judgment or gives a command, etc.

Justifiability implies that a person confronted with a practical statement can ask "why?" and thus demand reasons which support the statement. The faculty of asking "why?" is essential for our thinking and intersubjective communication.
  There are many ways to justify practical statements. Let me discuss three, one based on the causal relation between goals and means, another supported by weighing and balancing of various principles, and the third one based on the logical relation between practical and theoretical statements (see infra).
  The following, logically correct, inference exemplifies justification based on the causal relation between goals and means.

Premise 1 (a norm)   One ought to reduce the consumption of
                            drugs

Premise 2 (a   The consumption of drugs can be reduced,
theoretical   if and only if punishment for using drugs
proposition)   is stipulated

Conclusion: Punishment ought to be stipulated for
                            using drugs

Let me now give an example of a (logically correct)
inference supported by weighing and balancing of various
principles.

Premise 1 (a   Using drugs is a habit-forming practice and
theoretical   causes the user more pain than pleasure
proposition)

Premise 2 (a   If a practice is habit-forming and causes the
prima facie   user more pain than pleasure, then punishment
moral   ought to be stipulated for this practice, unless
principle)   other moral principles, justifying the contrary
                        conclusion, weigh more in this case

Premise 3   The moral principles, justifying the conclusion
(expressing a   that punishment ought not to be stipulated for
weighing of   using drugs, do not weigh more in this case than
principles   the reasons for stipulating punishment

Conclusion: Punishment ought to be stipulated for using drugs

The conclusion thus follows from a set of premises,
consisting of (1) a theoretical proposition, (2) a
prima-facie principle, and (3) a value statement,
expressing an act of weighing.

2.2.4. Theoretical Meaning of Practical Statements: L-, S- and D-rationality

An important component of the theoretical meaning of
practical statements can be characterised in the
following, more general and abstract, manner.

Although moral value statements and norm-expressive statements possess meaning related to some feelings and constitute reasons for action, various circumstances restrict arbitrariness of moral reasoning.

1. A moral statement can often be presented as a logically correct conclusion of a certain set of premises. One can also inquire whether these premises are (a) linguistically correct and (b) logically consistent.

2. One can also inquire whether the premises are sufficiently coherent.

3. Finally, different individuals can discuss moral questions in an impartial and otherwise objective way.

In brief, one can rationally justify moral statements.

Both philosophers and lawyers show recently an increased interest in rationality. The concept of rationality is, however, both ambiguous and applicable to vastly different areas. One speaks about deductive rationality, inductive rationality, scientific rationality in general, rationality of actions, goal rationality, norm rationality, system rationality, ethical rationality, legal rationality, rational reasoning etc. In this work, I will discuss rational reasoning, that is, rationality of conclusions, with particular attention to practical, inter alia moral and legal conclusions.

One can thus distinguish between three different demands of rationality. These demands are general but vague. I do not intend to formulate precise, contentually rich and generally valid rationality criteria. Only the moral discourse can show in concrete cases how rational particular conclusions are. The present work deals merely with conceptual and philosophical problems connected with some examples of rational moral and legal reasoning.

Logical rationality (in brief L-rationality; cf. Aarnio 1987, 189) of a conclusion means that it

1) follows logically of a set of premises that are

2) logically consistent and linguistically correct.

L-rationality is a minimum demand. A "justification" based on either inconsistent or linguistically incorrect premises is obviously worthless.

Logic comprises inferences whose truth depends on their form alone. that is, on concepts; e.g., the inference "if one is married than it is not so than one is not married" is true due to the meaning of such logical words as "if... then", and "not". I assume that all such inferences are logical, even if the inferential link is placed between norms or value statements lacking truth value.

Substantial or supportive rationality (S-rationality) constitutes the basic idea of rationality, its point. A perfect S-rationality of a conclusion means that it follows logically from a highly coherent set of premises. Inconsistent or linguistically incorrect premises are not S-rational. But the demand of S-rationality is stronger. It is also related to coherence.

I will return to coherence (cf. section 4.1 infra). But the main idea is that the degree of coherence is determined by balance between a number of criteria, inter alia, the following ones: the greatest possible number of supported statements belonging to the set of statements in question; the greatest possible length of chains of reasons belonging to it; the greatest possible number of connections between various supportive chains belonging to the set of statements; and the greatest possible number of preference relations between various principles belonging to it.

A conclusion may follow from a set of premises whose significant part constitutes a coherent theory. Other premises, belonging to this set, are perhaps coherent with this theory, but coherence is not proved. Such a conclusion is S-rational to a certain degree.

One can say that this conclusion has reasonable support. The statement p (weakly) supports the statement q if, and only if, q belongs to a set of premises, S, from which p follows logically. The support is reasonable, if all these premises are reasonable.

A reasonable statement is not falsified. Neither is it arbitrary. That is, the hypothesis is not to a sufficiently high degree corroborated that this statement does not logically follow from a highly coherent set of premises. In other words, the hypothesis is not to a sufficiently high degree corroborated that this statement is not perfectly S-rational.

The concept of reasonable support will be discussed in sections 2.7.4 and 3.2.4 infra.

Discursive rationality (in brief D-rationality; cf. Aarnio 1987, 190) of a conclusion means that it would not be refuted in a perfect discourse. D-rationality includes both S-rationality and some additional demands. In some cases, both the conclusion and its negation follow from highly coherent sets of premises. One can then hope that a discourse would determine which of these weighs more.

2.3. MORE ABOUT THEORETICAL MEANING OF PRACTICAL STATEMENTS. PRIMA-FACIE MORAL STATEMENTS

2.3.1. Criteria of Moral Goodness

There exists a considerable consensus of people, at least in the Western culture, that some principles are moral and that it is a morally good thing to pay attention to them. One can, e.g., mention the following principles.
   1) One ought not to injure other people.
   2) One ought to help other people.
   3) One ought to work efficiently.
   4) One ought to tell the truth.
   5) One ought to keep one´s promises.
   6) One ought to show courage.
Consequently, one can imagine a set of theoretical propositions about fulfilment of the principles, e.g.:
   1) A person, A, does not injure others people.
   2) A person, A, helps other people.
. . . .
   6) A person, A, shows courage.
Moreover, such statements as the following ones are meaningful:
   1) A is a morally good person, since he has a disposition not to injure other people.
   2) A is a morally good person, since he has a disposition to help other people.
   3) A is a morally good person, since he has a disposition to work efficiently.
   4) A is a morally good person, since he has a disposition to tell the truth.
   5) A is a morally good person, since he has a disposition to keep promises.
   6) A is a morally good person, since he has a disposition to show courage.
   These criteria fulfil the demand of L-rationality. In other words, they are meaningful in the following sense. The moral language is such that one can objectively (without relying on one´s emotions) state the following. The rules of moral language do not prohibit one to conclude that if A helps others, works efficiently, tells the truth, keeps promises, shows courage, etc., then he is prima-facie a good person. The content of the prima-facie conclusion is that he is a good person, provided that no reasons for the contrary conclusion are stronger.
   Theoretical propositions about some facts, such as a person´s disposition not to injure others or his

helpfulness etc., are thus meaningful reasons for the practical conclusion that this person is prima-facie morally good. In other words, criteria for the goodness are always determined, and not a matter of decision (cf. Jareborg 1975, 129 ff., quoting Philippa Foot and others).

Some other "moral criteria", on the other hand, would be ceteris-paribus linguistically unthinkable, that is meaningless without a special, often ad-hoc explanation, which goes beyond common sense. If somebody uttered the statement "A is a morally good person, since his nose is shorter than two centimetres", one would suspect that he is joking, does not know the language or is insane. To be sure, all absurdities can be saved by some ad-hoc hypotheses. For example, the absurd statement "A is a morally good person, since his nose is shorter than two centimetres" would gain some sense had one added to it a theory ascribing long noses evil qualities. But such a theory would be a strange one, indeed.

The established use of language thus determines some limits for arbitrariness of moral reasoning.

Moreover, the moral criteria are not only meaningful but also supported by coherent chains of reasons. One may argue for them. In this sense, they fulfil the demands of S-rationality.

2.3.2. General Theories of the Morally Good

Since a long time, philosophers regard such criteria as insufficiently profound and attempt at constructing general theories of moral goodness. These theories differ from mere criteria. Each general theory aims at stating an overriding formula, covering all morally good actions and persons. No concrete criterion implies such a claim.

It is plausible to say generally that morally good action has something to do with showing consideration for others. But the word "others" is vague. It certainly covers other people. One may argue that it also covers all creatures whose interests may be affected by the action regulated or evaluated by a moral statement. In other words, one may argue that it covers all creatures who can suffer, feel pleasure, think etc. The expression "showing consideration" is vague, too. One can show consideration to others by respecting their preferences, happiness, talents etc.

A special question concerns moral values attached to some products (in German philosophy called <u>Werkwerte</u>). One can argue that it is a morally good action to produce art, technology etc. But one may also argue that creating such cultural products is ggod only when it promotes interests of people, at least in the long run.

Several competing moral theories are thus admissible, each implying a definition of a good (or a right) action.

For the sake of simplicity, I disregard here a plausible distinction between the morally good and the morally right, according to which the former notion generally refers to the subjective dimension of actions: a good action is a virtuous action.

<u>Inter alia</u>, the following definitions are possible.
   1) If and only if an action, H, increases happiness of other people, then H is morally good.
   2) If and only if an action, H, fits a certain calculus of human preferences, then H is morally good.
   3) If and only if an action, H, promotes fulfilment of human talents, then H is morally good.
   4) If and only if an action, H, fits some goals and standards of perfection, inherent in established social practices, then H is morally good.
   Each general theory of this kind defines the morally good and, at the same time, stipulates a general norm for a moral action. The theories express, in other words, various <u>meaningful</u> (L-rational) and well <u>supported</u> (highly S-rational) premises, supporting the conclusion that one <u>prima-facie</u> ought to perform a certain action. I am omitting the complex question to what extent different theories imply different evaluation of concrete actions.
   Some "moral theories", on the other hand, would be <u>ceteris-paribus</u> meaningless without an explanation which goes beyond common sense. For example, the statement "an action, H, is morally good if and only if it increases the number of white stones in Scania" would gain some sense only if one had added to it a strange theory, e.g. ascribing white stones in Scania immortal souls.

2.3.3. <u>Prima-facie</u> Character of Moral Theories and Criteria

Many criteria and general theories of the moral good are both meaningful and reasonable. I will argue, however, that they have a provisional, <u>prima-facie</u> character. The argument consists of the following   steps.

Step 1 is to describe some well-known facts. Many criteria and theories of moral goodness compete with each other.

At the level of criteria, there exists "the well-known variation in moral codes from one society to another and from one period to another, and also the differences in moral beliefs between different groups and classes within a complex community" (Mackie 1977, 36). Moreover, a single individual often endorses mutually competing moral criteria. For example, a doctor endorses simultaneously the view that he ought to inform the patient about his sickness and the view that he ought to help him as efficiently as possible. But the doctor's disposition to tell the truth can in some cases harm his patient. The doctor must then make a choice between telling the truth and efficiently helping the patient. Or, a person making a moral judgment may "pick up" the peaceful disposition and helpfulness of a certain individual and concludes that this individual is morally good. He decides then not to use the other criteria (e.g., willingness to work, disposition to tell the truth etc.) when making moral evaluation in a concrete case.

At the level of general theories of moral good, there also exists a great variation. Sceptics disagree with objectivists. Rights theorists disagree with utilitarianists. Natural law theorists disagree with various kinds of historicists. Rule utilitarianists disagree with action utilitarianists. One can give reasons not only in favour of each theory but also against it.

Step 2 is the following hypothesis, explaining the described facts. Moral opinions of an individual do not constitute a consistent system of precise rules. Already Aristotle noticed the problem. "The Aristotelian approach starts with the premises that Practical Philosophy is concerned with principles of action and that the world in which we act is a world of 'things capable of being otherwise than they are' (EN. 1140 a31 and elsewhere.) In this untidy world of the contingent and the unforeseen, universal knowledge... is not to be had... 'To look for

demonstration in practical matters is as vulgar an error
as it is to accept less than demonstrative reasoning in
mathematics´" (EN. 1094 b26; quoted from Nowell-Smith
1973, 316).

Precise rules adapted to some cases of moral judgment
thus tend to conflict with other cases. "And despite the
prominence in recent philosophical ethics of...
utilitarian principles, and the like, these are very far
from constituting the whole of what is actually affirmed
as basis in ordinary moral thought" (Mackie 1977, 37.).
To be sure, a general theory may be changed and adapted
to counter-examples. But then, new counter-example would
appear. A gain of consistency at one end leads to loss at
the other.

Step 3 consists in the following hypothesis. A rational
choice of criteria and theories of moral good is often
based on <u>weighing and balancing</u>.

As regards criteria, this thesis is both plausible and
rather trivial. For example, a doctor performs an act of
weighing, which decides whether telling the truth (one
moral criterion) weighs in the actual case more or less
than avoiding harm (another criterion).

As regards general theories, the weighing hypothesis is
more controversial, yet in my opinion true. Assume, for
example, that an utilitarianist claims generally that an
an action which fits a certain calculus of preferences is
both good and obligatory. He decides then not to pay
attention to other normative theories, basing the moral
goodness and obligatoriness on happiness, established
practices, natural rights etc. Of course, he may employ
very different arguments to justify this choice. He may,
e.g., regard his theory as the only one logically
consistent, the only one correctly describing or
reflecting the established practice of moral judgment
etc. Such claims, however, have a rather intolerant
character. If a competing theory of the moral good
actually is inconsistent, it can very often be converted
into an improved theory, consistent and still competing
with the chosen one. At the end of a day, an advocate of
a certain moral theory states very often that it contains
<u>more important</u> moral insights than its competitors. This
judgment of importance implied an act of weighing and
balancing.

Step 4 consists in another hypothesis. The role of
weighing in moral contexts together with the empirical
fact that no general theory of moral goodness so far
succeeded to defend his assumed monopoly makes it
plausible to claim that <u>all</u> criteria and theories of

moral goodness have a <u>prima-facie</u> character. (Re the concept of "<u>prima facie</u>", cf. Ross, W.D., 27-28). That is, they are provisional, since other considerations, justifying an incompatible conclusion, may weigh more.

One can object to it and point out that many established systems of morality, as well as many philosophical theories of moral goodness, contain norms which, according to claims put forward in such systems or theories, have a definitive, not merely <u>prima-facie</u> character. Take, e.g., Catholic morality. It claims that the norm forbidding the intentional killing of an innocent is a definitive (not merely <u>prima-facie</u>) rule. Utilitarianists, e.g., claim often that one definitively ought to adapt one´s actions to preferences of other people. One can also imagine a perfectionist who claims that one definitively ought to perform actions promoting fulfilment of human talents, fitting some goals and standards of perfection, inherent in established social practices; etc.

Yet, it is not difficult to refute the objection. To be sure, such claims are actually put forward, but they are wrong. If life of billions could be saved by killing one innocent person, one ought to kill this person. If preferences of other people, or established social practices, include elements of cruelty, racial prejudices etc., one ought to disregard them. The impression of definitiveness is caused by a very great weight the rules in question have. But one can always imagine justifiable exceptions. Moreover, the exceptions are justifiable by recourse to weighing and balancing, showing that other considerations weigh more in certain situations than the main rule. Consequently, such rules may be regarded as merely <u>prima-facie</u>.

One must, however, make a distinction between the following concepts of <u>prima-facie</u>.

1. A practical statement has the <u>prima-facie-1</u> character (a <u>weak</u> <u>prima-facie</u>) if, and only if, the <u>language</u> in question <u>does not make it strange</u> for one to consider it within the act of weighing and balancing which determines one´s practical opinion or conduct (action or forbearance).

2. A practical statement has the <u>prima-facie-2</u> character (a <u>strong</u> <u>prima-facie</u>) if, and only if, the <u>culture</u> in question <u>compels</u> one to consider it within the act of weighing and balancing which determines one´s practical opinion or conduct (action or forbearance).

Without a serious attempt to make it precise, let me give two examples of reasonable interpretations of the

vague expression "the culture in question compels one to
consider a norm- or value-statement":

a. Any normal person, belonging to the culture, in any
particular case, to which this statement is applicable,
would regard it as strange not to consider this statement
and yet to insist that one has performed a justifiable
act of weighing and balancing in order to answer the
question whether H definitively is obligatory or good.

b. Any normal person, belonging to the culture, in any
particular case, to which this statement is applicable,
would act in a manner which implies that he obeys the
rule, according to which one ought to consider this
statement when performing such an act of weighing.

The following two concepts of prima-facie are less important.

3. A practical statement has the prima-facie-3 character if, and
only if, the culture in question does not make it strange for one to
consider it within the act of weighing which determines one's
practical opinion or conduct (action or forbearance).

4. A practical statement has the prima-facie-4 character if, and
only if, the language in question compels one to consider it within
the act of weighing and balancing which determines one's practical
opinion or conduct (action or forbearance).

Whenever I write "prima-facie" without index, I mean
prima-facie-1.

The following relations between these concepts of
prima-facie are plausible:

I. If a practical statement has the prima-facie-2
character (the strong prima-facie), it has also the
prima-facie-1 character (the weak prima-facie).

That is, if the culture in question compels one to
consider a practical statement within such an act of
weighing and balancing, the language in question does not
make it strange for one to consider it within this act of
weighing and balancing.

Indeed, one cannot imagine a situation in which the
language alone is sufficient to make it strange to
consider the statement, and yet any normal person,
belonging to the culture which uses this language, takes
for granted that one should consider it, that it is
strange not to consider it, etc.

II. If a practical statement has the prima-facie-4 character, it has
also the prima-facie-3 character.

That is, if the language in question compels one to consider a practical statement within such an act of weighing and balancing, the culture in question does not make it strange for one to consider it within this act of weighing and balancing.

One cannot imagine a situation in which the language alone compels one to consider the statement, and yet any normal person, belonging to the culture which uses this language, thinks that it is strange to consider it.

Logically incompatible actions can be, at the same time, prima facie good. One can also simultaneously have a prima facie duty to perform logically incompatible actions. The "normal" logic is thus not applicable to moral prima-facie statements. Suppose, e.g., that A killed B. One prima-facie reason, for instance circumstances of his act, can justify a life imprisonment of A, another, for instance A´s psychical condition, can support a milder punishment.

2.3.4. The Step From Theoretical Propositions To Prima-facie Practical Conclusions

This concept of prima-facie allows one to fruitfully discuss the question whether a practical statement can follow from a set of premises solely consisting of theoretical propositions. I will discuss here only moral norms and value-statements, thus leaving aside the problem whether other practical statements have the same properties. (Re theoretical meaning of moral value judgments in general, cf. Peczenik and Spector, 441 ff.).

(1) Ought- and Good-Making Facts

First of all, the language alone decides which facts are and which are not strange for one to consider in one´s act of weighing and balancing which answers the question whether A´s action H is obligatory or good. In principle, one does not need to make a recourse to weighing and balancing in order to find out which facts belong these two categories. Keeping in mind the definition of the "weak prima-facie" (prima-facie-1), one may claim that the following theses are plausible explications of analytic relations:

(1.1)   There exists at least one consistent description
            of an ought-making fact, such that the following
            holds good: if this fact takes place, then A
            ought <u>prima-facie</u> to do H, in the <u>weak</u> sense of
            "prima-facie"

and

(1.1*)   There exists at least one consistent description
            of a good-making fact, such that the following
            holds good: if this fact takes place, then the
            action H is <u>prima-facie</u> good, in the <u>weak</u> sense
            of "prima-facie".

Such relations may also be called "logical", provided
that one follows von Wright's advice (1963, 167) and
"enlarges the province of logic".

By the way, I disregard here the problem whether the
list of these ought- and good-making facts is finite or
infinite. I also disregard the question of mathematical
notation, one would need to express the idea of an
infinite list.

Let now the symbols $F_1 OUGHT(aH)$ - $F_n OUGHT(aH)$ stand for
all facts which are included in the complete list of
established moral criteria of what one ought to do; and
the symbols $F_1 GOOD(H)$ - $F_n GOOD(H)$ stand for all facts
which are included in the complete list of **established**
moral criteria of the good. Both lists are possible to
elaborate by a study of social practice, without any
recourse to weighing and balancing.

Now, one may claim that the following theses are
plausible explications of analytic relations between
practical statements and, on the other hand, good- and
ought-making facts:

(1.2)   If at least one ought-making fact $\{(F_1 OUGHT(aH)$
            or $F_2 OUGHT(aH)$ or, ... or $F_n OUGHT(aH)\}$ takes
            place, then A ought <u>prima-facie</u> to do H, in the
            <u>weak</u> sense of "prima-facie"

and

(1.2*)   if at least one good-making fact $\{F_1 GOOD(H)$ or
            $F_2 GOOD(H)$ or, ... or $F_n GOOD(H)\}$ takes place,
            then H is <u>prima-facie</u> good, in the <u>weak</u> sense of
            "prima-facie".

For example, if an action, H, increases happiness of other people, then H is prima-facie morally good or obligatory, in the weak sense of "prima-facie".

To avoid misunderstandings, let me emphasise the following. Since the weak prima-facie in this sense does not commit one to any action, the theses (1.1) - (1.2*) establish no bridge from the "Is" to the "Ought".

The following theses are also plausible explications of analytic relations:

(1.3)   If at least one ought-making fact $\{(F_1 OUGHT(aH)$ or $F_2 OUGHT(aH)$ or, ... or $F_n OUGHT(aH)\}$ takes place, then it is reasonable that A ought prima-facie to do H, in the strong sense of "prima-facie"

and

(1.3*)   if at least one good-making fact $\{F_1 GOOD(H)$ or $F_2 GOOD(H)$ or, ... or $F_n GOOD(H)\}$ takes place, then it is reasonable that H is prima-facie good, in the strong sense of "prima-facie".

As stated above, a practical statement has a prima-facie-2 character (the strong prima-facie) if, and only if, the culture in question compels one to consider it within the act of weighing and balancing which determines one's practical opinion or conduct (action or forbearance).

The theses 1.3 - 1.3* state that the culture in question compels one to consider in one's act of weighing any practical statement which the language does not make strange to consider. Such a statement may be refuted by arguments only, not simply ignored. This implies that if F is a fact which the language does not make strange to consider in an act of weighing concerning the question whether an action is definitively good or obligatory, then the hypothesis is reasonable that all normal people within the corresponding culture take for granted, at least implicitly, that F should be thus considered.

The strong prima-facie has a practical force. It commits one to consider some things when performing an act of weighing. Yet, the theses (1.3) and (1.3*) establish no bridge from the "Is" to the "Ought". The conclusions they validate are no practical statements, but merely meta-statements, according to which some practical statements are reasonable. "(W)ithin the context of a given moral discourse there are certain moves which are upheld, not by semantic rules, but rather by the conception of reasonability embedded in the moral discourse itself" (Peczenik and Spector, 473).

The statement "at least one good-making fact $\{F_1GOOD(H)$ or $F_2GOOD(H)$ or, ... or $F_nGOOD(H)\}$ takes place" is logically equivalent to the **propositional** content of the statement "H is prima-facie good, in the strong sense of "prima-facie". It is also equivalent to the **propositional content** of the statement "H is, all things considered, good". Moreover, the statement "at least one ought-making fact $\{F_1OUGHT(aH)$ or $F_2OUGHT(aH)$ or, ... or $F_nOUGHT(aH)\}$ takes place" is logically equivalent to the **propositional** content of the statement A ought prima-facie to do H, in the strong sense of "prima-facie" and to the **propositional content** of the statement "A ought, all things considered, to do H". (Cf. Peczenik and Spector, 451 ff.).

2.3.5. Permissibility-Making Facts

One can extend this discussion to other prima-facie norm statements, in particular concerning rights. There are not only ought-making but also permissibility-making, claim-making facts, etc.

Let me start with permissibility. How can a moral permissibility be justified? Let me divide the argument in two parts. 1) At first, I will report the well-known arguments, according to which a sphere of freedom is justified, because it is necessary for action and communication. 2) Then, I will discuss the problem, how extensive the free sphere ought to be.

I. Justification of a Sphere of Freedom

Let me, at first, consider the relation between freedom and action. The fact that one's sphere of freedom is necessary for one's action supports the conclusion that one ought to have a sphere of freedom. The following intellectual steps elucidate this idea:

(1) I do act intentionally, for my purposes.

(2) A sphere of freedom to act for my purposes is a necessary condition of all my actions.

(3) I ought prima-facie to have what is a necessary condition of all my actions.

(4) Consequently, I ought prima-facie to have a sphere of freedom.

(5) All people are similar in principle to myself.

(6) All people are purposive agents.

(7) A sphere of freedom to act for one's purposes is a necessary condition of all actions of anybody.

(8) Anyone ought prima-facie to have what is a necessary condition of one's actions.

(9) Thus, everybody ought prima-facie to have a sphere of freedom.

(This is a paraphrase of Gewirth's theory, cf. Hudson 1984, 115 ff. But I have added the assumptions 5-8).

This justification includes two assumptions, (3) and (8), from theoretical propositions to prima-facie ought-statements. The assumptions are plausible precisely because the conclusions have the prima-facie character. Moreover, (3) and (8) can be interpreted as meaning postulates, characterising a possible sense of the concept of "ought" within our moral culture.

Another justification of a sphere of freedom is based on requirements of human communication. Let me follow Robert Alexy's idea that a social order not taking individuals seriously, and thus not recognising any sphere of freedom at all, cannot be justified in a rational discourse. One may thus reason in the following way.

(I) Each participant of a rational discourse, in which one justifies norms, must take seriously the addressees of his argument. Otherwise the discourse would be impossible. Neither would it be possible to understand why a rational discourse is better than emotional manipulation. One must thus assume that other persons, in order to participate in the discourse, must be autonomous individuals, having a sphere of freedom. A society in which individuals do not have such a sphere, though logically possible, is discursively impossible, unjustifiable (cf. Alexy 1986).

The following intellectual steps elucidate this idea:

(1) I discuss the problem of justification of norms with others.

(2) Such a discourse is possible only if I assume that other persons, participating in it, have a sphere of freedom.

(3) Anyone ought prima-facie to have what is a necessary condition of one's capacity to participate in the practical discourse.

(4) Thus, everybody ought prima-facie to have a sphere of freedom.

Again, this justification includes an assumption, (3), which can be interpreted as a postulate, characterising a part of the meaning of the concept of "prima-facie ought" in our culture.

(II) Each participant of a practical discourse, thus qualified as an autonomous person, acts against his interest in preserving the autonomy, if he consents to establishment of a social order which does not recognise any sphere of freedom at all (cf. Alexy 1986).

The following intellectual steps elucidate this idea:

(1*) If I had consented to establishment of a social order which does not recognise any sphere of freedom of other people, I would have a small chance of my own sphere of freedom being accepted.

(2*) Acceptance of my own sphere of freedom by others is a necessary condition of preserving my autonomy as an individual.

(3*) I ought prima-facie to have what is a necessary condition of my preserving my status as an autonomous individual.

(4*) I ought prima-facie not to consent to establishment of a social order which does not recognise a sphere of freedom of others.

This justification, too, includes an assumption, (3*), which can be interpreted as a postulate, characterising a part of the meaning of the concept of "prima-facie ought" in our culture.

II. Justification of the Extension of Freedom

As regards the <u>extension</u> of freedom, one may regard the following thesis as a plausible explication of an analytic relation:

(2.1)   There exists at least one consistent description of a (permissibility-making) fact, such that the following holds good: if this fact takes place, then it is permissible for A to <u>prima-facie</u> do H (in the <u>weak</u> sense of <u>"prima-facie"</u>).

Moreover, one may base the answer to the question, What actions ought to be (morally) permissible?, on the complete list of socially established "permissibility-making" facts, such as basic human wants, needs, interests etc. Let the symbols $F_1PaH - F_nPaH$ indicate theoretical statements about these facts. If an action H of the person A is on this list, it follows that it is <u>prima-facie</u> permissible for A to do H (in the <u>weak</u> sense of <u>prima-facie</u>). It is thus not strange in the light of the language to consider these facts in one's act of weighing and balancing. One may assume that there is a plurality of permissibility-making facts. One may speak about them in an abstract way. On the other hand, it is difficult to state precisely what these facts are. One may give some examples, but it is doubtful whether they prove a theory of **fundamental values**, such as, e.g., <u>Finnis's</u> (1980, 59 ff. and 81 ff.).

One may then claim that the following theses are plausible explications of analytic relations:

(2.2)   If at least one permissibility-making fact $\{F_1\text{Permissibility}(aH)$ or $F_2\text{Permissibility}(aH)$ or, ... or $F_n\text{Permissibility}(aH)\}$ takes place, then it is <u>prima-facie</u> permissible for A to do H, in the <u>weak</u> sense of "prima-facie"; and

(2.3)   if at least one permissibility-making fact $\{F_1\text{Permissibility}(aH)$ or $F_2\text{Permissibility}(aH)$ or, ... or $F_n\text{Permissibility}(aH)\}$ takes place, then it is reasonable that it is <u>prima-facie</u> permissible for A to do H, in the <u>strong</u> sense of <u>"prima-facie"</u>.

This implies that if F is a fact which the language does not make strange to consider in an act of weighing concerning permissibility, then the hypothesis is reasonable that all normal people within the corresponding culture take for granted, at least implicitly, that F should be thus considered.

2.3.6. Claim-Making Facts

The concept "a moral right" is used, however, not only in the sense of freedom (permissibility) but also to cover a <u>claim</u>.

One person has a right, or a claim, not to be exposed to (not to bear, non pati) a given action of another person. This claim corresponds to a duty of the other to forbear from a given action (non facere). For example, a person, A, has a right not to be molested in his home, and others have a duty not to molest him. Cf. Petrazycki 1959-1960, vol. 1, 103 ff. Cf. Lindahl 1977, 15 ff. on Bentham's analogous concept.

This claim of A is not the same as his freedom to perform any action. What an action could it be? Neither is it the same as its competence (power) to do anything, e.g., to sue a trespasser. A claim of A not to be molested is satisfied (fulfilled) as no one molests him, without any necessity of A to do anything. Kelsen 1960, 133-134, calls such a claim a Reflexrecht, since it is merely a "mirror picture" of another person's duty. Cf. also Lindahl 1977, 26 on Hohfeld's corresponding concept. Also according to S. Kanger, A's claim against another person, B, that F means the same as B's duty to see to it that F, cf. Lindahl 1977, 44.

In a similar manner, one can discuss a claim of a person to receive (or to accept) something (accipere); this claim thus corresponds to a duty of another to perform a positive action (facere). One may thus say: "a baby has a claim to be fed by its mother" (cf. Petrazycki 1959-1960, vol. 1, 103 ff.). There is an interesting difference between the claims to forbearance and those to positive action. The former can be universal and unconditional, like A's claim that nobody may kill him. The latter, on the other hand, are almost always limited to some persons (cf. Levin, 91). The "social and economic rights", e.g., such as the right to work etc. make sense only if there exists, or at least ought to exist, an identifiable person, B, having the duty to give A work, and so on.

Let me now pass to the question of justification of claims. The answer to this question must have something to do with such facts as human wants, needs, interests etc. supporting this claim. Cf. Peczenik 1969b (1970, 154-5). Feinberg 1980 thinks that "the sort of beings who can have rights are precisely those who have (or can have) interests" (167), including animals but not vegetables (169).

One may thus attempt at elaborating an abstract justification of claims, based on claim-making facts. One may then claim that the following thesis is a plausible explication of an analytic relation:

(3.1)   There exists at least one consistent description of a (claim-making) fact, such that the following holds good: if this fact takes place, then A has a prima-facie claim that B does H, in the weak sense of "prima-facie".

If one assumes the list of socially established claim-making facts, one may also regard the following theses as plausible explications of analytic relations:

(3.2)   If at least one of the claim-making facts {F_1Claim(abH) or F_2Claim(abH) or, ..., or F_nClaim(abH)} takes place, then A has a prima-facie claim that B does H, in the weak sense of "prima-facie"; and

(3.3)   If at least one of the claim-making facts $\{F_1\text{Claim}(abH)$ or $F_2\text{Claim}(abH)$ or, ..., or $F_n\text{Claim}(abH)\}$ takes place, then it is reasonable that A has a prima-facie claim that B does H, in the strong sense of "prima-facie".

Moreover, it is plausible to state that if a person, A, has a claim that another person, B, does H, then B has a duty to do H.

The reverse implication is more complex. Sometimes a duty exists without a corresponding claim (cf. Petrazycki 1959-1960, vol. 1, 70 ff.; cf. Feinberg 1980, 144). But if a person, B, has a duty to do H, and a "claim-making" relation between B and another person, A, exists, then A has a prima-facie claim that B does H. Let me mention two kinds of these relations.

1) The duty constituting (legal or moral) norm may thus explicitly state that A's duty is related to B, e.g., the norm "a mother ought to feed her baby" states that it is the baby who is to be fed.

2) But a norm of the type "B has a duty to do H" may support a norm of the type "A has a claim that B does H", even though the first norm does not mention A. Assume that (1) B has a duty to do H and, at the same time, (2) some established "claim-making" relations between A and B exist, identifiable without recourse to weighing and balancing. Assume, e.g., that B's doing H importantly increases the degree of fulfilment of A's wants, needs, interests or benefits. This assumption implies three conclusions (1) A has a prima-facie claim that B does H; and (2) B has a duty to do H and (3) B has a duty to do H because A has a prima-facie claim that B does H.

One may thus conclude that the following thesis is a plausible explication of an analytic relation:

(4.1)   There exists at least one consistent description of a (claim-making) relation between A and B, such that the following holds good: if A and B are thus related to each other, then A has a prima-facie claim that B does H, in the weak sense of "prima-facie".

Furthermore, assuming an established list of claim-making relations, one may also regard the following theses as plausible explications of analytic relations:

(4.2)   If B ought to do H and at least one claim-making relation between A and B (F_1baH or F_2baH or, ... or F_nbaH) takes place, then A has a prima-facie claim that B does H, in the weak sense of "prima-facie"; and

(4.3)   If B ought to do H and at least one claim-making relation between A and B ($F_{1b}aH$ or F_2baH or, ... or F_nbaH) takes place, then it is reasonable that A has a prima-facie claim that B does H, in the strong sense of "prima-facie".

Such facts as wants, needs, interests etc. are not identical with the rights they support; cf., e.g., Opalek 1957, 302. To justify rights, they must be morally relevant. Cf., e.g., Martin 1986, 158.

2.3.7. Competence-Making Facts

One can also consider some theses relating <u>prima-facie</u> <u>competence</u> with some competence-making facts.

A has a competence to create B's deontic (normative) position D if, and only if, A <u>can</u> bring it about that B has the normative position D. The following abstract thesis seems to be plausible:

(5.1)   There exists at least one consistent description of a (competence-making) fact, such that if this fact takes place, then A has a <u>prima-facie</u> competence to create B's normative position D, in the <u>weak</u> sense of <u>"prima-facie"</u>.

Further theses are expressed with help of the following symbols. $\text{Competence}_{pf}\,aHbD$ means that a person, A, has a <u>prima-facie</u> competence to create through an action, H, another person's (B's) normative position, D. In other words, A can bring it about that another person, B, has a <u>prima-facie</u> normative position, D. (For more details, cf. Lindahl 1977, 212 etc.). The symbols $F_1\text{Competence}(aHbD)$ - $F_n\text{Competence}(aHbD)$ thus indicate what belongs to a certain list of competence-making facts. The following theses are thus plausible explications of an analytic relations:

(5.2)   If at least one competence-making fact, $F_1\text{Competence}(aHbD)$ or $F_2\text{Competence}(aHbD)$ or, ...or $F_n\text{Competence}(aHbD)$, takes place, then A has a <u>prima-facie</u> competence to create B's normative position, D, in the <u>weak</u> sense of <u>"prima-facie"</u>; and

(5.3)   If at least one competence-making fact, $F_1\text{Competence}(aHbD)$ or $F_2\text{Competence}(aHbD)$ or, ...or $F_n\text{Competence}(aHbD)$, takes place, then it is reasonable that A has a <u>prima-facie</u> competence to create B's normative position, D, in the <u>strong</u> sense of <u>"prima-facie"</u>.

2.3.8. Complex Right-Making Facts

"Rights to holdings" or "rights to a property" can be analysed as complexes of permissibility, claims and competences. Let me take the concept of "ownership" as an example. According to, e.g., Alf Ross (1958, 170 ff.), "ownership" is an "intermediate" concept, related to two clusters of norms, the first determining conditions of becoming an owner, the second prescribing legal consequences of being an owner. Let me pay attention to the first cluster only. Let me also restrict the discussion to ownership of material objects. (Concerning complex rights in general, cf. Lindahl 1977, 34 ff.). A thus has the right to the property G with regard to the person B if,
  -it is permissible for A to use the property G; and
  -A has the claim that B does not interfere with A's use of G; and
  -A has competence to create A's own claim against the court, C,

together with the duty of the court to perform a certain action
directed against B's interference with A's using G; and
  -A has competence to perform an action, such as entering into a
sale-purchase contract, shaping B's normative position, D, with
regard to the property G.
  A set of permissions, claims and competences is thus unified into
one right to a property. This unification makes it possible to
modify each component of the set without changing the identity of
the composite right itself (cf., e.g., Finnis 1980, 202). Now, one
can develop the following thesis regarding rights to holdings:

(6.1)   There exist at least one consistent description of a
         (right-making) fact, such that the following holds good: if
         this fact takes place, then A has a <u>prima-facie</u> right to
         the holding, in the <u>weak</u> sense of <u>"prima-facie"</u>.

Assuming an established list of right-making facts, one can state:

(6.2.)   If at least one complex right-making fact, $F_1aRight(G)$ or
         $F_2aRight(G)$ or, ...or $F_naRight(G)$, takes place, then A has
         a <u>prima-facie</u> right to the holding H, in the <u>weak</u> sense of
         <u>"prima-facie"</u>; and

(6.3)   if at least one complex right-making fact, $F_1aRight(G)$ or
         $F_2aRight(G)$ or, ...or $F_naRight(G)$, takes place, then it is
         reasonable that A has a <u>prima-facie</u> right to the holding H,
         in the <u>strong</u> sense of <u>"prima-facie"</u>.

2.4. WEIGHING AND BALANCING

2.4.1. Principles and Values

Some criteria of the morally good correspond to some
moral <u>principles</u> (see Section 2.3.1 supra). I will
discuss only the following sense of the ambiguous word
"principle". A <u>value principle</u>, establishes an <u>ideal</u>. The
ideal can be carried into effect to a certain degree. The
higher the degree, the better from the point of view of
the principle (cf. Alexy 1985, 76).

The word "principle" can also designate a general norm, an important
norm etc. (Cf. Alexy 1985, 72 ff.; Dworkin 1977, 14 ff.; Eckhoff
1980, 145 ff. with references to Scandinavian literature).
  Ch.1 Sec. 2 of the Swedish Constitution (The Instrument of
Government, <u>Regeringsformen</u>) thus stipulates, what follows: "The
public power shall be exercised with the respect for equal value of
all human beings and for each individual person's freedom and
dignity." The greater respect for equality, freedom and dignity, the

better from the point of view of the provision. In fact, the provision expresses three principles: (1) Those in power shall respect equal value of all human beings. (2) Those in power shall respect freedom of each individual. (3) Those in power shall respect dignity of each individual.

Each principle expresses an ideal, in other words a value, for instance it stipulates that equality, freedom and dignity are valuable. A value can be defined as a criterion of evaluation. Each criterion can be fulfilled to a certain degree, more or less (cf. Alexy 1985, 130 ff.). One can express nearly the same content in two different terminologies, speaking about principles or values. The difference is only this: a principle says what is prima-facie obligatory, a value decides what is prima-facie the best (Alexy 1985, 133).

Many principles express various individual values, such as individual standards of action (e.g., justice, inoffensiveness, benevolence, care or love) and individual goals (e.g., pleasure, happiness of an individual, fulfilment of his talents, dignity or virtue). Individual values correspond often to moral rights of an individual, e.g., right to a just treatment, protection of physical integrity and other forms of security, right to a certain private sphere including private property, freedom of opinion and many other forms of freedom, etc. Other principles protect such (indivisible) collective values and achievement values (Werkwerte; cf. Radbruch 1950, 147 ff.) as, e.g., environment, order, equality, culture and progress. The moral good is not reducible to a single value. The good in general is even less reducible. There is a variety of goodness (cf. von Wright 1963 passim).

Each principle, or value, can be a prima-facie reason of action. But they can collide in such a way that, e.g., an increased respect to equality in the particular case under consideration can cause a decrease of freedom and vice versa. One needs then meta-reasons ("super-reasons") to choose between them. Consequently, one has merely a provisional, prima facie duty to follow the wording of the principles. The same types of values and principles can be quoted on the "ground floor" of moral thinking, at its meta-level, at a meta-meta level etc.

The difference between value principles and rules is more important. (The following analysis is a result of a discussion with Aulis Aarnio). If one is in a situation regulated by a rule, one has only two possibilities, to

obey the rule in question or not. The rule thus
establishes a borderline - precise or vague - between the
obligatory and not obligatory, the forbidden and
permitted etc. If an action or a state of affairs is on
the right side of the borderline, the norm is obeyed, no
matter how close to the limit it is. The Swedish Road
Traffic Decree, Sec. 64, thus stipulates that the speed
of a vehicle in a built-up area should not exceed 50
kilometres per hour. In the light of this provision, it
does not matter whether one drives at the speed 49 kmh or
20 kmh. In both cases, one drives correctly. A rule
qualifies a human action as conforming to or violating
the rule. An important property of this mode of
qualification is its binary, either-or, 0-or-1 character.
A value principle, on the other hand, establishes an
ideal that can be carried into effect to a certain
degree, more or less. It qualifies an action, a person
etc. as more or less perfect in the light of the
principle. A principle is a yardstick of graded
qualification. This mode of qualification is not binary
but graded, more-or-less.

2.4.2. All-Things-Considered Practical Statements

One has an all-things-considered moral duty to follow the
best compromise, achieved through weighing and balancing
of different value-principles (or value-statements).

A practical statement is definitive only if by uttering
it one declares that one no longer is prepared to pay
attention to reasons which justify the contrary
conclusion. Our culture demands that definitive moral
statements are all-things-considered moral statements.

In order to state this demand more precisely, one needs
the following distinction.

A practical statement has the all-things-considered
quality sensu stricto, if and only if it has support of
considerations regarding (a) all morally relevant
circumstances, that is, all facts relevant in practical
reasoning about ethics, utilitarian morality, moral
principles, rights and duties, virtues, justice etc., and
(b) all criteria of coherent reasoning (cf. section 4.1
infra). No human being has resources sufficient to
formulate all-things-considered statements sensu stricto.

Our culture compels us merely to endorse definitive
moral statements only if these have the

all-things-considered quality <u>sensu largo</u>. A practical statement is all-things-considered <u>sensu largo</u>, if and only if it has support of considerations regarding (a) as many morally relevant circumstances as possible and (b) as many criteria of coherent reasoning as possible.

The expression "as many... as possible" indicates here that no moral consideration, and no criterion of coherent reasoning, is independently sufficient but must be weighed against other such criteria and other values. For example, in a case of emergency, one should spontaneously save a person in mortal danger rather then perform a time consuming moral reasoning.

Logically incompatible actions <u>cannot</u> be all-things-considered good at the same time. Neither can one simultaneously have a definitive duty to perform logically incompatible actions. If A, e.g., ought definitively to pay B 100 kronor, it is logically impossible that A ought not to do it. Logic is thus applicable to all-things-considered practical statements. In this manner, these differ from <u>prima-facie</u> statements, cf. section 2.3.3 supra.

2.4.3. Weighing and Balancing of Principles

In order to justify an all-things-considered practical statement, one must weigh and balance <u>prima-facie</u> practical statements which support it against such statements supporting the contrary conclusion.

One shall thus see to it that, e.g., a small increase of equality in the considered case does not cause a to great limitation of freedom; nor shall a small increase of liberty be "paid" by a too great inequality. In other words, the higher is the degree to which a particular action contradicts one principle, the more important is that it conforms to the other one. When freedom decreases, a greater and greater increase of equality is required to compensate a further decrease of freedom.

This duty to weigh and balance principles can also be expressed as a duty to weigh and balance corresponding <u>values</u> (cf. section 2.4.1 supra). In this context, one may consider two ways to express the same thing.

a) One may follow Alexy who regards principles themselves as commands to weigh (Alexy 1985, 71 ff.). Such a command is a <u>norm</u>, telling one what to weigh and balance. This norm differs from <u>rules</u> as regards its content: it demands that one performs an act of weighing, while a rule demands that one performs another action.

b) On the other hand, <u>Aulis Aarnio</u> claims that the command to perform weighing is not a part of the meaning of the principle, but a separate meta-norm, necessarily related to this meaning. This meta-norm is no principle but a <u>"technical" rule</u> having the following content. Whoever wishes to ascertain what is, all things considered, morally good, must weigh and balance all applicable value principles (or values), constituting <u>prima-facie</u> criteria of moral goodness, together with some established reasoning standards etc.

The difference between those two ways of speaking thus concerns the question whether the command to weigh, necessarily accompanying a principle, is "inside" or "outside" of the meaning of this principle. This difference has no material consequences in moral or legal philosophy.

Let me now give an example of weighing and balancing of principles - the Swedish case NJA 1984 p. 693. A foreigner A, who had considerable ties to both Sweden and the Federal Republic of Germany, owned a car, registered in the latter country. He borrowed a sum of money, giving the right to the car as security (a so-called "security transfer"). Later, a person rented the car and visited Sweden. The Swedish authorities sequestered the car as security for A's unpaid taxes. The dispute concerned the question whether the German security transfer should prevent sequestration in Sweden. The Supreme Court stated, what follows: "The demand for order and simplicity of the system together with difficulties for the creditors in Sweden to judge the credit risks otherwise than according to Swedish rules constitute the main reason against ascribing security transfer according to foreign law an effect against the transferor's creditors here in Sweden... The interest of the creditors in Sweden to be able to assess their credit risks according to Swedish law competes with the interest of the foreign transferee/creditor not to risk a loss of his right because the property without his participation has been moved to Sweden... One should weigh the proffered reasons against each other and one must then pay attention to the development of the international trade and to more and more intense commercial cooperation between various countries." The Supreme Court overruled the sequestration.

The reason consisted in the act of weighing and balancing of, <u>inter alia</u>, the following principles. (1) A right, acquired abroad, to property that without participation of the foreign transferee/creditor has been moved to Sweden, should <u>(prima-facie)</u> not be valid in Sweden if its validity would cause a relatively great increase of complexity of the Swedish legal system. (2) A right, acquired abroad, to property that without participation of the foreign transferee/creditor has been moved to Sweden, should (prima-facie) be valid in Sweden if its validity would cause a relatively great increase of legal certainty of the foreign creditor. In the case at bar, the Court performed a weighing and balancing of these two principles. In other words, it performed a reasoning whose conclusion was that one ought to recognise in such Swedish cases security transfer according to German law, since this recognition would cause a relatively great increase of legal certainty of the foreign creditor and only a relatively small increase of complexity of the Swedish legal system. One of the reasons, supporting this weighing of principles consisted of the thesis that the recognition of the German security transfer in Sweden would promote the development of the international trade and commercial cooperation between various countries. Other reasons are difficult to reconstruct but, no doubt, the Court paid attention to the assumptions concerning the sources of the law and legal method, characterising the contemporary legal culture or, technically speaking, legal paradigm in Sweden (see section 3.3.3 infra).

In brief, the decision is derivable from a set of statements containing some presupposed premises, characterising this paradigm, together with the additional statement claiming importance of international trade and commercial cooperation. However, international trade should not be the only factor, deciding about how the Swedish law treats rights, acquired abroad. One must consider other values and principles, as well, e.g., the claim of the foreign creditor to be treated fairly, the principle of reciprocity in relations between states, etc.

Most of such considerations can be graded, and then weighed against each other. One act of weighing depends on all other acts of weighing, included in the same chain of reasoning. For instance, weighing of legal certainty of the foreign creditor against simplicity of the Swedish legal system depends of weighing of the latter against international trade and commercial cooperation. Or weighing of freedom against equality may depend on weighing of equality against cultural progress. As a result, we have one relation of many components. Each case of weighing is characterised by such a relation.

A typical all-things-considered moral statement concerns an individual situation: a precisely determined person ought to perform a precisely determined action, H; or a precisely determined object is good, etc. Preciseness means here that all circumstances, all the context of this situation is considered.

One can now make a choice between two views.

1) One may assume that each situation is morally unique, that is, includes at least one morally relevant circumstance not shared by any other situation. Each case of moral weighing is then "contextual" (cf. Rentto 1988,

64 ff.), that is, unique, characterised by a unique
cluster of considerations to be weighed. We can say
something like this: In the situation s_1, the value v_1
fulfilled to the extent e_1 precedes the value v_2
fulfilled to the extent e_2; and in the situation s_2 the
opposite relation holds: the value v_2 fulfilled to the
extent e_2 precedes the value v_1 fulfilled to the extent
e_1.

2) One may assume that individual situations may be
classified into moral <u>types</u>. All situations belonging to
such a type are weighed in the same way. We can then say
<u>generally</u> that in the situation of the <u>type</u> S_1, the value
v_1 fulfilled to the extent e_1 precedes the value v_2
fulfilled to the extent e_2; etc. Under this assumption, a
general rule or a general value-statement can have a
<u>ceteris-paribus</u> all-things-considered character, in the
following sense: If circumstances remain unchanged, that
is, nothing new and morally relevant happens, then one
always ought to follow the rule. Or, if all morally
relevant circumstances remain unchanged, then an object
of a certain type is good, etc.

The choice between these assumptions is not easy. But
even if the second one is chosen, one may still claim
that no general rule at all can be, all thing considered,
<u>eternally</u> binding. Nor can a general value-statement be,
all things considered, eternally right. One may thus
claim that future can always bring new circumstances
which may gain moral relevance.

For that reason, I do not believe that even the best
philosophical minds ever can succeed in creating a
<u>calculus</u> which precisely determines the <u>content</u> of
weighing.

2.4.4. Weighing Rules

However, not only principles but also some <u>rules</u> create a
merely <u>prima facie</u> duty. This is true about both moral
and legal rules.

For example, one ought not to kill people. The moral
rule forbids <u>prima facie</u> all killing but to state that a
given individual, all things considered, ought not to be
killed, one must also pay attention to other rules,
stipulating exceptions; for instance, in a defensive war,
one may kill the aggressors. The all-things-considered
morality is then determined by a complex, consisting of

the main rule and the exceptions. In section 2.3.3 supra, I have discussed other examples, concerning rules formulated in general theories of moral goodness.

The natural way to identify such exceptions is to perform weighing and balancing of various considerations. A reasonable politician must, e.g., see to it that following preferences of the voters does not to an unacceptable degree impede development of human talents or set aside some important standards of perfection, inherent in established social practices. He has an all-things-considered duty to follow the best weighing and balancing of preferences, promotion of talents, established standards of perfection, and so on. In the same way, one can state that one, all things considered, ought to to follow the best weighing and balancing of the prohibition to kill, the prima facie duty to defend one´s country and perhaps some other considerations.

Weighing in the law also concerns both principles and rules. All socially established legal norms, expressed in statutes, precedents etc., have a merely prima facie character. The step from prima-facie legal rules to the all-things-considered legal (and moral) obligations, claims etc. involves evaluative interpretation, that is, weighing and balancing (see section 5.4.1 infra).

For that reason, one may doubt whether the distinction between rules and principles is important. To answer this question, one must evaluate the following differences between rules and principles. (The list of differences has been elaborated in cooperation with Aulis Aarnio).

1. Unlike a principle, the rule in question may be obeyed or not. There are no degrees of obedience. The rule does not claim to be obeyed as much as possible. It rather claims to be obeyed in so many cases as possible.

2. Unlike a principle, the rule in question does not express a single value but a compromise of many values (and corresponding principles). If, e.g., a legal rule says that an undue (unreasonable) contractual provision may be ignored, the determination of unreasonableness is to be made by weighing of many values and principles.

3. In routine ("easy") cases, one ought to follow socially established legal rules without any necessity of weighing and balancing. An act of weighing and balancing is then necessary only in order to ascertain whether the case under adjudication is an easy one or not. Only if the case is not easy but "hard", must one perform a value-laden legal reasoning, that is, an act of weighing and balancing. One the other had, no cases of application of principles are easy. All such cases are hard in this

sense. One must always pay attention to more then one
principle and perform an act of weighing and balancing.

4. A collision of rules has partly another character than a
collision of principles. A total logical incompatibility of rules
may be ascertained analytically and in abstracto, without concerning
particularities of the case; one rule prohibits exactly the same
another one permits or orders. On the other hand, there exists no
such, analytically demonstrable, incompatibility in abstracto of
principles. Collision of principles occurs only in particular cases:
in order to follow one principle to an increased degree, one must
decrease the degree of following another principle. In order to
ascertain whether such a collision occurs or not, one must pay
attention to the contingent facts of the case. And to decide the
case, one must weigh and balance various considerations.

2.4.5. Final Act of Weighing and Balancing

As soon one claims that a certain principle weighs more
than another, one faces the question "Why?". The answer
can be supported by further reasons, inter alia
principles. These, too, can be weighed and balanced
against thinkable counter-arguments. From the logical
point of view, the process of weighing can thus continue
ad infinitum. But in practice, one must finish the
reasoning, sooner or later.

If one aims at the best possible weighing, one must
take into account as many relevant reasons for and
against the conclusion in question as possible and
establish their relative weight. One can thus assume that
the objectively best weighing takes into consideration
all relevant reasons for the conclusion in question and
all relevant counter-argument (that is, reasons for the
opposite conclusion).

The hypothesis is not falsified that if one had
possessed

(1) more information about the use of moral language;

(2) better knowledge of how other people morally judge
various actual and hypothetical cases;

(3) more clarity as regards one´s own evaluation of
future cases; and

(4) more information about the logical connection
between one´s own judgments concerning various moral
questions;

then one would be able to use all this information to formulate objectively (that is, freely from emotional bias) a <u>complete list, containing all thinkable reasons for and against</u> the conclusion that a given action is <u>prima facie</u> good and obligatory. The fact that a so expanded list of reasons and counter-arguments is complete means that <u>no further reasons or counter-arguments can be added to it</u>.

This applies, among other things, to the moral theories and criteria, discussed above. The hypothesis is thus not falsified that if one had possessed more information, then one would be able to formulate objectively (that is, freely from emotional bias) a complete list, containing all thinkable moral theories and criteria.

Assume now for the sake of argument that one can formulate the <u>sufficient</u> condition for the conclusion that the action in question is, <u>all things considered</u>, (not only <u>prima facie</u>) good and obligatory. The fact that a moral reason or a combination of reasons is a sufficient condition for this conclusion means that <u>no thinkable counter-arguments weigh more</u>.

Such a sufficient condition would consist of (1) the complete list of <u>prima-facie</u> moral criteria and theories, established or newly created, applicable to the case under considerations, and (2) the complete list of statements determining the relative weight of these criteria and theories in this case.

To be sure, one can argue that

1) such complete lists of thinkable reasons for and sufficient conditions of goodness and obligatoriness cannot be finite, and

2) one has no way to formulate an infinite list.

Though plausible, the first thesis is, however, philosophically controversial. More important, the second thesis is probably false. Modern mathematics possesses means to deal with infinite sets. Analogously, it seems to be possible to find a finite method to formulate an infinite list of moral reasons.

Since the list is by definition complete, one cannot add more reasons to it. Any reasoning in favour of the conclusion that the listed reasons outweigh the counter-arguments must thus mean that one merely repeats some reasons already belonging to the list. <u>If all of these are already taken into consideration, the reasoning must stop</u>.

The discussed list may <u>consist of many levels</u>. At the
lowest level, there are reasons for and against the
conclusion that a given action is good and ought to be
performed. At a higher level, there are reasons of the
second order, for one or another weighing of the reasons
and counter-arguments. Some reasons of the second order
state, e.g., that certain reasons of the first order
outweigh the corresponding counter-arguments. The list
can, for instance, contain ten reasons for and twelve
against the conclusion that a given action ought to be
performed, and a "super-reason" stating that the ten
weigh more than the twelve. These "super-reasons", too,
can be weighed and balanced against thinkable
counter-arguments. There can thus exist reasons of the
third order, etc.

The list is complete and cannot be extended to further
reasons. This assumption applies to all the levels. One
cannot add to it any reasons at all, either of the first,
second or n-th order. A reasoning in favour of the
conclusion that the listed reasons outweigh the
counter-arguments means that one merely repeats some
reasons of a higher order, already belonging to the list.
If the listed reasons do not constitute a logical circle,
the list must thus include an ultimate reason of the n-th
order, fundamental for the whole argumentative structure.
This ultimate reason must be assumed without any
reasoning whatever.

In such a way, a reasoning ends with an arbitrary
assumption.

However, this fact does not make the weighing and balancing
worthless. Although its ultimate point is arbitrary, one knows at
least <u>what</u> is to be weighed and balanced (cf. Alexy 1985, 149-150).

The final step of weighing may consist of a concrete
judgment. If the contextuality thesis is not true (cf.
section 2.4.3 supra), then the final step in some cases
may also consist of an assumed general rule, determining
a priority order between principles in question. On the
other hand, it is inconsistent to say that a <u>principle</u>
constitutes the final step of weighing. A principle is,
as said before, no sufficient reason for a moral
conclusion; it must be weighed against other principles.
How then can it be the final <u>step</u> of weighing?

2.4.6. A Step From Theoretical Propositions to Definitive Practical Statements?

This role of weighing and balancing makes moral theories and criteria contestable. For that reason, it is interesting to discuss a minimal consensus theory, according to which an action is obligatory and good, if (although not only if) it simultaneously fulfils all such theories and criteria.

The hypothesis is not falsified that if one had a more extensive knowledge, one could be able to objectively (that is, freely from emotional bias) formulate an extended list, containing all meaningful moral theories and criteria which make the prima-facie moral goodness and moral obligatoriness dependent on some facts, described in theoretical propositions. One may now argue that moral value statements and norm-expressive statements are related to such theoretical propositions in the following way. The fact that an action simultaneously fulfils all the claims made by all thinkable moral theories and criteria of this kind is a sufficient condition for the conclusion that the following practical statements are reasonable: (a) the action in question is all-things-considered (not merely prima-facie) good; and (b) the action in question ought all-things-considered to be performed.

Let me, e.g., consider the following reasoning:

Premise	The action in question increases people's happiness and fulfilment of their talents; and it expresses people's preferences and fits various social practices; etc.

Conclusion	The action in question is (all things considered) morally good

The word "etc." indicates that the list of moral theories and criteria can be expanded to contain some additional, so far unknown ones. An important method to expand the list is to complete it with theories providing a foundation of those already listed. See section 3.2.5 infra!

This reasoning appears to be acceptable, although one may doubt whether it is logically correct. One can, however, add the following "bridging" premise 2: If the action in question increases people´s happiness and fulfilment of

their talents; <u>and</u> it expresses people´s preferences <u>and</u>
fits various social practices; etc., then the conclusion
is reasonable that the action in question is (all things
considered) morally good. In this way, one obtains the
following, logically correct, inference.

Premise 1   The action in question increases people's
                   happiness <u>and</u> fulfilment of their talents; <u>and</u> it
                   expresses people's preferences <u>and</u> fits various
                   social practices; etc.

Premise 2   If the action in question increases people's
                   happiness <u>and</u> fulfilment of their talents; <u>and</u> it
                   expresses people's preferences <u>and</u> fits various
                   social practices; etc., then the conclusion is
                   reasonable that the action in question is (all
                   things considered) morally good

Conclusion   The conclusion is reasonable that the action in
                   question is (all things considered) morally good

Apparently, it is reasonable to derive a practical
conclusion from some theoretical propositions. This
inference assumes, however, that premise 2 is true.
    One can also try to derive the conclusion that an
action, all things considered, ought to be performed.

Premise 1   The action in question increases people's
                   happiness <u>and</u> fulfilment of their talents; <u>and</u> it
                   expresses people's preferences <u>and</u> fits various
                   social practices; etc.

Premise 2   If an action increases people's happiness <u>and</u>
                   fulfilment of their talents; <u>and</u> expresses
                   people's preferences <u>and</u> fits various social
                   practices; etc., then the conclusion is reasonable
                   that the action ought, all things considered, to
                   be performed

Conclusion   The conclusion is reasonable that the action in
                   question ought, all things considered, to be
                   performed

Again, it seems to be reasonable to derive a practical
conclusion from some theoretical propositions, provided
that the additional premise 2 is true.

Both this conclusion and Premise 2 are not merely reasonable. It would also be unreasonable to deny them. In general, it is unreasonable to say: The action in question simultaneously fulfils all claims made by all thinkable moral theories and criteria, yet it is not (all things considered) good.

Let now the expressions "an ought-making fact" and "a good-making fact" refer to any fact of this kind <u>or any combination of such facts</u>, regardless its degree of complexity. One may then express the following theses:

(7.1)   There exists at least one consistent description of an ought-making fact, such that the following holds good: if this fact takes place, then it is reasonable that A ought all-things-considered to do H

and

(7.1*)   there exists at least one consistent description of a good-making fact, such that the following holds good: if this fact takes place, then it is reasonable that H is all-things-considered good.

Let me now assume that the symbols F_1OUGHT(aH) - F_nOUGHT(aH) and F_1GOOD(H) - F_nGOOD(H) once again indicate the facts that belong to a socially established list of facts which meaningfully can be proffered as reasons for the conclusion that an action is good and/or obligatory.

One can now argue that the following theses are plausible explanations of analytic relations:

(7.2)   If all the ought-making facts {F_1OUGHT(aH) and F_2OUGHT(aH) and, ... and F_nOUGHT(aH)} take place, then it is reasonable that A ought all-things-considered to do H

and

(7.2*)   if all the good-making facts {F_1GOOD(H) and F_2GOOD(H) and, ... and F_nGOOD(H)} take place, then it is reasonable that H is all-things-considered good.

The theses correspond to premise 2 in the examples, discussed above.

Though philosophically interesting, theses 7.2 and 7.2* are not _practically_ important for the following reason. Many moral theories and criteria are thinkable (linguistically meaningful), each indicating different properties of an action (i.e., different p´s) as deciding whether it is good and ought to be performed. One can doubt whether there exist such actions at all that simultaneously possess _all_ of these properties.

The following question is also philosophically interesting. Can one omit the words "it is reasonable that" and claim that the following theses

(a)   If all the ought-making facts $\{F_1\text{OUGHT}(aH)$ and $F_2\text{OUGHT}(aH)$ and, ... and $F_n\text{OUGHT}(aH)\}$ take place, then A ought all-things-considered to do H

and

(b)   if all the good-making facts $\{F_1\text{GOOD}(H)$ and $F_2\text{GOOD}(H)$ and, ... and $F_n\text{GOOD}(H)\}$ take place, then H is all-things-considered good

are plausible explanations of analytic relations?

An affirmative answer to this question would mean that there is a "bridge" from theoretical premises to practical conclusions. Many philosophers would regard this fact as a sufficient condition for the negative answer. Following Hume, they assume that ought-judgments are not implied by premises among which there are no ought-judgments. Yet, Hume´s "guillotine" is not beyond any doubt, as the following quotation exemplify:

("T)he role pf reason in the world as a survival mechanism for the agent (and his species) requires that it functions as a unitary mechanism capable of focusing fully on the fundamental unity of the world both as the subject matter of contemplative thinking and as the object of change by practical thinking.... There _must_, therefore, be bridging implications connecting propositions and practical noemata" (Castaneda 1975, 333).

However, the following reasons tell _against_ the view that (a) and (b) are logically true.

1) The _practical_ meaning of practical statements includes immediately that they are reasons for action,

whereas the meaning of the statements of fact does not. The meaning of the former is thus richer than that of the latter. A richer conclusion cannot follow from premises that have less extensive meaning (cf. Peczenik and Spector, 471).

One can answer this objection, as follows. Perhaps one can regard the conjunction-proposition describing coexistence of all thinkable ought- and good-making facts as a sufficient reason for action. One can perhaps argue that this conjunction, after all, has a practical meaning, making it logically contradictory to say "the action A fulfils all thinkable moral criteria of this kind and yet it is not good".

2) Two actions can at the same time fulfil all the claims made by the thinkable moral theories and criteria and still be incompatible, impossible to perform simultaneously. Suppose, e.g., that A sold the same thing twice to two different buyers, B and C. The moral theories demand perhaps that the thing is to be delivered to both B and C, but this is impossible. Consequently, it is not reasonable to conclude that A ought simultaneously to deliver the thing to both buyers.

One can answer this objection, as well. The moral obligation can, e.g., be formulated as an alternative: A ought to deliver the thing to B or C. Another solution is to assume that the moral criteria also include some collision norms, stating precisely the priority order between incompatible prima-facie obligations.

Although one can answer the objections, the answers can be criticised, as well. I thus do not commit myself in this work to the view that the theses (a) and (b) are logically (necessarily) true.

Such problems make it interesting to discuss another relation of moral goodness and obligatoriness to good- and ought-making facts. One may thus assume that an action, fulfilling the most important moral theory or criterion is (all things considered) good and obligatory. The following inference seems to be correct.

Premise 1   The action in question fulfils claims made by
                   the most important moral theory or criterion

Premise 2   If an action fulfils claims made by the most
                   important moral theory or criterion, then the
                   action is (all things considered) morally good
----

Conclusion   The action in question is (all things considered) morally good

Of course, one can, in the same way, derive the conclusion that an action, all things considered, ought to be performed.

Premise 1	The action in question fulfils claims made by the most important moral theory or criterion
Premise 2	If an action fulfils claims made by the most important moral theory or criterion, then the action, all things considered, ought to be performed

----

Conclusion	The action in question, all things considered, ought to be performed

Let me call the fact that the action in question fulfils claims made by the most important moral theory or criterion, "the most important ought-making fact" and "the most important good-making fact". The following theses are plausible explanations of logical relations:

(8.1)   If the most important ought-making fact takes place, then A, all things considered, ought to do H

and

(8.2)   If the most important good-making fact takes place, then H is, all things considered, good.

One may wonder whether there is a need to be cautious and, instead of the theses 8.1 and 82 merely state the following (see Peczenik and Spector, 474):

if the most important ought-making fact takes place, then it is reasonable that A, all things considered, ought to do H

and

if the most important good-making fact takes place, then it is reasonable that H is, all things considered, good.

The reference to reasonableness, weakening the link between the most important ought- and good-making fact and, on the other hand, the Ought and the Good, would be necessary if the statement "the action in question fulfils claims made by the most important moral theory or the most important moral criterion" were purely theoretical, lacking the practical component. It would be a mystery, if a purely theoretical statement implied the practical conclusion, expressing the ought or the good. But the statement in question is not purely theoretical, since it expresses the _evaluation_ of a moral theory or criterion as the most important one. The discussed inferences thus do _not_ constitute a step from a purely theoretical set of premises to a practical conclusion. The cautious addition "... then it is reasonable that..." is perhaps redundant, _if_ one assumes that the same process of weighing and balancing which determines which moral theory or criterion is the most important one decides what actions are all-things-considered (not merely _prima-facie_) good and obligatory. In both cases, one must weigh and balance various moral theories and criteria.

Consequently, the following direct inference is also logically correct.

Premise 1   The action in question fulfils claims made by
                   the most important moral theory or criterion
----

Conclusion   The action in question is (all things considered)
                   morally good and it ought (all things considered)
                   to be performed

Estimation of importance, and thus weighing, plays the same role in the context of all-things-considered _rights_. Consider the following example. It is wrong to kill an innocent in order to transplant his organs to several persons, whose lives thus will be saved. The innocent has an all-things-considered right not to be killed for the sake of transplants. On the other hand, it is right to kill an innocent to prevent a nuclear holocaust. The innocent has no _all-things-considered_ right not to be killed for the sake of preventing the nuclear holocaust. The difference is only how many lives one saves by killing one innocent person. This shows that the borderline between having and not having an all-things-considered right is a result of weighing and balancing of various considerations. (For this example, I am indebted to Robert Alexy). One may claim that the following theses are plausible interpretations of analytic relations:

(8.3)   If   the   most   important   permissibility-making   fact,
         justifying A's freedom to do H, takes place, then it is,
         all things considered, permissible for A to do H;

(8.4)   if B, all things considered, ought to do H and the most
         important claim-making relation between A and B takes
         place, all things considered, a claim that B
         does H;

(8.5)   if the most important claim-making fact takes place,
         justifying A's claim that B does H, then A has an
         all-things-considered claim that B does H;

(8.6)   if the most important competence-making fact takes place,
         justifying A's competence to create B's normative position
         D, then A has an all-things-considered competence to create
         B's normative position, D;

(8.7)   if the most important complex right-making fact takes
         place, justifying A's right to the holding G, then A has an
         all-things-considered right to the holding G.

The theses hold good, if one assumes that the same process of
weighing and balancing which determines what is "the most important"
decides what actions are the all-things-considered (not merely
prima-facie) rights.
     I have thus separately dealt with justifiable permissibility,
claims, competences and rights to holdings. But, at the prima-facie
level, these rights of different kinds can collide with each other.
One must then weigh them together. A certain permissibility-making
fact may, e.g., justify B's prima-facie freedom not to do H, and, at
the same time, a certain claim-making fact can justify A's
prima-facie claim that B does H. One can thus imagine the following
situation: a farmer, B, has an interest which justifies his
prima-facie liberty to use a certain kind of fertiliser. At the same
time, his neighbour, A, has a need to be protected from pollution
this fertiliser must cause; this need justifies A's prima-facie
claim that B does not use the fertiliser. However, such a weighing
is impossible at the level of all-things-considered rights. These
are a result of weighing, and cannot be subject to additional act of
weighing. When B has an all-things-considered liberty to use the
fertiliser, A cannot have an all-things-considered claim that B does
not use it, and vice versa. One must thus avoid contradictions
between all-things-considered rights. The best way is to
cumulatively consider all of them, each time one performs weighing
in order to decide which fact is the most important
permissibility-making fact, or claim-making fact, or
competence-making fact, or right-to-holdings-making fact. This means
that these importance-indicating concepts are mutually dependent.

Knowledge of the all-things-considered duties and rights thus presupposes a very complex act of weighing and balancing of several kinds of ought-, and right-making facts. Weighing is indispensable. Neither is it possible to definitively replace this complex act of weighing by a series of mutually independent simple acts.

2.4.7. The Step From Practical Statements To Theoretical Conclusions

The following (correct) inference elucidates further fragments of the theoretical meaning of practical statements.

Premise 1   The action in question is (all things considered) morally good

Premise 2   If the action in question is (all things considered) morally good, then it increases people's happiness or fulfilment of their talents; or it expresses people's preferences or fits various social practices; etc.

Conclusion   The action in question increases people's happiness or fulfilment of their talents; or it expresses people's preferences or fits various social practices; etc.

The same conclusion follows from the normative premise "the action in question ought (all things considered) to be performed" together with the appropriate premise 2.

The circumstance that the action in question is, all things considered, good or such that it ought to be performed is thus a sufficient condition for the thesis that this action fulfils claims made by at least one moral theory or criterion, established or possible to construct in the moral language.

The following theses, corresponding to premise 2 in the last example, are thus plausible explanations of analytic relations (cf. Peczenik and Spector, 467 ff):

(9.1)   If A ought, all things considered, to do H, then
           at least one ought-making fact takes place

and

(9.1*)   if H is all-things-considered good, then at
           least one good-making fact takes place.

In other words, there is a logical "bridge" from the
"ought" to the "is" (cf. Peczenik and Spector, 470).
   One may also formulate corresponding theses concerning
the prima-facie ought and good:

           If A ought prima-facie to do H, then at least
           one ought-making fact takes place

and

           if H is prima-facie good, then at least one
           good-making fact takes place.

These theses hold good both as regards the weak and the
strong sense of "prima-facie". Indeed, they follow from
the theses developed in the section 2.3.4 supra.

The "mirror picture" of the discussed example is this.

Premise 1   The action in question does not increase
                   people's happiness or fulfilment of their talents;
                   nor does it express people's preferences or fit
                   social practices; etc.

Premise 2   If an action does not increase people's
                   happiness or fulfilment of their talents; nor does
                   it express people's preferences or fit social
                   practices; etc. then this action is not morally
                   good nor ought it to be performed

Conclusion   The action in question is not morally good nor
                   such that it ought to be performed.

The fact that the action in question fulfils claims made by at least
one moral theory or criterion, established or thinkable, is thus a
necessary condition for the thesis that this action is good or such
that it ought to be performed.

Consequently, it is inconsistent to say that the action in question is good or such that it ought to be performed, yet it does not fulfil claims made by any, not even a single one, meaningful moral theory or criterion.

One can thus deduce an alternative of theoretical propositions from a practical statement! To this extent, our discussion supports the case of moral cognitivism. But the support is rather weak, since we cannot tell which moral theory or criterion must be fulfilled to make an action good or obligatory.

2.4.8. Concluding Remarks Concerning Logical Relations Between Theoretical and Practical Statements

The relations of various moral value-statements and norm-expressing statements to certain theoretical propositions, formulated in the discussed theses, constitute an important component of the theoretical meaning of these practical statements. The theoretical meaning of moral statements is, however, vague. Vagueness results from the following circumstances.

1) The description of the good-making, ought-making, right-making facts etc. is invariably vague or controversial. For instance, utilitarianists have done much work to state precisely what promotion of happiness or fulfilment of preferences mean. Yet, these problems are far from being solved.

2) There is no way to prove that a given list of such facts really is complete. To be sure, it is not logically inconsistent to believe that one can formulate a complete list of that kind. But how can one know that all important reasons for and against a given action have been taken into consideration? How can one know that no unknown counter-arguments weigh more? In other words, how can one know that the ultimate assumption of the moral reasoning in question is right? Due to such factors as limited knowledge and free will of human beings, one cannot by Reason alone, objectively (that is, freely from emotional bias) and, at the same time, definitively justify such beliefs.

The theory, developed above, is a synthesis of cognitivism and non-cognitivism. Among other things, the cognitivists are right that a prima-facie practical statement is derivable from some theoretical propositions. They are also right that some theoretical

propositions follow from   practical
statements. On the other hand, the non-cognitivists
rightly point out that an <u>all-things-considered</u> practical
statement does not follow from a set of premises solely
consisting of theoretical propositions. A practical
statement is related not only to facts but also to the
action, will and feelings. A practical statement thus has
both a theoretical and a practical meaning. If one sees
only one or another but not both simultaneously, one is,
so to say, one-eyed or half blind.

2.5. SOME EXAMPLES OF THE ROLE OF WEIGHING IN MORAL THEORIES

2.5.1. Introductory Remarks

Weighing and balancing thus plays an important role in
all moral contexts. Let me now give some more elaborate
examples. In fact, some examples have already been
discussed. In Section 1.4.1, I have thus pointed out that
the concept of legal certainty presupposes weighing and
balancing of predictability of legal decisions and other
moral considerations. Section 1.4.2 deals with weighing
and balancing of various criteria of democracy. More
examples would, however, make the situation clearer.

2.5.2. Weighing Preferences: Hare´s Utilitarianism

Although R.M. Hare's theory is a continuation of a long tradition of
British utilitarianism, including such thinkers as Bentham and Mill,
it shows a remarkable originality. Hare supports his theory with an
analysis of the moral language. He assumes that moral judgements are
1) overriding, 2) universalisable and 3) prescriptive.
   Moral judgements thus <u>override</u> other evaluative judgements. If an
action which follows a moral principle violates, e.g., an aesthetic
principle, one ought to follow the moral principle. Hare gives the
following example. Assume that Hare's wife gave him a magenta
cushion to put over his scarlet sofa in his room i college. An
aesthetic principle says that one ought to avoid such a combination
of colours. A moral principle states that one ought not to hurt
one's wife's feelings. The moral principle overrides the
aesthetical, and Hare thus ought to accept the gift (Hare 1981, 55).

Moral judgements are also <u>universalisable</u>. Any moral judgment follows from a universal principle applicable to <u>all</u> persons, situations, actions etc. of a certain kind. The like ought to be treated alike. If one makes different moral judgments about situations which one admits to be identical in their universal descriptive properties, one contradicts oneself (Hare 1981, 107 ff.). If one thinks, e.g., that John ought to earn more money than Peter, one must support this conclusion with a universal principle, e.g., that one's income ought to fit one's performance. Such a justification would be meaningless if only attached to individual names, e.g., "John ought to earn more because he is John". It follows that if a distinction between oneself and others is not universalisable, it lacks moral relevance. From the moral point of view, one ought to treat others in the same way as oneself.

Hare is thus a rule utilitarianist. He does not hold that one ought to evaluate individual actions directly by reference to their utility. One should not ask oneself whether breaking a promise particular, killing a particular person etc. would have the best consequences. Rather one ought to ask whether a universal rule permitting such actions would do it. This option allows Hare to avoid two forms of the standard anti-utilitarianist criticism. (1) First, a critic may point out that a particular action may have the best consequences, yet be morally unjustifiable because a universal practice to perform such actions would not have the best consequences. This criticism is fatal for act-utilitarianism, but not for rule-utilitarianism. (2) A critic may also ask, Why ought one to concern oneself with interests of other people at all? Hare could answer: Moral language is such that <u>if</u> I wish to use it, I must respect interests of others.

Finally, moral judgements are <u>prescriptive</u>; they entail norm-statements ("imperatives"). If a person assents orally to a moral judgment that an action ought to be performed in a certain situation, and yet does not perform it in this situation, he must be assenting insincerely. Prescriptivity is connected with the concept of preference. To have a preference is to accept a corresponding prescription (Hare 1981, 21 ff.).

Hare is thus a preference-utilitarianist, not a happiness-utilitarianist. He does not hold that one ought to evaluate actions by reference to happiness they may create. Rather one ought to ask whether they correspond to human preferences. This option allows Hare to avoid the standard anti-utilitarianist criticism, according to which a moral thinker may not impose own conception of happiness on everyone, including those who prefer <u>not</u> to be happy in the sense he has chosen.

A consequence of universalisability and prescriptivity of moral judgments is that <u>each person ought to adopt other people's preferences as his own</u>. "(T)he method of critical thinking which is imposed on us by the logical properties of the moral concepts requires us to pay attention to the satisfaction of the preferences of people (because moral judgements are prescriptive and to have a preference is to accept a prescription); and to pay attention equally to the equal preferences of all those affected (because moral principles have to be universal and therefore cannot pick out individuals)"; Hare 1981, 91.

Furthermore, it follows that one ought to treat others as they want to be treated. "It follows from universalisability that if I now say that I ought to do a certain thing to a certain person, I am committed to the view that the very some thing ought to be done to me, were I in exactly his situation, including having the same personal characteristics and in particular the same motivational states. But the motivational states he actually now has may run quite counter to my own present ones. For example, he may very much want not to have done to him what I am saying I ought to do with him... But... if I fully represent to myself his situation, including his motivations, I shall myself acquire a corresponding motivation..." (Hare 1981, 108-109).

In brief, one ought to treat others in accordance with a calculus of preferences, taking account of what they want, how many people have a certain preference, and how strong their preferences are.

Such a calculus of preferences is not the same as simple addition and subtraction. Had it been the case, the theory would be vulnerable for a standard criticism concerning distribution. Let us imagine that the society consists of three persons, A, B and C, who produce and consume certain "units of welfare", e.g., cakes. Let us then make a choice between two alternative organisations of this society, I and II, characterised by the following distribution:

    I. A gets 10 cakes. B gets 10 cakes. C gets 10 cakes.

    II. A gets 2 cakes. B gets 2 cakes. C gets 30 cakes.

In this situation, a person solely concerned with maximising welfare would have to choose II, although this choice contradicts moral intuitions of most people. Yet, a utilitarianist is not forced to do so. He must also pay attention to diminishing marginal utility (cf. Simmonds 1986, 32). He may thus easily point out that the additional 10 cakes given to the rich man will make a negligible contribution to satisfaction to his preferences, whereas additional cakes given to the poor would be much more significant, perhaps enabling him to avoid starvation.

This is, however, not the whole story of weighing and balancing of preferences. Other factors must also be weighed and balanced, for example the role of unequal distribution as an incentive to encourage people to work hard, the costs of maintaining some redistributive institutions and so on (cf. Simmonds 1986, 32 ff.)

The statement "x is morally good" is thus based on the statement "combined preferences of people for x weigh more that their combined preferences against x". Is the latter statement a theoretical proposition? Were this the case, Hare's theory would be naturalistic. But Hare denies it. To establish, e.g., that John's preference for freedom weighs more than Peter's preference for security, a moral thinker must not only describe the preferences but also decide to adopt them as his own and then weigh and balance them in the same manner as his own preferences for freedom and security.

This form of weighing creates some problems. It "involves putting oneself... thoroughly into other person's place, so that one takes on his desires, tastes, preferences, ideals, and values as well as his other qualities... But then it hardly makes sense to talk of putting <u>oneself</u> in his place; hardly any of oneself is retained. Rather, what one is trying to do is to look at things from one's own and from the other person's point of view at once, and to discover action-guiding principles... which one can accept from both points of view. Or rather, since there is not just one person but infinitely many, from all actual points of view... But... it is doubtful whether any principles will pass so severe a test... We must lower our sights a little, and look not for principles which can be wholeheartedly endorsed from every point of view, but for ones which represent an acceptable compromise between the different actual points of view" (Mackie 1977, 93).

One of Hare'e original contributions is the following theory of <u>two levels of moral thinking</u>. The <u>critical</u> level includes a complete knowledge of other people's preferences in all thinkable cases, together with weighing and balancing of these preferences. Only an "archangel" could perform such a task. The opposite of the "archangel", a "prole", lacks ability to think "critically". He must stay at the <u>intuitive</u> level, that is merely follow his own moral intuitions and some established moral principles, e.g., that one ought not to live at other person's expense, lie to one's friends, neglect one's children, torment one's dog etc. The archangel could show that some intuitions and principles more or less correspond to the calculus of preferences. The prole does not know it but still acts rightly. Ordinary people are neither archangels nor proles but rather an approximation of both. They have some moral intuitions, follow some principles <u>and</u> have some ability to check whether these correspond to what other people wish (Hare 1981, 44 ff.).

One often criticises utilitarianism in general and Hare's theory in particular by giving some counter-examples. Assume, e.g., that most people show a (consistent and universalisable) system of preferences including a preference to seek happiness in liquors. Ought we then to create a community of alcoholics where spiritous drinks are for free? Assume that such a system includes a preference to exterminate people regarded as endangering the purity of the race. Ought we to kill the "subhumans"?

One may regard such counter-examples as reasons for completing utilitarianism, regarded as a theory of the Good, with a theory of the Right, based on some fundamental norms. A special case of the latter can consist of a theory of <u>rights</u>. All people have thus a right to live, regardless others' preferences. But one can try to reconcile the rights with Hare's utilitarianism. One can, e.g., assume that an individual's preference for living is so strong that it outweighs the preference of a great number of racists for killing one. On the other hand, hypotheses concerning strength of preferences are not easy to test. Perhaps they must be based on some theories of human nature.

To answer such objections, Hare simply assumes that most people are neither drunks not murderers. In this way, his theory comes close to natural-law conceptions, based on assumptions concerning human nature. Moreover, if people actually had such preferences, the archangel would be able to show them that, in the long run, the results of drinking and killing would strongly jeopardise some other things they prefer even more. He would thus show that a system including a preference to abuse alcoholic drinks or to exterminate some people cannot be consistent and universalisable.

To be able to tell this, one must also make assumptions about human nature. But Hare could perhaps reply that <u>no</u> general moral theory is conceivable without such assumptions. Another known objection is that at least some preferences of different persons are incommensurable. One has no right to regard some person's satisfaction as a sufficient compensation of others' harm. In some cases, the objection is very plausible. One certainly ought not to kill John and transplant his organs to save five other people. In other cases, however, the utilitarian standpoints seems to prevail. It is plausible to assume that one <u>may</u> kill John, if this would prevent a nuclear holocaust with millions of victims. One needs weighing and balancing of various considerations to state which cases are which. And Hare would no doubt point out that an archangel would be able to perform such act of weighing.

On the other hand, a critic may say that Hare assumes things he cannot know, first that people are good and then that the archangel would be able to correctly weigh preferences of different persons.

Moreover, Hare assumes implicitly that the archangel would correctly weigh and balance John's and Peter's preferences, as if they were his own, and then state precisely that, e.g., his preference for liberty outweighs his preference for security. But can one make such weighing and balancing objectively correct, <u>entirely</u> rational? An act of weighing and balancing ultimately rests on one's will, feelings and emotions, cf. section 2.4.5 supra. Perhaps there can exist different archangels having different will and different emotions.

If Hare had assumed that the statement "H is a good action" is equivalent to the statement "H corresponds to an actual (consistent and universalisable) system of preferences of other people", his theory would be cognitivistic or, to put it more precisely, a naturalistic one. But he has not made such an assumption. His theory implies something else, namely that the former statement is equivalent to the statement "H corresponds to an actual (consistent and universalisable) system obtained through weighing and balancing of both other persons' and one's own preferences". This statement is not theoretical, since it expresses one's act of weighing, ultimately depending on one's will, emotions and feelings.

Hare's theory thus has both a theoretical and a practical meaning, the first related to the connection between goodness and other person's preferences, the second attached to the discussed role of weighing and balancing between them and one's own preferences.

2.5.3. Weighing Practices: MacIntyre´s Theory of Virtue

The central idea of <u>Alasdair MacIntyre's</u> theory (MacIntyre 1981) is that the moral good is analytically related to virtue. He received the idea from Aristotle. The virtue of a horse makes it a good horse which runs well, well bears the rider and well holds his ground against the enemy (Aristotle, 1105b; cf. Marc-Wogau 1970, vol.1, 217). Similarly, the virtue of a human being consists in the conduct through which he is a good person and carries out his work well.

The conceptual relation between "human being" and "good human being" resembles the relation between "chess player" and "good chess player". A good chess player is virtuous, since he is good at playing chess. In other words, he highly fulfils the standards of excellence characterising chess. He can find weak points in a chess position. If he has an advantage, he can find a winning plan of game. He can calculate many variants. He makes few mistakes etc. Such properties constitute <u>intrinsic values</u> of chess. They come into existence only when people play chess. Chess is a <u>practice</u>.

Other practices may be more difficult to analyse but one can always characterise them by some presupposed goals, standards of excellence and intrinsic values. When one, e.g., establishes a family, one starts a practice whose complex goal includes taking care of one's children. When one accepts a public position, one starts a practice whose intrinsic values include following the law.

In this way, MacIntyre's theory is based on the idea that x is good for some purpose, defined by a practice. Different practices influence each other and constitute a complex and changing system.

The same applies to actions of an individual. To understand the connections between actions, one must know his "narrative history". "We place the agent's intentions... in causal and temporal order with reference to their role in his or hers history; and we also place them with reference to their role in the history of the setting or settings to which they belong." (MacIntyre 1981, 194).

A morally good, that is, virtuous human being has both ability and disposition to find the golden mean between competing goals, standards of excellence and values characterising various, historically evolved, practices connected with his family, town, nation, duties, property etc. This connection between virtue and the golden mean is typical for Aristotle's philosophy.

But the balance is not easy to find. The process of finding out is like a spiral of learning. "The virtues... are to be understood as those dispositions which will not only sustain practices and enable us to achieve the goods internal to practices, but which will also sustain us in the relevant kind of quest for the good... (T)he good life for man is the life spent in seeking for the good life for man, and the virtues necessary for the seeking are those which enable us to understand what more and what else the good life for man is." (MacIntyre 1981, 204).

A virtuous chess player <u>deserves</u> to win against a less virtuous one. A virtuous parent deserves to have his children, a virtuous official deserves his position etc. It is <u>just</u> to give positions to virtuous officials. A morally virtuous person deserves praise.

MacIntyre thus differs from some moral philosophers eliminating the idea of desert, <u>inter alia</u> because virtue is allegedly a product of a genetic lottery (cf. section 2.6.2 infra).

MacIntyre's theory is intimately connected with weighing and balancing.

1) Weighing and balancing is necessary to state precisely the golden mean of intrinsic values, standards of excellence and goals expressed in various practices.

In this connection, one must ask two questions:

a) How can one state precisely the intrinsic values, standards of excellence and goals characterising such a complex practice as, e.g., political life? A utilitarianist would find its goal in maximising utility, a liberal in protecting liberty, a conservative in enforcement of historically developed order, and a socialist in equality. This is the case because different ideologies imply different weighing and balancing of prima-facie values, competing with each other in political life.

b) How can one find the golden mean of intrinsic values, standards of excellence and goals expressed in many different practices? Some people evaluate family life above all, others pursue professional career etc. Where does the golden mean lie between such ideals? The answer requires an act of weighing and balancing.

The central point of MacIntyre's theory can be summarised, as follows: The statement "A is a morally good person" is equivalent with the statement "A has both ability and disposition to find the golden mean between competing goals, standards of excellence and values characterising various, historically evolved, practices." If the latter statement had been a theoretical proposition, the theory would be cognitivistic or, to put it more precisely, a naturalistic one. One could then criticise it by means of Moore's "open question argument". One could thus meaningfully ask such questions as "To be sure, A has ability and disposition to find the golden mean between competing goals, standards of excellence and values characterising various practices, but is A a morally good person?". The meaningful character of the question reveals that to be good is not identical with having this ability and disposition.

But the statement "A has ability and disposition to find the golden mean... etc." is vague. More exactly, it is value-open. To interpret it in a precise manner assumes that one performs two acts of weighing and balancing, each ultimately depending on one's will, emotions and feelings. The first one is necessary to establish the goals, standards of excellence and values characterising various practices; the second is a necessary condition of finding the golden mean between the practices. In consequence, MacIntyre's theory has both a theoretical and a practical meaning, the first related to the connection between goodness and established practices, the second attached to the role of feelings etc.

2.6. EXAMPLES OF WEIGHING IN THEORIES OF JUSTICE

2.6.1. Justice, Equality and Weighing

The morally good is connected with the just. According to many authors, justice means that the like ought to be treated alike. This conception of justice is thus related to Hare's demand of universalisability of all moral statements; see section 2.5.2 supra. Chaim Perelman has thus formulated the "formal" principle of justice, according to which beings of one and the same essential category must be treated in the same way (Perelman 1963, 16).

This principle must be completed with a number of more precise norms for distributive justice, that is, just distribution of goods (or values), thus defining membership of the same essential category as determined by one's merits, works, needs etc. Perelman has discussed six "formulas of concrete justice". One may present these, as follows (Perelman 1963, 6 ff).

1) One ought to treat each individual in the same manner.
2) One ought to treat each individual according to his merits.
3) One ought to treat each individual according to his works.
4) One ought to treat each individual according to his needs.
5) One ought to treat each individual according to his rank.
6) One ought to treat each individual according to his legal entitlement.

Obviously, one may extend the list of such formulas through adding, e.g., the following ones:

7) One ought to treat each individual according to his sacrifices and suffering.
8) One ought to treat each individual according to his capability of using goods distributed or bear burdens imposed.
9) One ought to treat each individual according to his placing in time and space, e.g., in a queue (cf., e.g., Eckhoff 1971, 46; Rescher 1966, 73 and Lucas 1980, 164 ff.).

Since one cannot simultaneously distribute the goods in proportion to all such criteria, one must make a compromise between them. Perelman has pointed out that such a compromise is required by equity (Perelman 1963, 32 ff.). Of course, the compromise requires weighing and balancing.

In this connection, one may ask the question, What values are to be distributed justly, i.e. equally between equally entitled recipients?. The following alternatives may be considered (cf. Peczenik 1972, 523-524 and 1971b, 21; cf. Welinder 1974, 86-87 on Adolph Wagner, F.Y. Edgeworth and A.C. Pigou):

a. The goods to be distributed are these which are at the disposal of the distributor; an employer, for example, pays wages from his bank account.

b. The goods to be distributed are not only these which are at the disposal of the distributor but also goods which the recipient already has and which are to be redistributed. Such a corrective justice takes as its starting point that the recipients' position as a whole should be regulated in proportion to one's merits, works, needs etc. In agreement with this, social benefits and taxes, are distributed not equally but quite unequally, with a view to make people more equal.

An argument for corrective justice implies a political position as regards the question of redistribution. It is plausible to assume that such questions require weighing and balancing, inter alia of an individual's claim to keep what is his own and his claim to receive help when needed.

The Norwegian jurist <u>Torstein Eckhoff</u> has discussed another important question, that is, What relation is to exist between the possession of the relevant qualities (merits, needs etc.) and the share given to each person? One can think about the following possibilities (Eckhoff 1971, 44 ff.):

a. The distribution of values may be graded quantitatively in proportion to merits, works, needs etc.

b. The recipients may be divided into two classes, the entitled and the not entitled. If a person is entitled, i.e. has sufficiently large needs, merits etc., he will participate in the distribution of goods, otherwise not.

c. A hierarchy of recipients may be based on works, needs, merits etc.; a recipient who is higher in the hierarchy will get the goods in question earlier, but all will get an equal amount until the goods come to an end. Those who are lower in the hierarchy will get nothing.

One may argue for each of these solutions. But most such arguments imply weighing and balancing of various considerations. For example, in order to support dividing recipients of some goods in two classes only, instead of choosing a quantitative distribution in proportion to needs, merits etc., one may claim that welfare of the poor has a <u>greater weight</u> than all reasons for proportional distribution.

<u>Torstein Eckhoff</u> (1971, 38 ff.) has also discussed the following <u>principles of equal weight</u>:

1) Good ought to be repaid with good.

2) Evil may be repaid with evil.

3) Damage ought to be made good. (The optimal balance of considerations in the law of torts is, however, a matter of complex weighing, cf. Hellner 1972, 304 ff.).

4) A person whose interests are favoured by someone should also accept the fact that his benefactor assigns him some burdens.

Such principles of reciprocity and balance express the so-called <u>commutative justice</u>. One can imagine more such principles, e.g.:

5) Nobody should appropriate to himself a value if some other person will thereby lose a greater value (cf. also v. Wright 1963, 207 ff.).

One can also proffer principles demanding some balance between advantages and disadvantages (cf., e.g., Tammelo 1977, pp. 9, 39 and 54), e.g.:

6) A person whose interests are favoured by an action should also bear the costs of the action: <u>ubi emolumentum ibi onus</u> (cf., e.g., Esser 1964, 99 note 43).

7) Nobody should benefit from his own wrong (cf., e.g., Esser 1964, 99).

Some principles of justice are more difficult to analyse. Let me merely mention one example:

8) There must be a reasonable proportion between the crime and the punishment.

Both the norms for distributive justice and the norms for commutative justice are intimately connected with weighing and balancing. When various principles collide, one must weigh and balance them against each other. (Cf. Perelman 1963, 33: "pure compromise". Cf. Friedrich 1963, 43: "balanced evaluation... on the

ground of values prevalent in the political community concerned".
Cf. Weinberger 1978, 208).
The norms of justice thus have a prima-facie character. A
distributor of goods must certainly consider the question to what
extent the distribution fits the merits, works, needs etc. of the
recipients. But he has no clear criteria for definitive
distribution. The discussed theory identifies justice with the fact
that beings of one and the same essential category are treated in
the same way. The statement "A treats B justly" is thus equivalent
with the statement "A treats B equally with other members of the
same essential category". If the latter statement had been a
theoretical proposition, the theory would be cognitivistic or, to
put it more precisely, a naturalistic one. But this statement is
vague. To interpret it in a precise manner assumes that one tells
who belongs to the same essential category. To state this precisely,
one must perform an act of weighing. In consequence, the theory has
both a theoretical and a practical meaning, the first related to the
connection between justice, equality and several prima-facie
criteria of equality, the second attached to the role of weighing
and balancing in the process of deciding who is equal with whom.

2.6.2. The Role of Weighing In John Rawls's Theory of Justice

John Rawls has elaborated another conception of justice.
1. Rawls has not studied directly what a just action is but has
discussed the question of a just organisation of the society.
2. The starting point of the theory consists in a hypothetical
social contract. An organisation of the society is just if it would
be accepted by reasonable individuals in "the original position of
equality". Rawls has adapted this "position" to a compromise (a
"reflective equilibrium") of two conditions: 1) it must ascertain
impartiality, and 2) it must lead to unanimous acceptance of
reasonable principles of justice.
Rawls has characterised this "reflective equilibrium" as follows:
"By going back and forth, sometimes altering the conditions of the
contractual circumstances, at others withdrawing our judgments..., I
assume that eventually we shall find a description of the initial
situation that both expresses reasonable conditions and yields
principles which match our considered judgments duly pruned and
adjusted" (Rawls 1971, 20).
The original position of equality has the following properties.
a. Rationality. Whoever is in the original position performs a
rational choice between different organisation of the society.
b. Egoism. The choice is determined by the intention to protect
one's own interest.
c. The veil of ignorance. "Among the essential features of this
situation is that no one knows his place in society, his class
position or social status, nor does anyone know his fortune in the

distribution of natural assets and abilities, his intelligence, strength and the like... This ensures that no one is advantaged or disadvantaged in the choice of principles by the outcome of natural chance or the contingency of social circumstances" (Rawls 1971, 12).

d. Some information. The veil of ignorance does not eliminate all information. The discussed individuals know that their task is to make a choice of basic principles for the organisation of society. They also know which own interests they must protect (cf. Rawls 1971, 136 ff.). But since they do not know anything about their particular situation, they must conceive these interests in a very abstract manner. In consequence, the chosen principles of justice do not concern distribution of any goods whatever but merely some primary goods, such as liberty and opportunity, income and wealth, and, above all, self-respect (cf. Rawls 1971, 440 ff.).

4. The individuals in the original position would, according to Rawls, choose the following principles:

"(1) Each person is to have an equal right to the most extensive total system of equal basic liberties compatible with a similar system of liberty for all...

(2) Social and economic inequalities are to be arranged so that they are both:

(a) to the greatest benefit of the least advantaged, consistent with the just savings principle, and

(b) attached to offices and positions open to all under conditions of fair equality of opportunity" (cf. Rawls 1971, 302).

In my opinion, the Second Principle expresses the political point of the theory: it is just to protect the least advantaged.

5. The individuals in the original position would, moreover, accept the following priority rules. The first principle is "lexically" (unconditionally) prior to the second, and the second is "lexically" prior to efficiency, wealth etc. (cf. Rawls 1971, 302-303). This does not mean, however, that all kinds of freedom take priority over the second principle. Were it the case, the second principle could not support compulsory redistribution. Such a redistribution must restrict freedom of the persons whose goods are taken away. Since Rawls clearly admits compulsory redistribution, he must intend his first principle to protect, not liberty in general, but merely such specific civic liberties as freedom of speech, freedom of conscience etc. (cf. Simmonds 1986, 48-49).

6. These principles and their priority order define justice. Since Rawls also claims that justice is the highest value, they also define the idea of the right. "The right" is prior to "the good", 31 ff. The latter concept, but not the former, allows certain variations between different individuals, cf. Rawls 1971, 446 ff. Cf. Rawls 1980, 515 on "the Kantian roots of that conception".

Rawls's theory is, however, open for objections, each revealing the great role of weighing and balancing in a theory of justice.

1. The starting point of the theory consists in a set of initial assumptions concerning both the original position of equality and reasonable principles of justice. These initial assumptions are then adapted to each other by means of the "reflective equilibrium". The result is a highly coherent set of assumptions. But what happens if several coherent sets are possible? How should one make a choice

between them, if not through weighing and balancing of several prima-facie pro- and counter-arguments?

2. It is strange that the theory has no place for <u>desert</u>. No doubt, it is just to protect the least advantaged. But it is also just to recognise merits and desert. Rawls (1971, 311-2) claims that "the idea of rewarding desert is impracticable" because "the initial endowment of natural assets and the contingencies of their growth and nurture... are arbitrary from a moral point of view". This includes "the effort a person is willing to make" which also is "influenced by his natural abilities and skills". One's talents, willingness to make sacrifices, and thus one's merits, are results of a genetic lottery. However, should those who make sacrifices for the common good receive no more recognition than the individuals who do not care about anything but their own profit? (cf. Lucas 1980, 190 ff). To answer this question, one needs weighing and balancing of the genetical-lottery argument and the counter-arguments.

3. One can doubt whether rational individuals in the original position would choose Rawls's principles. They would certainly do it, were they afraid of taking risks. Otherwise, they might do something else. To be sure, they would protect themselves from the worst catastrophes, thus assigning the least advantaged a certain decent minimal standard of life. Once this "utility floor... below which no one should be pressed" (Rescher 1966, 29) is provided, they would rather try to maximise their chance to receive as great an amount of goods as possible. To determine this "utility floor", they would be forced to weigh and balance several moral considerations.

It may also be highly <u>improbable</u> that one becomes the least advantaged person. But the veil of ignorance is specifically designed to be "thick", not "thin", that is, to prohibit the individuals in question to pay attention to such probability. One may doubt whether this limitation is justifiable. "Rawls does nothing to establish that the original position makes probability calculations impossible because he gives no reason for thinking that a thick rather than a thin veil ought to be dropped over that situation of choice" (Pettit 1980, 173; cf. Simmonds 1986, 45.

One may wonder whether a choice between competing versions of the veil of ignorance can be rationally made without a kind of weighing and balancing of several considerations.

4. The principle of the greatest possible benefit of the least advantaged is just under some circumstances, but it might not be, were its price to consist of a radical decrease in the production of goods, and in losses for everyone except the least advantaged, perhaps losses exceeding profit. Since Rawls has neglected the connection between distribution and production, his theory best fits a society in which "things fall from heaven like manna". (Nozick 1974, 198; cf. Wolff 1977, 210; Weinberger 1978, 208).

Assume the following simple model. The society consists of three persons, A, B and C, who produce and consume cakes. Assume further that the production system is such that inequality highly promotes efficiency. More precisely, one has to make a choice between two alternative organisations of this society, I and II, characterised by the following distribution of cakes:

I. A gets 5 cakes. B gets 6 cakes. C gets 7 cakes.

II. A gets 4 cakes. B gets 8 cakes. C gets 16 cakes.

Rawls would choose I, thus assuring the greatest benefit of the least advantaged, A. But if already 4 cakes suffice for a decent standard of life, it is by no means clear why the production ought to be restricted to 18 cakes, instead of 28, in order to give A 5 cakes instead of 4.

In general, "(i)t may be said that (Rawls's) principles pay absurd attention to the position of the worst off person, and that they have the following intolerable results: that so long as the worst off are at the same level the principles would be indifferent between two systems in one of which people other than the worst off are much better treated than they are in the other, and that so long as it improved by a little the position of the worst off person, the principles would prefer a system that greatly impaired the lot of those other than the worst off" (Pettit 1980, 177). "(W)hereas Rawls is concerned only with the underdog, justice is concerned with everybody and seeks to maximise not only the minimum pay-off but every pay-off"; Lucas 1980, 67. Rawls's response is to say that "it seems probable that if the privileges and powers of legislators and judges, say, improve the situation of the less favored, they improve that of citizens generally. Chain connections may often be true, provided the other principles of justice are fulfilled" (Rawls 1971, 82). This rebuttal is nothing better than an ad-hoc empirical hypothesis, specifically designed to save the theory. No independent empirical reasons exist to assume that this hypothesis is true.

Indeed, the value of Rawls's principles can hardly be decided by purely empirical means. In my opinion, any choice between competing principles of justice requires not only empirical knowledge but also weighing of risks and gains their application would create.

5. Rawls's list of "primary goods" to be distributed according to the second principle of justice is vague. This is important, since the second principle is designed to justify redistribution or primary goods. Are one's organs, e.g., one's eyes and kidneys, primary goods? If so, may they be redistributed to save others? If not, why? (Simmonds 1986, 46 ff.; cf. Pettit 1980, 170 ff.). Obviously, one needs weighing and balancing of various considerations in order to ascertain what goods are and what are not primary.

6. It follows from Rawls's theory that the first principle is applicable only to some civic liberties, not to liberty in general. But what justifies the choice of just those basic liberties? Obviously, an answer to this question requires weighing and balancing of multiple considerations.

7. According to Rawls's priority rules, the first principle is unconditionally prior to the second, and the second is unconditionally prior to efficiency, wealth etc. This priority order is, however, very strange in starving societies, such as a great part of Africa. First of all, hungry people would prefer bread to liberty. Moreover, they may prefer to make sacrifices to assure continual progress and increasing prosperity of future generations.

Rawls (1971, 287), on the other hand, has expressed the following view: "When people are poor and saving is difficult, a lower rate of saving should be required; whereas in a wealthier society greater savings may reasonably be expected since the real burden is less. Eventually once just institutions are firmly established, the net accumulation required falls to zero."

Indeed, it is difficult to agree with any unconditional order of such values. It is more plausible to regard justice as a matter of weighing and balancing of many considerations.

Rawls's theory identifies justice with the fact that the organisation of society corresponds to his principles. One can then criticise it by means of Moore's "open question argument": "To be sure, the organisation of society S corresponds to the principles but is it just?" Since this question is meaningful, justice cannot be identical with fulfilment of these principles. Thus the following remark is fully justified: "Suppose somebody says 'In the original position I would opt for a social system ruled by the principle of utility, because this would maximise my chances; but morally I reject such system as unjust.' According to Rawls it would be self-contradictory to say such a thing, but it does not appear to be self-contradictory and may even be true" (Tugendhat 1979, 88-89; cf. Hare 1973, 249; Browne 1976, 1; Höffe 1977, 423).

No doubt, there exists a connection between justice and ideals of liberty, equality and protection of the least advantaged. The statement "The organisation of society S is just" has a similar (albeit not identical) meaning as the statement "S fulfils the demands impartial observers would formulate, concerning liberty, equality and protection of the least advantaged". But the latter statement is vague. To interpret it in a precise manner assumes that one performs an act of weighing of various properties of the society, ultimately depending on one's will, emotions and feelings. Rawls offers one interpretation but others are also possible.

In consequence, Rawls's theory has both a theoretical and a practical meaning. The first is related to the connection between justice and the ideals of liberty, equality and protection of the least advantaged. The second is attached to the role of weighing and balancing for deciding what the precise meaning these ideals ought to have.

2.6.3. The Role of Weighing In Robert Nozick's Theory of Justice

Robert Nozick has criticised, **inter alia**, Rawls's theory of distributive justice for not having recognised that many things are from the beginning attached to definite persons. Assume again that the society consists of three persons, A, B and C, who produce and consume cakes, and that one has to make a choice between two alternative organisations, I and II, characterised by the following distribution of cakes:

I. A gets 6 cakes. B gets 6 cakes. C gets 6 cakes.
II. A gets 4 cakes. B gets 4 cakes. C gets 10 cakes.

In this situation, any egalitarian would choose I but Nozick insist that II may, after all, be just if it has come about as a

result of voluntary exchanges from the starting point which
consisted of I. What determines justice is not the pattern of
distribution but "historical entitlement" (Nozick 1974, 155 ff).

1. Nozick thus assumes that people have rights, e.g., the property
right to justly acquired objects, independently from the positive
law, moral conventions and other social institutions. Each person
has an exclusive right in his own person and his own labour, and no
rights in other persons (cf. Nozick 1974, 174 ff.). This assumption
resembles the classical natural-law doctrine of the <u>suum</u>, including
a person's life, body, good reputation and actions. One has a
natural right to one's <u>suum</u>. According to Nozick, one has such a
right to justly acquired objects.

2. A just "historical entitlement" is determined by three sets of
principles, that is, (a) principles of acquisition, (b) principles
of transfer and (c) principles of rectification of injustice which
resulted from violation of a or b.

Nozick has thus formulated the following principles whose
fulfilment is a necessary condition of justice.

"If the world were wholly just, the following inductive definition
would exhaustively cover the subject of justice in holdings.

1) A person who acquires a holding in accordance with the
principle of justice in acquisition is entitled to that holding.

2) A person who acquires a holding in accordance with the
principle of justice in transfer, from one entitled to the holding,
is himself entitled to the holding.

3) No one is entitled to the holding except by (repeated)
application of 1 and 2" (Nozick 1974, 151).

3. In this connection, Nozick has developed the following ideas,
mostly corresponding to Locke's theory (Nozick 1974, 174 ff.).

a. An initial acquisition of an object is just if one has "mixed
one's labour with it". One's entitlement extends to the whole object
rather than to the added value one's labour has produced, provided
that no one suffers a loss in consequence of the acquisition.

b. A transfer is just if based on a free will of the entitled
person.

4. According to Nozick, a historical development of this kind,
that is, a free market, would inevitably upset any "patterned"
distribution, such as an equal distribution of money, freedom etc.
(Nozick 1974, 160 ff. and 219 ff.).

On the other hand, a perfect market, based on free will of the
persons involved, would promote equal chance of everybody to make a
free choice, that is, to use his resources to buy precisely the
goods he wants, whereas any redistributive mechanism rather gives
him the goods the deciders choose for him.

5. To apply these thoughts to the relation between individuals and
the state, Nozick has argued, as follows (Nozick 1974, 88 ff.):

a. In an imaginary state of nature, or a state of anarchy, no
institution restricts one's freedom.

b. The state of nature must evolve into an organised society.
Nozick imposes the following restrictions upon this transformation:
(ba) It should be a result of self-interested and rational actions
of various persons; and (bb) it should not include any violation of

the indicated principles of justice. No other moral restrictions are imposed.

c. In this situation, people will be forced to buy protection from various risks anarchy causes. A number of protective agencies will thus evolve. A natural selection of these would then lead to a dominating protective agency. This agency would be the same as an "ultra-minimal" state. At this stage, some people would stay unprotected. But those operating the ultra-minimal state would be morally required to organise taxation to provide some funds for people unable to buy the protection. They would also be required to buy out persons who do not want to be protected. Since people, in fact, would do what morality requires of them, a minimal state would evolve, giving everybody a minimum of protection but otherwise not engaged in any redistribution of goods (Nozick 1974, 149 ff.).

6. One can thus only justify the minimal state, not the modern welfare state, performing an extensive redistribution of goods.

Nozick's theory must, however, face the following objections, revealing the importance of weighing and balancing of several considerations of justice.

1. No doubt, a person is entitled to the full value of his labour. But why should he be entitled to the whole object with which he has "mixed his labour", e.g. to a natural resource he utilised, such as iron, oil and gas? (cf. Simmonds 1987, 56 ff.). Nozick may answer that the acquisition of the whole object is just if no one suffers a loss in consequence of it. This answer reveals, however, a consideration of an independent character, not connected with the principles of "historical entitlement". Such considerations must, indeed, be taken into account. But their weight must be determined by an act of weighing and balancing.

2. In the process of production, objects are refined by actions of interdependent individuals. In consequence, the principle of just acquisition applies not only to individual but also to collective ownership. One's option for private property must thus rest on other grounds than Nozick's. It is plausible that it must rest on weighing of pro- and counter-arguments for both systems of property.

3. A difficult question concerns new members of the society, born or immigrated after most things had already been acquired by others. Should these have no property at all? Or should one allow for a redistribution? (cf., e.g., Steiner 1977, 151). What is the extent to which redistribution is just? The answer to this question obviously requires weighing and balancing of several considerations.

4. Why must the "ultra-minimal" state evolve into a minimal state? No doubt, the people operating the former would be morally required to provide some funds for those unable to buy the protection. They would also be morally required to buy out persons who do not want to be protected. But how can Nozick know that they would do what morality requires? (cf. Pettit 1980, 98 ff.). The outlined evolution may, in fact, produce a society in which some people have no rights at all. Nozick's hypothesis that this would not happen is perhaps influenced by his moral opinion. No doubt, such a society would be unjust. But let me add that the best way to justify this moral opinion is to perform an act of weighing and balancing of several ethical considerations, some "historical", other "patterned".

Nozick's theory identifies justice with a result of a historical process, including the fact that some people "mixed their labour" with some things, voluntarily transferred the things to others, bought a kind of protection, and other such <u>facts</u>. One can then criticise it by means of Moore's "open question argument": "To be sure, all these facts occurred but is the resulting society just?" Since this question is meaningful, justice cannot be identical with these facts. Nor can it be identical with the causal result of them.

To be sure, there exists <u>a</u> connection between justice and such ideals as respect for work and free contracts. The statement "The organisation of society S is just" has a similar meaning as the statement "S evolved through a historical process consisting of productive work and voluntary agreements." But the latter statement is not identical with the former. Justice also demands paying attention to some other considerations, e.g., concerning the newly born and newly arrived members of the society. One must perform an act of weighing and balancing of various such considerations, ultimately depending on one's will, emotions and feelings.

In consequence, Nozick's theory has both a theoretical and a practical meaning. The first is related to the connection between justice and the respect for work and free agreements. The second is attached to the role of weighing and balancing these and other morally important considerations.

2.6.4. Some Concluding Remarks on Justice

Very little can be said about the most general idea of justice, except that its point is to make a justifiable distinction between what values different individuals ought to possess, what treatment they ought to receive etc. This point corresponds to a broad interpretation of the famous Roman distinction between what is one's own and what belongs to others. <u>Iustitia est constans et perpetua voluntas ius suum cuique tribuendi</u> (Ulpianus, Dig. I,I.10, pr; cf. Tammelo 1971, 95).

More precise definitions have little prospect of success. There are many competing theories of justice. Some of them were briefly discussed in the preceding sections. Different authors have thus proposed three theories which, in my opinion, attempt to state precisely some reasonable intuitions, <u>inter alia</u> expressed in the following vague principles:

1) relevantly like people ought to be treated alike (<u>see</u> equality theories, section 2.6.1.);

2) the least advantaged people ought to be protected (cf. Rawls's second principle, section 2.6.2.); and

3) rights acquired in a justifiable manner ought to be protected, cf. Nozick´s principles of justice, section 2.6.3.

One can support a just action or a just organisation of a society by each one of these principles, together with some other norms, e.g. demanding freedom (cf. Rawls´s first principle). The idea of "support" in this connection means that though the conclusion about justice of a particular action or society does not follow logically from the principle alone, it follows from a set of reasonable premises, to which the principle belongs (cf. sections 2.7 and 3.2 infra).

When A thus gives various reasons for his opinion that an action is just (or unjust), his quoting such a principle might increase "force" of the argument. This increase might create a problem for B, who disagrees with A, and might in some cases even justify reversal of the burden of argumentation: B must now show that A is wrong.

But none of such principles can grasp the idea of justice as a whole. Justice has many dimensions. To act justly is to take all relevant considerations. Justice is thus an optimal balance of considerations (cf., e.g., Tay 1979, 96). In other words, justice determines some all-things-considered moral duties. In many cases, the conclusion about justice of a particular action or a particular society follows logically from a set of reasonable premises containing more than one of the discussed principles of justice.

From each of these general and vague principles together with some reasonable premises, one can derive some more precise norms of justice, e.g. (a) One ought to treat each individual according to his merits; cf. section 2.6.1.; (b) Social and economic inequalities are to be arranged so that they provide the least advantaged with a decent standard of life; cf. section 2.6.2.; and, (c) A person who acquires a holding through his work is entitled to that holding; cf. section 2.6.3. But such more precise norms of justice do not make the vague and general principles unnecessary. The vague principles facilitate understanding of the more precise norms. They may also provide one with a starting point for a deliberation which results in the fact that one creates more precise norms. They thus give a deliberation and discussion concerning justice a point and a framework. But the estimation of whether a particular action or a

organisation of society is more just than another
requires weighing of several considerations.

One can also argue (in a manner indicated in section
2.3.3 supra) that justice is no supreme value.

Cf. Tammelo 1971, 51 and 57-58; 1980, 35 and 1977, 134-135; Feinberg
1975, 116 and Nowell-Smith 1973, 320 ff. Rawls 1971, 3, has
expressed a contrary opinion.

It is merely a component of the optimally balanced
ethical theory, that is, a theory which has support of
considerations regarding as many morally relevant
circumstances as possible, and as many criteria of
coherent reasoning as possible (cf. sections 2.4.2 supra
and 4.1 infra). Morally relevant circumstances concern
not only justice but also utilitarian morality, moral
principles, rights and duties, virtues, etc.

Judgements of justice, and moral judgments in general,
are based on both factual criteria and acts of weighing.
The former determine the theoretical meaning of the
concept, the latter its practical meaning. Cognitivists
emphasise the former, non-cognitivists the latter. We
need a synthesis.

2.7. SUPPORT IN MORAL REASONING

2.7.1. Gaps and Jumps in Moral Reasoning

Moral reasoning constitutes often a kind of a dialogue
where one presents, weighs and balances different reasons
and counter-arguments. One may, however, present the
final result of the reasoning as a logical conclusion of
the reasons that weigh more than the counter-arguments,
competing with them. To achieve logical correctness one
must, however, often supplement the reasoning with a
complex set of additional premises.

The preceding sections contain several examples of
reasonable but logically incorrect reasonings. They also
include examples showing how to convert some of these to
logically correct inferences.

A person making a moral judgment may, e.g., perform the
following reasoning:

Premise 1   B does not harm others

Premise 2   B usually helps others

Conclusion   B is a good person

The reasoning contains a gap. To make it logically correct, one must fill the gap with at least one set of additional premise. One can, e.g., formulate the following inference:

Premise 1   B does not harm others

Premise 2   B usually helps others

Premise 3   If B does not harm others and helps
                 them, then B is a good person

Conclusion   B is a good person

When the person making moral judgment formulates the premise 3, he decides, as stated before, to pay attention to some moral criteria and to ignore others (such as B´s disposition to work, keep promises, show courage etc., cf. Section 2.3.1). He would, e.g., regard B as a good person, even if B had been a lazy coward.

Though reasonable, premise 3 is neither certain, nor taken for granted in the culture under consideration, nor derived from certain and/or presupposed premises. This fact indicates that the step from the premises 1 and 2 to the conclusion is a jump.

Let me now introduce the concepts "jump", "reasonable jump" and "support". If the conclusion follows from many premises jointly but not from any of them separately, one can say, what follows. Each premise alone supports the conclusion. The step from any particular premise to the conclusion is a jump, provided that the rest of the set does not solely consist of certain, presupposed and/or proved premises. The jump is reasonable if all the premises are reasonable. The step from the whole set of premises to the conclusion is no jump.

2.7.2. The Concept of a Jump

A <u>jump</u> from a set of premises S to a conclusion q exists
if, and only if
   1) q does not follow deductively from S; and
   2) one cannot expand or change S in such a way that a
set of premises S1 occurs which fulfils the following
conditions:
   a) the conclusion q follows deductively from S1, and
   b) S1 consists solely of certain premises, premises
presupposed in the culture under consideration and proved
premises.

The discussed example can be modified. One can, e.g., formulate the
following inference:

Premise 1   B does not harm others

Premise 2   B usually helps others

Premise 3'   If B does not harm others and helps them, then it
                   is <u>reasonable</u> that B is a good person
----

Conclusion 2   It is reasonable that B is a good person

   If one regards premise 3' as analytically true, one must also
admit logical correctness of the following direct inference:

Premise 1   B does not harm others

Premise 2   B usually helps others

Conclusion 2   It is reasonable that B is a good person

In other words, the step from premises 1 and 2 to the
conclusion 2 is no jump, because one may convert this
step into logical deduction by adding a <u>certain</u> (in this
case, analytically true) premise 3´.

2.7.3. The Concept of a Reasonable Premise

A jump from the set of premises S to the conclusion q is reasonable if, and only if, one can convert the jump to a deductive inference through adding some reasonable premises. All such premises are meaningful and not falsified. But some meaningful and not falsified premises are not reasonable. The statement, e.g., "there are birds in the star system Alfa Centauri" , though not falsified, is unreasonable, since nothing indicates that it is true.

There are, however, many kinds of reasonable premises. Some are certain, some taken for granted within a particular practice belonging to the considered culture, some proved. But there also exist reasonable premises that do not belong to any of these three categories. A little more precisely, one can thus say, what follows:

A jump from the set of premises S to the conclusion q is reasonable, if one can convert the jump into a deductively correct inference through adding some new premises to S, or through changing some premises already belonging to S, and in this way create a finite and logically consistent set of premises that solely contains

1) old premises that already belong to S; and/or

2) new certain premises; and/or

3) new premises that are presupposed (taken for granted) within a particular practice belonging to the culture under consideration; and/or

4) new proved premises; and (always)

5) new premises that are reasonable, although neither certain, nor taken for granted in a particular practice belonging to the culture under consideration, nor proved.

Though the concept of reasonableness is difficult to define, one can claim that a reasonable premise is not falsified and not arbitrary. A premise is thus reasonable if, and only if, the following conditions are fulfilled:

1. The premise is not falsified; cf. section 3.3.2 infra on Popper´s theory. The more attempts to falsify a premise fail, the more reasonable the premise is.

2. The hypothesis is not to a sufficiently high degree corroborated that this premise does not logically follow from a highly coherent set of premises. Cf. section 4.2.2 infra re the relation of reasonable statements to data! In other words, the hypothesis is not sufficiently corroborated that this premise is not highly S-rational.

It is also not evidently improbable that a reasonable premise logically follows from a highly coherent set of statements.

General moral theories are reasonable in this sense. It
is, e.g., not evidently unlikely that utilitarianists can
show that their views follow from a highly coherent set
of premises. On the other hand, this theory of the
reasonable rules out much of political manipulation. It
is, e.g., very unlikely that one could show that whatever
promotes supremacy of the Arian race is morally good.

2.7.4. The Concept of Reasonable Support

Finally, let me introduce the concepts of weak support
and reasonable support. In section 3.2.4 infra, I will
add the important concept of strong support. All three
concepts will be defined as a logical relations between
premises and conclusion. A psychological fact that some
people regard p as support for q is not enough. Though
many people regarded epidemics as supporting the belief
that there were witches, this belief lacks any support.

The statement p weakly supports the statement q if, and
only if, p belongs to a set of premises, S, from which q
follows logically.

No doubt, any p1 together with an arbitrarily added
premise supports any conclusion whatever. Consider, e.g.,
the reasoning "since it is raining, I am the Chinese
emperor". Of course, the conclusion "I am the emperor"
does not follow from the premise "it is raining". Yet,
the reasoning will be logically correct, if one adds the
false premise "if it is raining, then I am the emperor".

One obtains then the following correct inference:

The original premise 1	It is raining
The added premise 2	If it is raining, then I am the Chinese emperor
Conclusion	I am the Chinese emperor

However, this weak concept of support may be used as a
starting point of discussion. Inappropriate additional
premises are to be eliminated by other means, among other
things the theory of coherence, discussed below, and the
theory of reasonable support.

The statement p reasonably supports the statement q if,
and only if, q belongs to a set of reasonable premises,
S, from which p follows logically.

CHAPTER 3
RATIONALITY OF LEGAL REASONING

3.1. SUPPORT OF LEGAL REASONING. INTRODUCTION AND AN EXAMPLE

3.1.1. Fixity of Law. Extensive Support of Legal Reasoning

In Chapter 2, I have discussed various circumstances restricting arbitrariness of moral reasoning.

1. A moral statement can often be presented as a logically correct conclusion of a set of premises. One can also inquire whether these premises are (a) linguistically correct and (b) logically consistent .

2. One can also inquire whether the premises are sufficiently coherent.

3. Finally, different individuals can discuss moral questions in an impartial and otherwise objective way.

Consequently, I have also put forward three different demands of rationality, that is, the demand that the conclusion is logically and linguistically valid (L-rationality), follows from a highly coherent set of statements (S-rationality), and would not be refuted in a a perfect discourse (D-rationality).

These demands of rationality thus restrict arbitrariness of moral reasoning, but they do not entirely eliminate it. Mutually incompatible moral statements can, simultaneously, to a high degree fulfil the rationality requirements. This fact explains the need of legal reasoning, more predictable than the moral one.

The law is more stable, so to say more "fixed" than morality. Legal decisions are more predictable than purely moral ones. This is the case because legal reasoning is supported by a more extensive set of reasonable premises than a pure moral reasoning. This support includes numerous statements about statutes, other socially established sources of the law and some traditional reasoning norms.

Since the relatively fixed law thus makes legal reasoning more predictable, it increases the chance of consensus in legal matters. However, the greater fixity

of law is not necessarily the same as its lesser
arbitrariness. An unjust but rigid law can be both highly
arbitrary and highly fixed. But fixity of the law,
resulting in predictability of legal decisions, has a
moral value, among other things because it promotes
peaceful cooperation between people, assures that like
cases are treated alike etc. If a result of legal
reasoning in a particular case is not worse from the
point of view of other moral values, then it is, all
things considered, better than a result of a purely moral
reasoning would be, and thus less arbitrary. In brief,
fixity of law makes legal reasoning ceteris-paribus less
arbitrary than moral reasoning.

3.1.2. An Example of Extensively Supported Legal Reasoning

Legal reasoning is thus supported by a more extensive set
of reasonable premises than purely moral reasoning. One
can give the following example, elucidating this thesis.
A haulage contractor´s, B, car was damaged. During the
time when the car underwent repairs, B could not provide
work for some employees. He could dismiss them
temporarily but did not do so, fearing that they would
not come back when needed again. Instead, he paid them
their full salaries. B´s claim for compensation for the
salaries was not granted by the Supreme Court. The
majority of the Justices pointed out that "no such
connection - between the damage and the mentioned
expenses of B - can be considered to have existed that
the compensation should be awarded" (NJA 1959 p. 552).
   Such a decision can be justified more or less
completely. To justify it as completely as possible, one
must weigh, inter alia, the following considerations:
   1) an analysis of some legal concepts, among other
things the concept of "adequate" (that is, not too
remote) causation;
   2) various substantive reasons (cf. Summers 1978
passim), among other things (a) moral principles, (b)
general moral theories and (c) moral judgments of a
concrete case; and
   3) legal authority reasons, that is, (a) such sources
of the law as statutes, precedents, legislative history
etc. and (b) norms of legal reasoning.

This role of legal concepts (item 1) and authority reasons (item 3) causes the relatively greater fixity of the results of legal reasoning in comparison with the purely moral one.

3.1.3. An Example of Analysis of Legal Concepts – the Concept of Adequacy

The expression "no such connection can be considered to have existed that the compensation should be awarded" suggests that the Supreme Court made a judgment of so-called adequacy of the causal connection in question. An unwritten principle of the Swedish law of torts stipulates that one has to compensate a damage only if it has been an "adequate" result of the action for which one is liable. But when is the causal connection "adequate"? The concept of adequacy is vague, perhaps ambiguous. To put it more precisely, it is value-open. To decide the case under consideration, one must thus make a choice between the different normative theories of adequacy (cf. Peczenik 1979, 153 ff.).

In this connection, one may make the following remarks.

I. There exists an established list of normative theories of adequacy.

Inter alia, the following theories of adequacy are established in the juristic literature:

1) The causal connection between an action and a damage is adequate if, and only if, any action of this kind is apt to bring about (or relevantly increases probability of) a damage of this type.

2) The causal connection between an action and a damage is adequate if, and only if, this action makes a damage of this type foreseeable for a very cautious and well informed person (a cautious expert, a vir optimus).

3) The causal connection between an action and a damage is adequate if, and only if, this action is a not too remote cause of the damage.

4) The causal connection between an action and a damage is adequate if, and only if, this action is a substantial (important) factor in producing the damage.

I am omitting here the complex question how often various theories imply different evaluation of adequacy in concrete cases.

II. Each formula of this kind has been proposed as the
general theory of adequacy, guaranteeing just and morally
acceptable decision making. But each one, although
reasonable, is not proved. One can give reasons not only
in favour of it but also against it. In order to avoid
rather futile controversies between them, one may thus
combine all these formulas with each other. More
precisely, one may regard them as mere <u>prima-facie</u>
reasons for, or <u>criteria</u> of adequacy, not general
theories.

A general theory claims to cover all cases of adequacy. A criterion
does not imply such a claim.
    Even if the theories of adequacy are regarded as mere criteria,
they imply some increase of fixity of the law and, <u>ceteris paribus</u>,
a restriction of arbitrariness of legal reasoning. One can
objectively (freely from emotional bias) study the legal language
and practice and thus show that all of them include both <u>meaningful</u>
(L-rational) and <u>reasonable</u> (highly S-rational) arguments for the
conclusion that the causal connection in question is adequate.

III. The hypothesis is not falsified that if one had
possessed
    (1) more information about the use of legal language;
    (2) better knowledge of how other lawyers judge various
actual and hypothetical cases;
    (3) more clarity as regards one´s own evaluation of
future legal cases; and
    (4) more information about the logical connection
between one´s own judgments concerning various legal
questions;
then one would be able to use all this information to
formulate objectively (that is, freely from emotional
bias) a <u>complete list, containing all thinkable normative</u>
<u>theories of adequacy.</u>
    IV. Yet, one cannot objectively (freely from emotional
bias) formulate the <u>sufficient</u> condition for the
conclusion that causal connection between an action and a
damage is, <u>all things considered</u>, (not only <u>prima facie</u>)
adequate.

Such a sufficient condition would consist of (1) the complete list
of <u>prima-facie</u> theories of adequacy, established or newly created,
applicable to the case under considerations, and (2) the complete
list of statements determining the relative weight of these theories
in this case.
    As soon one claims that a certain condition is, all things
considered, sufficient, one faces the question "Why?". The answer

can be supported by some reasons. But the reasons are open for weighing and balancing against some counter-arguments.

A special case is, what follows. When performing such an act of weighing and balancing, one may, inter alia say, what follows:

1) The causal connection between an action and a damage is adequate if any action of this kind is apt to bring about (or relevantly increases probability of) a damage of this type, unless

-this action did not make the damage sufficiently foreseeable for a vir optimus; or

-this action is a too remote cause of the damage; or

-this action is not a sufficiently important factor in producing the damage.

....

4) The causal connection between an action and a damage is adequate if this action is a substantial factor in producing the damage unless

-it is not so that any action of this kind is apt to bring about (or relevantly increases probability of) a damage of this type; or

-this action did not make the damage sufficiently foreseeable for a vir optimus; or

-this action is a too remote cause of the damage.

And so on...

The opinion that some reasons weigh more than others can also be weighed and balanced against thinkable counter-arguments. From the logical point of view, the process of weighing can thus continue infinitely. But in practice, one must finish the reasoning, sooner or later. If the reasoning does not constitute a logical circle, one must arrive at an ultimate reason, fundamental for the whole argumentative structure. This ultimate reason must be assumed without any reasoning whatsoever. Had one continued the reasoning, the "ultimate" reason would not have been ultimate.

In such a way, a reasoning ends with an arbitrary assumption. I assume that the ultimate reason for weighing involves feelings, the will etc.; cf. section 2.4.5 supra.

Sooner or later, a lawyer making a judgment of adequacy must thus under some influence of his will and feelings "pick up" some theories and disregards others. For example, he points out the importance of increased probability of damage and the foreseeability. He decides then not to pay attention to other normative theories, such as the theory of remoteness of damage, or the theory of substantial factor.

V. Another kind of weighing and balancing is necessary when one performs a precise interpretation of the notoriously vague terms the theories of adequacy contain, such as "a damage of this type", "a vir optimus", "a too remote cause of the damage" or "a sufficiently important factor in producing the damage". For example, it is easy to foresee that a traffic accident would lead to a result defined as "economic loss", but difficult to foresee that it might lead to "economic loss in consequence of paying salaries to temporarily dismissed employees".

The juristic activity, consisting in "picking up" a precise interpretation of the concept of adequate causation is thus to some extent similar to a moral activity, consisting in "picking up" some

theoretical propositions as reasons for the conclusion that an
action or a person is morally good.

3.1.4. An Example of Substantive Reasons in the Law. The Purpose of Protection. Influence of Moral Theories and Criteria

To some extent, one can proffer moral reasons justifying the choice
between thinkable criteria of adequacy. Moreover, one can find moral
reasons for the conclusion that a person shall not compensate a
damage, even if he had adequately caused it. According to the theory
of the "purpose of protection" (Schutzzweck), the tortfeasor is thus
liable only for the damage against which the norm in question is
intended to give protection. Schutzzweck is an extra condition of
liability, distinct from adequacy (cf. Peczenik 1979, 299 ff.).
    Does the purpose of compensation cover the situation in which a
traffic accident leads to economic loss in consequence of paying
salaries to temporarily dismissed employees? No clear rule answers
this question. One must rely upon weighing and balancing of various
considerations, including some moral judgments.
    We have seen how complex moral reasoning is. It is, among other
things, difficult to find some uncontested general theory of moral
goodness. Can one then, at least, find a normative theory that ought
to govern the law of torts? According to, inter alia, Calabresi
(1970 passim), the law of torts should be arranged so that it will
deter from causing damage. The purpose is not to impose all costs of
damage on the person who caused it but to make those liable who have
such a position that they can influence others not to cause damage.
But can one thus regard general deterrence as the ultimate goal of
the law of torts? It is not certain. One cannot dismiss, without any
reasoning, the view that, e.g., restitution of a situation existing
before the damage, or just distribution of losses constitute
independent goals of compensation (cf. Hellner 1972, 321 ff.).
    How can one then argue for the conclusion that something
constitutes the ultimate goal of compensation? If one wishes to
support the reasoning with something more than one's own intuitive
judgment, quotations of what others think or a description of the
use of language, one must leave the law of torts and search for
general moral theories of a wider range. The law of torts
constitutes a part of the legal order, and this order is merely a
component of the complex cluster of norms, regulating social life.
It is thus improbable that compensation has a single ultimate goal,
unconnected with other areas of human life. On the contrary, one
must argue for one's view of the purpose of the law of torts.
Restitution, distribution of losses, prevention etc. can constitute
a goal of compensation because they help to fulfil such ultimate
goals as satisfaction of human preferences, promotion of some social
practices, justice etc. (cf. section 2.5.2). The reasoning about the
goals of damage thus does not necessarily end in the law of torts
but may continue outside its limits, and must end first when

approaching the foundations of morality. "Behind" legal problems, one finds moral reasoning, with all its complexity, described in chapter 2 supra. It this way, legal reasoning "inherits" both practical and thus emotional and arbitrary components of morality and all L-, S- and D-rationality factors, restricting arbitrariness.

3.1.5. An Example of Legal Authority Reasons. Brief Remarks on Precedents

The analysis of our example would be incomplete if one omitted legal authority reasons, such as statutes, other sources of the law and reasoning norms. In legal reasoning, one thus has access to a more extensive set of premises than in the realm of morality. Together with a high fixity of the sources of law, this fact constitutes, ceteris paribus, an additional restriction of arbitrariness. Being supported by a more extensive set of premises, legal conclusions possess a higher degree of S-rationality and thus promote foreseeability of decisions, constituting an important component of the complex phenomenon of legal certainty; cf. section 1.4.1 supra. I will later return to the problem of the sources of law. Here, one may merely point out that many precedents deal with the question of adequacy and some approach the purpose of protection.

As regards the latter question, one may inter alia quote the following precedents: NJA 1950 p. 610, NJA 1962 p. 799, NJA 1968 p. 23, NJA 1974 p. 170 and NJA 1976 p. 458.

Different precedents can, however, support incompatible norms. The person interpreting them must then perform weighing and balancing, inter alia compare the weight of the precedents.

In this manner the act of weighing and balancing, connected with the concept of the purpose of protection, must be supplemented with another one, essential for interpretation of precedents. When the purpose of protection remains uncertain, the tortfeasor has to compensate the damage only if precedents supporting the liability weigh more than those which support the conclusion that the tortfeasor is not liable.

Finally, some authority reasons and some moral reasons in the law relate to administrative and procedural concerns, and only indirectly to the substantive question to be decided. One thus asks various questions regarding procedural rules applicable to the case, moral underpinning of such rules etc.

When performing such acts of weighing and balancing, one receives some guidance from various sources of the law. In same cases, however, this help is not sufficient. Ultimately, the decider must rely on moral reasoning.

3.2. ANALYSIS OF SUPPORT IN LEGAL REASONING

3.2.1. Legal Reasoning As a Dialogue. Reflective Equilibrium and Hermeneutical Circle

The goal and often the result of such weighing is a kind of reflective equilibrium of considerations.

One usually characterises the concept of reflective equilibrium as a balance of mutually adapted, general and individual, practical statements. One can thus argue in favour of general value statements and norm-expressive statements by showing that they are supported by (coherent with) some individual ones. On the other hand, one can argue in favour of the latter by showing that they are supported by the former. If there is no coherence, one can modify each of the components. Sometimes, an individual statement is easier to explain away; sometimes it is easier to stick to it and change a general one (cf. Rawls 1971, 20; Prawitz 1978, 153).

The idea of reflective equilibrium is similar in important respects to three other ideas; the first concerns the reciprocal relation between observation and language, the second the idea of the so-called theory circle and the third the "hermeneutical circle".

1) All observations are dependent on a language. Consider an example. My eye registers a changing field of colours and shapes and I recognise a datum, or a fact: this swan is white. But when I call something "a white swan", I do it in a language which contains general concepts. Observation of a swan is more than a registering of "flashes, sounds and bumps"; it is "a calculated meeting with these as flashes, sounds and bumps of a particular kind" (Hanson 1958, 24), determined by the concept of "swan". A "statement such as 'This swan here is white' may be said to be based on observation. Yet it transcends experience... For by calling something a 'swan', we attribute to it properties which go far beyond mere observation..." (Popper 1959, 423). Inter alia, the concept of "swan" refers to all swans, also those which nobody ever observed.

2) Consequently, all observations are dependent on theories which underly the concepts belonging to the language used by the person who makes the observation. In general, many thinkers emphasise the existence of a "theory circle": One judges a theory in view of data and data in view of a theory. "The unit of empirical significance is the whole of science" (Quine 1953, 42. Cf. Quine 1960, 40 ff.).

Yet, knowledge need dot be based on a vicious circle.

a) People do not literally justify p by q and q by p, at the same time, but rather are engaged in a justificatory "spiral": at first, p justifies q; later, q constitutes a reason justifying a modified version of p, say p'; still later, p' constitutes a reason justifying a modified version of q, say q'.

b) Consequently, the "theory circle" is rather a "theory spiral". Data$_1$ justifies Theory$_1$, which justifies Data$_2$ justifies Theory$_2$, which justifies Data$_3$, etc. The description of Data$_2$ thus presupposes theoretical terms with regard to Theory$_1$ but not with regard to Theory$_2$ (cf. Kutschera 1972 vol. 1, 258; Hermerén 1973, 73 ff.). In natural science, one can always make the conceptual distinction between data and theory.

3) As regards many humanistic theories, one cannot say clearly which propositions report observational data and which are expressions of theories. Stegmüller (1975, 84-85; cf. Aarnio 1979, 154-155) regards this property as an explication of the so-called hermeneutical circle,ordinarily characterised as follows: "the whole of a cultural product (be it literary or philosophical opus, or the entire work of a thinker or a period) can be only understood if one understands its component parts, while these parts in their turn can be understood only by understanding the whole" (Rescher 1977, 103).

In is thus not surprising that one may modify and thus mutually adapt one´s interpretation of various legal considerations, inter alia (a) theories and criteria elucidating such concepts as "adequate causation"; (b) substantive reasons concerning the goals of compensation etc.; and (c) various authority reasons, e.g., precedents pulling in different directions. Such an adaptation of reasons occurs often in a dialogue of different persons (a pro aut contra reasoning, cf. Naess 1981, 80 ff.).

One can, for instance, imagine the following dialogue.

B's pro-argument: A should compensate the damage because he negligently caused it.

A's counter-argument: But the causal connection was not adequate, since the result was too remote, cf. the adequacy criterion 3 (section 3.1.2). A is thus not liable in torts.

B's pro-argument: A should, after all, compensate the damage because his negligent action made the damage foreseeable for an expert, and thus adequate according to the criterion 2.

A's counter-argument: However, such a compensation is outside of the purpose of the law of torts (section 3.1.3). This makes A not liable.

B's pro-argument: Yet, some precedents support the conclusion that A should compensate the damage.

A's counter-argument: Nevertheless, a greater number of precedents support the opposite conclusion... Etc.

When one presents legal reasoning as a dialogue, one pays attention to the process of reasoning. The dynamic character of the dialogue expresses itself, inter alia, in the fact that one modifies some, originally quite

reckless, statements. Originally, B has perhaps said
simply: A caused the damage, and thus he must compensate
it. Later, he has modified his thesis and claimed, e.g.,
what follows: A should compensate the damage because he
negligently caused it; and his negligent action made the
damage foreseeable for an expert; and some precedents
support his duty to pay the compensation; etc.

3.2.2. Legal Reasoning As an Inference. An Example

If one, on the other hand, only considers the reasons
that "survived" the dialogue, one may present the <u>final
result</u> of the reasoning as a <u>logical conclusion</u> of them.

If the legal conclusion in question logically follows
from a consistent and highly coherent set of
linguistically correct premises, it fulfils important
demands of L- and S-rationality; cf. section 2.2.4 supra.
To achieve this form of rationality, one must, however,
often supplement the reasoning with a complex set of
additional premises.

For example, the following inference, constituting the
starting point of reasoning in the discussed case,
obviously constitutes a (logically <u>not</u> correct) jump.

(1) A non-controversial legal norm, cf. now Ch. 2 Sec.1 of the Tortious Liability Act, Sec. 18 of the Car Traffic Liability Act etc.
A person who caused damage in consequence of traffic with an engine-driven vehicle should compensate the damage if, and only if, there exists a legal ground therefor

(2) A non-controversial premise: the customary rule of adequacy
A legal ground for the conclusion that one should compensate the damage exists, if the causal connection between one's action and the damage was adequate

(3) A non-controversial premise: a description of facts
A caused negligently a traffic accident in which B's car was damaged. During the time when the car underwent repairs, B could not provide work for some employees. Yet, he paid them their full salaries, fearing that they would not come back when needed again.

Conclusion
A should not compensate B's loss in consequence of paying salaries to not working employees

If one expands the reasoning, for example through adding premises 4-11 quoted below, one obtains both deductive correctness and a more profound insight into the case. But not even the following inference pays attention to <u>all</u> considerations, relevant in the discussed case.

(1) A non-controversial legal norm, cf. now Ch. 2 Sec. 1 of the Tortious Liability Act, Sec. 18 of the Car Traffic Liability Act etc.

A person who caused damage in consequence of traffic with an engine-driven vehicle should compensate the damage if, and only if, there exists a legal ground therefor.

(2) A non-controversial premise: the customary rule of adequacy

A legal ground for the conclusion that the tortfeasor should compensate a damage exists, if the causal connection between his action and the damage was adequate.

(3) A non-controversial premise: a description of facts

A caused negligently a traffic accident in which B's car was damaged. During the time when the car underwent repairs, B could not provide work for some employees. Yet, he paid them their full full salaries, fearing that they would not come back when needed again.

(4) An added non-controversial: premise: a list of established criteria of adequacy

One may choose the following facts as reasons for the conclusion that the causal connection between an action and a damage is adequate: 1) any action of this kind is apt to bring about (or relevantly increases probability of) a damage of this type; 2) this action makes a damage of this type foreseeable for a very cautious and well informed person; 3) this action is a not too remote cause of the damage; 4) this action is a substantial (important) factor in producing the damage.

(5) An added and reasonable premise: the chosen criterion of adequacy

The following criterion of adequacy should be used in the case under consideration:
(2) the causal connection between an action and a damage is adequate, if the action makes the damage of the type T foreseeable for a very cautious and well informed person.

(6) An added and reasonable premise: restriction of liability which exceeds the purpose of protection

The tortfeasor shall not compensate the damage, not even the adequately caused one, if the law of torts is not intended to give protection against it.

(7) An added and reasonable premise: an authority

When the purpose of protection remains uncertain, the tortfeasor has to compensate the damage only if precedents supporting the liability weigh more

reason	than those which support the conclusion that the tortfeasor is not liable.
(8) An added and reasonable premise: an estimation of adequacy	The action in question made a damage of the type T (that is, a loss in consequence of paying salaries to not working employees) foreseeable for a very cautious and well informed person.
(9) An added and reasonable premise: a judgment of the purpose of protection	It is uncertain whether the law of torts is intended to give protection against a damage of the type T.
(10) An added and reasonable premise: an interpretation of precedents	Precedents supporting the liability do not weigh more than those which support the conclusion that the tortfeasor is not not liable.
(11) An added and reasonable premise: a description of valid law	No other legal ground exists for the conclusion that A should compensate B's loss in consequence of paying salaries to not working employees.
Conclusion	A should not compensate B's loss in consequence of paying salaries to not working employees

This extended inference contains the initial and non-controversial premises 1-3 together with a set of additional premises 4-11. The additional premises convert the jump to a logically correct inference. But many of the additional premises are <u>contestable</u>. For example, premises 5, 6 and 10 are neither certain, nor presupposed within the legal "paradigm" (that is, within the established tradition of legal reasoning, cf. section 3.3.3 infra), nor proved within this paradigm. One must thus either deduce the conclusion from contestable premises or perform non-deductive, logically incorrect, reasonings from non-controversial premises.

3.2.3. Legal Reasoning As a Reasonable Jump

In section 2.7 supra, I have defined the concepts of "jump" and "reasonable jump". Let me repeat the definitions together with some comments concerning the discussed example.

A <u>jump</u> from a set of premises S to a conclusion q exists if, and only if (1) q does not follow deductively from S; and (2) one cannot expand or change S in such a way that a set of premises S1 occurs

which fulfils the following conditions: (a) the conclusion q follows
deductively from S1, and (b) S1 consists solely of certain premises,
premises presupposed in the culture under consideration and proved
premises. A jump from the set of premises S to the conclusion q is
reasonable, if one can convert the jump into a deductively correct
inference through adding some new premises to S or through changing
some premises already belonging to S, and in this way create a
finite and logically consistent set of premises that solely contains
(1) some old premises that already belong to S; and (2) new
reasonable premises.

In our example, one thus had to add premises 4-11, that is, a list
of established criteria of adequacy; a statement expressing a choice
between such criteria; an established norm concerning the so-called
purpose of protection; an authority reason concerning precedents;
some premises concerning the facts of the case; an interpretation of
the relevant precedents and a general description of the law in
force. We will see below that all these premises are reasonable.

I have also defined the concept of "support" and
"reasonable support". Using these concepts, one can state
the following. A legal conclusion in a hard case does not
follow from set of premises solely consisting of legal
norms and a description of facts. The conclusion follows,
however, from an extended set, including additional
reasonable premises, some analytical or empirical, some
normative or evaluative. Some are perhaps certain, or
presupposed within the tradition ("paradigm") of legal
reasoning, or proved. Some other are neither.

One may thus conclude, what follows. (1) Each premise
alone weakly supports the conclusion. (2) The step from
any particular premise to the conclusion is a jump. In
particular, the step from the legal norm to the
conclusion is a jump. (3) The jump is reasonable if all
the premises,including the added moral norms and value
statements, are reasonable. (4) The step from the whole
set of premises to the conclusion is no jump.

3.2.4. Strong Support

Let me now add the following:
5) The set of premises includes a legal norm which
strongly supports the conclusion. One can thus express
the legally important thesis that the conclusion has a
strong legal, often statutory support.

The point of the concept "strong support" is this. In
legal reasoning, statutory provisions and other

established norms have a <u>privileged position</u>. Within this
form of reasoning, one cannot replace them with premises
of another type, and yet obtain the same conclusion.

As regards a general and informal account of the idea of
propositions with privileged status within a theory cf. Quine 1961,
xii ff.; cf. Lakatos 1970, 132 ff.

One may now conceive a set of statements, S, containing
all premises belonging to a certain form of reasoning,
such as the legal reasoning. Such a set is extremely
extensive. One may argue that it is infinite. Keeping
this in mind, one may propose the following definition.

The statement p <u>strongly supports</u> the statement q if,
and only if, p belongs to a set of premises, S, having
the following properties:

1) all these premises are reasonable; and
2) at least one subset of S is such that
a) q logically follows from it, and
b) all members of the subset are necessary to infer q
from this subset (that is, q does not follow, if any
premise belonging to the subset is removed from it); and
3) each member of S belongs to at least one such
subset; and
4) p is necessary in the following stronger sense: q
does not follow from any subset of S at all to which p
does not belong.

Each subset mentioned in the condition 2) consists of
premises of a thinkable correct inference within S, e.g.,
within the legal reasoning.

The condition 4) implies that q does not follow if p is
removed from S. Thus, p's membership in the set of
premises S is a necessary condition for the fact that the
conclusion follows from <u>this</u> set, e.g., the total set of
premises reasonable within the <u>legal</u> reasoning. But
obviously, the conclusion may also independently follow
from <u>another</u> set of premises, e.g., reasonable within
<u>moral</u> reasoning, albeit this set does not include p.

The concept of <u>strong support</u> is especially important
in legal reasoning. Lawyers often argue that a decision
should be supported by an established legal norm,
explicitly included in or at least derivable from a
statute. The same statute may support many decisions. To
be sure, many other premises are also included in the
supportive structure. Assume, e.g., that the conclusion
follows from a set of premises containing an established
norm derivable from some statutes concerning torts (see

premise 1 of our example), a description of the case and some <u>precedents</u> (see premises 7 and 10). Any particular statement, belonging to this set, supports the conclusion in the discussed manner. Within the legal reasoning, however, such sources of the law as a statute often have a special position. The same decision may follow from another set of premises containing the same established norm, supported by the statute, the same description of the case and some quotations from <u>travaux préparatoires</u>. In this sense, neither the precedents nor the <u>travaux préparatoires</u> are necessary for the derivation.

One may also imagine a situation when the same conclusion follows from two independent inferences, the first containing the established norm together with a certain conceptual assumption, the second containing the same norm together with another such assumption. One can thus imagine the following two inferences.

I

An assumption p, belonging to the set S	The causal connection between an action and a damage is adequate, if the action action makes the damage of the actual kind foreseeable for a very cautious and well informed person.
Other premises belonging to the set S	A caused negligently a traffic accident in which B's car was damaged. During the time the car underwent repairs, B could not provide work for some employees. Yet, he paid them full salaries, fearing that they would not return when needed again. The action in question made a damage of the type described above (that is, a loss in consequence of paying salaries to not working employees) foreseeable for a very cautious and well informed person.

Conclusion	The causal connection between A's action and B's damage was adequate.

The conclusion does not follow from set S, if one removes premise p.

II

An assumption p1, belonging to the set S1	The causal connection between an action and a damage is adequate, if precedents supporting the adequacy weigh more than those which support the conclusion that the causal connection is not adequate.
Other premises belonging to the set S1	A caused negligently a traffic accident in which B's car was damaged. During the time the car underwent repairs, B could

> not provide work for some employees. Yet,
> he paid them full salaries, fearing that
> they would not return when needed again.
> Precedents supporting the adequacy of
> causation in such cases as described
> above weigh more than those which support
> the conclusion that the causal connection
> is not adequate.

Conclusion   The causal connection between A's action
                              and B's damage was adequate.

The conclusion does not follow from set S1, if one removes premise p1.

In some cases, no _single_ established legal norm has such a special position. Yet, one can say that, within legal reasoning, the conclusion does not follow from any subset of S at all to which no established legal norm of some kind belongs. The same conclusion may thus follow from a set of premises containing either a provision of the Tortious Liability Act, or a provision of the Traffic Liability Act; but the conclusion does not follow from any set of legally acceptable premises which does not contain either of these provisions.

The concept "strong support" may play a role not only within legal reasoning but also in other causal and normative contexts which include the question "why?". Natural science, e.g., often states that x occurs _because_ of y. The words "why?" and "because" may indicate a _causal_ relation. The logic of conditions has no means to define causal necessity which seems to have an _a-priori_ quality (Cf. Kant 1983, B 233-235; Burks 1977, 619). Yet, laws of nature might serve as criteria of causation (cf. Peczenik 1979, 333 ff.). One might perhaps construct a reasonable interpretation of at least some laws of nature as expressing a relation of strong support between a statement of cause and an statement of effect. The concept of "strong support" might also be useful to explain the notoriously obscure distinction between _conditio sine qua non_ and _conditio per quam_, made by Kelsen (e.g. 1960, 197). One might perhaps construct a reasonable interpretation, according to which only the latter, not the former, gives the conclusion strong support.

The following example elucidates the role of strong support in moral theory. Even if some moral systems require that one helps one's enemies, it is strange to say "A ought to help B _because_ B is A's enemy". One may only plausibly say "A ought to help B <u>in spite</u> of the fact that B is A's enemy". To state this distinction precisely, one needs the concept of "strong support". To obtain a useful idea of when p strongly supports q, it is not enough to require that p belongs to a set of reasonable premises from which q logically follows. Indeed, even the premise "B is A's enemy" together with the Christian principle "one ought to help one's enemies" entails the conclusion "A ought to help B". On the other hand, one may say the following. The statement "B is A's friend" <u>strongly supports</u> the statement "A ought to help B" <u>relatively to the set of premises characterising an ethical system based on loyalty to one's friends,</u> in brief – the Friend Ethics, since (1) the statement "B is A's friend" belongs to the Friendship Ethic; and all the premises belonging to the Friendship Ethic are reasonable; and (2) at least one subset of the Friendship Ethic is such that (a) the conclusion "A ought to help B" logically follows from it, and (b) all members of the subset are necessary to infer the conclusion "A ought to help B" from this subset (that is, this conclusion does not follow, if any premise belonging to the subset is removed from it); and (3) each statement of the Friendship Ethic belongs to at least one such subset; and (4) the statement "B is A's friend" is necessary in the following stronger sense: the conclusion "A ought to help B" does not follow from any subset of the Friendship Ethic at all to which p1 does not belong.

Within the Friendship Ethic, there can exist many different sets of additional premises, each warranting the derivation. The only thing they must have in common is the statement "B is A's friend". I have thus assigned a special role to this statement. This is the only premise which one cannot replace by any other, belonging to the Friendship Ethic, and yet obtain the conclusion.

But cannot one in the same manner construct a Hostility Ethic, giving a similar privileged position to the statement "B is A's enemy"? I assume here the hypothesis that such an Hostility Ethic could not consist solely of reasonable premises: No set of such premises implies the conclusion "A ought to help B" <u>only</u> together with the statement "B is A's enemy". Testing of this hypothesis constitutes an important challenge for future research.

3.2.5. Depth of Reasoning

To convert a jump into a deductive inference, one may add a different number premises, depending on how profound the reasoning is. One can, for example, think that the following inference is satisfactory:

| Premise 1, see above | A person who caused damage in consequence of traffic with an |

	engine-driven vehicle should compensate the damage if, and only if, there exists a legal ground therefor.
Premise 2, see above	A legal ground for the conclusion that the tortfeasor should compensate the damage exists, if the causal connection between his action and the damage was adequate.
Premise 3, see above	A caused negligently a traffic accident in which B's car was damaged. During the time the car underwent repairs, B could not provide work for some employees. Yet, he paid them full salaries, fearing that they would not come back when needed again.
Premise 4*	The causal connection between the traffic accident and B's loss in consequence of paying salaries to not working employees was adequate.
Premise 6 see above	The tortfeasor shall not compensate the damage, not even the adequately caused one, if the law of torts is not intended to give protection against it.
Premise 9*	The law of torts is not intended to give protection against damage of the actual kind.
Premise 11, see above	No other legal ground exists for the conclusion that A should compensate B's loss in consequence of paying salaries to not working employees.

Conclusion	A should not compensate B's loss resulting from paying salaries to not working employees.

If one doubts premise 4*, one may argue in a more profound way and thus replace it with the premises (4, 5 and 8) from which it follows. In the same manner, if one doubts premise 9*, one may replace it with premises 6, 7, 9 and 10. In the latter case, the more profound reasoning leads to a change of an originally assumed premise 9*. One is no longer sure whether the law of torts is not intended to give protection against damage of the actual kind.

One may also expand in this manner the complex inference, proffered above. One may, e.g., replace premise 10 with a set of premises, justifying the outcome of weighing and balancing of various precedents.

One may thus reason more and more profoundly, completing the actual set of premises with an increasing number of statements which provide support, often a strong support, for those already belonging to it.

The idea of such a chain of support allows to answer an important question. Let us assume that a chain of reasons exists, that is, that p1 supports p2, p2 supports p3, etc. To put it more precisely, this would imply that p1 together with some other premises, say r1 and s1, logically entails p2; p2 together with another set of premises, say, r2 and s2, logically entails p3 etc. But what if we omitted the intermediate step, p2, and simply stated that p3 follows from p1 together with r1, s1, r2 and s2? This would effectively dissolve the chain of support. What remained would be a conclusion and a set of premises, without intermediate links.

This would have the effect of invalidating a central point of the theory defended in the present work. In order to defend the idea of chains of support, one may refer to the progress of thinking, in history of science as well as in the mind of an individual (cf. Alexy and Peczenik 1989). Knowledge evolves step by step. Longer and longer chains of support are developed. However, historical and psychological insights are not sufficient to justify a logical reconstruction of knowledge. Only logical or, at least, epistemological reasons serve this purpose. The concept of strong support makes it possible to develop such reasons. The concept of strong support thus matches the fact that there are statements, as for instance norm-statements in legal reasoning, which play a special role in justification in a given context. If there is such a statement, it can be used to establish a certain step of reasoning, which can be distinguished from other steps. First, one indicates that p2 strongly supports p3 and then, perhaps within another theory, one states that a deeper premise, p1, strongly supports p2. In this way, one organises the totality of knowledge into different levels, such as, e.g., biology and physics, each characterised by its own core of premises which strongly support conclusions. Were the levels eliminated, one would lose important insights in the structure of our knowledge. A supportive structure which expresses such a knowledge is better than one which does not. This is the reason for introducing the concept of supportive chains instead of simply talking about classes of premises.

3.3. LEGAL RATIONALITY AND LEGAL PARADIGM

3.3.1. Introductory Remarks on Legal Paradigm

The observation that knowledge evolves step by step has far reaching consequences. As stated above, there are statements, as for instance norm-statements in legal reasoning, which play a special role in justification in a given context. In this way, one organises the totality of knowledge into different levels, such as, e.g., biology and physics, or, let me add now, legal reasoning and legal philosophy. For example, when sentencing Charlie for a petty larceny, the judge may safely rely on the Penal Code and the established tradition of its interpretation. It would be absurd for him to embark on a philosophical discussion of the validity of the penal provision applied, the problem of validity in general, the demands of rationality which restrict arbitrariness of practical reasoning etc. Such questions are, however, of a vital importance for philosophy of law.

In Chapter 2 supra, I have thus discussed various demands of rationality, restricting arbitrariness in moral reasoning. A moral statement can thus be presented as a logically correct conclusion from logically consistent, linguistically correct and reasonable premises, weighing more than some counter-arguments. One can also discuss moral questions in an impartial and otherwise rational way. Mutually incompatible moral statements can, however, simultaneously fulfil the demands of rationality. Legal reasoning, on the other hand, is more predictable and thus, ceteris paribus, less arbitrary than the moral one. In legal reasoning, one thus has access to a more extensive set of premises, such as statutes, other sources of the law and reasoning norms. The sources of the law are relatively fixed; cf. section 3.1.1 and 3.1.5 supra. These premises have been characterised as certain, presupposed, proved or otherwise reasonable; cf. Section 3.2.3 supra. I must now explain what these expressions mean. This task requires some remarks concerning philosophy of science.

3.3.2. Some Theories of Science

The older theory of science was dominated by the so-called inductivism. According to this view, a theory is probably true if it constitutes an inductive generalisation of observational data. However, all philosophers know, at least since Hume, that justification of induction is difficult to provide, since it is not certain that the unknown objects resemble the known ones. "All food is milk", said the baby. The more observation the baby gathered for support of this conclusion, the closer was the time approaching when the first cake would falsify the inductive generalisation.

No doubt, disciplines such as biology and sociology provide reasons for the correctness of induction. But if they are themselves inductive, they can only justify induction in a circular way. To be sure, this does not make induction useless. Some philosophers of science have thus argued that if order rules the universe, induction is the only method of foreseeing the order (Reichenbach 1940, 97 ff.; Feigl 1962, 29 and 31); they also claimed that it is sufficient to reconstruct all scientific reasonings (Reichenbach 1949, 429 ff.) and involved in statistical reasoning (Hempel 1962, 133 ff.).

Other thinkers are highly sceptical as regards induction. One of them is sir Karl Popper (cf., e.g., 1959, 28 ff.). He claims that the proper method of scientific research consists of creating bold hypotheses. One should try to falsify the hypotheses. One accepts them conditionally, as long as they are not falsified (Popper 1959, 40 ff.). The growth of knowledge is the result of a process closely resembling what Darwin called natural selection, that is, the natural selection of hypotheses (Popper 1959, 108 and 1972, 261).

But not even Popper's falsificationism is free of difficulties. Pierre Duhem noticed already before Popper's time that one may criticise and eliminate the observations, apparently falsifying a hypothesis. Suppose the theory T combined with the auxiliary hypothesis A implies e but observation suggests non-e. For instance, physics (T) combined with the hypothesis of expanded universe (A) implies a given position of a start (e), but the star is not exactly where it should be (non-e). What should one do? (1) One may challenge the derivation by showing that e does not follow from T and A. (2) one may show that the observation which purports to show non-e is unreliable ("the telescope is wrong"). (3) One may reject the auxiliary hypothesis A. (4) One may reject the theory T. How should one choose? (cf. Koertge 1978, 255).

To solve this problem, Popper (1959, 83) has formulated some methodological rules. The most important is the rule that ad hoc auxiliary hypotheses, introduced in order to save the theory while not explaining anything else are forbidden. An ad hoc hypothesis thus does not increase the informational content of the theory, which Popper interprets as a degree of its falsifiability. Some science theorists give, nevertheless, examples of acceptable ad hoc hypotheses (cf. Nordin 1980, 113 ff. on Agassi).

Some philosophers of science try to enrich the list of methodological rules. Knut Erik Tranöy (1976, 131 ff. and 1980, 191 ff.) thus discussed "norms of inquiry" which have nor only methodological character, but express distinct traditions, each concentrated around different value: self-realisation, public welfare, value-neutrality, testability, intersubjective controllability, honesty, sincerity, exactitude, completeness, simplicity, order, coherence, system and academic freedom.

According to <u>Thomas Kuhn</u> (1970, 23 ff.), one should judge scientific theories as parts of a broader totality called a <u>paradigm</u>. Each paradigm includes, <u>inter alia</u>, (1) some examples of concrete scientific achievements imitated by scientists in subsequent research, e.g. Einstein's research; (2) some value judgments, norms and basic beliefs shared by scientists, e.g. the criteria of correctness of physical experiments; and (3) the so-called symbolic generalisations, concerning the sense of scientific terms, such as "mass", "energy" etc. See also Popper 1959, 13: "a structure of scientific doctrines is already in existence;... This is why (a scientist) may leave it to others to fit his contribution into the framework of scientific knowledge." Cf. Popper 1970, 51 ff.

If a scientist cannot solve a problem within the paradigm, this does not falsify either the whole paradigm or theories essential to it but it "falsifies" his scientific skill.

Paradigms are incommensurable. In the transition from one paradigm to the next words change their meaning or conditions of application. Each paradigm then satisfies the criteria it dictates for itself and fall short of a few of those dictated by its opponent (Kuhn 1970, 109-110). The old paradigm gives way to the new one not <u>via</u> a rational debate but because the advocates of the old one die out. The choice of paradigms depends on weighing and balancing of values; "the relative weight placed on different values by different individuals can play a decisive role in individual choice" (Kuhn 1970, 262; cf. Sintonen 1986, 364 ff.).

In his later works, Kuhn introduced also the concept of "disciplinary matrix" (cf. Kuhn 1979, 293 ff.). Each matrix defines a scientific discipline. Within the same matrix, one paradigm can replace another. Normal science is bound to its paradigm. A paradigm shift happens only during a scientific revolution. But scientific revolution "need not be a large change", and "occurs regularly on a smaller scale", Kuhn 1970, 180-181.

According to <u>Imre Lakatos</u> (1970, 132 ff.), a given research program (a series of theories) contains a hard <u>core</u>, including some central propositions, e.g. the main points of the relativity theory. The core is protected by auxiliary hypotheses. One thus ought to direct counter-examples against the auxiliary hypotheses, never against the hard core. In Lakatos's theory, the core thus plays a role similar to that paradigms have in Kuhn's system.

The research program is fruitful ("progressive"), if it continually produces theories with greater and greater empirical content, explaining more and more observations. A degenerative research program is no longer able to do it. In such a case, the program often gives way to another one, with another hard core. Classical physics thus stagnated at the end of 19th century. All questions were apparently solved, no new theories appeared. Somewhat later, it gave way to the new physics, based on relativity.

In the present work, I have no chance and no reason to adopt any position in the controversies between different theories of science. Perhaps each one has a sound core. Let me thus inquire what each of them can teach a law theorist.

3.3.3. Theory of Science and Legal Reasoning

Theory of science helps one to understand and deeply justify legal reasoning, among other things to clarify the idea that legal premises can be characterised as certain, presupposed, proved or otherwise reasonable. However, to obtain these profits, one must perform some modification and generalisation of the applicable theses of theory of science. A _literal_ application of theory of science to legal reasoning is fruitless due to some peculiarities of the latter, _inter alia_ because the goal of science consists in true description of facts, while the purpose of legal reasoning is more complex. Moreover, at least natural science is invariant in time and space, while the law is bound to a given society.

The modified theory of science is, first of all, fruitfully applicable to _legal dogmatics_. To a certain degree, it is also applicable to the legal practice, since its methods of reasoning are fairly similar to those of legal dogmatic; cf. section 1.1 supra.

All competing theories of science can to some extent help one to understand legal reasoning.

I. Legal dogmatics is filled with examples of generalising the statutory provisions and other norms of established law _via_ the so-called "legal induction". One can express the "legal induction" in the following manner:

Premise	Cases $c_1 - c_n$ which belong to the type C ought to be treated in the way P
Conclusion	All cases (c_{n+1} etc.) which belong to the type C ought to be treated in the way P

One can interpret both the premise and the conclusion either as norms or as theoretical propositions stating that an established norm exists, for instance that a certain source of law actually expresses not only the norm (1) but also the norm (2). The first interpretation is more correct, since a jurist can draw the conclusion (2) even if he does not believe that there is an already established norm (2), expressed in the sources of the law, in various practices, etc. In other words, whereas the "normal" induction leads to theories or hypotheses concerning preexistent facts, the legal induction, and the legal reasoning _ex analogia_, often leads from a norm to the creation of a new norm. The problem then occurs, how to justify this act of creation. The ordinary induction can be justified, if at all, by the metaphysical assumption that nature is uniform (cf., e.g., Braithwaite 1960, 259). One cannot justify the creation of a new norm in such a manner. Its justification is rather based on another norm, for example, on the principle of formal justice: the like should be treated alike (cf. Peczenik 1966, 50-72 and 1967, 135 ff.). In this way, a modified inductionist pattern of thinking leads a philosopher of law to a deeper understanding of the peculiarities of practical, inter alia legal justification.

II. Falsificationism brings a law theorist to a similar conclusion. It is doubtful whether legal research consists of testing falsifiable hypotheses, since it is not clear what observational data these hypotheses would explain. This is especially doubtful when one considers the fact that legal research contains the discussed component of creating new norms. Neither is it clear what the term "to falsify" means in the present context. The goal of legal research is different, that is, to create as coherent systems of practical statements as possible, see below.

III. The theory of norms of inquiry gives a law theorist more promise of success. The most important lesson a law theorist receives from this theory is the insight that normative and conventional components are by no means specific for legal research. This is important, because many critics of legal research claimed that these components make it unscientific. One can also find analogies between norms of enquiry in natural science and legal research. Such values as self-realisation, public welfare, testability, intersubjective controllability, honesty, sincerity, exactitude, completeness, simplicity, order, coherence, system and academic freedom are certainly not alien to a legal researcher. On the other hand, value-neutrality rather is, for the reasons mentioned above. There are important analogies between natural science and legal research but it would be very strange to expect identity.

IV. The paradigm theory leads to similar conclusions. One can thus find analogies between matrices (and paradigms) in natural science and legal research. According to Aulis Aarnio (e.g., 1984, 25 ff.), the matrix of legal dogmatics, in a modified Kuhnian sense, consists of the following four components.

1) A set of philosophical background presuppositions, inter alia the assumption that legal reasoning is based on valid law.

2) Presuppositions concerning the sources of the law. One assumes that some of these are either binding or at least constituting authority reasons.

3) Presuppositions concerning legal method. One thus assumes that legal reasoning is and should be governed by some methodological norms.

I will return to this problem in chapters 6 and 7 infra but let me give some examples. All courts and authorities must use statutes in the justification of their decisions, if any are applicable. They should use applicable precedents and legislative preparatory materials. One should not construe extensively provisions imposing penalties, taxes or other burdens on a person. When interpreting a statute, one must pay attention to its purpose.

4) A set of values, first of all concerning legal certainty (cf. section 1.4.1 supra) and justice.

Each legal **paradigm** contains a particular interpretation of the matrix. (Re description of various paradigms of legal research, cf. Dalberg-Larsen 1977, 513 ff.). Legal reasoning of different times and societies is underpinned by different sets of assumptions concerning valid law, legal sources, legal method, legal certainty etc. But all legal reasoning is based on some presuppositions of these kinds.

V. One can also view legal reasoning in the light of a properly adapted theory of research programs. (I presented a different version of this view in Peczenik 1983, 126 ff. and 1985, 296 ff.). To achieve this adaptation, let me assume that the following kinds of entities, relevant for legal research, are analogous to the observational data:

a) data concerning facts of the case, sociological and other data concerning the community etc.;

b) statutes and other sources of the law, authoritatively recognised in the legal system; and

c) prima-facie moral norms and value statements, commonly endorsed within the community.

Moreover, a fourth component is to some extent analogous to the data. This component comprises

d) prima-facie moral norms and value statements, endorsed by the person performing the concrete act of legal reasoning.

This analogy is based, <u>inter alia</u>, on the fact that these norms and value statements are discussed by the lawyers and explained by theories they create. (One could regard these value statements and normative statements as data in the literal sense had one believed that people possess a "moral sense" enabling them to "see" values, cf. section 2.1 supra).

Let me also assume that two kinds of entities are analogous to theory cores in Lakatos´s sense:

a) theory cores of auxiliary sciences employed in the law, such as economics, medicine etc.; and

b) norms and other assumptions, concerning legal sources and methods, for example the assumption that legislative preparatory materials, (<u>travaux préparatoires</u>) should be treated as seriously in the process of statutory interpretation as judicial precedents.

A scientist tries to interpret observational data as mutually consistent and coherent with the "hard core" of the assumed theory. Analogously, a legal researcher tries to interpret the established legal norms and the <u>prima-facie</u> moral statement as mutually consistent and coherent with the core assumptions concerning legal sources and methods.

According to de Wild 1980, 55 ff., a series of juristic theories is progressive in Lakatos's sense, if the next theory within the series explains and sets aside a greater number of deontic incompatibilities as its predecessor. This conception is compatible with the one presented above, provided that one extends de Wild's list of legal data.

These core assumptions determine the employed research program. The research program is fruitful ("progressive"), if it continually produces coherent theories covering more and more established legal norms, more and more commonly endorsed moral statements, as well as more and more moral statements endorsed by the legal researcher in question. A degenerative legal research program is no longer able to do it.

The norms and other assumptions concerning legal sources and methods can thus be viewed both as components of a legal paradigm and as components of a theory core of legal research. <u>Some</u> of them are so well established that they constitute a component of the <u>matrix</u> of legal research. They must thus be included in theory cores of <u>all</u> legal research programs. To be sure, one may doubt

each such assumption. But the total set of them is not only
established in the legal practice and legal research but also
related to the concept of legal reasoning. It would be strange to
simultaneously refute a significant part of the set of such norms
and assumptions, and still try to perform a legal reasoning.

To some extent, these assumptions are also similar to material
inference rules in Toulmin's sense (cf. 1964, 109.). Although not
logically true, they are presupposed in the everyday life. Some
material inference rules are based on probability. Toulmin's example
of such a rule is this: If someone is a Suede, one may assume that
he is almost certainly not a Catholic. The reason for the norm is
that less than 2% of Suedes are Catholics. The norm makes it
possible to utilise the premise "Peterson is a Swede" as a support
for the conclusion "Peterson is almost certainly no Catholic".

3.3.4. Certain Premises

The survey of analogies and differences between natural
science and legal research draws our attention to the
central role some assumptions play in both fields. Both
fields thus include some statements, commonly regarded as
certain, or at least taken for granted.

The idea of certain and assumed statements thus appears
once again in our discussion. I have already claimed that
premises supporting legal reasoning can be reasonable ,
that is, neither falsified nor arbitrary. There are many
kinds of reasonable premises, characterised as certain,
presupposed, proved or otherwise reasonable.

The problem of "certain" premises is recognised as very
difficult. Foundationalists believe that an ultimate and
certain ground for knowledge exists (cf., e.g., Chisholm
1957 and 1966). Some truths are evident, not merely
reasonable. The key criticism of foundationalism is,
however, "that the basic beliefs required by
foundationalism turn out to be no more privileged and
have no better justification than many other beliefs"
(Kekes 1979, 407). Coherentists thus conclude that no
beliefs are certain and that knowledge thus constitutes a
totality whose fragments support each other.

Several versions of coherentism are defended among other by Quine 1953 and 1960, Sellars 1963, Lehrer 1974, Rescher 1973 and 1977 and Winch 1958. Between foundationalism and coherentism there are also intermediate positions. Cf. Kekes 1979, 405 ff.

But to that, one objects "that... false beliefs may also cohere. The coherentist has no rational way of choosing between equally coherent systems" (Kekes 1979, 406, reporting the foundationalists´ views).

A synthesis of foundationalism and coherentism has been suggested by Ludwig Wittgenstein.

Firstly, his remarks concerning doubt and certainty reveal some foundationalist insights. One cannot doubt everything (cf. Wittgenstein 1979 No. 115 and 1 ff.), because doubt needs undoubted grounds (cf. Wittgenstein 1979 No. 122 and 217; Aarnio 1977, 100 ff.). "If you are not certain of any fact, you cannot be certain of the meaning of your words, either" (cf. Wittgenstein 1979 No. 114, cf. No. 231 and 1953 No. 481). Consequently: "The game of doubting itself presupposes certainty" (Wittgenstein 1979 No. 115. Cf. No. 124 and 253). In the system of our knowledge, "some things stand unshakeably fast and some are more or less liable to shift" (Wittgenstein 1979 No. 144. Cf. No. 136). These "fast" things are more certain than any grounds which one can give in favour of them (Wittgenstein 1979 No. 307) and one can accept nothing as evidence against them. We can ask whether it can make sense to doubt them (Wittgenstein 1969 No. 2. Cf. No. 154).

Let me add the following. "Certain" statements are taken for granted by all normal people, perhaps under influence of innate mechanisms, or at least all normal people belonging to the culture under consideration. (If necessary, one may explicate the requirement of normality by recourse to psychiatry and medicine.) An innate mechanism seems to lie behind learning (Popper 1972, 71; Lorenz 1973 Ch. IV), abstract thinking, culture (cf. Lorenz 1973 Chs. V and VII) and language.

Cf. Chomsky 1970 and 1967, 87 ff. Not even Wittgenstein intended to rule out the possibility of innate knowledge, cf. Kenny 1975, 184. To be sure, such views are controversial. "What must be 'innate' are... learning strategies", not grammar; Putnam 1967, 100. Cf. Goodman 1967, 107 and Katz 1966, 269.

In this context, one may also mention the Kantian tradition. According to Kant, one cannot empirically demonstrate that space and time exist, because such an empirical demonstration already presupposes space and time (Kant 1983, A 22 ff., B 37 ff., A 30 ff., B 46 ff.; cf. Kemp 1968, 16 ff.). Although mathematical theories change (cf., e.g., Popper 1972, 135), all of them must assume that objects of experience are located in some kind of space and time (cf. Patzig 1976, 32 ff. and Trigg 1973, 164-165). Our intellect, then, uses "categories" to actively organise spatially and temporally ordered sensations and enables us to experience objects. "We are indeed given certain things in sensation, but it is not given that this object before us is a table, and that a dog; before we can know this our understanding must have formed the concept of table and dog" (Kemp 1968, 24). Kant has formulated a list of categories, that is, logical forms and types of judgment (1983, A 80, B 106) including, inter alia, unity, substance and causality.

According to Kant's principle of causality, all alterations thus take place in accordance with the law of cause and effect (A 189, B 232; cf. Burks 1967, 608 ff.). To be sure, the list of categories is controversial (cf., e.g. Strawson 1966, 79 and 266 ff.). Advanced physics, philosophy etc., may modify the category of causality, but the resultant concept must be useful for making distinctions similar to those made by the concept of causality in the ordinary sense.

It is natural to assume that such categories are innate.
   Certainty based on culture is even more complex. The cultural tradition includes intricate relationships between beliefs, action and language. In this context, one may speak about the "form of life". The concept, created by Wittgenstein, has been introduced to theory of law by Aulis Aarnio. To be sure, references to the form of life do not fulfil standards of clarity, usual in analytical philosophy. They suggest something important but unclear, "the presence of things partly hidden and not yet fully disclosed" (Black 1978, 330; cf. Black 1980 passim). Yet, one may state that our picture of the world - the Weltanschauung - including our most certain and most central views - continually manifests itself in everyday action (cf. Aarnio 1979b, 34). This action is then the same thing as the form of life. The form of life is thus our picture of the world expressed in our everyday actions and in our everyday concepts. In this

way, "certain" statements are linked with the form of
life. Cognition is related to action.

At the same time, cognition is related to language. In
other words, "experience cannot escape its being moulded
by language" (Castaneda 1980, 36).

Yet, language "cannot be the limit of one's experience"; id. We must
admit that human beings have far more concepts (distinctive
cognitive capacities) than words for expressing them - as the
example of colors amply shows", black 1962, 249. Finally, infant and
animals have cognition but no language, cf. Churchland 1979, 137.

Finally, language is also related to action. "The
speaking of language is a part of an activity, or of a
form of life" (Wittgenstein 1953 No. 23. The term "form
of life" has been used also by Spranger 1950). "Giving
grounds... comes to an end; but the end is not certain
propositions striking us immediately as true...; it is
our acting, which lies at the bottom of the
language-game" (Wittgenstein 1979 No. 204. Cf. No. 344).
The language-game is "the whole, consisting of language
and the actions into which it is woven".

Wittgenstein 1953 No. 7 in fine. Cf. No. 23: "multiplicity of
language-games..., giving order..., describing..., reporting...,
speculating about an event, forming and testing a hypothesis...,
play-acting, singing catches,... making a joke" etc. Cf.
Wittgenstein 1953 No. 19, 23 and 241, and pp. 174 and 226;
Wittgenstein 1979 No. 204.

Language-games are related to one another (Wittgenstein 1953 No.
65), "form a family" (id. No. 67), and show "a complicated network
of similarities" (id. No. 66).

Cf. Aarnio 1979b, 34: "(T)he world picture, or more correctly
speaking, the fragment of a world-picture forms the foundation for a
(certain) language-game. It forms the pre-knowledge upon which we
rest ourselves when playing our language-game. Cf. Aarnio 1977, 126
ff.; von Wright 1972 sections 4-6 re "pre-propositional stage".

Many concepts would therefore be impossible to understand
without some knowledge of action to which they are
related. "Our talk gets its meaning from the rest of our
proceedings" (Wittgenstein 1979 No. 229. Cf. No. 476).
Knowing nothing about the practice of legislation and
adjudication, one would have difficulties to understand,
e.g., the concept of law. In fact, action is at the

bottom of <u>all</u> cognition. "At the beginning was the deed" (Wittgenstein 1979 No. 402, quoting Goethe, Faust I).

Conversely, many actions would be incomprehensible had one not at least a vague idea of some concepts. In this context one may repeat a more or less Kantian list of concepts such as "time", "space", "truth", "cause", "reason", "number", "substance" etc. No person belonging to our culture (and perhaps no human being at all, see above) can dismiss such concepts without replacement by counterparts having partly the some meaning.

Some certain statements are single axioms, each certain in isolation from other information. No normal person, e.g., doubts such propositions as "here is one hand and here is another". One takes for granted that one´s hand is a hand, not an illusion, since one uses one´s hand to eat and work. One takes also for granted that other people partly resemble oneself, since otherwise one could not talk with them. Neither does a normal person doubt that the earth existed a hundred years ago.

However, Wittgenstein also made some coherentist remarks. Most statements, taken for granted as certain, are certain as members of a system. One may doubt each one of them but no normal person at the same time puts in question an extensive part of the system. Wittgenstein has thus pointed out that our "knowledge forms an enormous system. And only within this system has a particular bit the value we give it" (Wittgenstein 1979 No. 410. Cf. No. 144, 152 and 225). No single axioms are as certain as a system in which consequences and premises give each other mutual support (Wittgenstein 1979 No. 142). One cannot simultaneously doubt all the "fast" things, but one could every single separately (Wittgenstein 1979 No. 232. Cf. Aarnio 1979b, 29 ff.). One could thus doubt p_1 when assuming p_2 and p_3, and doubt p_3 when assuming p_1 and p_2. The <u>Weltanschauung</u> is like the bank of the river of our fluid and changing experiences. "And the bank of that river consists partly of hard rock, subject to no alteration or only to imperceptible one, partly of sand, which now in one place now in another gets washed away, or deposited" (Wittgenstein 1979 No. 99. Cf. No. 256). Some concepts are thus such that if one changed a great number of them at the same time, one also had to change our life in a radical, unacceptable and perhaps incomprehensible manner. And some beliefs are such that their negation would commit us to actions we are not prepare to perform and perhaps to silence and passivity.

Such obvious insights, intertwined with everyday action, are the "end station" of all reasoning. The term "form of life" thus refers to the end-points of justification, often unknown and perhaps even impossible to state precisely.

In other words, the form of life is a reification of the end-points of justification. To understand this idea, a jurist may consider that analogously, the state in Kelsen's sense is a personification of the legal order, Kelsen 1960, 294 ff.

As regards such "certain" knowledge of <u>nature</u>, the form of life is the same for all, at least for all educated people belonging to the Western culture. No sane person doubts that one can travel to America, that the fastest way to do it is to take a plane, and that the plane can fly. Such common insights, shared by all, are perhaps less frequent as regards <u>society</u> but they exist. Some of them concern <u>values</u>, e.g., no sane person thinks that it is a good thing to burn babies alive. Moreover, many actions would be incomprehensible had one not at least a vague idea of some social, economic and legal concepts. One, e.g., "buys" food in a shop "owned" by a "company" and "pays" with "money". Indeed, one can hardly conceive a world in which nobody "owned" anything nor could "buy" anything. (For that reason, Pol Pot had no chance in Cambodia.)

3.3.5. Presupposed Premises

"Presupposed" premises are taken for granted within a particular practice belonging to the culture under consideration, e.g. within the legal paradigm; see the preceding section. The concept of "practice", here used to define presupposed premises, differs from the concept of "culture", implemented above to define the certain ones. A culture thus covers many areas of life while a practice covers a single one, such as chemical research, legal dogmatics etc.

More precisely, presupposed premises are taken for granted within, so to say, a <u>necessary</u> practice, that is a practice in which one must participate if one wishes to

well perform certain kind of action. For example, a
member of our society who wishes to discover an unknown
star must participate in the kind of astronomical
research our universities teach. He has no choice, e.g.
he cannot involve himself in astrology, instead of
astronomy.

When defining presupposed premises, I thus disregard such practices
as a definite religion. Who wishes to participate in religious
activity <u>has</u> a choice; he can, e.g., convert from the Swedish
Lutheran Church to Islam.

One can repeat here the discussed distinction between
single axioms and systems. Very few presupposed premises
are taken for granted as single axioms, in isolation from
other information. One may thus doubt almost any
presupposed premise but one cannot simultaneously put in
question an extensive part of the system.
    Certain and presupposed premises are of two kinds,
substantive and procedural. The former describe
intuitions, observations, intentions, evaluations,
interests, interpretations etc. The latter describe
procedures of rational reworking of the former, through
weighing and balancing of various criteria of <u>coherence</u>,
perhaps together with other considerations concerning
rational <u>discourse</u> (cf. section 4.3 infra) or <u>scientific</u>
method, such as Popper´s method conjectures and
refutations (cf. section 3.3.2 supra). Such procedures
possess a content-generating capacity. Their existence
make our knowledge to change and grow.
    As stated before, premises presupposed by lawyers
belong to the legal paradigm. Let me add that <u>certain</u>
premises, too, belong to this paradigm, not in the sense
of having a peculiar legal character but because of not
being contradicted by any normal jurist. Moreover,
certain and presupposed premises jointly constitute the
juristic <u>theory core</u>, to some extent resembling theory
cores in Lakatos´s sense. This core thus includes some
fundamental moral views, commonly accepted by both
lawyers and people who make moral judgments. Furthermore,
it includes the assumption that legal reasoning is
supported by valid law. It also contains fundamental
juristic views on the authority of the sources of the law
and legal norms of reasoning. Finally, it includes some
fundamental evaluative views, first of all concerning
legal certainty and justice. If one wishes to perform a

<u>legal</u> reasoning, one cannot at the same time put in question an extensive part of this theory core.

Neither can one simultaneously doubt an extensive part of valid statutes, precedents and other important sources of the law. The sources of the law can thus be regarded as another part of the juristic theory core, if one does not wish to regard them, instead, as observational data of the lawyers.

The great role of presupposed premises in legal reasoning makes the law more fixed than the purely moral reasoning. The latter is more fluid, it does not rest on any established paradigm.

3.3.6. Proved Premises of Legal Reasoning

"Proved" premises follow from a consistent set of certain premises and/or premises taken for granted within the particular practice, such as the legal paradigm. The word "proved" means here "proved within the paradigm", <u>not</u> "proved in an absolute, philosophically unquestionable way". Not even theories of natural science are proved in the latter sense.

In the discussed example of legal reasoning concerning the question of remoteness of damage, the following premise, e.g., is proved:

(1) A non-controversial   A person who caused damage in
    legal norm, cf. now   consequence of traffic with an
    Ch. 2 Sec.1 of the   engine-driven vehicle should
    Tortious Liability Act,   compensate the damage if, and
    Sec. 18 of the Car   only if, there exists a legal
    Traffic Liability Act etc.   ground therefor

This premise follows from the statutes and established interpretation norms, and one can prove that the statutes under consideration have been enacted according to the constitution; in the legal paradigm, one takes for granted the established interpretation norms and assumes that the constitution should be obeyed.

A lawyer thus hopes that faithfulness to juristic assumptions may help him to escape the need to pay attention to vague moral values. And he hopes this is a way to create legal certainty.

But not all interpretation norms and presuppositions, constituting the legal paradigm, are explicitly formulated in commonly accepted texts. Many are implicit, assumed in a tacit way. Nobody spells them out, but if they had been formulated, no jurist would refute them.

The list of statements, thus proved in the legal paradigm, is not fixed. One must argue for them, sometimes in general terms, sometimes in concrete cases. They thus reveal themselves step by step in the legal discourse. An attempt to completely describe them resembles the work of Sisyphus. As soon as one problem is solved another occurs. One hopes to be able to definitively solve all the problems, but no one has done it so far.

3.3.7. Other Reasonable Premises of Legal Reasoning

In hard cases, however, presuppositions commonly accepted within the legal paradigm do not liberate the lawyer from the necessity to make a moral choice. This is the lawyer´s dilemma. Most premises, added in order to make the reasoning in the discussed example of legal reasoning logically correct, must be called "reasonable, although neither certain, presupposed, nor proved".

As stated above, a premise is reasonable if, and only if, the following conditions are fulfilled:

1. The premise is not falsified.
2. The hypothesis is not to a sufficiently high degree corroborated that this premise does not logically follow from a highly coherent set of premises. In other words, the hypothesis is not sufficiently corroborated that the premise is not perfectly S-rational.

Such a highly coherent set need not solely consist of certain premises, premises presupposed within the legal paradigm and proved premises. To be sure, a lawyer who regards a premise or a conclusion as reasonable has often a disposition to assume that if he had more information then he would be able to show that it logically follows from a set of such premises. For instance, he may assume in some cases that the juristic choice between criteria of adequacy follows from such a set. Yet one cannot prove the additional premises, consisting of norm-expressive statements or value statements.

Certainly, one can show that the norm-expressive statement or the value statement in question constitutes

a meaningful <u>prima-facie</u> moral reason, cf. sections 2.3.1
- 2.3.3 supra. One can also show that the norm-expressive
statement or the value statement in question is logically
related to some theoretical propositions; cf. sections
2.3.4 and 2.4.6 - 2.4.8 supra.

But such logical relations are too week to constitute
the proof. In a hard case, one must also argue that no
thinkable   counter-arguments   weigh   more   than   the
norm-expressive   statement   or   the   value   statement   in
question. Such an argument requires a definitive act of
weighing and balancing of reasons and counter-arguments;
cf. section 2.4.5 supra. In other words, it is based on
an unargued assumption. To be sure, one must be able to
incorporate such assumptions into a highly <u>coherent</u> value
system; cf. section 4.1 infra. But more then one system
can   fulfil   this   condition.   Such   systems   may   be
incompatible; and it may be impossible to show which one
of them is the most coherent one; cf. section 5.9.4
infra. The assumptions which underly a juristic act of
weighing are thus reasonable, but neither certain, nor
presupposed, nor proved.

The set of reasonable, although neither certain, presupposed, nor
proved premises contains also some analytic, empirical and practical
statements. As an example, one can proffer the additional premise 5,
see the discussed example of a case concerning adequate causation.

(5) An added and   The following criterion of adequacy
    reasonable   should be used in the case under
    premise: the   consideration:
    chosen   (2) the causal connection between an
    criterion of   action and a damage is adequate, if
    adequacy   the action makes the damage of the type T
                         foreseeable for a very cautious and well
                         informed person.

The hypothesis is not to a sufficiently high degree corroborated
that this premise does not logically follow from a consistent set
containing:
   1) an analytic proposition which says that this criterium of
adequacy can meaningfully be proffered as a <u>prima-facie</u> reason for
the conclusion that the connection is adequate;
   2) an empirical proposition which describes the choice of criteria
of adequacy, often made in the legal practice; and
   3) a moral value statement concerning the appropriateness of the
choice of this criterion, endorsed by the person who performs the
legal reasoning in question.

3.3.8. Reasonableness and Falsification

At this moment, a supporter of Popper´s philosophy (see section 3.3.2. supra) may retort: Facing these difficulties, is it not better to abandon the theory of reasonable support in the legal paradigm? Is it not better to assume, that a legal view is to be accepted as a hypothesis, until it is falsified?

Let me answer this objection in the following way: One must make a choice between two philosophical theories, both contestable, Popper´s falsificationism and, on the other hand, the theory of reasonable support in the legal paradigm. One may prefer the former but only within a limit: it is an excellent theory of science but neither a theory of ultimate basis of all knowledge nor a plausible theory of moral and legal justification. Outside of the proper limit of Popper´s falsificationism, it is better to choose the theory of reasonable support.

Although Popper's theory is plausible as regards scientific theories, it fails to answer the question of its own foundation. How to justify Popper's philosophical views, including his methodological rules? One cannot interpret these as another hypothesis, falsifiable but not verifiable. What would be regarded as a falsification of this philosophical hypothesis? Any answer to this question is controversial. One must perhaps regard Popper's theory, which connects science with possibility of falsification, as itself unfalsifiable. Ultimate philosophical statements , such as Popper's methodological rules, have a special character. They are not hypotheses but assumptions, taken for granted, with no intention to test them. One may also hope to present them as plausible interpretations of analytical theses, whose refutation would create logical contradictions. As regards ultimate justification, cf. Apel 1976b; Kuhlmann 1985, 60 ff.; Apel 1986.

The theory of reasonable support is to be preferred as regards practical, inter alia moral and legal, views because the idea of falsification of practical statements faces the following problems.

1. It is not clear whether one may speak about truth and falsehood of practical statements. How can one then falsify them, that is, prove that they are false? Cf. sections 3.3.3 supra and 4.2.6 infra.

2. The role of weighing in practical reasoning is incompatible with falsificationism. Each act of weighing ultimately rests on an unfalsifiable assumption one chooses in a particular case; cf. section 2.4.5 supra.

3. It is not clear what component of the practice of legal reasoning is analogous to proffering observational data as a proof that a theory is false. To be sure, some borderline between legal observations and legal theories may be determined, but it is by no means so sharp and clear as within the natural science. This fact makes an application of Popper´s theory to the law difficult.

Cf. section 3.3.3 supra. From a certain point of view, the sources of the law seem to be analogous to observational data. But legal data include also information about various facts, e.g. the facts disputed in the legal case under consideration, the fact that the legislator and some other persons expressed some value statements etc. The value statements and normative statements uttered by the lawyer who performs the legal reasoning in question show, too, a vague resemblance to propositions reporting observational data.

4. On the other hand, the practice of moral and legal reasoning provides many examples of giving reasons, reasons for reasons, etc. It thus fits well the model of reasonable support.

3.3.9. The Problem of Fundamental Justification of Legal Reasoning

The theory of reasonable support and legal paradigm, outlined above, makes it possible to better understand the problem of deep justification of legal reasoning. "Justification" is defined as giving sufficient reasons for a conclusion. But what reasons should one regard as sufficient? Reasons sufficient for a lawyer may be insufficient for a moralist, a political opponent, a philosopher, etc. The latter three might demand a justification of premises that the lawyer takes for granted. Juristic conclusions, judicial decisions and the like can thus be either justified

a) within the framework of legal reasoning, in other words, within the established legal tradition, or paradigm; or

b) outside it.

The former is <u>contextually sufficient legal justification</u>. It has a support of such premises as
-statutes, precedents and other sources of the law;
-traditional legal reasons, such as statutory analogy;
-various legal methods, such as teleological interpretation of statutes;
-traditional reasoning norms, e.g., if an earlier statute is incompatible with the later, one shall apply the latter; and
-legal value judgments, concerning, e.g., legal certainty, justice, reasonableness etc.

The latter can be a <u>deep (fundamental) justification</u> which provides support or criticism to the premises that the lawyer takes for granted (cf. Peczenik 1983, 1).

I disregard here a possibility of justification of another type, e.g., historical.

Various parts of the legal tradition or paradigm may thus - for various purposes and in various contexts - require the deep justification. For example, the question, Why shall we follow the Swedish Constitution?, makes no sense if asked during a legal trial. The court simply takes for granted that one should do it. On the other hand, the question may be pertinent at a political meeting where one answers an objection posed by an Anarchist.

As regards deep (fundamental) justification of legal reasoning, I have already stated the following. Various demands of rationality restrict arbitrariness of moral and legal reasoning. A moral or a legal statement thus can be presented as a logically correct conclusion from logically consistent, linguistically correct and reasonable premises. Moreover, in the law, one has access to an extensive set of reasonable premises, both moral and specifically legal. In the next chapter, I will pass to a still deeper problem one must face when analysing the idea of a reasonable premise.

CHAPTER 4
THE ULTIMATE JUSTIFICATION
OF MORAL AND LEGAL REASONING

4.1. COHERENCE

4.1.1. Introductory Remarks

As stated before, legal reasoning is supported by reasonable premises. A reasonable premise is not falsified and not arbitrary. A premise is thus reasonable if, and only if, the following conditions are fulfilled:
  1. The premise is not falsified.
  2. The hypothesis is not to a sufficiently high degree corroborated that this premise does not logically follow from a highly coherent set of premises.
   In consequence of this definition of reasonableness, the theory of rationality, presented above, is logically dependent upon a theory of coherence. One must thus make the justification even deeper and discuss the concept of coherence. The discussion of this concept, presented in this section (4.1), follows closely a paper on the subject, jointly prepared by <u>Robert Alexy</u> and myself (Alexy and Peczenik 1989).
   Since a long time, the idea of coherence has been regarded as an attractive tool for solving epistemological problems (cf., e.g., Hegel 1970, 24). The idea is applicable in many different contexts. A theory can thus be coherent with data. One theory can be coherent with another. Legal rules can be coherent with moral principles. Interpretation of a statute can be coherent with moral principles and such sources of the law as precedents; and so on.
   Many thinkers also agree that coherence is more than logical consistency. They are right. To be more precise, consistency is a necessary but not sufficient condition of coherence. Physics and chemistry, e.g., are highly coherent with each other, whereas there is a lesser degree of mutual coherence between physics and religion though it cannot be said that they contradict each other.
   Philosophers face great difficulties when attempting to formulate the precise concept and criteria of coherence. There is a tendency to avoid the term altogether, or to

characterise a coherent set of statements metaphorically as a "tightly knit unit" etc.

Some influential theories of coherence assume that more general statements create coherence in the less general ones they support. According to Neil MacCormick's conception of normative coherence in the law (1984, 235 ff.), some principles support a number of legal rules, and thus make them coherent.

Already Savigny (1814, 22) has pointed out that "von ihnen (the leading principles   ) ausgehend den inneren Zusammenhang und die Art der Verwandschaft aller juristischen Begriffe und Sätze zu erkennen, gehört eben zu den schwersten Aufgaben unsrer Wissenschaft, ja es ist eigentlich dasjenige, was unsrer Arbeit den wissenschaftlichen Charakter giebt".

On the other hand, some other theories assume that particular data-statements make general theories coherent. According to Nicholas Rescher, a proposition is thus true if and only if it follows from consistent data. However, the total set of accessible data-statements will be inconsistent, for at least two reasons. Firstly, there is always the possibility of a mistake. Secondly, one may obtain inconsistent data, depending on which of the competing theories of scientific method one applies. Rescher thus determines various maximal consistent subsets inherent in the (inconsistent) set of data. Some of those are to be preferred. A proposition, p, maximally coheres with data, if it invariably follows from all preferred maximal consistent subsets of data (Rescher 1973, 169 ff.). One can thus say that the preferred subsets of data support this proposition.

Ronald Dworkin's theory of "integrity" (that is, coherence) of law includes MacCormick's idea that principles make rules coherent. But Dworkin's theory seems to be more general. He compares a lawyer with a novelist, participating in writing a "chain novel" seriatim. Each novelist, and each lawyer, aims to make his additions fit not only general principles but all the material he has been given, the predictions of what his successors will want or be able to add to it, and his substantive value judgments (cf. Dworkin 1986, 225 ff.).

4.1.2. The Concept and Criteria of Coherence

I will now analyse the concept and criteria of coherence. The order of presentation is the following. Firstly, I will state the main idea of coherence, though the concept remains a vague one. Secondly, I will present some criteria and principles which need to be weighed and balanced against each other to determine coherence of a theory.

The main idea or the <u>concept</u> of coherence can be expressed in the following way.

The more the statements belonging to a given theory approximate a perfect supportive structure, the more coherent the theory.

As regards the connection between coherence and support cf. Peczenik 1983, 88 ff.; Aarnio 1987, 198 ff.

One must explain the meaning of the terms "theory", "support", "supportive structure" and "better support".

1) The word <u>"theory"</u> is used here in a broad sense, covering both descriptive, for example empirical theories, and normative or evaluative theories (norm systems or value systems).

2) The concept of support used here is a weak one. It has already been characterised (cf. section 2.7.4 supra) in the following manner: The statement p <u>supports</u> the statement q if, and only if, p belongs to a set of premises, S, from which q follows logically.

In an extreme case, q follows from p alone. A stronger concept of support will be introduced below.

Certainly, any p1 together with an arbitrarily added premise supports any conclusion whatever. However, this weak concept of support may be used as a starting point of discussion. Inappropriate additional premises are to be eliminated by the criteria of coherence, discussed below, and perhaps by further means.

3) Supportive <u>structure</u> depends on supportive relations between statements belonging to the theory in question. That is to say that the supportive structure of a theory is the same as the class of formal properties of the supportive relations between statements belonging to it.

4) The degree of <u>perfection</u> of a supportive structure depends on the degree to which the criteria of coherence are fulfilled.

Criteria of coherence make the concept of coherence more precise. The criteria are related to each other. The degree of coherence depends on weighing them up and balancing them against each other. The following discussion of these criteria constitutes one conception of coherence. Since the concept of coherence is vague and contested, it is possible to conceive of coherence in different ways.

The criteria of coherence can be divided into three classes, i.e., the properties of the supportive structure constituted by the theory, the properties of concepts applied by it and the properties of the scope covered by it.

4.1.3. Properties of the Supportive Structure

(1) The Number of Supportive Relations

The minimum condition of coherence is that a coherent theory contains statements supported by reasons. The following criterion and principle of coherence clarify this. Although they may differ in form, the criterion and the principle are merely different expressions of the same requirement of coherence.

1.   Ceteris paribus the more statements belonging to a theory are supported, the more coherent the theory.

1*.   One should justify as many statements as possible.

The clause "ceteris paribus" and the expression "as many... as possible" indicate here the same thing; no principle or criterion of coherence is independently sufficient but must be weighed against others. For example, other principles of coherence may explain the fact that relatively many statements belonging to the theory are not justified but merely taken for granted. Moreover, the quality of coherence can be weighed and balanced against other values. For example, in a case of emergency, a fireman should obey orders rather than continually demand a time consuming explanation.

Speaking about numbers, two questions occur. Firstly, what is a single statement?, Secondly, how to treat

numerous but trivial and perhaps redundant statements?
The first question may be answered in many ways
depending, among other things, on the subject of the
theory. One possible answer is this: A single statement
<u>sensu stricto</u> is the smallest unit of a theory which can
be confronted with the question "why?", and, therefore,
is capable of being justified. As regards the second
problem, the <u>ceteris-paribus</u> clause in criterion 1
implies that it can and must be solved by the other
criteria of coherence, and perhaps by other means.

(2) Length of the Supportive Chains

Coherence depends also upon the length of the supportive
chains belonging to the supportive structure. A statement
p1 thus supports p2, p2 supports p3, etc.
   Longer chains make the supportive structure more
complex. In other words, they make the theory more
structured. They can also make it more profound.
   The following criterion and principle of coherence help
to clarify this idea.

2.   <u>Ceteris paribus</u>, the longer the chains of
            reasons belonging to a theory are, the more
            coherent the theory.

2*.   When justifying a statement, one should support
            it with as long a chain of reasons as possible.

   The principle 2* demands a long series of
justifications. Together with the definition of support,
it assumes deductive correctness and they jointly imply a
complex criterion of coherence. This comprises
completeness of deductive trees, obtained as a result of
a logical reconstruction of the supportive chain.

(3) Strong Support

A premise may occupy a peculiar position. To state this
special position precisely, I have already defined the
concept of strong support.

The statement p <u>strongly supports</u> q if, and only if, p belongs to a
set of premises, S, having the following properties: (1) all these
premises are reasonable; and (2) at least one subset of S is such

that (a) q logically follows from it, and (b) all members of the subset are necessary to infer q from this subset (that is, q does not follow, if any premise belonging to the subset is removed from it); and (3) each member of S belongs to at least one such subset; and (4) p is necessary in the following stronger sense: q does not follow from any subset of S at all to which p does not belong.

I have also given examples of the role of strong support in moral and legal reasoning. *Inter alia*, the concept of strong support fits the fact that some norm-statements play a special role in legal reasoning. One may also claim that each general moral theory expresses a statement which strongly supports moral conclusions. In this way, one organises the totality of knowledge, justification, reasoning etc. into different levels, matrices and paradigms, such as, e.g., moral and legal reasoning, each characterised by its own core of premises which strongly support conclusions. Some of these premises may be characterised as *presupposed* within the paradigm in question; cf. section 3.3.5 supra. The concepts of "paradigm" and "presupposed premise" are thus linked to the concept of strong support. The examples make it plausible that the degree of coherence increases when not only weak but also strong support occurs. The following criterion and principle of coherence express this idea.

3.   *Ceteris paribus*, the more statements belonging to a theory are strongly supported by other statements, the more coherent the theory.

3*.   One should formulate statements which strongly support as many statements as possible.

(4) Connection Between Supportive Chains

Coherence depends also upon the connection between various supportive chains belonging to the supportive structure. We will discuss two kinds of connections. Firstly, the same premise may support different conclusions. Secondly, the same conclusion may follow from different sets of premises.

A connection of the first kind occurs, e.g., when the same principle supports a number of legal rules, and thus makes them coherent. The following criterion and principle of coherence corresponds to this idea:

4.1.   <u>Ceteris paribus</u>, the greater the number of conclusions which are supported by the same premise belonging to the theory in question, the more coherent the theory.

4.1*.   When justifying a statement, one should formulate premises supporting as many different conclusions as possible.

Cumulation of reasons within the supportive structure is also a criterion of coherence. It is well known that in judicial practice the decision often is justified by a cluster of reasons, none of which are sufficient in themselves, but which when taken along with others provide fairly good evidence. In other cases, the same conclusion follows from a number of independent reasons, each one sufficient. For example, the <u>Bundesverfassungsgericht</u> supported a conclusion concerning the position of a statute in the German legal order by three independent reasons: the principle that the state should be based on the law <u>(Rechtsstaat)</u>, the principle of parliamentary democracy, and the basic rights {BVerfGE 49, 89 (126 f.)}.

The following criterion and principle of coherence express this idea:

4.2.   <u>Ceteris paribus</u>, the greater the number of independent sets of premises within the theory in question, such that the same conclusion follows from each one of these sets, the more coherent the theory.

4.2*.   When justifying a statement, one should formulate as many independent sets of premises supporting it as possible.

(5) Priority Orders Between Reasons

Moreover, coherence of some theories depends on priority orders between reasons. <u>Inter alia</u>, priority orders are important when one faces a collision of principles, e.g., when an individual right collides with the demand to protect the environment. The relevant question is then, How to optimalise both principles within the system? This is the question of creating coherence. The only possible answer is to establish conditional, more or less general, all-things-considered priority relations and <u>prima-facie</u>

priority orders. This is the case regardless the fact that one can never establish an unconditional priority order, applicable to all thinkable cases of a collision between the principles in question. To establish a conditional priority order is the only way to avoid the risk that the system will be used to justify incoherent decisions. Incoherence would consist in the fact that though the decisions are logically compatible, their relation to each other is arbitrary. The following criterion and principle of coherence express this idea:

5.   If the theory in question contains principles then, _ceteris paribus_, the greater the number of priority relations between the principles, the more coherent the theory.

5*.   When using principles belonging to a theory as premises which justify a statement, one should formulate as many priority relations between the principles as possible.

(6) Reciprocal Justification

Reciprocal justification constitutes another criterion of coherence. One of the most fascinating and, at the same time, most controversial ideas connected with coherence is that of a system in which any statement supports each other one. It is easy to see the problem. The idea would be untenable had one defined support as logical entailment between p1 and p2 alone. Mutual support would then mean that p2 follows from p1 and p1 follows from p2. This is the case only when p1 and p2 are equivalent. The idea of a system in which each statement supports each other would thus lead to the conclusion that the system contains only logically equivalent statements, that is, it contains only one single statement. This is one of the reasons why we have chosen another definition of support, according to which p1 might support p2 even if p2 does not follow from p1 alone. Thus, p1 supports p2 if, and only if, p1 belongs to a set of premises, S, from which p2 follows logically. At the same time, p2 might support p1, that is, p2 might belong to another set of premises, S´, from which p1 follows logically.

An important distinction is the one between three different kinds of mutual support: empirical, analytic and normative.

An empirical reciprocal support exists, e.g., when institutional enforcement of basic rights constitutes a factual condition of democratic procedure of legislation and the latter constitutes a factual condition of the former. Such empirical connections are normatively relevant. A normative theory which contains them is richer and connects its elements in a better manner. The following criterion and principle of coherence express this idea:

6.1.   Ceteris paribus, the greater the number of reciprocal empirical relations between statements belonging to a theory, the more coherent the theory.

6.1*.   When using a theory to justify a statement, one should see to it that the theory covers as many reciprocal empirical relations between statements belonging it as possible.

As an example for a mutual analytic support, one can proffer the relation between basic rights and the well-known institution called in the Continental political philosophy "Rechtsstaat" (the state based on the law). Many reasons support the conclusion that legal validity of basic rights constitutes a conceptually necessary condition of a fully developed Rechtsstaat and, at the same time, when no Rechtsstaat at all exists, one cannot, for conceptual reasons, speak about the validity of the basic rights. A system which contains such conceptual relations connects its elements in a better manner than a one which does not. The following criterion and principle of coherence express this idea:

6.2.   Ceteris paribus, the greater the number of reciprocal analytic relations between statements belonging to a theory, the more coherent the theory.

6.2*.   When using a theory to justify a statement, one should see to it that the theory covers as many reciprocal analytic relations between statements belonging it as possible.

A normative reciprocal support exists when a relatively general statement supports a number of relatively special ones and the latter support the former. A connection of the first kind occurs, e.g., when a general legal norm supports a number of legal rules (see the criterion 4.1 supra). It is often called "deductive". A connection of the second kind, often called "inductive", may be made deductively complete by an addition of some premises. The relatively general conclusion follows then logically from the relatively less general statements together with the added premises.

The cumulation of both kinds of support is interesting because it leads to what Rawls calls "reflective equilibrium" (Rawls 1971, 48). I have already mentioned this concept in section 3.2.1 supra. The following example elucidates it a little more. During a long period, the Bundesverfassungsgericht interpreted the constitutional guarantee of human dignity as follows: "It contradicts human dignity to make a person a mere object" {BVerfGE 27, 1 (6)} of the activity of the state authorities. In spite of its vagueness, this formula supported the solution of many cases, and the cases were regarded as a support for the formula. However, in a case concerning an interception of a telephone conversation, the Court found that human dignity is contradicted first when the action of the authorities not only makes a person a mere object but also constitutes a contempt {BVerfGE 30, 1 (26)}. The new formula helped to justify the change of the law, according to which a person whose conversation was intercepted no longer could appeal to a court, only to a special parliamentary body. Yet, one may find this change to be wrong and regard this evaluation as a reason against the new formula. Moreover, one may imagine a series of cases where an activity of the authorities violates human dignity in spite of the fact that it does not constitute a contempt. Thus, the old formula seems to be better than the new one. Consequently, the Court returned to it in later decisions {BVerfGE 45, 187 (228)}.

A creation of reciprocal normative relations, that is, a reflective equilibrium of the type described above, is not a perfect justificatory procedure, since it leaves open the priority order between general and special statements. Sometimes, a more special statement is easier to give up; sometimes it is easier to stick to it and change a more general one. Yet, one can hardly deny that this procedure is rational and contributes to the creation of a coherent system; cf. section 3.2.1 supra. The following criterion and principle of coherence correspond to this insight:

6.3.   Ceteris paribus, the greater the number of reciprocal normative relations between statements belonging to a theory, the more coherent the theory.

6.3*.   When using a theory to justify a statement, one
             should see to it that the theory covers as many
             reciprocal   normative   relations   between
             statements belonging to it as possible.

   A   more   complex   reciprocal   justification   is   also
conceivable. Imagine, e.g., the following inferences, a,
b and c.

a.

p1
s & p1 -> p2
s

Conclusion: p2

b.

p2
s & p2 -> p3
s

Conclusion: p3

c.

p3
s & p3 -> p1
s

Conclusion: p1

Let me give two examples, the first containing causal propositions,
the second including statements of many different kinds.

Example 1.

Imagine the following inferences, A, B and C.

A.

p1   Urbania has a greater number scientists per capita
                        than any other country

s & p1 -> p2   If a country has an efficient economic
                        system and a greater number scientists per

	capita than any other country, it also has a higher BSP per capita than any other country
s	Urbania has an efficient economic system
Conclusion (p2)	Urbania has a higher BSP per capita than any other country

B.

p2	Urbania has a higher BSP per capita than any other country
s & p2 -> p3	If a country has an efficient economic system and a higher BSP per capita than any other country, it also spends higher percent BSP for research than any other country
s	Urbania has an efficient economic system
Conclusion (p3)	Urbania spends a higher percent BSP for research than any other country

C.

p3	Urbania spends higher percent BSP for research than any other country
s & p3 -> p1	If a country has an efficient economic system and spends a higher percent BSP for research than any other country, it also has a greater number scientists per capita than any other country
s	Urbania has an efficient economic system
Conclusion (p1)	Urbania has a greater number scientists per capita than any other country

In this example, A, B and C reveal a causal feedback: ceteris paribus, the number of scientists influences causally the BSP, the latter influences causally the amount of money spent for research and this influences causally the number of scientists.

Example 2.

Imagine now the following inferences, A', B' and C'.

A'.

p1	Urbanian legal system contains the prima-facie negligence principle N_1, according to which one is liable for the damage one caused only if one's action made a damage (of any kind) foreseeable for a cautious person (a bonus pater familias).

s & p1 -> p2   If the law is fairly just, a legal system which
                      contains the prima-facie negligence principle
                      N_1 also   contains   the   prima-facie   principle
                      concerning adequacy A_1 according to which one is
                      liable in torts for the damage one caused only if
                      one's   action   made   a   damage   of   this   type
                      foreseeable for a very cautious and well informed
                      person (a cautious expert, a vir optimus)

s   The legal system of Urbania is fairly just

Conclusion (p2)   Urbanian legal system contains the prima-facie
                      adequacy principle A_1

By the way, the second premise is justifiable in the following way.
In a system of liability based on negligence without adequacy, one
must face such cases as the famous story by von Kries: A horse-cart
driver slept when driving, the horse chose a different way home, and
the passenger was killed by a thunder. The driver was negligent,
since he certainly could foresee a damage, but should he be held
liable for the thunder? To adjust liability to moral evaluations,
one then must introduce the rule of adequacy, based, e.g., on
foreseeability of a definite type of damage.

B'.

p2   Urbanian legal system contains the prima-facie
                      adequacy principle A_1

s & p2 -> p3   If the law is fairly just, a legal system
                      which contains the prima-facie adequacy principle
                      A_1 also   contains   the   prima-facie   causation
                      principle C_1 according to which one is liable not
                      only if one's action was a necessary condition of
                      the damage but sometimes also if one's action was
                      a sufficient but not necessary condition therefor.

s   The legal system of Urbania is fairly just

Conclusion (p3)   Urbanian legal system contains the prima-facie
                      causation principle C_1

Concerning the second premise, let me give the following example. A
challenger, A, gives the champion poison, in order to lower his
capacity. He is very careful not to endanger the victim's life.
Another competitor, C, does the same. The cumulated amount of poison
kills the victim. A's action was not an adequate cause of the
victim's death, since not even an expert could have foreseen that
also C would have the same idea. For the same reason, C's action was
not an adequate cause the fatal result either. Yet, it would be
obviously unjust to let both A and C go free from liability.

C'.

p2   Urbanian legal system contains the prima-facie
                      adequacy principle A_1

p3   Urbanian legal system contains the <u>prima-facie</u>
                        causation principle C_1

                        If the law is fairly just, a legal system
s & p3 -> p1   which contains the <u>prima-facie</u> causation
                        principle C_1 also contains the <u>prima-facie</u>
                        negligence principle N_1

s   The law of Urbania is fairly just

Conclusion (p1)   Urbanian legal system contains the <u>prima-facie</u>
                        negligence principle N_1

As regards the question how to justify the second premise, let me
merely state that a legal system containing complex rules on causal
overdetermination would be unjust if totally lacking the principle
of negligence. Indeed, this would be a pure system of strict
liability. In other words, one would be liable though only a <u>vir
optimus</u>, certainly not oneself, would be able to foresee a damage.

4.1.4. Properties of Concepts

There are intrinsic connections between the properties of
supportive structure and the properties of concepts. All
supportive structures presuppose some logical concepts
such as "if... then" etc. Besides, many supportive
structures are possible only because of relations
between some other, e.g., moral or legal, concepts. In
the history of philosophy, there are examples of thinkers
who emphasise concepts, e.g., Hegel, and those who
emphasise statements, e.g., many logicians of the first
half of 20th century. The classical German
Begriffsjurisprudenz (Conceptual Jurisprudence)
emphasised concepts, though many of its theses could be
reconstructed as concerning support between statements.
In this context, let us discuss the following criteria
and principles of coherence.

(7) Generality

A criterion of coherence is thus what could be described
as generality in the broad sense, generality of concepts
and, consequently, arguments. In this context, one may
refer to (a) universality, (b) generality in the strict
sense, and (c) resemblances.

a. Universality consists in the fact that one uses concepts designating <u>all</u> things belonging to a certain class, not merely names of individual objects. Universality, that is, the use of concepts, is a necessary condition of all coherence. Therefore, the criterion 7.1, formulated below, only declares what the criteria discussed above already imply.

Universality is relevant for all concepts and theories. When using concepts, we put the same label on a class of things. The concept "swan" thus denotes <u>all</u> swans. One cannot think without concept, solely using individual names.

Universalisability of a statement is often defined as the fact that it follows logically from a universal statement. Morality requires universalisability of norms and value judgments.

b. Generality, in contrast to universality, can be graded. The more general the concept in question, the greater the number of objects it covers (cf. Hare 1972/73, 2 ff.).

In the law, this form of coherence manifests itself, <u>inter alia</u>, in the so-called general parts of criminal codes of many countries, dealing generally with negligence, intent, self-defence, and so on. Civil codes, such as the German BGB, also have a general part. Moreover, in legal reasoning, one often uses general arguments, rooted in moral philosophy, e.g., when the defendant pleads not guilty on the grounds that he was not negligent, and argues that responsibility without negligence would be unjust.

The moral idea that the like ought to be treated alike is not purely logical but rather involves generality. A judgement that two persons ought to be treated differently is thus no moral one, unless it can be completed with a set of <u>reasonable</u> premises pointing out relevant differences between these persons and thus <u>supporting</u> the different treatment. This requirement of reasonable support is stronger than mere universalisability (cf. Alexy 1985, 357 ff.).

By the way, Kant's categorical imperative, demanding that one ought to act only according to the maxim about which one could wish that it be a general law, is not purely logical either. "Der tragende Gedanke der Lehrstücks vom kategorischen Imperativ scheint folgende zu sein: Eine vieltahl von menschlichen Individuen, die in einer Gesellschaft vereinigt sind, besitzen eine Fülle von gegenläufigen Interessen... Wäre das freie Spiel der Kräfte und Interessen das

einzige regulativ... , so wäre ein Chaos ... die Folge... Hiergegen
ist nun nach Kant die vernünftige Reflexion auf die Maximen des
Handelns das einzige, aber auch ausreichende Hilfsmittel." (Patzig
1980, 162-163).

c. A conceptual family exists when the concept in
question refers to a cluster of phenomena, one similar to
another, this to a third one etc.

In legal reasoning, this kind of generality and thus
coherence, shows itself when one argues _ex analogia_.
Amongst these forms of argumentation is the so-called
analogia intra legem, that is, the argument that a
certain case is so similar to the cases the statute
typically covers that it must itself be counted as
covered by the linguistic meaning of it. Another form of
argument is the so-called statutory analogy, which uses
various similarities to extend the area of application of
a statutory norm beyond its purely linguistic limits.
Last but not least, there is reasoning by analogy, which
applies a precedent to a subsequent case which is similar
to the prior one.

The criteria of generality in the broad sense apply
both to general theories and particular legal decisions.
The latter must also be supported by coherent theories
which use general concepts. In some cases, the court must
formulate an explicit and general justification, in
others it is enough that such a justification is
possible.

Therefore, the following criteria and principles of
coherence hold good.

7.1.   _Ceteris paribus_, the more statements without
         individual names a theory uses, the more
         coherent the theory.

7.1*.   When using a theory to justify a statement, one
         should see to it that the theory is expressed in
         as many statements without individual names as
         possible.

7.2.   _Ceteris paribus_, the greater number of general
         concepts belong to a theory, and the higher
         their degree of generality, the more coherent
         the theory.

7.2*.   When using a theory to justify a statement, one
         should see to it that the theory is expressed in

as many general concepts as possible and in as highly general concepts as possible.

7.3.   Ceteris paribus, the more resemblances between concepts used within a theory, the more coherent the theory.

7.3*.   When using a theory to justify a statement, one should make as complete a list as possible of the resemblances between the concepts belonging to the theory.

8. Conceptual Cross-connections

Conceptual cross-connections between parts of the structure constitute a further criterion of coherence. Ceteris paribus, two theories are thus coherent to the extent that they use the same or analogous concepts, structures, rules etc.

For example, due to such structural similarity, modal logic, which deals with the concepts of necessity and possibility, is highly coherent with deontic logic, which deals with the concepts of obligation and permission. This fact helped logicians to solve many ancient problems connected with the relations between such concepts as obligation, prohibition and permission, on the analogy of relations between necessity, impossibility and possibility (cf. the fundamental paper, v. Wright 1957). Another example is the fact that conceptual tools elaborated in economics, such as Pareto-optimality and indifference curves, can be used to analyse the weighing and balancing in legal and moral reasoning (cf. Alexy 1985, 100 ff., 145 ff.).

The criteria and principles of coherence which emerge from this idea are the following:

8.1.   Ceteris paribus, the more concepts a given theory, T1, has in common with another theory, T2, the more coherent these theories are with each other.

8.1*.   When using a theory to justify a statement, one should see to it that the theory is expressed in as many concepts belonging to other theories as possible.

8.2.   <u>Ceteris paribus</u>, the more concepts a given
            theory, T1, contains which resemble concepts
            used in another theory, T2, the more coherent
            these theories are with each other.

8.2*.   When using a theory to justify a statement, one
            should see to it that the theory is expressed in
            as many concepts similar to those used in other
            theories as possible.

4.1.5. Properties of the Objects the Theory Deals With

(9) Number of Cases

A further criterion of coherence is the number of cases a
theory covers. This criterion has a connection with the
idea of a "certain" premise (section 3.3.4 supra). Some
certain premises concern particular cases. They are
particular statements, expressing an intuition,
observation, intention, evaluation, interest,
interpretation etc. involved in a particular case. If
they express an observation, they may be regarded as data
statements. Coherence increases when a theory covers an
increased number of alleged certain premises, among other
things an increased number of alleged data, that is,
"data candidates". I do not assume here any strong theory
of data. Instead, I think that the criteria of coherence
may contribute to establish the required difference
between proper candidates to the data status, e.g.,
physical experiment, and improper candidates, such as
dreams and spiritual revelations.
    The following criterion and principle of coherence
correspond to this idea.

9.   <u>Ceteris paribus</u>, the greater number of
            individual cases a theory covers the more
            coherent the theory.

9*.   When using a theory to justify a statement, one
            should see to it that the theory covers as many
            individual cases as possible.

To some extent, the number of cases a theory covers
depends both on the dimensions of the supportive
structure in question and the generality of the applied

concepts. To this extent, the criterion 9 is a corollary
of the criteria 1-8 discussed above.

(10) Diversity of Fields of Life

From another point of view, however, a theory has a
greater scope if the cases to which it applies are more
diversified, that is, belong to more different areas of
knowledge. A particular logical calculus is thus
especially important if applicable to very different
areas, e.g., to modal and deontic logic. A theory of
weighing and balancing is particularly important if
applicable to such different fields as economics, law and
practical philosophy.

The theory or the cluster of theories in question
should be as wide-ranging as possible. Indeed, the most
important theories, formulated in physics, chemistry,
biology etc., are supportively and conceptually linked
together in such a manner that they jointly constitute a
coherent set of propositions covering a great number of
fields of life and showing some supportive and conceptual
connections with many fields of life.

The following criterion and principle of coherence are
thus justifiable.

10.   Ceteris paribus, the more fields of life a
           theory covers the more coherent the theory.

10*.   When using a theory to justify a statement, one
           should see to it that the theory covers as many
           fields of life as possible.

To be sure, the connections between sciences and, on
the other hand, social institutions, history etc. are
not sufficient to conclude that, for example, physics and
history jointly constitute one coherent whole. Yet, our
institutions and history have some connections with,
e.g., physics and biology. At the very least, they exist
in a universe following the laws of physics, and they
must fit the biological limitations of human beings.
Social institutions which aim at the achievement of the
physically or biologically impossible are, of course,
doomed.

On the other hand, some science fiction stories, or
even political ideologies, may to a high degree fulfil
other criteria of coherence, yet they lack connection
with many fields of life. If such a story covered our

life so well that, among other things, a person
performing his everyday actions had to pay attention to
it in a similar manner as to his physical, chemical and
biological characteristics and conditions, it would no
longer be a science fiction but a coherent, and probably
true, theory.

4.1.6. Weighing and Balancing of Criteria of Coherence

The degree of coherence is determined by weighing and
balancing of the discussed criteria. One should not
follow any of the principles of coherence in isolation
from others. In some cases, the higher the degree of
fulfilment of one criterion, the lower that of another.
For example, the supportive chain of reasons may be
particularly long when one uses less general concepts,
and shrink substantially when the concepts applied become
more general. In such a case, one must perform a
complicated act of weighing in order to answer the
question which theory is more coherent, the more general
one, or the one containing the longer chain of reasons.

4.2. COHERENCE, CORRECTNESS AND TRUTH

4.2.1. Coherence and Rational Thinking

What is the importance and the full impact of coherence?
In the present context, I cannot discuss this complex
problem in a comprehensive manner. I will limit myself to
a few brief remarks (which follow closely the quoted
paper, Alexy and Peczenik 1989).

To clarify the contribution of coherence to practical
rationality, one can discuss the difference between a
legal justification which is supported by a fairly
coherent system and such a justification which has no
such support. A legal justification which neither
explicitly nor implicitly refers to a system is an ad-hoc
justification. Neither universal nor general, it would
not fulfil elementary demands of justice (MacCormick
1984, 243). Justice requires that legal justification is
embedded in a fairly coherent system. Moreover, the
connection with a system has a number of further results

to be positively evaluated from the point of view of
practical rationality (cf. Alexy 1989, 266 ff.): Legal
dogmatics creates a system of concepts and statements
which enables one to collect, test and improve opinions
expressed by many generations of jurists. In this way, it
contributes to stability and progress. Within such a
system statements are tested in a much more efficient way
than within an unsystematic ad-hoc justification.
Moreover, construction of the system results in new
insights which persons solely engaged in an ad-hoc
justification would hardly gain. Finally, the system
makes the work of the decision-maker easier. He can rely
upon statements which have already been tested many
times, and has no need to return in each case to the
hopeless task of justifying everything at once.

Generally, it can be said that the concept of
justification is related to that of support.
Justification in a strong sense includes support and
additional requirements. A central one is that of
coherence. Moreover, such concepts as rationality and
correctness are related to that of justification and thus
coherence. Therefore one can say that coherence is a
central element of a fully-fledged concept of
justification, rationality and correctness. This relation
can be expressed as follows.

If the norm- or value-system in question is more
coherent than any competing system, then it is
prima facie better justified and more rational
than any competing system. If the norm- or
value-system in question is more coherent than
any competing system, then there exists a prima
facie reason that it is correct.

These analytical connections between coherence,
justification, rationality and correctness might,
however, not convince a sceptic. He might say that all
this talk about justification, rationality and
correctness is an illusion while the plain fact is that
practical statements merely express our arbitrary
feelings.

However, one can advance the following arguments
against this kind of scepticism. The fact that one can
arrange one´s opinions concerning practical problems into
a coherent whole means that one can rationally think
about these problems. One could try to explicate the very
concept of rational thinking as an effort to obtain a
balance between the following criteria of coherence: (1)

the greatest possible number of supported statements belonging to the theory in question; (2) the greatest possible length of chains of reasons: belonging to it ; (3) the greatest possible number of strongly supported statements belonging to the theory; (4) the greatest possible number of connections between various supportive chains belonging to the theory; (5) the greatest possible number of preference relations between various principles belonging to it; (6) the greatest possible number and complexity of reciprocal supportive relations between various statements belonging to the theory; (7) the greatest possible number of universal statements belonging to the theory; the greatest possible number of general concepts belonging to it; the highest possible degree of generality of concepts implemented within it; the greatest possible number of resemblances between concepts used within it; (8) the greatest possible number of conceptual cross-connections between various theories; (9) the greatest possible number of cases covered by the theory; and (10) the greatest possible number of fields of life covered by the theory.

Thus, it seems to be sufficiently clear that we can have not only feelings and emotions concerning practical matters but also more or less well grounded judgments. Certainly, a judgment based exclusively on feelings and emotions may have some advantages. For example, it may be better than a well grounded judgment insofar as it is easier to obtain. But it is difficult to doubt that a judgment which is supported by argument is better in what concerns rationality and correctness than a judgment which has no such support.

4.2.2. Coherence, Data, Presuppositions and Correctness

A sceptic, however, may insist that a theory can be coherent and still have no contact with reality. But this objection is easy to answer. The contact with reality is provided by criteria of coherence. Criterion 9 thus demands that a coherent theory covers a great number of "data candidates", or "certain statements". Criterion 3 relates coherence to presupposed statements, which characterise a certain practice, such as legal reasoning.

"Certain" statements are taken for granted by all people or at least all normal people belonging to the culture under consideration. Some certain statements concern particular cases. They express intuitions, observations, evaluations etc. involved in a particular case. If they express an observation, they may be regarded as data statements.

Other certain statements describe procedures of rational reworking of the observations, evaluations etc. The procedures are justifiable through weighing and balancing of all criteria of coherence, perhaps together with other considerations.

"Presupposed" statements are taken for granted within a particular practice belonging to the culture under consideration, e.g. within the legal paradigm. Their link with the criteria of coherence includes the following. One organises the totality of knowledge, justification, reasoning etc. into different levels, matrices and paradigms, such as, e.g., moral and legal reasoning, each characterised by its own core of premises which strongly support conclusions. Some of these premises may be characterised as presupposed within the paradigm in question. The concepts of "paradigm" and "presupposed premise" are thus linked to the concept of strong support. But strong support is the third criterion of coherence. Coherence increases when not only weak but also strong support occurs.

"Proved" statements follow from a consistent set of certain premises and/or premises presupposed within the particular practice, such as the legal paradigm. They are thus indirectly connected with criteria of coherence.

Finally, all reasonable statements are linked to the ideas of coherence and certainty in the following manner. The hypothesis is not sufficiently corroborated that they do not follow from a coherent set of premises.

To be sure, practical reasoning involves often weighing and balancing of considerations. The final step of such a reasoning is to be chosen under influence of will and feelings; cf. section 2.4.5. However, the act of weighing is rational only if the considerations to be balanced are organised in coherent systems. Moreover, the fifth criterion of coherence explicitly deals with weighing and balancing. It thus makes coherence dependent on the number of preference relations between various considerations to be weighed.

One may now restate the discussion of correctness of legal reasoning in a manner emphasising its connection with coherence. To be sure, deep justification of legal reasoning is problematic because this form of reasoning constitutes a peculiar mixture of theoretical propositions and practical (normative or evaluative) statements, and yet is supposed to give knowledge of valid law or of juristic meaning of the sources of the law. It is difficult to see how value judgments can lead to (true) knowledge of the law. On the other hand, they certainly can be included in a highly coherent set of statements. Such a set has the discussed contact with "certain" and presupposed statements. Its supportive structure possesses a high degree of perfection. Why not to regard this kind of perfection as correctness of legal reasoning?

4.2.3. Theories of Truth

However, what is the relation between coherence and truth?

To answer this question, one must, at first, say something about the concept of truth.

It is controversial whether, and in what sense, scientific theories succeed in their pursuit of truth. Do theories formulate correct models or interpretations of reality? Are theories irreplaceable: must replacing them by observational propositions lead to loss of true knowledge? (cf., e.g., Kutschera 1972 vol. 2, 391 ff.). Epistemological realism answers these questions in the affirmative, instrumentalism in the negative (cf. Hempel 1958, 49, on the paradox of theorising; cf. Gärdenfors 1980, 78 ff.). The controversies should not, however, obscure the central point, namely that the "regulative" idea of truth gives purpose to theoretical thinking, inter alia to science (cf. Popper 1972, 29-30.).

Ordinary people understand truth as correspondence between beliefs and facts. Roughly speaking, a statement is true if and only if facts are such as it states them to be. This is the core of the classical theory of truth, often called the correspondence theory.

The correspondence theory of truth faces, inter alia, the following difficulty, emphasised already by ancient sceptics, René Descartes, George Berkeley and many other philosophers. We can report our beliefs. But can we compare them with the facts? The only way to know the facts is to rely upon experience and reason, but how can we know that these sources of knowledge are reliable? If an evil demon all the time had deceived us, we could not notice it but would believe in fictions, not in facts. One can thus argue for the conclusion that an individual solely knows his own psychical experiences, not the facts.

In consequence of such and other difficulties, many philosophers defend non-classical theories of truth.

According to the coherence theory of truth, p is true if and only if it belongs to a highly coherent set of statements. But must a highly coherent theory be true? An obvious objection is that even a novel, although not true, can be highly coherent. A sophisticated coherence theory of truth claims thus that a true statement must be included in a set of statements covering almost all fields of life; cf. criterion 10 of coherence.

The <u>consensus theory</u> defines truth, as follows. A statement, p, is true if and only if people agree that p. The fact that the proposition "the Earth is round" is true is thus the same as the fact that everybody agrees that the Earth is round. An obvious objection is that the Earth were round already in the period when everybody thought it was flat. Some philosophers, among others <u>Karl-Otto Apel</u> and <u>Jürgen Habermas</u> thus have elaborated more sophisticated consensus theories of truth. According to <u>Habermas</u> (1973, 218), a proposition is true, if the validity claim with which we utter it is justifiable. This claim is justifiable if and only if people participating in the rational discourse would agree that p (id. 240). The perfectly rational discourse would exist in the ideal speech situation in which intellectual communication of people would not be impeded by violence and everybody would have the same chance to ask and answer questions, interpret others' views, recommend actions etc. (id. 252 ff.). Alexy's theory of optimal discourse, discussed in Section 4.3 infra, was inspired by Habermas's theory.

According to the <u>pragmatic theory</u> of truth, p is true if and only if, roughly speaking, it is useful to believe in p. In other words, p is true if the belief in p helps one to achieve one's goals. Physics, e.g., is true because it helps engineers to build machines that work. The obvious difficulty is that even false beliefs can be useful in some situations. For instance, an engineer's belief that God requires of him at least seventy hours work pro week would certainly increase his chance of success. A sophisticated theory of truth must thus assume that only true beliefs <u>invariably</u> lead to pragmatic success, that is, help one to achieve one's goals. This assumption is, however, controversial. One must state the connection between truth and pragmatic success in a very careful way.

The non-classical theories of truth face the following difficulty (analogous to Moore's "open question argument, cf. Section 2.1 supra). It is meaningful to ask such questions as "To be sure, p belongs to a coherent world picture, but is p true?; "To be sure, p would be accepted in an optimal discourse, but is p true?"; etc. If the non-classical theories correctly reported the meaning of the word "true", such questions would be as meaningless as "To be sure, John is a bachelor but is he not married?" The latter question is meaningless because the word "bachelor" means the same as "a man who never married". The questions concerning truth are, on the other hand, meaningful because the word "true" does <u>not</u> mean the same as "coherent", "accepted" etc. Good reasons thus exist, in spite of all problems, for accepting the correspondence theory. This theory elucidates the sense of "truth". The non-classical theories of truth give mere criteria of truth, not the concept of truth.

4.2.4. More About the Correspondence Theory of Truth

One must, however, briefly discuss some additional difficulties the correspondence theory faces. Let me return to the preliminary formulation that a statement is true if and only if facts are such as it states them to be. The following questions then occur.

1. What are the facts? Among other things, what facts do correspond to such statements as "x can happen", "x causes y" or to mathematical propositions? Assume for a moment that the world is the totality of facts, not things (Wittgenstein 1922, No. 1.1). Does the world itself consist of modalities, causal relations etc.?

2. One may also argue that any fact, e.g., the fact that x causes y, is theory-laden, dependent on our language, theories etc. (cf. Strawson, 1964, 32 ff.; Habermas 1973, 211 ff.).

Among other things, a fact is not the same as an event. The event that Brutus killed Caesar took place in 44 B.C. but today, two thousand years later, one can say that it is (not merely "was") a fact that Brutus killed Caesar. Facts are "that-entities". It is a fact that Brutus killed Caesar (cf., e.g., Patzig 1980, 20, 34 ff.). The "that" is a language-dependent component. The world itself contains no "that" (cf. Mulligan, Simons and Smith 1987, 210 ff.).

3. One must also discuss alleged impossibility of comparing so different entities as statements and facts. Wittgenstein (1922, No. 2.1. ff. and 4.01. ff.) probably assumed that statements correspond to facts, if they have the same structure. However, this thesis is highly metaphysical, and also open for criticism (cf., e.g., Bunge 1974, 93). One objection is founded on the vagueness and continual change of the language: Are the facts themselves vague? Do they change when the language changes? (Apel 1976, 124-5).

In the present context, nevertheless, one may avoid such problems and simply state the following. **By regarding a statement as true, one makes recourse to the external world, quite independently of the question what the world consists of.**

"(I)n making any kind of truth-claim or knowledge-claim, we are committed to holding that certain objects, which the assertion is ultimately about, exist"; Black 1977, 57.

There is something in the world which makes a given statement true or false. This "something" is the same as truth-conditions of the statement. Though one cannot grasp these truth-conditions without having formulated the corresponding statement, they can exist before one uttered the statement (cf. Patzig 1980, 38). They "there outside" in the world, not merely in our statements. Let me call them truth-makers (cf. Mulligan, Simons and Smith 1987, 210 ff.).

Let me thus understand the correspondence theory of truth and its relation to coherence in the following manner:

a) If something in the world, a "truth-maker", makes the statement p true, then p is true.

b) If p is true then there exists a "truth-maker" making it true (cf. Mulligan, Simons and Smith 1987, 246).

c) The truth-maker is impossible to describe; to emphasise this impossibility, one may call it a truth-maker in itself.

d) The statement p thus describes something else, say a knowable fact, e.g., that Brutus killed Caesar.

e) The statement p can describe the knowable fact correctly or not.

f) If and only if the description is correct, p is true.

g) If we wish to make the ordinary use of the word "true" understandable, we must **postulate** that there is a correspondence between the truth-maker and the knowable fact.

h) What we call thinking is an approximation of the ideal of coherence.

i) Thinking, and hence coherence, is adapted to the task of representing knowable facts.

The fact that one can arrange one´s beliefs into a coherent whole means that one possesses knowledge of connections, logical and causal. One may perhaps assume with <u>Hegel</u> that a complete knowledge of connections is an approximation of that what actually exists.

4.2.5. Conclusions About Truth and Coherence

In consequence, the following metaphysical assumptions are (not proved but) reasonable:

1)   If a theory is perfectly coherent then it corresponds to knowable facts.

Moreover:

2)   If a theory <u>can</u> be made highly coherent, then there exist truth-makers which decide about this possibility.

Something in the world, some truth-makers, are necessary conditions of coherence. The truth-makers decide that some statements can be ordered into a coherent set while others cannot.

Finally:

3)   If a theory is perfectly coherent, then it corresponds to truth-makers, that is, to the world.

Coherence thus is a sufficient condition of this correspondence. In other words, correspondence between a theory and truth-makers is a necessary condition of coherence. (I am grateful to <u>Risto Hilpinen</u> who expressed this idea in an oral discussion).

To show that the latter thesis is plausible, let me state the following.

1. To be sure, one also needs some external contact of a theory. For example, a political ideology can be very coherent, yet false because it lacks empirical foundations, or is so vague that it can "explain" all thinkable phenomena. I have already stated (in section 3.3 supra) that knowledge must have something to do with empirical data, or at least with some "certain" and presupposed statements.

2. However, the class of certain and presupposed premises contains not only shared intuitions, observations, intentions, evaluations, interests, interpretations etc. but also procedures of rational reworking of them. The latter include arranging the observations, evaluations etc. in <u>coherent</u> theories, submitting them to a rational <u>discourse</u> and criticising them according to scientific methods, such as Popper´s conjectures and refutations. The main idea of coherence thus constitutes a certain or at least presupposed statement in the discussed sense.

3. Moreover, the class of certain and presupposed statements is sufficient to bear the whole edifice of knowledge only if it is understood in the broad sense, including the main idea of coherence as well as other basic assumptions concerning the concept and criteria of truth. Paraphrasing <u>Kant</u>, one can say: Without observations etc., our knowledge is empty, without reworking procedures it is blind.

4. Assume, finally, that one takes into account <u>all</u> beliefs and standpoints, existing within one´s surrounding, including observational data, other "certain" statements, presuppositions of various scientific disciplines and everyday practices, hypotheses and guesses, indeed even dreams and religious revelation etc. In this way, one perfectly fulfils two criteria of coherence, that is, those concerning <u>scope</u> of theory (criteria 9 and 10 supra). The hypothesis is plausible that the other criteria of coherence, demanding complexity and preciseness of supportive structure (criteria 1-6) and generality of concepts (criteria 7 and 8) are then sufficient to sort out such things as dreams. What is left within a coherent theory is, indeed, only

"certain" and presupposed premises, and conclusions following of them.

5. The hypothesis is also plausible, that such a coherent theory would explain the special status of observational data in natural science, in opposition to theories (cf. section 4.2.2 supra). Among other things, criterion 9 requires that a coherent theory covers as many individual cases as possible. One can reasonably interpret the expression "individual cases" as covering observational data.

One may wonder whether another thesis is not justifiable, as well, namely that something in the world, some truth-makers, are <u>sufficient</u> conditions of coherence. In other words, coherence of a theory is a necessary condition of its correspondence with the world:

4)   If a theory corresponds to the world, then it is highly coherent.

This thesis would be false had the world been chaotic. But <u>if</u> one assumes that the world is relatively ordered and stable, then it is plausible.

These reflections about truth make the following theses plausible:

5)   <u>Ceteris paribus</u>, the more coherent a theory, the greater amount of true information it gives.

6)   <u>Ceteris paribus</u>, the more coherent a theory, the closer it comes to true information.

In his recent paper, (1985), Rescher modified his earlier views and developed similar ideas: There exists essential connection between truth and coherence. If a statement which belongs to a data basis possessing certain formal qualities is optimally coherent, then it corresponds to reality.

4.2.6. Truth and Correctness of Practical Statements

Comparing the role of coherence in practical and theoretical contexts, one may state, what follows.

Generally speaking, "truth" is an <u>ontological</u> concept, that is, a concept presupposing something about the real facts. For that reason, it is doubtful whether norms and value statements, _inter alia_ legal interpretative statements, possessing not only theoretical but also practical meaning, can be true. Practical meaning of norms and value statements is partly independent of their theoretical meaning. All-things-considered (not merely _prima facie_) norms and value statements presuppose weighing and balancing of reasons and counter-arguments, ultimately involving the will and feelings (cf. Section 2.4.5 supra).

At the same time, the concept of truth has a certain function in epistemology and philosophy of science, that is, determines the purpose of such practices as science. The purpose it to tell the truth. Similarly, one can say that the purpose of legal reasoning is to state precisely what is right.

Cf. Popper 1966, vol. 2, 384-5: "First, both proposals and propositions are alike in that we can discuss them, criticize them, and come to some decision about them. Second, there is some kind of regulative idea about both. In the realm of facts it is the idea of correspondence between a statement or a proposition and a fact; that is, the idea of truth. In the realm of standards, or of proposals, the regulative idea may be described in many ways, and called by many terms, for example by the terms 'right' or 'good'."

Finally, the concept of truth has a function in formal logic. Logicians thus construct calculi with two values, 0 and 1, where 1 means "true" in the formal sense. In spite of some known objections, I am of the opinion that such a calculus, appropriately modified in formal respects, can be applied to value statements, as well.

But on the other hand, norms and value statements, _inter alia_ in the law, can to a high degree fulfil the criteria of coherence. Fulfilment of these criteria indicates that they are _correct._

4.3. RATIONAL DISCOURSE

4.3.1. Introductory Remarks on D-Rationality

Let me now present some remarks concerning the relation between coherence and rational discourse. The remarks follow closely the already mentioned paper prepared jointly with _Robert Alexy_ (Alexy and Peczenik 1989).

Advantages of a coherent system are limited by three
necessary disadvantages.

The first one follows from the concept of coherence.
Coherence is a matter of degree. It also depends on
weighing and balancing of partly incompatible demands.
The criteria of coherence do not always lead to a unique
answer to the question of whether one system is more
coherent than another. In some cases, they only decide
that one system is more coherent in one respect, another
system in another respect. The choice between the systems
requires then an evaluation which cannot be based solely
on criteria of coherence.

The second limitation follows from the formal character
of coherence. The criteria of coherence do not say
anything about the content of normative systems.
Certainly, the criteria comprise generality and
universality. Moreover, a fully elaborated justification
is apt to contribute to rationality and justice rather
than to irrationality and injustice. Thus, fulfilment of
the criteria restricts irrationality and contributes to
justice. Yet, it cannot entirely eliminate unjust and
unreasonable content of a normative system.

The third limitation is the most important in practice.
It results from the necessary incompleteness ("open
texture") of all normative systems, regardless their
degree of coherence. A creation as well as an application
of a normative system makes it necessary to formulate
some new norm-statements and value-statements. This fact
is particularly important when the following steps are
concerned: the step from relatively general to relatively
special norms (4.1), the weighing and balancing of
principles (5.) and the creation of a reflective
equilibrium (6.3).

These limitations do not destroy the idea of a coherent
system of statements. However, they show that another
level is also important, that is, the procedural level,
in which persons and their acts of reasoning play the
decisive role. The idea of justification connects these
levels with each other. Justification requires two
things. Firstly, it requires the creation of an as
coherent system of statements as possible. Therefore, it
is true, perhaps even analytically true that if a norm-
or value-system in question is more coherent than any
competing system, then consensus about it would be prima
facie rational. Secondly, justification requires an as
rational procedure of argumentation as possible which
aims at a reasonable consensus. A theory of rational
discourse deals with this requirement. Coherence is a

property concerning statements only. On the other hand, discursive rationality concerns both relations between statements and between persons dealing with them. Discursive rationality thus comprises coherence and additional demands of procedural rationality, such as freedom from violence, equal respect etc.

A rational discourse results in a rational <u>consensus</u>. In this context, one may also express the following thesis about the link between coherence and consensus:

> If a norm- or value-system is more coherent than any competing system, then consensus about it is <u>prima facie</u> rational.

As regards rationality of <u>practical</u> reasoning, consensus has also an independent importance. Practical reasoning depends on weighing and balancing; the ultimate step consists in an act of will, cf. section 2.4.5 supra. For that reason, an individual may only guess, but can never be entirely sure of, the result of weighing and balancing performed by another individual. But one needs no guesses when other people tell one what conclusions their acts of weighing support (cf. Alexy 1988).

Rationality thus depends on both coherence and consensus. Briefly speaking, a legal view is rational, and in this sense correct, if it unanimously would be accepted by lawyers who support their conclusions with a highly coherent set of certain, presupposed, proved and/or otherwise reasonable premises.

This idea is very different from the primitive consensus theory, holding that the actual majority opinion is always right. What matters for rationality is not actual consensus but acceptability (cf. Aarnio 1987, 185 ff.) within the relevant group of people, that is, "audience" (cf. Aarnio 1987, 221 ff.), colleagues, peers etc. These persons accept p or at least agree that p is acceptable according to the standards they accept; p is acceptable to a person, A, if he finds it legitimate (or permitted) for another person, B, to accept and assert p even if A himself prefers not to accept and not to assert it. <u>Tranöy</u> (1980, 191 ff.) claims that one judges acceptability in view of <u>norms of inquiry</u>, and it is these which A and B actually accept. Let me add that the <u>principles of coherence</u> (see above) constitute the most important norms of inquiry. On the other hand, A can always ask himself <u>why</u> he should follow the accepted norms of inquiry, <u>inter alia</u> the principles of coherence, why he should follow the socially accepted sense of the

word "knowledge" etc. A´s total system of beliefs,
standpoints etc., and nothing else, ultimately determines
what are the yardsticks of acceptability with which A is
satisfied. B´s total system determines the yardsticks of
acceptability with which B is satisfied. One cannot "jump
out" of one´s system of beliefs etc.

In general, the relationship between coherence and
consensus is thus the following. The idea of coherence is
not sufficient to solve some epistemological problems. To
go deeper, one needs the idea of consensus. On the other
hand, the idea of consensus is not sufficient, either. To
go deeper, one needs the idea of coherence.

The role of consensus is also linked with the idea of form of life
(cf. section 3.3.4 supra). Systems of beliefs, values etc. of
different people often stand in the relation of causal
interdependence and relevant similarity as regards concepts,
accessible empirical data and endorsed values. When this requirement
is not fulfilled, "then each man declares the other as fool and
heretic. There can thus be some topics about which a maximal
discussion in A's system will lead to the conclusion p while in B's
system it would lead to the conclusion non-p. This rules out
rational discussion and rational consensus between A and B. A and B
belong to the same form of life if their system of beliefs,
standpoints, values etc. are in such a relation of causal
interdependence and relevant similarity that they can rationally
discuss about most of the relevant topics of their respective
lives. When A and B can rationally discuss about x (for instance,
physics) but not about y (for instance, justice), they belong to the
same aspect of the form of life as regards x, and to two different
aspects as regards y.

For such reasons, the theory of correct legal reasoning,
developed above, has a prepared place for Discursive
rationality, connected with the idea of consensus. It is
also connected with consensus in a more particular
manner: The idea of presupposed premises, which plays a
great role in the theory, is related to "culture under
consideration" and "legal paradigm", and thus to a kind
of consensus within the culture.

4.3.2. Robert Alexy´s Rules for Rational Practical Discourse

Robert Alexy has elaborated a well-known theory of rational practical discourse. A practical discourse concerns evaluative and normative questions. It is perfectly rational, if it follows some rationality rules he formulated. The more frequently these rules are violated, the less rational the discourse. Alexy´s rationality norms can be interpreted as guaranteeing that the outcome of the debate solely depends on reasons, that is, on coherence, not on violence or emotions. A perfect practical discourse is precisely the kind of discussion in which conclusions solely depend on coherence of reasons. A D-rational discourse must thus be S-rational.

Let me quote the rules in an abbreviate manner, and provide them with some comments.

The set of rules is divided into five classes. I am omitting some problems, concerning the basis of the classification.

1. The Basic Rules (Alexy 1989, 188 ff.)

(1.1) No speaker may contradict him or herself.

This rule expresses the demand of Logical rationality, cf. section 2.2.4 supra.

(1.2) Every speaker may only assert what he or she actually believes.

The following considerations, inter alia, justify this rule.

a) One may efficiently lie only if others believe one tells the truth. Without expectation of sincerity, not even a lie would make sense.

b) To be sure, a lie can constitute a rational action. It is thus rational to lie for dangerous enemies. But in a perfect discourse, there are no enemies. A lie is no correct reason. A discourse full of lies is not perfect as a discourse.

(1.3) Every speaker who applies a predicate F to an object a must be prepared to apply F to every other object which is like a in all relevant respects.

This rule expresses the idea of generality. As stated before, generality is a criterion of coherence; cf. section 4.1.4 supra.

A special case is this:

(1.3') Every speaker may assert only those value judgments or judgments of obligation in a given case which he or she is willing to assert in the same terms for every case which resembles the given case in all relevant respects.

(1.4) Different speakers should not use the same expression in different senses.

2. The Rationality Rules (Alexy 1989, 191 ff.)

(2) Every speaker must give reasons for what he or she asserts when asked to do so, unless he or she can cite reasons which justify a refusal to provide a justification.

This rule expresses the idea of S-rationality: In a perfectly rational debate, one's views are supported by reasons. Of course, this is the central idea of coherence; cf. section 4.1.2 supra.

This requirement supports, inter alia, the more and more frequent claims that judicial decisions should be provided with comprehensive justification, cf. section 6.5 infra.

(2.1) Everyone who can speak may take part in discourse.

A perfectly rational discourse is thus open for everybody. It thus fits the idea of universalisability. If anybody may discuss, the probability also increases that all relevant reasons are considered.

One may, of course, for some reasons, introduce some restrictions, e.g., only the parliament members may participate in parliamentary debates. But then, the debate is not perfectly rational.

(2.2) (a) Everyone may problematize any assertion. (b) Everyone may introduce any assertion into the discourse. (c) Everyone may express his or her attitudes, wishes and needs.

(2.3) No speaker may be prevented from exercising the rights laid down in (2.1) and (2.2) by any kind of coercion internal or external to the discourse.

The reason-rules (2) and (2.1)-(2.3) are connected with criterion 1 of coherence, since they result in introducing to the debate a maximal number of reasons; cf. section 4.1.3 supra. Moreover, these rules flow from the idea that violence is no reason. An optimally rational debate, by definition governed by reasons alone, must thus be free of violence.

One may, of course, find reasons to introduce some violence, e.g., in order to stop a terrorist propaganda. But then, the debate is not perfectly rational. No terrorists participate in a perfect debate.

3. Rules for Allocating the Burden of Argument (Alexy 1989, 195 ff.)

(3.1) Whoever proposes to treat a person A differently from a person B is obliged to provide justification for so doing.

(3.2) Whoever attacks a statement or norm which is not the subject of the discussion must state a reason for so doing.

(3.3) Whoever has put forward an argument is only obliged to produce further arguments in the event of counter-arguments.

(3.4) Whoever introduces an assertion... which does not stand as an argument in relation to prior utterance, must justify this interjection when required to do so.

The rule 3.1 expresses the idea of generality, and thus a criterion of coherence; cf. section 4.1.4 supra. All the rules of the burden of argumentation express S-rationality, i.e. the idea that the perfectly rational debate is entirely determined by reasons. One must thus give reasons for such moves as treating various persons differently, introducing new topics, demanding repeated argumentation etc. Let me state again that this is the central requirement of coherence. They also express criterion 1 of coherence, since they result in introducing to the debate a maximal number of reasons; cf. section 4.1.3 supra.

4. The Argument Forms (Alexy 1989, 197 ff.) are omitted here.

5. The Justification Rules (Alexy 1989, 202 ff.)

(5.1.1) Everyone who makes a normative statement that presupposes a rule with certain consequences for... other persons must be able to accept these consequences even in the hypothetical situation where he or she is in the position of those persons.
(5.1.2) The consequences of every rule for the satisfaction of interests of each and every individual must be acceptable to everyone.
(5.1.3) Every rule must be openly and universally teachable.
A perfectly rational debate is thus, by definition, entirely determined by reasons accessible to and testable by everybody.
The rules (5.1.1) - (5.1.3) express, again, the principle of generality and thus coherence.
(5.2.1) The moral rules underlying the moral views of a speaker must be able to withstand critical testing in terms of their historical genesis. A moral rule cannot stand up to such testing if: (a) even though originally amenable to rational justification, it has in the mean time lost its justification, or (b) it was not originally amenable to rational justification and no adequate new grounds have been discovered for it in the mean time.
(5.2.2) The moral rules underlying the moral views of a speaker must be able to withstand critical testing in terms of their individual genesis. A moral rule does not stand up to such testing if it has only been adopted on grounds of some unjustifiable conditions of socialization.
(5.3.) The actually given limits of realizability are to be taken into account.

6. The Transition Rules (Alexy 1989, 206.)

The perfectly rational discourse is determined by different kinds of reasons, practical, empirical and analytic (cf. section 3.3 supra). Consequently, the following rationality rules apply to it.
(6.1) It is possible for any speaker at any time to make a transition into a theoretical (empirical) discourse.
(6.2) It is possible for any speaker at any time to make a transition into a linguistic-analytical discourse.
(6.3) It is possible for any speaker at any time to make a transition into a discourse-theoretical discourse.
The rules (6.1) - (6.3) extend the scope of discourse and thus are connected with criteria 9 and 10 of coherence.

4.3.3. Robert Alexy´s Principles of Rationality

Alexy´s system of rationality rules is thus complex. Later, however, he has formulated the following six principles, underpinning the rules (Aarnio, Alexy and Peczenik 1981, 266 ff.)

1. The principle of consistency demands that statements uttered in a rational debate must be logically consistent (free of contradiction). This is, of course, a demand of L-rationality, cf. the rule (1.1). It is also a minimum requirement of coherence.

2. The principle of coherence requires that statements uttered in a rational debate must constitute a coherent system. I have already indicated the connections between several rules of practical rationality and coherence.

3. The principle of generality claims that, in a rational debate, the like must be treated alike. Generality is also a criterion of coherence. I have already mentioned its connection with several rules of rational discourse.

The following principles, 4 and 5, concern the relation between different participants in the discourse. But they have also some connection with coherence.

4. The principle of sincerity demands that one tells the truth {cf. rule (1.2)}. Understood broadly, it also claims that one does not use violence {cf. the rule (2.3)}.

This principle expresses the idea that a perfectly rational debate is entirely determined by reasons, and thus S-rationality. It also provides support (and hence coherence) between two levels: that of belief and that of speech.

5. The principle of testability demands that each speaker can test reasons, supporting views of other participants.

In this way, the principle is related to support, that is, to S-rationality, and hence to coherence.

6. The principle of goal-rationality (efficiency) in practical sphere has a special character. It comprises two requirements: efficiency of communication between people {cf. the rules (1.4), (2), (3.2)-(3.4) and indirectly (6.2)-(6.3)}, and efficient fulfilment of the goals, established in the debate {cf. the form (4.2)}.

Cf. the rules and forms (1.4), (5.1.3), and indirectly (4.1)-(4.3), (2)-(2.3), (3.1)-(3.2) and (3.4).

4.3.4. Robert Alexy´s Rules For Rational Legal Discourse

Alexy regards legal reasoning as a kind of practical reasoning because it answers practical questions, concerning what one should or may do (Alexy 1989, 16 and 212 ff.). He considers, however, legal reasoning as a special case, since its goal is not to show that a normative statement, e.g., a judicial decision, is absolutely reasonable, but only that it is reasonable within the framework of valid law. (See, however, section 5.4 infra on the relations between the law and morality).

At the same time, he points out that legal reasoning aims at rationality (cf. Alexy 1989, 214 ff.). Whoever performs legal reasoning, tries to give reasons supporting his conclusions. Everybody expects that legal conclusions are thus supported. The courts have an extensive duty to justify their decisions. Finally, such expressions as "the court hereby sentences A to ten years in prison, although no reasons support the decision" are strange, that is, constitute conceptual anomalies. Of course, all this contributes to coherence of legal reasoning.

Alexy elaborated the following forms and rules for the rational legal discourse.

1. Rules and forms of the so-called internal justification (cf. Alexy 1989, 221 ff.) are the following.

There are two forms of the internal legal justification, simple subsumption and chain subsumption. This problem may be omitted here. Let me merely refer to the examples already given in section 1.2.1 supra.

Alexy formulates the following rules for internal legal justification:

(J.2.1) At least one universal norm must be adduced in the justification of a legal judgment.

(J.2.2) A legal judgment must follow logically from at least one universal norm together with further statements.

(J.2.3) Whenever it is open to doubt whether a given rule covers the considered case, a rule must be put forward which settles this question.

(J.2.4) The number of decompositional steps required, is that number which makes possible the use of expressions whose application to a given case admits no further dispute.

These rules state precisely the idea that legal reasoning must be supported by general rules, and thus conform to a criterion of coherence (cf. section 4.1.5 supra).

2. Rules and forms of the so-called external justification (cf. Alexy 1989, 230 ff.) concern questions of evidence and interpretation.

Alexy assumes that some rationality rules may govern questions of evidence but he does not formulate such rules.

Alexy's forms of interpretation are the following.

At first, he correctly points out that semantical reasons may support the conclusion that one must (J.3.1), must not (J.3.2) or may (J.3.3) accept a given interpretation. Then, he deals with "genetic" interpretation in the light of the intention of the "historical" lawgiver (J.4.1 and J.4.2). Finally, he discusses

"teleological" interpretation which helps one to establish the
purpose of the rule objectively, independently of the intention of
the "historical" lawgiver (J.5).

Alexy assumes that some reasoning forms govern historical,
comparative and systematical interpretation but he does not
formulate such forms. However, he formulates the following
rationality rules for the optimal legal interpretation.

(J.6) Saturation - that is a full statement of reasons - is
required in every argument which belongs among the canons of
interpretation.

(J.7) Arguments which give expression to a link with the actual
words of the law, or the will of the historical legislator take
precedence over other arguments, unless rational grounds can be
cited for granting precedence to the other arguments.

One can perhaps doubt universal validity of this rationality rule.
Some legal scholars, inter alia Per Olof Ekelöf, propose
interpretation methods incompatible with it, cf. section 7.4 infra.
Although these methods are controversial, one cannot simply label
them as irrational.

(J.8) Determinations of the relative weight of arguments different
in form must conform to weighing rules.

(J.9) Every possibly proposable argument of such a form that it
can be counted as one of the canons of interpretation must be given
due consideration.

Rules (J.6), (J.8) and (J.9) have a relation to the criteria of
coherence, discussed in the section 4.1.4 supra.

Alexy's rationality rules for the optimal reasoning in legal
dogmatics are, what follows.

(J.10) Every dogmatic proposition must be justified by recourse to
at least one general practical argument whenever it is subjected to
doubt.

(J.11) Every dogmatic proposition must be able to stand up to a
systematic testing...

In this testing, one checks whether the proposition is logically
compatible with and justifiable by other statements of legal
dogmatics.

This test is, of course, a test of coherence.

(J.12) Whenever dogmatic arguments are possible they should be
used.

This is also a special case of a criterion of coherence, that is,
the criterion requiring a great number of justified statements; cf.
section 4.1.4 supra.

Alexy formulates also the following rationality rules for
interpretation of precedents.

(J.13) If a precedent can be cited in favour or against a decision
it should be so cited.

(J.14) Whoever wishes to depart from a precedent carries the
burden of argument.

These rules are, again, connected with the criterion of coherence
which requires a great number of justified statements; cf. section
4.1.4 supra.

Alexy's system includes also two, especially legal, argument forms (J.15 and J.16), constituting logically correct components of the arguments e contrario and ex analogia (see section 7.4 infra).

Finally, Alexy formulates the following rationality rule.

(J.18) Special legal argument forms must have the reasons for them stated in full - that is, must achieve saturation.

This rule, too, is connected with the criterion of coherence which requires a great number of justified statements; cf. section 4.1.4 supra.

4.4. WHY SHALL LEGAL REASONING BE RATIONAL?

4.4.1. Introduction. Why Shall Theoretical Propositions Be Consistent and Highly Coherent?

Let me now turn to normative problems concerning rationality. Why should legal reasoning be rational? I will discuss the question in two steps, corresponding to the two components of legal reasoning, theoretical propositions and practical statements.

Let me start from some more or less established theses concerning rationality of theoretical propositions.

1) Why should theoretical propositions be Logically rational? In particular, why should theoretical propositions formulated within the legal reasoning, e.g. propositions about the literal sense of a statute, constitute a logically consistent set, that is, a set of propositions free from logical contradictions? If a set of theoretical propositions does not fulfil the demands of L-rationality, in particular the demand of logical consistency, then it cannot be true. There is only one world. If p constitutes an accurate description of a given part of the world, non-p cannot do it. The words "non-", "not" and other negation words have a meaning which excludes simultaneous truth of p and non-p.

The following technical norm corresponds to these analytic remarks. If one intends to use the negation words in accordance with their actual meaning, one must not utter theoretical propositions violating the demands of L-rationality.

2) Why should theoretical propositions be Supportively rational? In particular, why should theoretical propositions formulated within the legal reasoning, e.g. propositions about the literal sense of a statute, belong to a highly coherent set of statements? These answer has already been formulated in the section 4.2 supra: Ceteris paribus, the more coherent a theory, the greater amount of true information it gives and the closer it comes to true information.

If one wishes to approximate truth, one must have a disposition to formulate coherent sets of theoretical propositions.

This use of the concept of "disposition" is affected by a lecture
Horacio M. Spector gave in Buenos Aires in August 1984, let it be
that he dealt with a different problem.

Moreover, "to argue" means to give reasons supporting the
conclusion. If one wishes to argue, one must have a disposition to
support theoretical propositions one utters with reasons. Such a
support is the first criterion of coherence.

4.4.2. Why Shall Practical Statements Be Logically Consistent?

The problems are more complex in connection with
practical statements. Why should practical statements be
L-rational? In particular, why should value statements
and norm-statements formulated within the legal
reasoning, e.g. "The Liability for Damages Act is a good
law" or "One ought to follow the Liability for Damages
Act", constitute a logically consistent set?

Such a value statement has both a practical and a
theoretical meaning. Its theoretical meaning consists,
inter alia, of the fact that some theoretical
propositions are prima facie reasons for the conclusion
that, e.g., "the Liability for Damages Act is a good
law". The demand of L-rationality is certainly
justifiable if the same reason is chosen in connection
with a value statement and its negation. One should not
simultaneously say "The Liability for Damages Act is a
good law" and "The Liability for Damages Act is not a
good law", if one actually means "The Liability for
Damages Act is a good law, since it prevents damage of
the the type T" and "The Liability for Damages Act is not
a good law, since it does not prevent damage of the the
type T". In such a case, one would utter inconsistent
theoretical propositions, and I have already argued for
the conclusion that one should not do it.

The situation is more complex when one simultaneously
says "The Liability for Damages Act is a good law" and
"The Liability for Damages Act is not a good law", and
means "good in one respect, not good in another", e.g.
"The Liability for Damages Act is a good law, since it
increases security of the persons suffering damage of the
type T" and "The Liability for Damages Act is not a good
law, since it does not prevent damage of the the type T".
As stated in section 2.3.3 supra, the problem is actual
only as regards all-things-considered practical

statements, not _prima-facie_ practical statements. Logically incompatible actions can thus be, at the same time, _prima facie_ good. One can also simultaneously have a _prima facie_ duty to perform logically incompatible actions. The "normal" logic is thus not applicable to moral _prima-facie_ statements. Suppose, e.g., that A killed B. One _prima-facie_ reason, for instance circumstances of his act, can justify a life imprisonment of A, another, for instance A´s psychical condition, can support a milder penalty.

One can then argue, as follows. Assume that a given person, A, sincerely utters the following statement: "x is all-things-considered good and x is all-things-considered not good". Or assume that he sincerely utters the statement "B ought all-things-considered to do H and B ought all-things-considered not to do H". Formal logic expresses the meaning of propositional connectives such as "not", "if... then" or "and". Such connectives are applicable not only in the theoretical but also in the practical context. The words "not", "if... then" , "and" etc. have such a meaning that a conceptual anomaly occurs if one accepts both an all-things-considered value statement and its negation, or if one accepts an all-things-considered value statement but does not accept its logical consequences (cf., e.g., Weinberger and Weinberger 1979, 96 ff.). In brief, formal logic is applicable to all-things-considered practical statements. Consequently, if one does not wish to create a conceptual anomaly, one should not sincerely utter value statements that violate the demands of L-rationality.

But _is_ formal logic applicable to all-things-considered practical statements? Perhaps the meaning of the words "good" and "ought" is such that the logical words "not", "or" etc. mean something else in connection with them as in the theoretical context? Though strange, this view deserves some discussion. Let me thus say something about the relation between the meaning of "ought" and "good" with the meaning of logical connectives.

As stated above (cf. section 2.2.1 supra), norm-expressive statements qualify human actions, events etc. as prescribed, permitted, forbidden etc. I disregard here more complex types of normative qualification. The statement "A should not park his car here" thus qualifies A´s action of "parking the car here" as prohibited. One can regard normative qualification as, so to say, inverted truth. A theoretical proposition, p, is true if and only if p describes the facts in a given way, and the

facts are such as p describes them. Consequently, a
theoretical proposition is false if it does not
correspond to the facts.

In the present context, I disregard the relation between facts and
"truth-makers", cf. section 4.2.4 supra.

The relation between a norm-expressive statement and
actions, events etc. it qualifies is reverse. The
norm-expressive statements are not qualified as true or
false. On the contrary, a norm-expressive statement
qualifies some actions, events etc., e.g. as conforming
to or violating the norm in question. Now, one may
perhaps use this qualification as a foundation of a logic
of norms. Assume, for example, that the meaning of two
norm-expressive statements, n_1 and n_2, is such that each
action etc. qualified in a given way by n_2 is qualified
in the same way by n_1. It is then plausible to assume
that n_1 entails n_2 (cf. Peczenik 1967, 133; 1968, 119 and
1969, 46 ff.; = 1970 pp. 31, 11 and 60 ff).
  In a similar manner, one may generally define the
logical connective "if... then" in the realm of norms.
Then, one may also define other logical connectives, such
as "not", "and" etc., in a manner importantly analogous
to corresponding definitions in the realm of theoretical
propositions.

However, analogy is limited. In the realm of theoretical
propositions, only one kind of qualification is relevant for
entailment: propositions are qualified as true or false. A
theoretical proposition, p, entails another one, q, if these
propositions are qualified by truth-makers in such a way that p
cannot be true and q simultaneously false. In the realm of
norm-expressive statements, on the other hand, two kinds of
qualification are relevant. One compares the actions etc. p
qualifies as prescribed etc. with those q thus qualifies; but the
purpose of this comparison is to establish such a relation between p
and q that if p **is qualified** as valid, correct, right etc., then q
is thus qualified.

A further important reason against the anti-logical view
of "ought" allows for a moral duty to do the logically
impossible, for example "B ought to do H and B ought not
to do H". The postulate "No one has an
all-things-considered (not only prima-facie) duty to do
what is impossible" is in such a way linked to the idea

of "moral ought" that it is conceptually strange, anomalous, to sincerely claim that B ought all-things-considered to do H and yet ought all-things-considered not to do H.

If one does not wish to create a conceptual anomaly, one should not assume views whose consequence is that one has an all-things-considered duty to do the impossible.

To be sure, one can conceive a moral or legal predicament. Assume that B sold his dog to C and then to D. He ought to give C the dog, and yet he ought not to give it to C (but to D). Whatever he does, he violates his moral duty. But this moral duty is a merely a prima-facie one. B must now weigh and balance his prima-facie duties and achieve the final conclusion whether or not he, all things considered, ought to give C the dog. A moral philosopher who thinks that such predicaments are definitive, not merely prima-facie, simply does not share my view that moral thinking is intimately connected with weighing and balancing. An established legal rule, for example a statutory provision, can also demanding of one to do the impossible. But this demand is only a prima-facie legal duty. The corresponding all-things-considered duty is a result of weighing and balancing the contradictory demands posed by the law.

Another reason against the anti-logical view of "ought" and "good" is the link between these words and wants, goals and intentions. If a given person, A, sincerely claims that x is all-things-considered good, then he has a disposition to want definitively (not only prima facie) that x exists (unless something else, incompatible with x, is even better). If A then sincerely claims that x is good and, at the same time, sincerely claims that x is not good, then he has at the same time a disposition to definitively want that the mutually contradictory propositions "x exists" and "x does not exist" be true. But these propositions cannot be simultaneously true (cf., e.g., Moritz 1954, 95 ff.; Alchourrón and Bulygin 1981, 106 ff.); this is the case because of the meaning of logical connectives such as "not". The incompatible goals cannot be simultaneously fulfilled. Consequently, it is an anomaly to utter logically incompatible (mutually contradictory) definitive and, consequently, all-things-considered (not only prima facie) value statements.

I assume here that the concepts "to want" "to intend" and the like have a reasonable interpretation in which they mean "to definitively want", "to definitively

intend" etc. Then, the following is true: if a person
knows that something is impossible, then it is anomaly
for this person to definitively want it.

But another interpretation is also reasonable, in which such words
merely mean "to prima-facie intent" etc. So is the case especially
if one uses such words as "to wish", instead of "to want"; e.g. "I
wish I were more intelligent than Albert Einstein, although I know
it is impossible". This statement expresses a prima-facie wish, not
a definitive one.

If one does not wish to create a conceptual anomaly, one
should not sincerely utter value statements that violate
the demands of L-rationality.

4.4.3. Why Shall Practical Statements Be Highly Coherent? Some Conceptual Reasons

Why should practical statements be S-rational? In
particular, why should value statements and
norm-statements formulated within the legal reasoning,
e.g. "The Liability for Damages Act is a good law" or
"One ought to follow the Liability for Damages Act",
belong to a highly coherent set of statements?
   One answer to this question is based on some properties
of language and thus resembles a "definitional
justification" in Alexy´s sense, cf. section 4.4.4 infra.
   1. The fact that one can arrange one´s norm- and
value-statements concerning a certain practical problem
into a coherent whole means that one can think about this
problem in an intensive and extensive way. As stated in
section 4.2.1 supra, one could try to explicate the very
concept of rational thinking as an effort to obtain a
balance between various criteria of coherence. If one
intends to think about practical matters, one should have
a disposition to arrange one´s practical opinions into a
coherent system.
   2. At the same time, that there is a correspondence
between coherent thinking and correctness, see section
4.2.1 supra: It is difficult to doubt that a judgment
which is supported by argument is better in what concerns
rationality and correctness than a judgment which has no
such support. If one intends to correctly think about

practical matters, one should have a disposition to arrange one´s practical opinions into a coherent system.

3. Let me now elucidate the connection of S-rationality of practical statements with support as the first criterion of coherence. Why should one support practical statements with reasons? If one does not wish to create a conceptual anomaly concerning the concept of "arguing", one should have a disposition to argue S-rationally, that is, only by proffering reasons supporting one´s conclusion. An important property of the meaning of most, if not all, practical statements is that they may be justified. One can meaningfully argue for them, and "to argue" means to give reasons supporting the conclusion. The language is thus adapted to the practice of supporting practical statements by reasons. Consequently, it is an anomaly to sincerely utter legal or moral value-statements or norms and yet refuse to argue for them. For example, it would be strange to say "A is liable for damage in question although no reasons support the conclusion that he is liable". One may also consider the following example. Assume that a political leader, Adolf, thinks that killing Jews is a good action. One asks him repeatedly for reasons for this judgment and gets none except "I know that it is so" and "Your question shows that the Jews already have corrupted you". One may now say that Adolf uses the word "good" in a strange sense, perhaps different from the sense this word has to rational people.

4. Another argument concerns weighing and balancing. We all assume that an act of weighing and balancing can be right or wrong. It is right only if justifiable by further reasons. It would be strange to say "x weighs more than y although no reasons support the conclusion that x weighs more than y". If one does not wish to create a conceptual anomaly concerning the concept of "weighing", one should have a disposition to proffer reasons supporting one´s acts of weighing and balancing. The only exception is the final, ultimate act of weighing; see section 2.4.4.

5. Passing to universalisability (that is, another criterion of coherence), one may state the following. Universalisability of a statement is the same as the fact that it follows from a universal statement, the latter concerning all members of a certain kind. Morality requires that the like should be treated alike. A judgement that two persons ought to be treated differently is thus no moral one, unless it can be completed with a set of reasonable premises pointing out

relevant differences between them. In legal reasoning, universalisability implies that similar cases should be solved in a similar way.

A conceptual anomaly would thus occur if one seriously uttered a moral or legal value statement, and yet claimed that no universal principle supports this view. It would be strange to say: "Peter and John are similar in all respects, yet they ought to be treated differently".

If one does not wish to create a conceptual anomaly, one should have a disposition to support moral and legal practical statements with universalisable reasons.

4.4.4. Some Conceptual Reasons For Rationality of a Practical Discourse

One must also ask the question why to follow Alexy´s rules of rational practical discourse. To justify his theory, Alexy introduced four mutually combined methods of justification, technical, definitional, empirical and universal-pragmatic. Let me, at first, discuss the definitional justification. This form of justification can be described, as follows. Firstly, one presents the system of rules of rational practical discourse. Secondly, one hopes that the presentation of this system will "constitute a reason or motive for its acceptance, regardless of whether or not any further reasons are given" (Alexy 1989, 184).

Let me further elucidate this mode of justification. What does "rational discourse" mean? The answer is given in terms of Alexy´s rationality rules. To "argue" in a manner violating D-rationality, for example by using lies, random changes of the sense of words, violence, and so on, means that one "argues" by other means as reasons. This means that one does not argue at all. If one then intends to argue, that is, to utter a highly coherent, S-rational cluster of statements, one should have a disposition to follow the rules of D-rationality.

4.4.5. Why Shall Practical Statements Uttered Within Legal Reasoning Be Rational? Some Conceptual Reasons

Legal reasoning is a chain of arguments consisting of theoretical and practical statements. It thus consists, inter alia, of the following components:

1) theoretical statements about the literal sense of socially established norms (a) contained in such sources of the law as statutes, precedents, etc., and (b) embodied in the tradition of legal reasoning;

2) (moral) value- and norm-statements, endorsed by the person who performs the reasoning, stating precisely what is a right interpretation of the socially established norms and how one ought to interpret these norms.

The theoretical part of legal reasoning should be rational for the same reasons as other theoretical propositions. The practical part of legal reasoning should be rational for the same reasons as moral statements. In particular, practical statements belonging to legal reasoning are related to rationality for the following conceptual reason. It is a conceptual anomaly to sincerely express a legal opinion, and yet not to have a disposition to support it by legal reasons. Practical statements in the law are justifiable. As already stated, in section 2.2.3 supra, justifiability implies that a person confronted with a practical statement can ask "why?" and thus demand reasons which support the statement. The statement "B ought legally to pay income tax, though no legal reasons exist for his paying income tax" is thus strange. It is also strange not to intend to make the reasons as coherent as possible. If one does not wish to create a conceptual anomaly, one must have a disposition to support one's legal opinions by highly coherent reasons, that is, by S-rational thinking.

But there also exist some special reasons for rationality of legal reasoning. One of them concerns the concept "valid law". This concept refers not only to the socially established law but also to the interpreted law. For example, many Swedish norms concerning causation in torts are commonly recognised as valid law, albeit they exist merely in some influential textbooks, whose purpose is to creatively interpret statutes and precedents, not merely to describe their literal content; cf. section 5.5.7 infra. This interpretation is commonly expected to be rational. The expression "this interpretation of a statute is valid law, yet it is not rational" is strange and thus constitutes a conceptual anomaly. If one does not wish to create a conceptual anomaly, one must have a

disposition to regard a result of a legal interpretation
as valid law only if this interpretation is rational.

4.4.6. The Concepts and Life

In sections 4.4.2 - 4.4.5, I thus have formulated, inter
alia, the following "technical norms", stating necessary
means for assumed purposes.
  1) Concerning L-rationality: If one does not wish to
create a conceptual anomaly, one should not sincerely
utter value statements that violate the demands of
Logical rationality. In particular: If one does not wish
to create a conceptual anomaly, one should not assume
views whose consequence is that one has an
all-things-considered duty to do the impossible.
  2) Concerning S-rationality: If one intends to think at
all about practical matters, one should have a
disposition to arrange one´s practical opinions into a
coherent system. If one intends to correctly think about
practical matters, one should have a disposition to
arrange one´s practical opinions into a coherent system.
If one does not wish to create a conceptual anomaly
concerning the concept of "arguing", one should have a
disposition to argue S-rationally, that is, only by
proffering reasons supporting one´s conclusion. If one
does not wish to create a conceptual anomaly concerning
the concept of "weighing", one should have a disposition
to proffer reasons supporting one´s acts of weighing. If
one does not wish to create a conceptual anomaly, one
should have a disposition to support moral and legal
practical statements with universalisable reasons.
  3) Concerning S- and D-rationality: If one intends to
argue, that is, to utter a Supportively rational cluster
of statements, one should have a disposition to follow
the rules of Discursive rationality.
  4) Concerning rationality of legal reasoning: If one
does not wish to create a conceptual anomaly (concerning
the concept "valid law"), one should have a disposition
to regard a result of a legal interpretation as valid law
only if this interpretation is rational.
  The basis of these technical norms consists of some
concepts, such as "value statement", "moral reasons",
"legal duty", "weighing", "arguing", "valid law", "legal
interpretation" etc. But cannot our concepts be
misleading? Should one not rather change the concepts in

order to separate them from the difficult, vague and
controversial demands of rationality? In fact, members of
such philosophical movements as the Uppsala school did
precisely that. For example, they defined value
statements as a pure expression of feelings. In this
context, let me make the following brief comments.

A radical change of some concepts would change our life
in a manner difficult to imagine. In this context, one
may speak about "a form of life" (cf. section 3.3.4
supra). The form of life is our picture of the world
expressed in our everyday actions and concepts. Many
actions would be incomprehensible had one not at least a
vague idea of some legal concepts. One, e.g., "buys" food
in a shop "owned" by a "company" and "pays" with "money".

But would the form of life change radically had we
abandoned the discussed, quite abstract, moral and legal
concepts, such as "weighing", "valid law", "legal
interpretation" etc.? One can present the following
hypothesis. If these concepts were abandoned, rational
discourse of legal and moral problems would be
impossible. This would in particular be the case, if the
idea of moral duty were changed so that the statements
such as "B ought (all things considered) to do H and yet
B ought not (all things considered) do H" no longer
constituted a conceptual anomaly. This would also happen
if moral and legal concepts acquired a new meaning, no
longer presupposing any possibility of justification of
moral value-statements and normative statements.

In consequence, fatal chaos would occur. This applies
particularly to the _legal_ concepts, because of the
connection between the law and organised force. Political
life would thus be dominated by manipulators who would
directly affect emotions of people. (Imagine a mob at a
football ground shouting "one people, one state, one
leader". Or consider political songs as a means to win
elections.) The lawyers, emotionally unstable and
susceptible to irrational manipulation, would arouse
common contempt. One could win legal disputes only by
being most pleasant to the judge and sharing his
opinions, tastes and prejudices. At the end, no one would
trust anybody. People would be isolated form each other.
Our culture, our form of life, would change radically.

If one does not with to create a radical change of our
form of life, one should have a disposition to avoid
anomalies concerning practical, especially legal,
concepts. Indeed, if the meaning of these concept no
longer were related to reason, one had to create new
concepts, practical and yet thus related. Since these

concepts presuppose rationality, legal reasoning should
be rational.

4.4.7. Why Shall Practical Statements Be Highly Coherent? Some Empirical And Technical Reasons

In addition to conceptual reasons for S-rationality, that
is, a high degree of coherence, of practical statements,
one may also state the following empirical and technical
reasons.

1) People often arrange practical statements in
coherent systems; in particular, everybody often supports
practical statements with reasons. To be sure, one can
emotionally reject a set of norms and/or value statements
highly fulfilling the criteria of coherence. But most
human beings have a disposition to endorse coherent
systems. I omit the question whether this disposition is
determined genetically or merely socially. In the first
case, human nature is perhaps rational. In the second
case, one can at least say that modern people have a
disposition to think rationally, that is, coherently. In
both cases, one may explain this disposition by
biological and/or social evolution.

Can everybody be wrong? This justification by recourse
to a common practice constitutes a kind of empirical
justification in Alexy's sense (cf. 1989, 182 ff.).

2) One can also present a technical, (teleological,
goal-oriented) justification in Alexy's sense (cf. 1989,
181-2). To arrange practical statements in a coherent
system is thus important for the following reasons.

a) Coherence makes our opinions stable. First of all,
the very concept of coherence implies that, ceteris
paribus, the most coherent theory available in a given
situation is the most stable one. At least two criteria
of coherence include a temporal dimension, broadness of
scope covered by the theory in question and generality of
concepts. Ceteris paribus, general concepts are
applicable to a class of situations invariable in time,
or at least extending for a long period. Another
connection between coherence and stability is this.
Ceteris paribus, a more coherent norm- or value-system
contains a greater number of statements and connections
between them. This makes the hypothesis plausible that it
is more difficult for an individual to reject such a

system than to reject an isolated statement. Increased coherence thus causes an increased stability.

If one intends to make one´s practical opinions stable, one should have a disposition to arrange one´s practical opinions into a coherent system.

b) Various individuals can then compare their systems and state precisely how much these resemble each other. A comprehensive resemblance of whole systems tends to endure longer than a similarity concerning a single practical statement. If one intends to create stable consensus concerning practical matters, one should have a disposition to arrange one´s practical opinions into a coherent system.

One may assume that the pursue of stable consensus is the point of practical reasoning. We aim at constructing normative systems and value systems which others may endorse during a long period. If the reasoning, on the other hand, shows that the value systems of various individuals are different, the persons in question gain a better knowledge about what they disagree. This facilitates the use of various consensus-generating procedures, such as voting.

c) Moreover, a stable consensus facilitates achievement of such goals as efficient organisation, minimisation of violence and, ultimately, survival of the species.

In a chaotic crowd of people, where consensus appears and disappears in an unexplainable manner, one would never know how others react to one´s action. Such a crowd would never constitute a community complex enough to create and maintain a civilisation. In an extreme case, it would not be able to survive. Practical reasoning, on the other hand, makes a stable consensus within a community likely, and thus promotes survival of mankind. Assuming that survival of people in general, or at least survival of our modern culture is a good thing, one may also justify coherence of practical theories as a condition of survival.

If one intends to increase the chance of survival of mankind, one should have a disposition to arrange one´s practical opinions into a coherent system.

4.4.8. Why Should a Discourse be Rational? Empirical, Technical and Universally-Pragmatic Reasons

In addition to conceptual reasons for D-rationality, one may point out some empirical, technical and universal-pragmatic reasons.
1. The theory of rational discourse based on Alexy´s rules may be checked empirically, by showing that people often act as if they had applied these rules.

I disregard here some problems, e.g., does the widespread practice of "arguing" by irrational means, e.g., populist manipulations in politics, weaken the empirical justification?

2. One may also argue ("technically") that by using this kind of rationality, people can survive and often achieve such goals as efficient organisation, minimisation of violence, some forms of justice, and so on.
3. Finally, one may point out that rationality rules are necessary conditions for knowledge, understanding and intersubjective communication. This is the "transcendental" or "universal-pragmatic" justification (cf. Alexy 1989, 185-6). Since knowledge, understanding and communication are here assumed as goals, and rationality rules are treated as means, this mode of justification is a special case of the "technical" one.
The universal-pragmatic justification is particularly important. Let me thus make some further remark related to it.
Why shall theoretical propositions be D-rational? If a set of such propositions fulfils the demands of D-rationality, it probably has a better chance to approximate truth than a set of propositions which does not fulfil these demands would have. The closer a discourse comes to such ideals as sincerity, uniform use of words, openness, non-violence, testability, impartiality etc., the greater is the chance that the discourse generates true knowledge. (Such a hypothesis is also the core of a rationalist version of the theory of consensus as a criterion of truth, cf. section 4.2.2). If one wishes to approximate truth, one should have a disposition to obey the demands of D-rationality.
Why should practical statements also be D-rational? In particular, why should one submit value statements and norm-statements formulated within the legal reasoning, e.g. "The Liability for Damages Act is a good law" or

"One ought to follow the Liability for Damages Act", a discourse following Alexy´s rationality rules? The closer a discourse comes to the ideals of sincerity, uniform use of words, openness, non-violence, intersubjective testability, impartiality etc., the greater is the chance that the discourse generates efficient communication and stable consensus of people, and thus increases the chance of survival of the society etc.; cf. section 4.4.7 supra.

4.4.9. Why Should Practical Statements Uttered Within Legal Reasoning be Rational? Some Further Reasons

In addition to the conceptual reasons for rationality of legal statements, one may state the following.

An important reason for rationality consists in the following connection between rationality and legal certainty. People expect in general that legal decisions fulfil the demands of legal certainty, that is, are highly predictable and, at the same time, highly acceptable from the point of view of other moral considerations (cf. section 1.4.1 supra). S-rationality of legal decisions is a necessary condition for existence of a high degree of legal certainty.

a) If legal reasoning had not highly fulfilled the demands of rationality, its results would be unpredictable. Rational reasoning based on relatively fixed rules makes legal reasoning relatively more certain, more predictable than the moral one.

One can thus present a legal conclusion as logically following from a set of consistent, linguistically correct and reasonable premises. In legal reasoning, one also has access to a more extensive set of premises, such as statutes, other sources of the law and reasoning norms; cf. Section 3.1.1 and 3.1.5 supra. These premises can be characterised as certain, presupposed, proved or otherwise reasonable; cf. Section 3.3 supra. A rational discourse about legal problems further increases predictability of juristic conclusions.

b) If legal reasoning had not highly fulfilled the demands of rationality, its results would be arbitrary and thus unacceptable from the moral point of view. Moral acceptability would be out of question if the lawyers had no disposition at all to fulfil demands of S-rationality, that is, to support their conclusions by highly coherent reasons.

Legal interpretatory statements are not true in the literal sense. But they can fulfil to a high degree the requirements of _L_ogical, _S_upportive and _D_iscursive rationality. They thus can be both <u>coherent</u> and <u>acceptable</u> in the light of both morality and the legal paradigm. Consequently, they can fulfil important criteria of <u>truth</u>, coherence and consensus. For that reason, L-, S-, and D-rationality are indications of their <u>correctness</u>.

To be sure, one may emotionally reject a set of value statements which to a high degree fulfils demands of coherence and consensus. But at the present state of development of human societies, most people have a disposition to endorse a coherent and commonly accepted value system. In this broad sense, the human <u>nature</u> is rational.

But if human nature had been more servile than rational, the obligation to obey the law would be better justifiable by reference to commands, of God or the authorities.

CHAPTER 5
WHAT IS VALID LAW?

5.1. WHAT IS VALID LAW? - INTRODUCTORY REMARKS

5.1.1. Starting Point: Rationality and Fixity

We are now prepared to discuss the classical question, What is valid law? As a starting point, let me make an abbreviated restatement of theses defended in the preceding chapters.

1. Most human beings actually have a disposition to endorse coherent systems and to act as if they had intended to approximate a perfectly rational discourse.

2. An analysis of some moral and theoretical concepts justifies the conclusion that if one intends to correctly think about practical matters, one should have a disposition to arrange one's practical opinions into a coherent system and to follow the rules of discursive rationality. If the concepts were abandoned, rational discourse of legal and moral problems would be impossible. In consequence, our form of life would change radically.

3. Coherence makes our opinions stable. The hypothesis is plausible that it is more difficult for an individual to reject a highly coherent system than an isolated statement. If one intends to make one's practical opinions stable, one should have a disposition to arrange them into a coherent system.

4. If one intends to create stable consensus concerning practical matters, one should have a disposition to arrange one's practical opinions into a coherent system and to follow the rules of rational discourse.

5. A stable consensus facilitates achievement of such goals as efficient organisation, minimisation of violence and, ultimately, survival of the species. If one intends to increase the chance of survival of mankind, one should have a disposition to arrange one's practical opinions into a coherent system and to follow the rules of rational discourse.

All this is applicable not only to purely moral but also to legal reasoning. Not only the former but also the latter should be highly coherent and discursively

rational. In consequence, it is plausible that the very
concept of valid law should contribute to coherence and
discursive rationality of the law.

Moreover, analysis of the concept of valid law
justifies the conclusion that if one does not wish to
create a conceptual anomaly, one should have a
disposition to regard a result of a legal interpretation
as valid law only if this interpretation is rational.

Finally, people expect in general that legal decisions
are highly predictable and, at the same time, highly
acceptable from the point of view of other moral
considerations. If legal reasoning had not fulfilled the
demands of coherence and discursive rationality, its
results would be unacceptable from the moral point of
view; in particular, they would be unpredictable.
Predictability is more important in legal reasoning than
in a purely moral reasoning. To assure predictability,
the law itself must be relatively stable, fixed.

In brief, one needs a theory of legal validity and the
concept "valid law" which simultaneously fit two
postulates: rationality of legal reasoning and fixity of
the law.

5.1.2. The Purpose of Our Theory of Valid Law

A purely reportive (analytic, lexical) definition of
valid law would faithfully describe the use of this term
in the legal language. A stipulative definition would
prescribe a new use of the term, without any attention to
the established language. Our theory of valid law is
neither fully descriptive nor arbitrarily prescriptive
but reconciles description and prescription. It thus
reconciles the following demands (cf. Peczenik 1966, 13
ff.)

 1. It should be logically consistent.
 2. It should establish a fixed sense of "valid law" and
stick to it in various contexts.

The ordinary language of lawyers does not fulfil these demands. One
utters apparently incompatible theses about valid law. For example,
one sometimes regards statutory norms as legally valid if, and only
if, they were enacted in the correct way, regardless whether the
courts are actually applying them or not. Sometimes one regards the
judicial application of the norms as the necessary and sufficient

condition of their validity, regardless whether they were enacted correctly or not. At best, one must conclude that the lawyers use the term "valid law" in different, mutually inconsistent senses, each one internally consistent (cf. Wedberg 1951, 257 - no reasonably exact definition of legal system can be formulated; cf. Jörgensen 1970, 6 ff.

3. Provided that the demands 1 and 2 are fulfilled, our theory of valid law should identify as legally valid all and only the phenomena ordinarily enumerated as valid law.

"Ordinarily" refers either to ordinary language or to its specialised branch - legal terminology. Consequently, our theory of "valid law" will be better adapted to juristic discourse than, for instance, to empirical sociology.

4. Provided that the demands 1 and 2 are fulfilled, our theory of valid law should also regard as essential to the concept "valid law" all and only the properties
   a) common for all or almost all legally valid norms; and
   b) ordinarily regarded as essential.

Our theory is not merely concerned with the words "law", "valid law", "legal", etc. I will rather arrange the use of many words in a way showing what we in our culture regard as important properties of all or nearly all systems of valid law.

5. Provided that the demands 1 and 2 are fulfilled, our theory should, finally, contribute to the optimal weighing and balancing of two postulates, the first demanding that legal reasoning should be as coherent and discursively rational as possible, the second requiring that the law should be as fixed as possible.

The theory is not value-free, since it presupposes "an evaluative judgment about the relative importance of various features" of the law (cf. Raz 1982, 124). It thus goes beyond the "linguistic approach", as it must do, since the law theorists are no lexicographers and "should be concerned with explaining law within the wider context of social and political institutions"; cf. Raz 1982, 107 ff. and 122-3.

5.1.3. Normative Character of the Concept "Valid Law"

Although lawyers can easily give examples of valid law,
they face problems when attempting to define the concept.
The main cause of the difficulties is vagueness of the
concept "valid law", particularly its value-openness. The
concept of valid law has not only the theoretical
meaning, expressed in various criteria for making a
distinction between legal and non-legal norms, but also a
practical meaning, that is, a normative aspect. To say
that a norm is valid means that it ought to be observed.

Cf. Lang 1962, 112 ff. and 128 ff.; Olivecrona 1971, 112 and von
Wright 1963b, 196. Ofstad 1980, 166-8, made several distinction: a
norm is valid, if it (a) ideally viewed, ought to be accepted, or
(b) is generally accepted, or (c) is acceptable, or (d) is supported
by good reasons, etc.

An idea of valid norm that ought not to be observed is
like a "married bachelor" or a "square circle", that is,
inconsistent and self-destroying (cf. Marantz 1979). In
consequence, one often attempts to answer two different
questions simultaneously, What is valid law?, and Why
ought one to obey the law?. The first concerns a
definition of valid law, the second its deep
justification. The first presupposes some ontology, that
is a theory of what is real. I am thus going to use the
term "the question of definition and existence".
    The second question requires a clarification. The
"valid" law is considered as "binding" but it is
difficult state precisely what the latter concept means
either. What does it mean that a norm, N, is binding,
that is, ought to be observed? It cannot mean anything
but the fact that another norm, a "super-norm", says that
N ought to be observed. In this sense, legal validity is
relative, in other words "derivative". Legal validity is
thus no natural property but a normative one, necessarily
related to, and derived from, a "super-norm", stating
that a certain norm ought to be obeyed. In order to
meaningfully speak about a valid norm, one must assume at
least two norms, one determining validity of another.
This logically (analytically, necessarily) true thesis
concerns all norms, inter alia legal and moral.
    The relative character of validity causes a problem
which Georg Henrik von Wright described in the following
manner: "If validity of a norm is validity relative to

the validity of another norm of higher order, the
validity of this higher order norm will in its turn mean
validity relative to a third norm of a still higher
order, and so forth. If this chain is infinite the
concept of validity would seem to lose all meaning, or be
hanging in the air. If the chain is not infinite, then
the validity of the norm in which the chain terminates
cannot mean ´validity relative to some other valid norm´,
since there are no other norms to refer to." Von Wright´s
solution (1963b, 196-7) is the following: "The validity
of a norm... is not validity relative to the validity of
another norm. It is validity relative to the existence of
another norm, hierarchically related to the first in a
certain way". I will return to this problem in sections
5.3.1, 5.3.2 and 5.8.4.

The norm determining validity of a legal norm can
itself belong to different systems. (1) It can be a legal
norm. A constitutional norm thus determines validity of
statutory norms. (2) It can be a moral norm. A moral norm
decides, e.g., whether an old statute is to be regarded
as obsolete, or even derogated by means of desuetudo.

On the other hand, it cannot be a norm of language. No
doubt, a complex of such norms determines what kind of
structure, content and efficacy of a normative system is
sufficient to call it "valid law". But the meaning of the
word "valid" is either legal or moral, not linguistic.
The language merely refers to the law or morality.

One can classify different opinions of the concept
"valid law" into three categories: Natural Law, Legal
Positivism and Legal Realism, cf. sections 5.2, 5.3 and
5.5 infra. Natural Law tends to find the super-norm for
the law in morality, Legal Positivism in the law itself,
Legal Realism regards the whole problem as not rational.

5.2. LAW AND MORALITY - ON NATURAL LAW

5.2.1. Introductory Remarks

Many advocates of Natural Law have distinguished between
the "positive" law, created by the authorities, and the
truly valid or binding law, conforming to the natural
law. In other words, they have made two assumptions.

1. The statement "n is a valid legal norm" implies the
statement "n is binding" and "n belongs to a normative
system roughly corresponding to the natural law".

2. One ought to obey valid legal norms precisely because they belong to a normative system roughly corresponding to the natural law.

But what is natural law? Though the concept is vague, one can assume that it refers to especially important moral norms.

But not all moral norms belong to the natural law. Some classical natural-law thinkers thus distinguished between the natural law, deciding what is iustum, and morality, deciding what is honestum (Mautner 1979, quoting Thomasius).

As regards the content and the sources of natural law, one can distinguish the following standpoints.

1. A natural-law theory is religious, if its important parts are supported by some religious assumptions, even if they also have an analytic or empirical support.

Thomas Aquinas's theory is thus religious, despite the fact that it also contains the following, profoundly reasonable, theses independent from the religion. Knowledge is supported both by observational data, provided by senses, and by a creative reworking of these, provided by reason. Reason creates concepts and enables one to grasp the essence of things. Reason also makes it possible to distinguish right and wrong. Human nature includes three kinds of dispositions, to self-preservation, to satisfying biological needs such as procreation, and to fulfilment of rational goals, such as knowledge and respect for the interests of others. Reason also tells us that these dispositions are good, provided that they are kept within limits. But why are they good? Here comes the religious component: They are good because God asks us to follow our nature.

Aquinas's theory of law corresponds to these views. The human law is binding only if corresponding to the natural law. The natural law, revealed in the Bible, reflects some parts of the eternal law, made by God to rule the universe. Since the eternal law is inaccessible to our reason, we need both the natural and the human law. On the other hand, the eternal law is imprinted in our nature. We can thus follow it to some extent, if we listen to reason.

It is not my intention to quote innumerable restatements of Aquinas's views about the law, not to speak about his original works. Brief and simple reports can be found, e.g., in 1980, 398 ff. and Stone 1965, 51 ff.

2. A natural-law theory is rationalistic, if it fulfils the following conditions.

a) The most important parts of it are supported by statements which in one way or another are given by reason. Such statement can be analytic (reporting the sense of some concepts) or otherwise obvious, acceptable for anyone who possesses a coherent world picture etc.

b) The theory can also have an empirical support (but this is perhaps not necessary).

c) No important parts of the theory require a support of religious assumptions.

The classical Natural Law of 17th and 18th centuries provides many examples. One assumed that human beings had a natural right to the suum, that is, his own or his due, including one's life, body, thoughts, dignity, reputation, honour and freedom of actions (cf. Olivecrona 1969, 176 ff.; 1971, 275 ff.; 1973, 197 ff. and 1977, 81 ff.). The idea of the suum justified the binding force of promises, including the social contract. The content of the law was regarded as justifiable by recourse to such a contract. No wonder that, e.g., Grotius, regarded the principle that contracts should be respected (pacta sunt servanda) as the most important principle of natural law. People living in the original "state of nature" could enter a social contract, and thus give the ruler a part of their suum, e.g., the right to regulate their actions. In this manner, a hypothetical contract which rational people would enter in the state of nature, could justify the duty to follow the law. The ruler's legal power to enact binding laws was thus based on the "obvious" idea of the suum and the "obvious" assumptions concerning the content of a hypothetical social contract.

Contractarian thoughts are unusually persistent. They appeared long before the classical Natural Law and persist until our days. Mention can be made of the Hebrew belief in the Covenant established between Jahve and the Israeli people and the ancient Germanic belief concerning the contract between the ruled and the ruler (cf., e.g., Strömberg 1981, 15). At the other end of the time scale, John Rawls claims that reason alone would be a sufficient condition for various individuals to unanimously accept certain principles of justice etc., if the following conditions were fulfilled: (1) they were placed in "the original position of equality", assuring impartiality; and (2) their views were satisfactorily balanced, that is, in the "reflective equilibrium"; cf. section 2.6.2 supra.

3. A natural-law theory is empirical, if it fulfils the following conditions.

a) The most important parts of it are supported by empirical statements.

b) The theory can also have some support of statement which in one way or another are "given by reason".

c) No important parts of the theory require a support of religious assumptions.

5.2.2. An Example of Empirical Theory of Natural Law

<u>Alfred Verdross</u> (1971, 92 ff.) elaborated a moderate version of such an empirical theory of natural law. The theory contains four parts.

1. The first part is based on the thesis that all normal human beings feel certain basic needs and exhibit some primary wants.

a) They all want to live. Though circumstances can force one to suicide, the disposition to self-preservation is natural.

b) All normal people want to avoid being exposed to physical injury, defamation or economic loss.

c) Though some people have a disposition to follow a leader, all normal human beings want to have some freedom to fulfil their intentions and not to be forced to act .

d) They all want to be able to rely on the help of others, if needed.

The following norms of the so-called social morality express these needs and wants.

a) Each individual <u>ought to</u> abstain from attacking life of others.

b) Each individual <u>ought to</u> abstain from attacking health, reputation and property of others.

c) Each individual <u>ought to</u> abstain from attacking liberty of others.

d) Each individual <u>ought to</u> help others, if this is required.

The following reasoning underpins this theory:

Premise 1   All normal human beings want that each
                   individual acts in the way x

Conclusion   Each individual <u>ought to</u> act in the way x

The conclusion does not follow from premise 1. But one can add a premise 2, and obtain the following logically correct inference:

Premise 1   All normal human beings want that each
                   individual acts in the way x

Premise 2   If all normal human beings want that each
                   individual acts in the way x then each
                   individual <u>ought to</u> act in the way x
----
Conclusion   Each individual <u>ought to</u> act in the way x

One can interpret premise 2 in many ways, <u>inter alia</u> as a more or less arbitrary norm, or as a value-naturalist definition of the concept of "ought". To be sure, the word "ought" has a more complex and unclear meaning. The following view is, however, plausible. If all normal human beings want that x happens, then each individual prima facie ought to act in the way bringing about x (in the weak sense of prima-facie, cf. section 2.3.3 and 2.3.4 supra). Moreover, it is then reasonable to conclude that one must take this prima-facie Ought into account when deliberating whether one ought all-things-considered to act in the way x or not. (This is the strong sense of prima-facie; cf. id.)

2. Primary natural law, discussed in the second part of Verdros's theory, is a special case of social morality. It thus consists of norms which (a) belong to social morality and (b) regulate legal problems. One identifies the legal character of problems according to two criteria. While social morality includes norms stipulating duties, the norms of primary natural law stipulate both duties of certain persons, other persons' rights corresponding to them, and competences of authorities to use means necessary to enforce the rights and duties.

Primary natural law is eternal, since it belongs to social morality, based on equally eternal primary needs and wants.

3. Secondary natural law indicates how the aims for the legal system which are derived from primary natural law can best be realised in the given social conditions. Secondary natural law changes continually, since it must fit changing social facts.

Before nuclear weapons were discovered, the primary natural-law goal of bringing good-neighbour relations between nations might sometimes be realised through war, either purely defensive or aiming at removing such a menace as Hitler. Consequently, just wars were permissible from the point of view of natural law. In the nuclear age a war can no longer lead to anything valuable. The doctrine of the just war must thus be abandoned.

4. Positive law, given in statutes, precedents etc. and enforced by sanctions is valid only when it is in accord with the secondary natural law.

5.2.3. Some Critical Remarks on Natural-Law Theories

Natural-law theories face, among other things, some empirical problems. We should all accept natural-law norms as both reasonable and deciding about validity of positive law, if social science could show us that if we observe these norms we could effectively satisfy needs and fulfil wants of everybody. But does science give us such evidence? Many critics claim that people living in different times and societies endorse different values and, first of all, different value hierarchies. The goals all recognise, e.g., to protect life, are vague. Moreover, one may choose several alternative means for realising the goals. One can protect life, e.g., through developing a more efficient health service or through more efficiently fighting crimes. To justify such a choice, one needs an act of weighing and balancing, ultimately connected with one´s will and feelings.

No doubt, the law is indirectly connected with human nature. Human nature creates limits for human forms of life. The forms of life in their turn provide limits for what can constitute acceptable prima-facie moral reasons. Inter alia, it creates some rational limits for a hypothetical social contract. It is not plausible to assume that such a contract could have any arbitrary content possible to imagine. In effect, human nature creates some limits for a rationally justifiable content of valid law. But all those limits are flexible. They are not so precise as, e.g., Rawls assumes (cf. section 2.6.2 supra). Still smaller is the chance to deduce from these vague limits a content of a complex system of natural law. Fuzziness of such limits makes the requirement of correspondence between positive law and a contentually characterised system of "natural law" almost empty. In brief, natural-law theories tend to make too strong analytical and/or empirical assumptions.

One can also criticise many kinds of natural-law theories for making too strong assumptions concerning theoretical content of practical statements, e.g., for attempts to derive practical (normative or evaluative) conclusions from theoretical propositions about human nature etc. I have already discussed serious difficulties such a derivation must face, cf. sections 2.1 and 2.4.6 supra: The step from theoretical propositions to all-things-considered practical statements is not analytic but requires a judgment of reasonableness.

These problems create a paradoxical situation. Though intending to be precise, natural-law theories are peculiarly vague, that is, unable to elaborate a clear test of Natural Law. In consequence, if the concept "valid law" is defined as conforming to Natural Law, then the system of law becomes more vague, less fixed. This contradicts the postulate of fixity formulated in the section 5.1 supra.

5.3. LAW AND MORALITY - LEGAL POSITIVISM

5.3.1. Hans Kelsen´s "Pure" Theory of Law

Legal Positivism accepts the natural-law assumption that valid law is binding, that is, ought to be obeyed. At the same time, the positivists reject any analytic connection between law and morality. They claim that the legal system can be thoroughly immoral and yet valid. From the legal point of view, one ought to observe even norms belonging to such a systematically immoral system. Consequently, they must explain the sense of this "legal ought", different from a moral obligation. If the validity of legal norms is "derivative" (cf. section 5.1.3 supra), and if it cannot be derived from morality, from what, then, can it be derived?

The standard positivistic answer is: from the sovereign power which can enforce the law. One can mention the Sophists (cf., e.g., Dias 1976, 79) and Ulpianus: <u>quod principi placuit, legis habet vigorem</u> (Dig. I,4,1 pr.). Within the framework of Natural Law, this connection was emphasised also by Hobbes (cf. Olivecrona 1971, 19). Systematic Legal Positivism is, nevertheless, comparatively new; the term "philosophy of positive law" was first used by Gustav Hugo in 1798.

According to Bentham and Austin, the law consists of commands of the habitually obeyed sovereign, ensured by the threat of punishment. Its existence as law entails no moral justification at all (cf. Olivecrona 1971, 27 ff.) On the other hand, according to the traditional German Legal Positivism, the positive law has binding force by virtue of the will of the state. For instance, Bergbohm held that the material source of positive law consists of the legal consciousness (an influence of Savigny and Hegel) and its formal source of the will of the state (cf. Olivecrona 1971, 39 ff.) Such theories, however, encounter two further problems. First, one cannot define precisely "the will" of such an abstract entity as a state (cf. Olivecrona 1971, 71 ff. and 73 ff.). Second, entities such as the "sovereign" and the state are legal creatures; how, then, can existence of the state and the sovereign make the law binding if they are themselves made by the law? (cf. Olivecrona 1971, 65 ff.).

<u>Hans Kelsen</u> created the most perfect positivist theory of law. According to Kelsen, the actual legal research is an unjustifiable mixture of juristic, moral, sociological and other components. Consequently, one must liberate it from alien influence. Kelsen's pure theory of law is so to say a general part of thus purified legal research.

The pure theory of law deals with what <u>ought to</u> be done from the point of view of the positive law, not what people actually do. Consequently, it studies legal norms, and only legal norms.

A norm is the sense of an act of will, directed at another person's conduct. (Cf. section 2.2.2 supra.)

"Whoever gives an order, <u>means</u> something. He expects that the other understands <u>it</u>. Giving the order, he means <u>that</u> the other ought to act in a certain way. This is the <u>meaning</u> of his act of will" (Kelsen 1979, 25).

A legal norm functions as a scheme of interpretation. A juristic interpretation differs from interpretation in the natural science in the following manner: The former only, not the latter, regards a course of events from the point of view of a valid norm.

"The quality of an action to be an execution, not a murder, cannot be grasped by senses but follows first from a process of thinking,

that is, from a confrontation with the criminal statute and the
order of criminal process" (Kelsen 1960, 4.).

Kelsen makes a distinction between a legal norm and a legal
statement. This distinction corresponds closely to the difference
between the so-called genuine and spurious legal statements, cf.
section 1.5.1. Legal science according to Kelsen utters legal
statements, not legal norms.

"The difference shows itself in the fact that the
ought-statements, formulated in legal science..., which neither
oblige nor entitle anyone to anything, can be true or false, while
the ought-norms, enacted by a legal authority - which oblige or
entitle legal subjects - neither can be true nor false but only
valid or invalid" (Kelsen 1960, 75 f.).

A legal scholar thus attempts at telling the truth about the
content and validity of legal norms.

One expresses both legal norms and legal statements in the
language of "ought", "may" etc. In both cases, one has to do with
"the ought", not with natural facts. The difference is particularly
clear in comparison with causal laws. While a causal law says "if
there is A, B must necessarily occur", a legal statement says "if
there is A, B ought to (should) occur".

"A legal statement connects two elements with each other in a
similar manner as a (causal) law of nature. But the connection
expressed in the legal statement has an entirely different content
than the causal one described in the natural law... In the legal
statement, one does not state that if A then B occurs, but that if A
then B ought to occur" (Kelsen 1960, 80).

When evaluating Kelsen's views, one must make a distinction
between two components. The first is a very plausible advice, given
a legal scholar: Study valid legal norms, not anything else! The
second is the controversial philosophical thesis that legal norms
constitute a particular "world of the ought" etc. The second may
imply the first, but the first has also an independent
justification.

From a philosophical point of view, one can regard "the world of
the ought" as a special case of Popper's "world 3", cf. section
5.5.6 infra.

"Purity" of Kelsen's theory means also that it has been liberated
from moral elements. Morality differs according to Kelsen from the
law, since only the latter is provided with an organised sanction.
Moreover, several moral systems can coexist in the same society,
e.g. a Christian and an Islamic one. One cannot scientifically prove
which one is better. The law thus creates own criteria of the good
and the ought, independent from any morality. A moral system may
causally influence the content of the law, but has nothing to do
with its legal validity.

"If one assumes that values are relative and thus claims that law
and morality in general, and law and justice in particular, differ
from each other, this claim does not mean that the concept of law
has nothing to do with morality and justice, nor that the concept
'law' does not come under the concept 'good'. For the concept 'good'
cannot be defined in any other way as 'that which ought to be', that
is, that which corresponds to a norm; and if one defines the law as

norm, it follows that what conforms to the law is good. The... claim
to separate the law from morality and... justice means only that if
one evaluates a legal order as moral or immoral, just or unjust, one
expresses a relation of the legal order to one of many possible
moral systems and not to 'the only one' morality... (V)alidity of a
positive legal order is independent from its correspondence... with
any moral system" (Kelsen 1960, 68-69).

"When discussing validity of a positive legal norm, one must
disregard validity of a moral norm incompatible with it, and when
discussing validity of a norm of justice, one must disregard
validity of a positive legal norm incompatible with it. One cannot
simultaneously regard both as valid" (Kelsen 1960, 361).

Though contestable, the thesis that there are many moral systems
is plausible. But it does not imply that the concept "valid law" is
independent from morality. One can, e.g., interpret the concept
"valid law" as implying that an extremely immoral "law" is no valid
law. Each individual would then regard a normative system as valid
law or not, depending on whether it does fulfil or not some minimal
requirements of the moral system he endorses. I will return to this
question later on; cf. section 5.8.3.

According to Kelsen, a legal order is an order of force, a
sanctioned order. He concludes, what follows: "(A)ll norms which do
not stipulate an act of force... are incomplete norms... valid only
in connection with norms which do stipulate an act of force" (Kelsen
1960, 59).

The norms of private law are thus valid due to the fact that other
norms enact sanctions for their violation, that is, sequestration,
punishment etc.

One may wonder whether this theory fits the contemporary welfare
state as well as the "minimal state" or 19th century night-watchman
state. No doubt, the modern state still claims monopoly of using
force, yet its activity has expanded to cover health service,
education, redistribution and what not. It is by no means clear what
the "essence" or, to put it more cautiously, the point, the most
fruitful definition etc. of the law and state is. The safest course
is to assume a plurality of criteria, none sufficient and none
necessary, cf. section 5.8 infra.

One of the most important elements of Kelsen's theory is the idea
that legal norms constitute a hierarchy of a peculiar kind. A norm
is legally valid if it has been created in accordance with valid
norms of higher standing which determine who is authorised to make
the norm and how this should be done (cf. Kelsen 1960, 228 ff. and
section 5.6.2 infra). The higher norm itself is valid if it has been
made in a way prescribed by a still higher valid norm, and so on.
But the highest legal norms, belonging to the constitution, cannot
derive their validity from validity of still higher legal norms,
since no such norms are valid in the legal system. The lawyers take
for granted the validity of the highest legal norm. For a law
theorist, however, it is a puzzle.

According to Kelsen, the highest legal norms must derive their
validity from the Grundnorm, the basic or apex norm. One formulation
of this norm is, as follows: the constitution ought to be observed.
More precisely: "Acts of force ought to be performed under the

conditions and in the manner which have been stipulated by the
historically first constitution of the state and by the norms
enacted in agreement with it. (In an abbreviated form: one ought to
behave as the constitution prescribes.)" - Kelsen 1960, 203-204.

This is a regulative norm, imposing a duty. Raz 1974, 97, has
written, however, that the nature of the Grundnorm is power
conferring, that is, in our terminology, a kind of qualification
norm). Cf. Paulson 1980, 177.

As an alternative, Kelsen admits a construction in which legal
validity is based on international law whose Grundnorm is the
following: The states ought to behave in the way which corresponds
to the international custom; cf. Kelsen 1960, 222.

According to Kelsen, any apex norm whatever can be assumed
provided it meets the requirement of efficacy (cf., e.g., Kelsen
1960, 215 ff.),, namely that the majority of rules which are based
on it are applied by a given power-exercising organisation.

In the Soviet Union, e.g., one may assume the Grundnorm "The
Soviet constitution ought to be observed", but not "The constitution
of the (czarist) Russian Empire ought to be observed".

Efficacy is thus the main criterion of legal validity. But why did
Kelsen not say that it entirely determines the validity? Why had he
also referred to the Grundnorm? One reason is that power systems
exist (e.g. the Mafia organisation) which are not regarded as valid
law. Secondly, legal validity is a normative quality, which cannot
be identified with factual efficacy. Only "if the Grundnorm... is
presupposed, can the constitution... be recognised as binding legal
norms" (Kelsen 1928, 339; cf. Kelsen 1951, 1391; 1958, 1397 ff.;
1960b, 1422 ff.; 1960, 204 ff.; 1961, 827).

The apex norm is not legally valid because it has not come into
existence in a legally prescribed way. It is only conceptually
presupposed by anyone engaged in legal reasoning about valid law.
Cf. Kelsen 1945, 116: The Grundnorm is "the necessary presupposition
of any positivistic interpretation of the legal material"; my
italics. Cf. Kelsen 1960, 209. Cf. Walter 1968, 339: Pure theory of
law is a theory of legal dogmatics, not a theory of legal history or
legal politics.

Kelsen has always regarded the Grundnorm as a presupposition.
However, sometimes he also called it hypothetical, cf. Kelsen 1934,
66 ff. This interpretation inspired, e.g., Lachmayer 1977, 207 and
Marcic 1963, 69 ff. But one can doubt whether this "hypothesis" is
falsifiable. Cf. Verdross 1930, 1308 and Walter 1968, 339. Besides:
"It is sometimes the case that two alternative scientific hypotheses
may be equally apt to explain the phenomena in question. But there
is no room for alternative Grundnormen", Dias 1976, 499-500.

After 1962, Kelsen regarded the Grundnorm as a fictitious norm
presupposing a fictitious act of will creating this norm; cf. Kelsen
1964, 1977 and 1979, 206-7. Cf. Olivecrona 1971, 114. This was
perhaps an influence of Vaihinger (cf. 1922, 24), or a compromise
with Legal Realism, cf. Hägerström 1953, 277: The Grundnorm "merely
hovers in the air".

Neither the idea of a hypothesis nor the idea of a fiction can be
considered as improvements of Kelsen's main theory.

We all think that the constitution is valid law. If one seriously claims that the constitution is valid law, one thereby means that it ought to be observed. A law theorist thus concluded: "If the law become something that people were not obliged to obey then it would no longer be the law"(Marantz 1979). The expression "The constitution is valid law", can be defined as equivalent to "The constitution ought to be observed". The fact that we all call the constitution valid thus implies that we presuppose, take for granted, that it ought to be observed. The <u>Grundnorm</u> says precisely the same, that the constitution ought to be observed.

One can agree with Kelsen that the <u>Grundnorm</u> is thus conceptually presupposed by anyone engaged in legal reasoning about valid law. But according to Kelsen it also is a "ground" for legal validity. "If one asks for the ground of a legal norm, belonging to a certain legal order, the answer can only consist in a reference to the <u>Grundnorm</u> of this legal order, namely in the statement that this norm has been enacted in accordance with the <u>Grundnorm</u>" (Kelsen 1960, 202).

In this manner, Kelsen succeeded to answer the natural-law question, Why is the law binding?, and yet to reject any analytic connection between law and morals.

But how can a mere presupposition constitute a ground for legal validity?

In my opinion, one can regard the <u>Grundnorm</u> as a conclusion derived from two premises, the first stating what the lawyers have a disposition to regard as valid law, second explaining the meaning of the word "valid". One can imagine the following inference.

Premise 1, stating what the lawyers have a disposition to regard as valid law	The constitution is valid law
Premise 2, a definition of the concept "valid"	"Valid" means "such that one ought to observe it"
Conclusion – the <u>Grundnorm</u>	One ought to observe the constitution

To put it simply: "The constitution ought to be observed because we lawyers have a disposition to think that it ought to be observed".

One can regard this disposition of the lawyers as identical with the <u>existence</u> of the social norm "the constitution ought to be observed". Consequently, the <u>Grundnorm</u> can be said to exist in the legal practice in which it is presupposed; cf. Peczenik 1981, 294.

If this interpretation is accepted, Kelsen's views become a special case of von Wright's theory of validity (cf. section 5.1.3 supra): The validity of the constitution is not validity relative to the <u>validity</u> of another norm. It is validity relative to the

<u>existence</u> of another norm, namely the social norm "the constitution ought to be observed".

Yet, one can deny that the existence of <u>this</u> social norm is sufficient for derivation of legal validity of the constitution. One can ask the question: To be sure, the lawyers think that the constitution ought to be observed, but ought it, really, to be observed? Within the - contextually sufficient - legal reasoning, the latter question is meaningless, since one takes for granted that the constitution ought to be observed. But within a deep justification of legal reasoning, the question is vital.

One can answer it, e.g., by stating that positive law is valid only if its content corresponds to natural law. A better answer is, in my opinion, this: The constitution ought to be observed because it is a necessary condition for coherence of the legal order. <u>Chaos</u> would occur in a society in which no coherent legal order existed. Chaos is morally worse than order, provided that order is not extremely immoral; <u>see</u> section 5.8.2 infra.

Kelsen did not solve the problem of the deep justification of the law. He has merely pointed out that the problem not a <u>legal</u> one.

Moreover, though Kelsen admitted that morality causally affects the content, interpretation and efficacy of the law, he regarded moral judgments as exceeding the limits of the pure theory of law. In consequence, evaluative interpretation of law was uninteresting for a "pure" theorist. Practical lawyers were thus left alone, to cope with such problems without any theoretical aid. The hypothesis is plausible that such a disinterest must cause a lesser degree of rationality of legal interpretation, thus contradicting the postulate of rationality, expressed in section 5.1.1 supra. Paradoxically, it may also cause a lesser degree of fixity of the law. Since the pure theory of law emphasises the role of will and fiat in the process of legislation, a Kelsenian legislator would not be particularly inclined to submit his judgment to rational testing. He would rather freely change the law and thus make it less fixed.

5.3.2. Herbert Hart´s Theory of Law

<u>Herbert Hart</u> has followed Kelsen in many respects.

According to Hart, the law consists of social rules, written or not. A custom to obey rules differs from a mere custom to behave in a certain manner. To obey rules presupposes that one also has a certain attitude of acceptance. This does not mean that one continually experiences emotions, "analogous to those of restriction or compulsion... There is no contradiction in saying that people accept certain rules but experience no such feelings of compulsion. What is necessary is that there should be a critical reflective attitude to certain patterns of behaviour as a common standard, and that this should display itself in criticism (including self-criticism), demands for conformity, and in acknowledgements that such criticism and demands are justified, all of which find their characteristic expression in the normative terminology of 'ought', 'must', and 'should', 'right' and 'wrong'" (Hart 1961, 56).

One can regard legal rules from the external and the internal point of view, that is, "either merely as an observer who does not himself accept them, or as a member of the group which accepts and uses them as guides to conduct" (Hart 1961, 86).

The law differs from other social rules. It thus consists of primary and secondary rules. "(W)hile primary rules are concerned with the actions that individuals must or must not do, the secondary rules are all concerned with the primary rules themselves. They specify the ways in which the primary rules may be conclusively ascertained, introduced, eliminated, varied, and the fact of their violation conclusively determined" (Hart 1961, 92). Hart makes a distinction between three kinds of secondary rules. The rules of adjudication determine the procedure of conclusive ascertaining whether the primary rules have been violated. The rules of change determine the procedure of changing the primary rules. The rule of recognition, finally, prescribes the criteria by which the validity of other rules of the system is assessed (cf. Hart 1961, 92 ff.).

This view resembles Kelsen's hierarchy of legal norms. Both Kelsen and Hart accept the idea that the validity of a legal rule depends on its having been made in accordance with higher rules.

Ronald Dworkin, on the other hand, admits two kinds of valid legal norms. Legal rules are valid because some competent institution enacted them. Legal principles must to a high degree simultaneously fulfil two demands. They must conform to "a sense of appropriateness developed in the profession and the public over time". At the same time, they must fit statutes, judicial decisions and their "institutional history"; cf. section 5.9 infra.

According to Hart, most parts of the rule of recognition are "not stated, but its existence is shown in the way in which particular rules are identified, either by courts or other officials or private persons or their advisers" (Hart 1961, 98).

The rule of recognition is similar to Kelsen's Grundnorm. To be sure, Hart has claimed, what follows: "The question whether a rule of recognition exists and what its content is..., is regarded... as an empirical, though complex, question of fact. This is true even though... a lawyer... does not explicitly state but tacitly presupposes the fact that the rule of recognition... exists as the accepted rule of recognition of the system... Kelsen's terminology classifying the basic norm as a...'postulated ultimate rule'... obscures the point stressed in this book, viz. that the question what criteria of legal validity in any legal system are is a question of fact" (Hart 1961, 245). But Hart has also claimed that the lawyers cognise the law from internal point of view, "and that is a point of view which regards the law as a body of standards that ought to be complied with. Does it not follow that propositions about legal rights, duties, validity, and so on, express conclusions about what ought to be done?" But how can this be if the lawyer does only study facts and does not assume the Grundnorm?

At the same time, Hart's "question of fact" is the same in Kelsen's theory. It is a fact that the lawyers assume the Grundnorm. In other words, it is a fact that their use of language and their practice of reasoning, making decisions etc. show that they (1) have a disposition to regard the constitution as valid, and (2) understand the word "valid law" as "the law one ought to observe".

The difference is perhaps this only. The Grundnorm states precisely what all the lawyers presuppose. The presupposition is therefore abstract and formal; it has always the same content, that is, one ought to observe the constitution, whatever it may contain. Hart tends, on the other hand, to give his "rule of recognition" a richer content which may vary from one legal order to another. But this makes Hart's theory open to the following objection, expressed by Summers: "Hart has claimed that 'at the foundations' of a modern legal system we find one accepted rule of recognition (or a few such rules) specifying all criteria of valid law. This vastly oversimplifies the actual phenomena. Instead, we find many particular tests of validity" (Summers 1985, 71) and these are "fluid and changing" (id., 75).; cf. section 5.8 infra.

Hart's theory also resembles Kelsen's views concerning the separation of law and morals.

The following ideas of Hart are, however, more original. Any moral rule has the following characteristics: 1) It is regarded as something of great importance. 2) It has evolved spontaneously, and cannot be brought into being or changed by deliberate enactment. 3) It makes moral blame dependent on intent or negligence of the person blamed. 4) Finally, it is sanctioned by criticism of immoral actions, not by force. Hart has also made a distinction between the commonly accepted morality and a critical morality of an individual. The latter "must satisfy two formal conditions, one of rationality and the other of generality", the former may in some cases fail to do it. The latter may thus constitute the basis of criticising the former. Critical morality also "has its private aspect, shown in the individual's recognition of ideals which he need not either share with others or regard as a source of criticism of others... Lives may be ruled by dedication to the pursuit of heroic, romantic, aesthetic or scholarly ideals..." (Hart 1961, 179).

No doubt, morality causally affects the content, interpretation and efficacy of the law. But according to Hart, no necessary conceptual link exists between the law and morality. The basis of legal validity consists in the factual existence of the social practice determining the rule of recognition, not in moral values. The content of the law thus can be immoral. In this connection, Hart has pointed out, what follows.

1. When such normative words as "ought to" are used in the law, they need not carry any moral judgment whatever.

"Those who accept the authority of a legal system look upon it from the internal point of view, and express their sense of its requirements in internal statements couched in the normative language which is common to both law and morals: 'I (You) ought', 'I (he) must', 'I (they) have an obligation'. Yet they are not thereby committed to a moral judgment, that it is morally right to do what the law requires" (Hart 1961, 199).

2. The conceptual separation of law and morals makes it possible to criticise the law from the moral point of view.

"What surely is most needed in order to make men clear sighted in
confronting the official abuse of power, is that they should
preserve the sense that the certification of something as legally
valid is not conclusive of the question of obedience, and that,
however great the aura of majesty or authority which the official
system may have, its demands must in the end be submitted to a moral
scrutiny" (Hart 1961, 206).

By the way, Kelsen (1960, 68) expressed a similar view.

One may, however, criticise Hart's theory on the following
grounds.

1. "As the common terminology of legal and moral discourse
indicates, the elements of moral and legal reasoning share a common
framework even though they have considerable differences of internal
detail. This means exactly that there is at least one necessary
conceptual link between the legal and the moral, namely that legal
standards and moral standards both belong within the genus of
practical reasons for action, whatever be their weight as such"
(MacCormick 1981, 161).

This fact causes a tendency to mutual adaptation of the law and
morality. No doubt, one can say "from the legal point of view, I
ought to pay tax amounting to 102 % of my income, yet from the moral
point of view I ought not to do it". One cannot, however, both pay
and not to pay the tax. The conflicting demands create a predicament
which one must solve, either by assuming a priority order between
the legal and moral norms in question or by reinterpreting,
modifying and thus reconciling the moral and legal claims. A natural
result of this harmonisation is to permit a minimum of morality to
serve as a criterion of legal validity, according to the maxim
"extremely immoral 'law' is no valid law"; cf. section 5.8.2 infra.

2. This fact does not exclude the possibility of moral scrutiny of
law. One may express a critical attitude towards valid law in the
following ways.

a) One may criticise a particular legal decision, without denying
that the legal system as a whole is morally acceptable. In this way,
one may criticise Swedish tax laws, without doubting that the
Swedish law as a whole is fairly good.

b) One may also criticise a great number of legal norms and
conclude that the whole legal order is objectionable, yet valid. In
this manner, one may criticise South African or Soviet law, still
without expressing doubts as regard its legal validity.

c) Finally, one may criticise the legal system as a whole in a
particularly severe way, i.e., as extremely and extensively immoral.
First such an extremely severe criticism of, e.g., Hitler's or Pol
Pot's "law" may lead one to denying its validity.

Hart's theory resembles Kelsen's views concerning another problem,
too, namely judicial discretion. His starting point is that the law
is vague, it has an "open texture".

"Whichever device, precedent or legislation, is chosen for the
communication of standards of behaviour, these, however smoothly
they work over the great mass of ordinary cases, will, at some point
where their application is in question, prove indeterminate; they
will have what has been termed an open texture... Natural languages

like English are when so used irreducibly open textured" (Hart 1961, 124-125).

This vagueness is a result of two factors, the discussed properties of the language and the functions of the law.

"In fact all systems... compromise between two social needs: the need for certain rules which can, over great areas of conduct, safely be applied by private individuals to themselves without fresh official guidance or weighing up of social issues, and the need to leave open, for latter settlement by an informed, official choice, issues which can only be properly appreciated and settled when they arise in a concrete case" (Hart 1961, 127).

The vagueness of the law makes judicial discretion necessary.

"The open texture of law leaves to courts a law-creating power... Whatever courts decide..., stands till altered by legislation; and over the interpretation of that, courts will again have the same last authoritative voice" (Hart 1961, 141).

In this connection, one may notice that Dworkin rejects the idea of "strong" judicial discretion. He recognises vagueness of the legal language, yet insists that a perfect judge, bound by the enacted law, can interpret it in the light of legal principles together with his moral judgment, and thus find the one right answer to all legal questions. The enactment together with the principles give the judge a precise directive. The enactment must thus be precise in the context of the principles. In other words, Dworkin claims that almost all legal norms are contextually precise, though they may be lexically vague; cf. section 5.9.3 infra.

In my opinion, the truth lies between Hart's and Dworkin's positions. Dworkin is right that the judge is bound, not only by enacted rules but also by results of coherent thinking which involves weighing and balancing of the enacted law and one's own moral evaluations. Hart, on the other hand, is right when implying that such an act of rational weighing and balancing cannot generate the one right answer to all difficult legal questions. Sooner or later, discretion is necessary. The main reason for it is that weighing and balancing ultimately are based on one's will and feelings, cf. section 2.4.5 supra. Yet, the role of feelings is restricted. They may govern a choice between highly coherent norm- and value-systems but they cannot justify a a random cluster of incoherent solutions of particular cases.

In other words, Hart's theory plays down the postulate of rationality of practical reasoning in the law. Having the "law-creating power" to make "official choice" a judge might find it easy to follow rather his moral intuitions than the bounds of reason. This would also lower the degree of fixity of the law.

Although Hart certainly is a legal positivist, let me end this presentation with a brief discussion of his natural-law theory (Hart 1961, 189 ff). In fact, Hart recognises that important reasons exist, given survival as an aim, for the conclusion that both law and morals should include the following "minimum content of natural law". (a) Human vulnerability is a reason for the norm "Thou shalt not kill". (b) Approximate equality of people "makes obvious the necessity for a system of mutual forbearance and compromise which is the base of both legal and moral obligation". (c) Limited altruism of people, the fact that they occupy an intermediate position between angels and devils, create both the necessity of rules and prospect of their efficacy. (d) Limited resources justify the institution of property "(though not necessarily individual property"; Hart 1961, 192). (e) Limited understanding and strength of will create necessity of sanctions.

When a positivist finds it necessary to discuss such problems, doesn't it show that the positivistic jacket is too tight for his juristic body?

5.3.3. The Institutionalist Legal Positivism

Neil MacCormick and Ota Weinberger have elaborated a more moderate version of Legal Positivism. Though MacCormick's "roots" include Hart while Weinberger's starting points are closer to Kelsen, their theories resemble each other to the extent that has enabled them to publish a common book.

An important inspiration for both theorists has been provided by Anscombe's and Searle's theory of institutional facts (cf. Anscombe 1958, 69-72 and Searle 1969, 50-53; cf. MacCormick and Weinberger 1986, 9 ff.). Institutional facts are products of human activity, such as state, law, duties, rights, money, calender, contracts, promises, marriage, citizenship, knowledge, science, culture, literature, etc. If one intends to understand the world in which people perform their actions, one must have information about institutional facts.

Institutional facts differ from brute facts, such as the fact that Peter is now running from Malmö to Lund. The existence of an institutional fact depends partly on a brute fact, partly on norms, deciding, e.g., that Peter is participating in a marathon competition. Disregarding the relevant norms one cannot understand the difference between a valid thousand-kronor bill and forged money either. Such norms decide, e.g., who counts as an owner of a thing and what competences the owner has. They also decide what counts as an establishment of a court, what powers a court has and under what circumstances a judge once appointed may or must demit his office (cf. MacCormick 1978, 57).

By the way, the best analysis of this difference between institutional and brute facts has been provided by Legal Realists (cf. section 5.5 infra). For example, according to Hägerström, ownership is not identical with the use of force against a person who infringes upon that right because the right comes first and the use of force later (if, for instance, someone has stolen the property). Nor is it identical with the fact that the owner uses the property. (The owner can lose it, and a thief can use it). Neither is ownership identical with the legal rules governing ownership. The language itself argues against any such identification. One may claim that one _has_ the right of ownership, but not that one _has_ legal rules.

Cf. Hägerström 1953, 322 ff. and Olivecrona 1959, 127 ff. See also Olivecrona 1939, 75 ff. and 1971, 182 ff. and 186 ff. Ross 1958, 172; Ekelöf 1952, 546 ff.

However, the Realists concluded that there are no such facts as ownership, whereas the Institutional Positivists recognise them as a special class of facts.

Knowledge of institutional facts requires an internal point of view.

MacCormick has improved Hart's theory of the internal point of view. Hart pointed out that a lawyer views legal norms "as a member of the group which accepts and uses them as guides to conduct" (Hart 1961, 86). MacCormick has added the following distinction. There is "cognitively internal" point of view, from which an observer appreciates and understands another person's conduct "in terms of the standards which are being used by the agent as guiding standards: that is sufficient for an understanding of norms and the normative. But it is parasitic on - because it presupposes - the 'volitionally internal' point of view: the point of view an agent, who... has a volitional commitment to observance" (MacCormick 1978, 292) of these standards.

Institutional facts exist in time, e.g., a contract can be valid one year. They are, however, difficult to locate in space. Such questions as, How bread, high and long the contract between John and Peter is?, have no plausible meaning. Weinberger has concluded that institutional facts are "ideal", existing in time but not in space, while brute facts are "material", extant both in time and space. Though ideal, institutional facts are "real", since they can <u>cause</u> brute facts. A contract can thus affect human behaviour and through this a performance of a machine etc. On the other hand, institutional facts also can enter logical relations. A contract can thus have certain logical implications (cf., e.g., Weinberger 1979, 45).

To explain and understand brute facts, one needs theories; physics thus explains the movement of the planets etc. To explain and understand institutional facts, on the other hand, one also needs practical statements, first of all norms, and practical concepts, such as "intention", "action" and "value" (cf. Weinberger's introduction to MacCormick and Weinberger 1985, 17).

To understand a chess game one must both know the rules of chess and understand the players' plans, strength of their moves etc.

Let me add that one grasps institutional facts through stating some brute facts and interpreting these in the light of some practical statements and concepts. One can thus imagine an inference from a set of premises including a description of a brute fact to a conclusion about an institutional fact. The description of a brute fact thus supports the conclusion about an institutional fact. Such an inference is a jump, reasonable if the required additional premises are reasonable.

<u>Norms</u> constitute an important class of institutional facts. But MacCormick's and Weinberger's theory of law "expands the frontiers of the legal beyond what has traditionally been dealt with by positivists" (MacCormick's introduction to MacCormick and Weinberger 1986, 8). They thus assume that the <u>positive law</u> includes not only

legal norms but also institutional facts these determine, such as state, rights, legal dogmatics etc. Moreover, the class of legal norms includes not only explicitly enacted rules but also principles and goal-expressing norms, supporting and justifying the rules (MacCormick's introduction to MacCormick and Weinberger 1986, 19).

The institutional positivists approve of the positivistic separation of law and morals, yet express this view in a very moderate manner.

1. To be sure, they do not share the conviction of, _inter alia_, advocates of Natural Law as regards the conceptual relation between the law and objective values. MacCormick and Weinberger thus "do not think the normativity of law presupposes or is necessarily rooted in objective values or immanent principles of right" (MacCormick's introduction to MacCormick and Weinberger 1986, 7).

Neither do they share Dworkin's more radical view that the law also includes moral principles which so far have not been expressed in either legislation or judicial practice.

2. Moreover, they claim that there are many types of normative systems, e.g., the law, morality, games etc. Different systems may regulate the same thing, e.g. law and morality may regulate the same action. If a collision occurs, one needs a super-system of norms determining the choice between the systems. Weinberger calls it a _Zusammenschlussystem_ (cf. Weinberger 1971, 399 ff. and 423 ff.). Any person has own super-system, perhaps causally influenced by other persons.

Let me add that such a super-system must regulate weighing and balancing of prescriptions given by the competing normative systems. One can explain the personal, "private" character of the super-system by the fact that the ultimate act of weighing involves feelings and the will, cf. section 2.4.5 supra.

3. Yet, they recognise the fact that vagueness of the concept of the law permits different definitions of the concept. There may exist _evaluative_ "underpinning reasons" (MacCormick 1978, 138) which justify the choice of a positivistic, that is, value-free definition of law.

Let me exemplify this point by recourse to Hart's above-mentioned reason for Legal Positivism. According to Hart, a value-free definition of law makes it easier for a legal positivist to criticise the law from the moral point of view. Since such a criticism is valuable, one ought to opt for Legal Positivism; cf. section 5.3.2 supra.

The following theses, asserted by Weinberger, constitute the reasons which, _inter alia_, decide that he regards himself as a legal positivist: (1) The law is a social fact, and its content is a product of social structures and human will. (2) There exists no content-determining practical reason. (3) The law is conceptually independent from morality (cf. Weinberger's introduction to MacCormick and Weinberger 1985, 49 ff.). (4) There is no bridge between the "ought" and the "is". The institutional positivists thus reject Searle's theory of such a bridge (cf. id. 22 ff.).

As regards reasoning in legal dogmatics and judicial practice, MacCormick and Weinberger accept the well-known distinction between a descriptive (theoretical) knowledge of pre-existing law and evaluative (practical) activity of making the law morally better, more rational etc. But despite this, they "believe in the possibility of practical reasoning, of rational deliberation upon practical problems, and rational application of attitudes and values in settling personal and interpersonal problems of how to act...(R)eason guides and restricts but does not wholly determine the range of action which can be considered as right or justified..." (MacCormick's introduction to MacCormick and Weinberger 1986, 8-9). The rational element, restricting arbitrariness of practical reasoning in the law, consists in the possibility to derive logical conclusions from sets of premises including, _inter alia_, theoretical propositions and positive legal norms. This rational component is sufficient for a rich set of conclusions, because the law has extensive content, comprising not only statutes but also unwritten principles and systems of goals. The set of conclusions becomes even more enriched, if one accepts MacCormick's requirement of coherence (MacCormick 1984, 235 ff.), according to which general principles thus make legal rules coherent, helping one to understand and to explain them. In brief, MacCormick and Weinberger might call themselves "rationalistic non-cognitivists" (MacCormick's introduction to MacCormick and Weinberger 1986, 8-9).

I am prepared to accept most of these ideas, with two significant exceptions.

1. Certainly, one must agree with MacCormick and Weinberger that practical conclusions often follow from a mixed set of premises, including both theoretical and practical statements. One must also emphatically agree with MacCormick's insight that the requirement of coherence helps one to make a choice between thus justified practical conclusions. But one must also recognise the theoretical meaning of practical statements, implying, among other things, the following. The language alone makes some facts _prima-facie_ ought- and good-making in a weak sense. The culture makes some facts _prima-facie_ ought- and good-making in a strong sense (section 2.3 supra). Recognition of these limits of arbitrariness as regards the choice of practical premises must increase the degree of rationality of legal reasoning and, consequently, the degree of fixity of the law.

2. It is not certain that a value-free definition of law is the best one. To be sure, it may contribute in some cases to fixity of law. Yet, when the enacted system of norms is as immoral as Pol Pot's "law", other moral considerations may prevail and they may force one not to regard this system as valid law. Indeed, such a "system of law" would probably _not_ conform to the postulate of fixity. The law-givers not bound by moral constraints and the subjects not bound by loyalty to the system would rather create chaos than stable order.

5.3.4. Limitations of Classical Theories of Valid Law

A study of classical theories of valid law leaves the reader in despair. One gets an impression that the theories destroyed each other.

Legal Positivism is superior from the ontological point of view and from the point of view of fixity of the law. The Natural Law theory claims that some correspondence of a normative system to the natural law is necessary for legal validity of the system. Only a very complex ontology admits existence of so intricate and indeterminate entities as natural law. Moreover, the indeterminacy is hardly compatible with the postulate of fixity of the law. Legal Positivism, regarding all positive law as valid, thus has the following advantages. (1) From the point of view of an ordinary lawyer, the ontology of Legal Positivism is highly plausible. He regards positive law as real but cannot imagine any natural law. To be sure, the ontology of Legal Positivism is also complex, but it is simpler than that of the Natural Law. (2) Independence of positive law from the obscure idea of natural law also tends to contribute to the postulate of fixity of the former. These advantages weigh more than the fact that the separation of law and morality forces a positivist to recognise legal validity of extremely immoral orders, which would possess a low degree of fixity.

However, the answer of Legal Positivism to the normative question, Why ought one to obey the law?, is less convincing. A positivist tries to answer the question, Why ought one to obey the law?, without mentioning either morality or the natural law. Instead, he bases legal validity on the Grundnorm, the rule of recognition or the like. But in this way, nothing more is said than "one ought to obey the law because we lawyers have a disposition to believe that one ought to obey the law" (cf. sections 5.3.1 and 5.3.2 supra). If one wants to check whether this legal belief is right or not, one must rely on ones subjective judgment, concerning weighing and balancing of different normative systems (cf. section 5.3.3). Positivist theories do not contribute very much to rationality of this judgment. Neither do they contribute much to rationality of interpretation of valid law.

In brief, only the Natural Law theory answers the normative question, thus claiming that one ought to obey valid legal norms because they belong to a normative

system to some extent corresponding to the natural law.
Moreover, Natural Law is also expected to give important
help to an interpreted of enacted norms. But Natural Law
theories face insuperable difficulties when attempting at
stating precisely the content of the Natural Law,
regardless whether one seeks support of religious,
analytical or empirical theses. No doubt, human nature
creates limits for the content of valid law. But the
limits are flexible. They are not the same as
correspondence between positive law and a contentually
characterised system of "natural law".

One thus needs a "third theory of law" (Mackie´s term
applied to Dworkin´s theory; 1977b, 3), providing for a
reasonable middle way between Legal Positivism and
Natural-Law theories. In my opinion, the theory of
prima-facie and all-things-considered morality (cf.
sections 2.3 and 2.4 supra), together with the discussion
of rationality of legal reasoning (cf. Chapters 3 and 4
supra), greatly facilitates construction of such a
theory.

5.4. MORE ABOUT LAW AND MORALITY

5.4.1. Prima-facie Law And Its Relation to Prima-facie Morality

The Starting Point: Evaluative Interpretation in the Law

The starting point is this. I have already described the
great role a value-laden interpretation actually plays in
the practice of legal reasoning. This practice is by no
means surprising. One can find the following support for
the conclusion that the law ought to be interpreted, and
that such an interpretation ought to constitute a
weighing and balancing of the socially established
(prima-facie) law and substantive moral prima-facie
principles. If the mission of the lawyer had consisted in
merely following the wording of the established law, he
could easily become a servant of an unjust legislator.
But if the mission of the lawyer only consisted in
performing a free moral discourse, such a discourse could
easily result in chaos. It is improbable that a free
moral discourse would lead to consensus. Although the
legal reasoning, too, is ultimately dependent upon
feelings and will, I have already pointed out that it is

relatively more certain than the moral one. One can
perform a highly rational - and hence intersubjectively
controllable - reasoning that supports one´s weighing of
the established law and substantive moral principles. For
this reason, chaos is not the only alternative to blind
obedience. In brief, a good lawyer can and must find the
middle way between Scylla of anarchism and Charybdis of
servility.

Legal certainty thus demands a division of labour
between the legislator and the courts: The latter have to
use interpretation to correct the meaning of the law.

In this context, one can repeat the points made in Section 1.4.1
supra. The legislator cannot predict in advance or acceptably
regulate all cases that can occur in future practice. The
evaluations to be done in legal practice, among other things
concerning the question whether a decision of a given kind is just,
are easier to make in concrete cases, not in abstracto. Historical
evolution of the method of legal reasoning has adapted it to the
purpose of weighing and balancing of the wording of the law and
moral demands. The judge has a far greater practical experience in
applying this method to concrete cases than any legislative agency
can have.

The First Consequence: The Prima-facie Character of the Socially Established Law

The great role of value-laden interpretation in legal
reasoning makes the following thesis plausible. The
socially established law, stated in such sources as
statutes, precedents, travaux préparatoires etc., has a
prima-facie character. The liberties, duties, claims
etc., explicitly stated in the socially established law
are merely prima-facie legal ones, since other
considerations may justify the contrary conclusion
concerning legal duties, claims etc.

The thesis that the socially established law has a
prima-facie character must be interpreted in the light of
our discussion of legal paradigms, research cores and
presupposed premises (cf. sections 3.3.3 and 3.3.5
supra). The jurists and lawyers thus take for granted
some statements, jointly constituting the legal paradigm
or, in other words, the juristic theory core. This core
thus includes some fundamental moral statements, commonly
accepted by both lawyers and people who make moral
judgments. Furthermore, it includes the assumption that

legal reasoning is supported by valid law. It also
contains fundamental juristic views on the authority of
the sources of the law and legal reasoning-norms.
Finally, it includes some fundamental evaluative views,
first of all concerning legal certainty and justice. If
one wishes to perform a legal reasoning, one cannot at
the same time put in question an extensive part of this
theory core. The content of these core assumptions of the
law implies that one cannot simultaneously doubt an
extensive part of the set of norms, expressed in valid
statutes, precedents and other important sources of the
law. Yet, one can doubt each presupposition of this kind
and each legal norm separately. But doubt needs
justification. To justify such doubt, one must rely upon
other reasons. In brief, the established legal
presuppositions and norms have a prima-facie character:
They constitute prima-facie reasons, to be weighed and
balanced against other reasons.

These prima-facie reasons are first-order ones, for
performance of a certain action, H, and/or second-order
ones. The latter demand prima-facie an exclusion of
prima-facie first-order reasons, e.g., for doing H. All
things considered, such a second-order reason may justify
in some cases not doing what ought to be done on the
balance of first-order reasons. For example, a legal
provision, prohibiting immigration, may justify my action
of not helping poor Poles to establish themselves in
Sweden.

Within the contextually sufficient legal justification,
that is, within the legal paradigm, legal reasons of both
kinds are immune from some doubts. Such a reason thus is
immune from the claim that its character of a prima-facie
reason should be re-examined with a view to possible
revision on every occasion to which it applies . For
instance, a lawyer may not continually doubt validity of
each statutory provision. But it is not immune from the
claim that it must give priority to other prima-facie
reasons, if these are sufficiently powerful. Nor is it
immune from the claim to possible revision within a deep
justification, outside of the legal paradigm.

By the way, this view is a paraphrase of Joseph Raz's theory of
exclusionary reasons in the law. I cannot tell whether he would
accept this paraphrase. In any case, he has claimed the following:
An exclusionary reason is a second-order reason for disregarding a
first-order one. "Directly", it is a reason for excluding another
reason, R, for performing an action, H. "Indirectly, it weakens the

case for" doing H. An exclusionary reason "never justifies abandoning one's autonomy, that is, one's right and duty to act on one's judgment of what ought to be done, all things considered." But it may justify in some cases "not doing what ought to be done on the balance of first-order reasons". An exclusionary reason "is immune from the claim that it should be re-examined with a view to possible revision on every occasion to which it applies" (Raz 1979, pp. 18, 27 and 33).

In brief, legal interpretation is creative and value-laden. "Interpretation" in the law is not a mere interpretation sensu stricto, establishing the linguistic (lexical or contextual) sense of a legal text. It includes something more, i.e., an improvement of the law, its adaptation to critical morality. Such an improvement is a common practice in "hard" cases. In the light of this practice, the enacted law is merely prima-facie, and the improved law is all-things-considered.

To be sure, one may criticise this theory of a prima-facie character of the established law. A critic may assume that, given any interpretation of a text expressing a legal rule, there arises the independent question whether the rule is prima-facie or all-things-considered. In particular, he may admit that interpretation of legal rules can lead to a meaning opposite to the literal meaning and still deny the prima-facie character of the rules. The reason is that the law claims for its duties and liberties a definitive status, not a merely a prima-facie one.

The critic may then present the following alternatives:

1. The established law overrides morality. The fact that other considerations can justify a contrary conclusion implies the moral invalidity of these considerations, not the prima-facie character of the law.

2. The established law is a valid system of norms, which can be incompatible with valid morality. The "corrective interpretation" of the established law is in this view no improvement of the law but a creation of moral rules. These can be morally valid or not. If valid, they have a moral all-things-considered quality but may be incompatible with the all-things-considered law.

Both versions of the objection imply a contradiction between what the law claims to be and what the law must be in view of the practice of its corrective (moral, value-laden) interpretation. To resolve this contradiction, I give priority to the practice. The critic does the opposite, but why?

An additional argument answers the second version. Even

if one recognises the distinction between the legal and
moral all-things-considered, cf. section 5.4.5 _infra_, one
cannot consistently say that they are logically
incompatible with each other. The concept of
"_all_-things-considered" excludes such a possibility. "All
things" are _all_ things which ought to guide one´s action,
nothing less. The expression "all things considered"
means that _all_ practically relevant things have been
considered, explicitly or implicitly. It follows that one
can merely _think_ about incompatible normative systems,
but one cannot simultaneously _act_ in accordance with
them. And the "all-things-considered" norms are precisely
the norms which ought to govern one´s action.

**The Second Consequence: The General _Prima-facie_ Moral
Obligation to Obey the Law**

Moreover, there exists a general _prima-facie_ moral
obligation to obey the law. More precisely:

(1)   If the _prima-facie_ law explicitly contains,
         implies or otherwise supports the conclusion
         that A has a certain _legal_ duty, claim,
         competence or right to a holding, then A has a
         moral _prima-facie_ duty, claim, competence or
         right of the same content.

This is an _inclusion-thesis_ concerning the relationship
between the legal and moral _prima-facie_: The _prima-facie_
law is thus a part of the _prima-facie_ morality.

This view differs both from legalist theories, stating that one has
a definitive (not merely prima facie) obligation to obey the law;
cf., e.g., Oakeshott 1983, 117 ff. It also differs from purely
moralist theories, denying any obligation to follow the law
whatever; cf., e.g. Wolff 1971, 60 ff.

I will return to justification of this inclusion thesis.
At this place, it is sufficient to repeat the central
point. There exists a general _prima-facie_ moral
obligation to obey the law because general disobedience
would create chaos. This would be the case, even if
everybody followed moral considerations. It is improbable
that a free moral discourse would lead to so much
consensus as obedience to the reasonably interpreted law.
It is more probable that it would result in chaos.

To be sure, one may imagine some counter-examples. Assume, e.g., that a Nazi law explicitly contains the provision that the police have a legal duty to kill anybody who is a Jew. Have then the police also the moral prima-facie duty to kill Jews? Paradoxically but truly, the answer is "yes!". The very fact that this deeply immoral provision belongs to the socially established law converts it, by definition, into a meaningful prima-facie moral reason which is, of course, easy to override by means other moral prima-facie reasons. This is the case unless one denies that the Nazi "law" is a legal system at all. To be sure, one may deny it for moral reasons, but the immorality must then systematically underlie the total system, including its technical provision of private law etc. One immoral provision, or one systematically immoral branch of the system is not enough; see infra.

But the moral duty etc. to follow the law is merely a prima-facie one. The step from it to the conclusion about a corresponding all-things-considered moral duty etc. presupposes at least an additional premise, expressing an act of weighing and balancing of the legal source in question and other considerations. By introducing the institution of legal order, the society thus can restrict, yet not entirely eliminate the necessity of weighing and balancing.

5.4.2. The Justification of the Relation Between the Law and Prima-Facie Moral Norms. Why Ought One To Follow the Law?

A. Some Reasons Supporting the General Prima-Facie Moral Obligation to Obey the Law

One may propose the following justification of these relations between the law and prima-facie moral duties, claims etc.

1. Moral reasoning is relatively uncertain, as a result of its ultimate dependence upon feelings and will.

To be sure, the connections between moral statements and, on the other hand, various theoretical statements about morally relevant facts, that is, ought-, good-, and right-making facts restrict the arbitrariness of moral reasoning. In the established moral language, a theoretical statement about some good-making facts thus implies a value-statement (and, consequently, a principle) stating that a certain person, action, event, object etc. is prima-facie good in the weak sense of "prima-facie". This means that it is natural in view of the language to proffer such facts as moral reasons. A theoretical statement about such facts also implies that it is reasonable to state that a person, object etc. is prima-facie good in a strong sense. In other words, our culture compels one to consider these facts in one´s act of moral weighing and balancing of considerations. Consequently, one can proffer these facts as (insufficient but meaningful) reasons for the conclusion that it is all-things-considered good. Moreover, since this value statement is a reason for action, theoretical statements about "good-making" facts also are (indirect) reasons for action. Several moral theories are thus admissible, formulating or implying various definitions of or at least criteria for a good action etc.

Yet, the connections between moral statements and ought-making, good-making, claim-making and other morally relevant facts do not entirely eliminate arbitrariness of moral reasoning. Morally relevant facts imply only prima-facie duties, competences etc., not all-things-considered ones. The step to the latter involves weighing and balancing. In other words: Morality consists, first of all, of principles that one must weigh and balance against each other. Mutually incompatible moral statements can thus simultaneously possess support of both moral principles and morally relevant facts. Different persons may agree what principles and facts are relevant to the moral question under consideration, yet disagree as regards weighing and balancing of them.

The law, on the other hand, is more fixed. The legislator compares the weight of several morally relevant facts and moral principles and thus creates some more or less exact rules, telling one what to do. The courts deciding individual cases create relatively precise premises supporting general legal norms. Moreover, the traditional legal method (the legal paradigm) imposes restrictions on legal reasoning. In particular, it contains certain fundamental assumptions concerning authority of the sources of law and some traditional reasoning-norms, telling one how to interpret statutes, precedents etc.; cf. section 3.3.3 supra.

As stated in section 3.1.1 supra, fixity makes the law, ceteris paribus, less arbitrary than morality. To be sure, an unjust but rigid law can be both highly arbitrary and highly fixed. But fixity of the law and predictability of legal decisions has a moral value. <u>If</u> a result of legal reasoning in a particular case is not worse from the point of view of other moral values, then it is, all things considered, less arbitrary, than a result of a purely moral reasoning would be.

Within legal reasoning, one thus gains access to a <u>more extensive set of premises</u>, supporting one´s practical conclusions. Only in so-called hard cases, not in routine cases, must one complete such a set of established legal premises with a freely created norm- or value-statement. Only in hard cases is such a free act necessary to perform an act of weighing, in order to state precisely whether a given legal rule applies or not.

2. A morally objectionable <u>chaos</u> would thus occur in a modern society, if it no longer possessed a legal order, that is a normative system which is highly fixed and public. As stated above, such a system has, <u>inter alia</u>, the following properties: (a) it consists of several levels, higher norms deciding how the lower are to be created; (b) it claims to be complete, sovereign and in possession of the monopoly of using force; and (c) it is to a great extent obeyed by people and applied by authorities. It is thus morally better to have a society possessing a legal order which <u>in some cases</u> leads to morally wrong decisions than to force individual persons to rely upon own moral judgments in all cases.

3. Still stronger reasons support one´s duty to obey the law in a <u>democratic</u> society. The authority of the democratically created laws is, <u>inter alia</u> supported by the majority principle. The latter is an approximation of a calculus of human preferences, itself approximating the idea of the morally good; cf. Section 1.4.2 supra.

B. Morality 1 and Morality 2

Somehow paradoxically, one can thus say that moral reasons call for obeying the law, instead of solely obeying morality.

In this context, one may perhaps distinguish between two kinds of moral considerations, and thus between "morality 1" and "morality 2". Morality 1 contains some general principles, e.g. "one ought not to denunciate one´s neighbour for the authorities". Morality 2 determines the compromise between these principles and the law. It thus may support the following conclusion "one may in some cases denunciate one´s neighbour for the authorities, since a statute demands this"; this

conclusion is right only if the value of obedience to the
law weighs more than the principle under consideration.

Only morality 2, not morality 1, establishes
all-things-considered, not merely prima-facie, duties and
values. In morality 1, one disregards the law. The law is
a morally relevant factor. How can one then say that one
considered all morally relevant things?

C. Clarification: More Than An Obligation Not To Set Bad Examples

The central point of the theory presented above is this:

> There exists a general prima-facie moral obligation
> to obey the law because general disobedience would
> create chaos.

In other words: I have a prima-facie moral obligation to
obey the law, because chaos would occur if all people in
all cases violated all applicable laws. To justify this
obligation, one needs the following universal premise:

> I have a prima-facie moral obligation to act in such
> a way that my action could be repeated by everybody
> without creating morally wrong consequences.

This premise is a consequence of universalisable
character of morality, cf. sections 2.5.2 and 4.1.1
supra.

This justification does not require hypotheses about
causal connections between my action and actions of other
persons. Consequently, the theory developed above should
not be confused with another one, easy to criticise.
According to this theory, which I do not advocate,

> there exists a general prima-facie moral obligation
> to obey the law because each act of disobedience
> would set bad examples and thus increase probability
> of chaos.

This thesis has been criticised in the following key
passage by **Joseph Raz**: "Some philosophers... tried to
show that... (d)isobedience, even to a bad law, ... sets
an example and inclines other people to disobey... Hence
one has an obligation to obey." But, "though the argument
applies in many cases it fails to apply to many others.
There are offences which when committed by certain people

or in certain circumstances do actually revolt people and strengthen the law-abiding inclinations in the population... Moreover, in many cases it is practically certain in advance that the offence, if committed, will remain undetected. Such offences do not set any example whatsoever. Hence the argument from setting a bad example fails to apply to many instances of possible offences" (Raz 1979, 237-8). However, Raz´s criticism does not affect my theory, which says nothing about causal consequences of setting bad examples.

D. An Objection: No **Prima-facie** Obligation to Obey Immoral Laws

A critic may object that only <u>some</u>, not all, legal provisions create <u>prima-facie</u> moral duties. He may give the following set of examples. (1) One has a <u>prima-facie</u> moral duty to obey, e.g., a rule forbidding parking cars in the middle of a frequently used road, since violation of this rule would invariably create chaos. (2) In some but not all cases, a driver has a <u>prima-facie</u> moral duty to obey a red-light stop signal. A violation would often create chaos but would have no morally significant effects on an empty road. (3) One has no <u>prima-facie</u> moral duty to obey, e.g., a legal rule which stipulates that some contracts must be concluded in a written form. This rule is "morally neutral". (4) Finally, one has a <u>prima-facie</u> moral duty to disobey a Nazi rule, forbidding Jews to marry "Arians". This rule is <u>prima-facie</u> immoral.

He may add that the collision between this Nazi rule and a corresponding <u>prima-facie</u> moral principle of equality is total, in the sense that no instance of obeying the Nazi rule is consistent with equality. This is different from collisions of moral <u>prima-facie</u> principles which are always partial, never total. Moreover, the Nazi provision can never win the game of weighing and balancing, performed in order to determine all-things-considered duties. The critic may thus find it meaningless to assign a <u>prima-facie</u> moral character to such a provision.
  Yet, this <u>prima-facie</u> moral duty has the following point. To conclude that the Nazi provision never wins the competition with moral counter-arguments, one must perform an act of weighing. In this act of weighing, the Nazi provision must be taken seriously. After the weighing is performed, not before, one concludes that the provision has lost the competition.

Unlike such a critic, I have assumed a _prima-facie_ moral
duty to follow **any** law, regardless its content. The
content matters very much, but only as regards
all-things-considered moral duties, not the _prima-facie_
ones. All things considered, one ought **not** to follow some
Nazi rules, but _prima-facie_ one **ought** to do it. This
interpretation of the vague expression "a _prima-facie_
moral duty" has the following consequences: An act of
weighing and balancing is necessary to determine
all-things-considered moral duties. It may also be
necessary to determine whether a certain normative order
as a whole is or is not valid law. It thus would not be
valid law, if it is so extremely immoral that it creates
chaos, not order. Neither would it be valid law if the
order it creates is worse than chaos; cf. section 5.8.2
infra. But an act of weighing is not necessary to
establish a _prima-facie_ moral duty to follow provisions
which already have been recognised as legally valid. Such
a provision may, indeed, create a bad order, or even
chaos. But one still has a _prima-facie_ moral duty to
follow it, since it belongs to a system which **totally**, as
a whole, produces order and this order is better than
chaos.

The critic, on the other hand, must always perform two
acts of weighing: the first in order to establish whether
a legal rule is _prima-facie_ morally binding, the second
to ascertain whether it is all-things-considered morally
binding.

In this manner, I admit two kinds of relatively certain points of
departure, taken for granted when one performs an act of moral
weighing: The first kind consists of relatively certain knowledge of
what particular types of action etc. are _prima-facie_ morally
obligatory. The second consists of a highly abstract knowledge of
what types of normative orders are legally valid and thus
prima-facie morally binding. To admit so abstract points of
departure is coherent with the assumptions made in the section 3.3.4
supra.

E. A Consequence: Extremely Immoral Normative System is No Valid Law

The critic may insist that the _prima-facie_ moral
obligation to obey a rule always depends on a content of
the rule. He thus finds it strange to assume that a mere
authority has a moral significance. On the other hand, I
claim that once a provision is legally binding, it is
also _prima-facie_ to be obeyed in the moral sense,
regardless its content. Yet, this assumption becomes less

strange, if one admits that **legal** validity of a normative
system as a whole is not entirely independent of its
content. I will argue in section 5.8.2 infra that an
extremely immoral normative system is not legally valid.
This view eliminates the most striking counter-examples,
directed against the discussed inclusion thesis; e.g.,
provisions of a Pol-Pot "law" did not create prima-facie
moral duties, because they were no valid law at all.

Due to vagueness of all involved terms, such as "moral",
"prima-facie", and "valid law", the critic can now make a choice
between several possibilities. Among other things, he may choose one
of the following two alternatives.
   1. He may refute the assumption that an extremely immoral
normative system is not legally valid. That is, he may recognise
only purely descriptive criteria of legal validity. The expression
"valid law" is sufficiently fuzzy to permit such an interpretation.
   In this case, one may reply that even if such a "value-free"
definition of valid law is assumed, one may still insist that any
norm belonging to any system of valid law ought prima-facie to be
observed in a weak but clearly moral sense of the "ought".
   Indeed, one may even insist that fulfilment of each particular
criterion of legal validity (cf. sections 5.8.1 and 5.8.2) gives a
normative system a (still weaker) prima-facie moral obligatoriness.
   2. On the other hand, even if the critic accepts the premise that
a legal order as a whole is prima-facie morally binding, he may
reply that I make an illicit step. He thus may insist that this
premise merely implies that each legal provision **probably** ought
prima-facie to be obeyed (in the moral sense of the "ought"). He
would still deny that the stronger conclusion follows, that is, that
each such provision is prima-facie morally binding.
   However, this objection is unclear, since it presupposes the
notion "probably ought to be obeyed". It is not clear what this
notion means in the present context.

5.4.3. Weighing Legal Rules

A greater degree of fixity in the law is connected with
the fact that the law often replaces moral principles
with rules. This restricts the need of weighing and
balancing. However, not only principles but also legal
rules require weighing against other considerations.
Indeed, all socially established legal norms, expressed
in the sources of the law, have a merely prima facie
character. The step from prima-facie legal rules to the
all-things-considered obligations, freedoms, claims etc.
involves weighing and balancing (cf. sections 5.4.1 and

2.4.4 supra). In other words, it involves a value-laden
legal reasoning.

For that reason, one may doubt whether legal rules
actually make the normative system sufficiently fixed.
Yet, the doubt is unjustified. The main advantage of
legal rules is the fact that they create "easy" cases. In
easy (routine) cases, one ought to follow socially
established legal rules without any necessity of weighing
and balancing. An act of weighing and balancing is then
necessary only in order to ascertain whether the case
under adjudication is an easy one or not. Only if the
case is not easy but "hard", must one perform a
value-laden legal reasoning, that is, an act of weighing
and balancing. One the other had, no cases of application
of principles are easy. All such cases are hard in this
sense. One must always pay attention to more then one
principle and perform an act of weighing and balancing.
The point of the law is to create routine (easy) cases,
though not to make all cases easy.

5.4.4. All-Things-Considered Law As Interpreted Law

In this connection, one may also speak about
all-things-considered legal duties, claims etc.

The socially established law explicitly contains some
prima-facie legal norm-statements. Within the legal
reasoning, such a prima-facie legal norm-statement
strongly supports the conclusion that one has an
all-things-considered legal duty, freedom, claim,
competence etc. On the other hand, some other prima-facie
legal norm-statements or moral statements may support
different conclusions. One needs weighing and balancing
of various prima-facie legal and moral statements. The
all-things-considered law is a result of this weighing.
It is a result of interpretation of the prima-facie law.

The word "all-things-considered" implies that one would
recognise the norm-statement in question as legally
binding, if one had a complete information about all
legally relevant circumstances. If a legal norm-statement
has all-things-considered character, then it is
reasonable to assume that it also has definitive
character. When recognising definitive character of such
an all-things-considered legal norm-statement, one
declares that one no longer is prepared to pay attention
to reasons which justify the contrary conclusion

concerning <u>legal</u> duties, claims etc. Indeed, what reasons
can it be, if all things had already been considered?

Of course, interpretation may also result in another <u>prima-facie</u>
rule. But a decision to apply a legal rule to a concrete case is
<u>definitive</u>, and in this sense no longer <u>prima-facie</u>. The decision
leads to an action, and an action cannot be <u>prima-facie</u>. An
optimally justified decision must thus have the
all-things-considered character.

The all-things-considered law is an **idealisation**. In
practice, nobody can consider all things. But the more
the interpreted law approximates the
all-things-considered law, the better the interpretation.
   A special problem occurs because a legal discourse may
be defined as **not** considering some things. Certainly, the
judge ought not to consider reasons for and against the
assumption that the constitution of the country is valid
law, cf. section 3.3.5 supra.
   **The all-things-considered law is thus a product of an
optimal interpretation which**
   **a) considers all things which are relevant within the
legal discourse; and**
   **b) takes for granted all things which are constitutive
for the legal discourse.**
   The very concept "valid law" is ambiguous. It refers
not only to socially established, <u>prima-facie</u> law but
also to all-things-considered, that is, <u>optimally
interpreted law</u>.
   As regards legal interpretation and its result, the
interpreted law, one may state the following.
   1. Interpretation of the socially established law is
and ought to be permeated by moral evaluations, performed
by the interpreter.
   2. At the same time, the lawyers presuppose that the
result of the interpretation, that is, the interpreted
law, needs support of reasons and thus must be rational
in the sense developed in chapter 3 supra.
   3. Influenced by value judgments, legal interpretation
can cause a new understanding of the law and a change of
legal practice.
   4. Still, the result of interpretation is frequently
called valid law. In this sense, one can regard some
"unwritten" norms concerning remoteness of damage
(section 3.1) as valid law, although one needs
interpretation to state precisely their content.

5.4.5. The Relation Between the All-Things-Considered Legal Norms and All-Things-Considered Moral Norms

One may now consider an <u>inclusion-thesis</u> concerning the relationship between the <u>legal</u> all-things-considered and the <u>moral</u> all-things-considered:

(2)   If a person, A, has a legal all-things-considered duty, liberty, claim etc., concerning an action, H, then he also has a moral all-things-considered duty, liberty, claim etc. of the same content.

The all-things-considered law, that is, the optimally interpreted law, is thus a part of the all-things-considered morality.

Certainly, one may try to avoid this conclusion by the following argument. Both legal and moral all-things-considered duties, liberties, claims etc. are determined by a weighing and balancing of morality 1 (which disregards the law) against the socially established law, but the <u>result</u> of this weighing still is different within morality 2 than within the law itself. The reason for this dualism can consist in the different weight the social practice of legislation and adjudication has within these two systems. One could say something like this. A weighing of a Nazi provision, unfairly differentiating Jews, against moral considerations would lead to a total elimination of it from morality 2 but merely to a restrictive interpretation within the law itself. However, such a distinction would create a moral predicament for any person applying or interpreting the Nazi law. How ought he to act? If all-things-considered law and morality 2 are different things, which one ought he to follow? Such a dualism would contradict the point of the law which is to facilitate decision making, not to create insoluble predicaments. On the other hand, the inclusion thesis fits this point very well. The Nazi provision is a <u>prima-facie</u> moral reason. Its weighing against other <u>prima-facie</u> moral reasons may lead to its restrictive interpretation or total elimination. In the first case, there is a moral and reasonable interpretation of the provision, and the interpretation constitutes an all-things-considered moral and legal norm. In the second case, there is no such interpretation. The all-things-considered moral norm would then be the same as it would have been had the provision not existed. And

there would be <u>no</u> all-things-considered legal norm of
this content at all.

To be sure, one may utter a <u>definitive</u> legal norm of
this content. One may thus proclaim that one endorses
this norm as definitively binding in a legal sense, and
is not prepared to discuss it. But such a norm would not
be correct. It would be based on an unjustified act of
political power, not on reason.

The inclusion of all-things-considered law in
all-things-considered morality is, however, no matter of
identity, for the following reasons:

1. If a person has no legal all-things-considered duty,
liberty, claim etc. of a certain content, he can still
have a moral all-things-considered duty, liberty, claim
etc. of the same content.

2. If a person has a legal all-things-considered duty,
claim etc. of a certain content, and, consequently, a
moral all-things-considered duty, claim etc. of the same
content, the identity concerns only the content, not the
reasons which ought to be explicitly proffered in order
to support it. The same content thus receives a legal
support within the legal reasoning and a different
support within a moral reasoning. If the latter is
complete, it must include the former. On the other hand,
some moral reasons may be omitted in an explicit legal
argumentation. It is the case even if the argumentation
is optimal. An optimal legal argumentation does not
require an explicit support of all morally relevant
reasons, though it certainly requires an <u>implicit</u> support
of all of them.

3. Following <u>Aarnio</u>, one may also emphasise the fact
that legal premises, supporting a conclusion, are often
more precise, concise and easier to formulate than the
non-legal ones. Assume, e.g., that the court has an
all-things-considered legal duty to ignore oral contracts
concerning the sale of real estate. The main legal reason
for this duty is, of course, that the law imposes a
written form of such contracts. Now, one <u>may</u> support this
duty by substantive moral reasons. But to justify such a
moral duty, independently from the law, one must adopt a
broad view of the society as a whole, and thus speculate
about the immoral consequences of uncertainty concerning
ownership of real estate, allegedly resulting from
recognition of such oral contracts etc. Such substantive
considerations may be appropriate in legal reasoning, as
well, but not even the optimal legal justification must
contain so much of them as a free moral justification.

This distinction is much more profound than the trivial
thesis that explicitly provided reasons in the law are
not identical with explicitly provided reasons in moral
justification. Explicitly provided reasons may be
irrelevant for a theory of moral and legal reasoning, and
merely relevant for a sociological study of the
rhetorical techniques employed by jurists. But the
distinction concerns something else, that is, the reasons
that should be proffered in the special form of
justification called legal. The background assumption
here is that of plurality of types of practical
justification. Legal justification is a special case of
moral justification. This relation is parallel to the
relation between general common-sense cognitive
considerations and a specialised science. Each science
makes initial assumptions, justifiable only within a
broader form of deliberation. The profound question of
the justificatory force of specialised sciences and
discourses is perhaps the most difficult philosophical
problem of all, which unfortunately remains unsolved.

5.4.6. Gaps In Interpreted Law. Legal Interpretation and Moral Criticism

The socially established (prima-facie) law constitutes
prima-facie moral reasons. One has a prima-facie duty to
follow the established law. But there is a limit. This
prima-facie duty must be weighed against other moral
prima-facie reasons. One has no all-things-considered
duty to follow and unjust legal norm.

Unjust law can be enacted not only in a totalitarian state but also
in a democratic one. The democratic legislation process is fallible.
The law does not always reflect the opinion of the majority.
Moreover, a law reflecting the opinion of a momentary majority can
have so grave disadvantages that the majority would have changed its
views, if it more carefully thought about the problem. The right is
not what most people happen to think but what they would think had
they thought rationally (cf., e.g., Tranöy 1985, 385 ff.)

This conception of law, morality and rationality implies
that an individual ought to adopt a critical attitude

towards the law. He may criticise a particular decision, a number of legal norms or the legal system as a whole.

One can perform such a criticism within the framework of legal reasoning ("de lege lata") or outside of it, thus adopting the so-called "legally-political" point of view ("de lege ferenda"). Already the former permits a lawyer to reduce injustice of law. A person who applies the established law may thus weigh its literal content against other prima-facie moral reasons. But when the immoral law is clear, a legal interpreter cannot do much. Weighing does not lead to any result at all. It is then impossible to formulate a norm which simultaneously would fulfil two necessary conditions of legal interpretation, that is, 1) would have a strong support of socially established legal norms and, 2) would have a sufficient support of prima-facie moral norms. In such a case, an all-things-considered legal norm simply does not exist. As soon one pays attention to the established law, one must disregard morality and vice versa. No all-things-considered legal norm at all can be based on the socially established legal norm in question. Consequently, no definitive legal norm one adopts can be correct. There is a gap in the law, not merely in the prima-facie law, socially established (cf. section 1.2.3 supra) but in the interpreted, all-things-considered law.

On the other hand, one can criticise any law in the "legally-political" manner. A legal interpretation of an immoral provision may be impossible, its moral criticism is always possible. Yet, even in the latter case, one´s thinking must partly resemble that of a lawyer. One must thus support the criticism with both established (legal) authority reasons and moral (substantive) reasons. The difference consists in the fact that the relative weight of the latter increases at the expense of the former.

5.4.7. The Right to Resist Oppression

In some cases, not even the "legally-political" criticism is morally sufficient and one may or ought to pass to non-verbal resistance. Let me distinguish between the following forms of such a resistance.

1. Silent resistance. Silent resistance is practically efficient and morally acceptable, inter alia when the law too deeply affects the private sphere of an individual, including his family life, property etc. One can also find reasons to silently disobey norms that for incomprehensible reasons regulate thousands of everyday trivialities. If, e.g., no legal parking exists close to one's

office, one parks the car illegally at a big square which until
recently used to serve as a parking.

But a single individual can easily misjudge the moral reasons
against obeying the law. Only if acting openly, one can learn for
sure whether others are ready to accept one's views.

2. <u>Demonstrative "civil" disobedience</u>. In some cases, one can
consider public and collective (but nonviolent) disobedience. The
controversial question in many such cases concerns <u>political issues</u>,
e.g., environment, economy, taxes, warfare etc. In this way, e.g.,
Mohandas Gandhi organised resistance against British salt monopoly
in India. Conscripts may thus desert from an unjust war. Taxpayers
may return tax-forms. Voters may boycott undemocratic general
elections, etc. (cf. examples quoted by Bay 1968, 45 ff.).

Civil disobedience presupposes that the state is to some extent
democratic. If one, on the other hand, has to do with such a regime
as in Eastern Europe, this form of resistance is less promising. A
military deserter, e.g., would be punished severely. An environment
protection activist would lose his job, etc. If one in this
situation wishes to resist unjust laws, one may choose either silent
disobedience or - in extreme cases - violent revolution.

3. <u>Violent revolution</u>. Violent revolution causes always some
degree of chaos. I have already concluded that order is <u>prima facie</u>
better than chaos. But if order is so repulsive as Hitler's or Pol
Pot's, it loses this moral justification. (At the same time, it
loses the character of valid law, cf. section 5.8.2 infra). In such
a situation, one can find sufficient reasons for using weapons.

Non-verbal resistance, even in its mildest forms, is a serious
thing. One must thus carefully consider conditions of its justified
use. Two conditions have general applicability. (1) Moral reasons
for resistance must weigh clearly more than counter-arguments. (2)
Verbal reasoning must lack any prospect of success (cf., e.g., Rawls
1971, 373).

1. <u>Prevalence of moral reasons for disobedience</u>. As stated above,
one has a <u>prima facie</u> duty to obey the law. Strong moral
counter-arguments may outweigh this duty. Non-verbal resistance,
however, is justified only if consequences of obeying the bad laws
are in the long run <u>clearly</u> worse than the negative consequences
disobedience always causes. Young people lacking any prospect to
rent an apartment may perhaps occupy empty houses, but they ought
not to throw Molotov cocktails.

2. <u>Inefficiency of reasoning</u>. Non-verbal resistance is justifiable
only if verbal reasoning lacks any prospect of success.

The role of reasoning hangs together with the above-mentioned
<u>prima facie</u> character of the duty to obey the law. In most hard
cases, only a free debate can generate reasons, sufficient for
answering the question what (if any) interpretation of the legal
norm in question is all-things-considered, not only <u>prima facie</u>,
justifiable and thus morally binding one's action. If an individual
participating in such a debate finds that <u>no</u> interpretation is thus
justifiable, he may demand a legislative change. But if the debate
is impossible, an individual has no possibility of resistance but a
non-verbal action, creating accomplished facts. If he then finds the
law unjust, he may in some cases disobey it.

Reasoning may be impossible, e.g., due to the following factors.
a) Censorship and other legal prohibitions. It was, e.g., a futile
enterprise to criticise Pol Pot's "laws". One would be shot for
this. Non-verbal resistance was the only choice.
b) Opinion monopoly in mass media. Opinion monopoly in mass media
can eliminate any effective criticism. Assume that a statute is
enacted in order to permit sale of weapons, otherwise forbidden, to
a certain aggressive and undemocratic state. Assume, furthermore,
that the press, entirely controlled by the friends of this state,
suppresses information about its actual nature. In such a case, a
critic may consider spectacular measures to prevent delivery.
c) Incapacity of the addressee to consider the reasoning.
Non-verbal resistance is also justifiable if the addressee of the
criticism lacks capacity to seriously consider it when making
decisions. Of course, it is not enough that one failed to convince
the authorities. But the reason of the failure may consist in the
fact that the authorities possess ideological means to define away
criticism (cf., e.g., Tranöy 1985, 395-396). In a deeply religious
society, e.g., a liberal may be regarded as a pagan whose reasons
for the freedom of religion are not to be considered. The discursive
community breaks down and splits into isolated parts or "forms of
life". Non-verbal resistance is the only way to be heard.
   One thus must pay attention to these conditions when considering
non-verbal resistance and making a choice between its different
kinds and forms. Some authors have formulated other conditions, too,
e.g., have regarded non-verbal resistance as justified only if
compatible with the principles of the state governed by the law
(Rechtsstaat). Cf., e.g., Dreier 1981, 201; Singer 1974, 64 ff.
Singer admits some exceptions from this restriction. One may
interpret such conditions as a special case in the following sense.
If they are not fulfilled, the requirement of prevalence of moral
reasons for disobedience is not fulfilled either. Besides, these
conditions tend to be vague. One needs weighing of various criteria
of democracy to be able to tell, e.g., what is and what is not
compatible with the principles of the state governed by the law.
   The degree of prevalence of moral reasons for disobedience and the
gravity of the obstacles to argue decide jointly how strong
resistance is to be chosen. But in consequence to the prima facie
duty to obey the law, the person performing an act of non-verbal
resistance has the burden of argumentation. He must be able to
justify his action. Other members of the society have no duty to try
to persuade him that reasoning is better than accomplished facts
(cf. Dreier 1981, 199). Among other things, he must argue for the
conclusion that verbal reasoning is futile. In some cases, one may
regard this duty to argue as fulfilled, when the critic used all
possible legal means to fight the unjust law and failed.
   The critic, resorting to non-verbal resistance, must thus have
access to two sets of reasons, one for the conclusion that the law
is unjust, and another for the conclusion that reasoning is futile.
This is no contradiction. To be sure, it would be irrational to try
to convince a Pol Pot that Pol Pot is not accessible for reasons.
But one must possess reasons which rational persons would accept.

Circumstances may force one not to spell out these reasons but one
must be prepared to proffer them, given the opportunity.

5.5. THE QUESTION OF EXISTENCE OF THE LAW. LEGAL REALISM

5.5.1. Introductory Remarks. Axel Hägerström´s Philosophical Starting Points

The theory presented in section 5.4 supra is a synthesis
of natural-law and positivist approach to the relation
between the law and morality. However, theory of valid
law must also include another kind of considerations,
concerning the mode of existence of valid law. The
questions such a theory must answer were formulated
mostly within the tradition of Legal Realism. Recent
philosophy of law tends to ignore the heritage of Legal
Realism. As I will argue, disagreement with Legal Realism
is justifiable. To ignore it is, however, another thing.
Legal Realists, especially in Scandinavia, argued on a
very high level, certainly deserving a serious attention.
     As stated above, Legal Positivism accepts the
natural-law assumption that valid law is binding but
rejects any analytic connection between law and morals.
Legal Realism is even more sceptical, since it also
rejects any possibility of scientific establishment of
the binding force or validity of the law.

From the beginning of the 20th century, Legal Realism presented
itself in many countries, especially in the United States and
Scandinavia. Let me deal with one line of its evolution, the
Scandinavian, from Hägerström to Olivecrona, Strömberg and Alf Ross.
     The founder of the so-called Uppsala School, Axel Hägerström,
built up his theory around the following theses concerning reality.
All knowledge concerns something real.
     Cf. Hägerström 1929, 116. Hägerström thus rejected Kant's
distinction between the thing in itself and the thing as it appears
to us, cf. id. 114 ff. and Hägerström 1908, 73 ff.
     Metaphysics in general consists of mere strings of words, about
whose character the metaphysician knows nothing; Hägerström 1929,
136. Metaphysical statements are self-contradictory; Hägerström
1964, 42; cf. Bjarup 1980, 152-3. The conclusion: preterea censeo
metaphysicam esse delendam; Hägerström 1929, 111 and 158. And:
"materialism is actually the only possible world-view", Hägerström
1964, 299; cf. Bjarup 1980, 153.

Only one reality exists and it includes objects located in time and space. A human being is thus real, since he exists during a certain time, and always occupies some position in space. Mental processes exist because they are indirectly related to time and space: they are experienced by people existing in time and space. According to a well justified interpretation of Hägerström, he also accepted existence of the content of thoughts, since the thoughts are experienced by people existing in time and space. In this manner, even an imaginary concept like "drake" exists. Some concepts are, moreover, useful for describing things extant in time and space (cf. Marc-Wogau 1968, 113 ff.).

Time and space are objective. What cannot be placed in time and space does not exist. The reason why some concepts cannot be thus placed is their self-contradictory character. According to Hägerström, value concepts like "good", "beautiful" etc. are self-contradictory, if one interprets them in an objectivist manner. They apparently tell something about the objects (e.g., "this picture is beautiful") but in fact they do not do it at all, and merely express feelings (such as "I am expressing my admiration of this picture"). Moreover, value statements lack truth values, since they "describe" something outside of time and space. The value "existing" in an object, e.g., goodness "existing" in it, does not exist in any definite sense at all. Suppose that a person, A, gave bread to a poor man, B, and this was a good action. It is meaningless to inquire where the goodness does exist, it A's hand, in the bread, in B's mouth etc. Neither can values exist in a particular world, outside time and space, since no such world can exist. The expression "the world outside time and space" is self-contradictory.

This was the foundation of Hägerström's criticism of the lawyers' belief in valid law, rights etc. Among other things, he refuted the popular view that positive law expresses the will of the state. The state is, according to Hägerström, merely a product of imagination, not capable of having a will (cf. Hägerström 1953, 17 ff.).

Hägerström's ideas gained influence among the lawyers due to their reception by Vilhelm Lundstedt and Karl Olivecrona.

5.5.2. Karl Olivecrona On Independent Imperatives and Their Functions

According to Karl Olivecrona, both Natural Law and Legal Positivism are voluntarist theories, since they assume that the law is an expression of will (cf. Olivecrona 1971, 79 ff.). But one cannot identify the person whose will the law is supposed to express. A command expresses the will of a person who utters it. It presupposes that a definite individual tells another one to do something. A legal norm, on the other hand, can be issued in the name of an institution, e.g., the parliament, and addressed to an open class of persons, for example taxpayers. "(I)t is impossible to define law as the content of the will of any particular person or persons. Those who for the moment are in power (as kings, presidents, members of

the government or of parliament) have many other things to do than
going about willing what is said in the laws. They do not even know
more than a certain limited part of the law, often quite a small
part" (Olivecrona 1939, 24).

But an utterance or an endorsement of a legal norm causes the fact
that some people think of someone's command, corresponding to it. A
legal norm thus expresses a so-called independent imperative (an
independent command). Its meaning is such that one understands it as
if it were a command (Olivecrona 1939, 42 ff. and 1971, 128 ff.).

In Olivecrona's opinion, the law has no binding force. It merely
causes feelings of being bound. The belief in "binding force" is
merely an expression of respect for the law. But the respect for the
law has important social functions.

"Rights" and "duties" are, according to Olivecrona, mere words,
lacking reference, not describing any facts. However, Olivecrona
permitted the use of concepts such as "valid law", "rights",
"duties" etc. in general commerce, administration of justice and
legislation, and emphasised that the concepts have socially
beneficial functions. A belief in rights has thus a directive
function, it affects human conduct. It also has an informative
function, although the information provided by phrases like "A is
the owner of this house" is vague.

"The statement that A is the owner of this house tells me nothing
about the actual relationship between A and the house. It does not
say that A is living in the house, that he takes care of it, or
draws an income from it... The owner may, indeed, be ignorant of the
existence of the house... Nevertheless, it seems that I receive some
information through the statement... I know that, in the usual
course of things, a person to whom the ownership of a house is
correctly ascribed exercises some control over it. Therefore I
assume that this is the case here, too, unless I know something to
the contrary... I cannot conclude what kind of control A is
exercising; only a vague idea of control is associated with the
phrase that A is the owner of the house... The statement will
(also)... be useful because it shows with whom one has to make
contact if some legal transaction with regard to the house is
contemplated. Whether the statement itself will be sufficient as a
prerequisite for entering into an agreement is another question; in
many cases something more will be needed" (Olivecrona 1971, 194-5).

In legislation, a belief in rights has, finally, a connecting
function. "Since a right, according to the law, can often be
acquired in several different ways and a great many rules can refer
to the situation where a person is in the possession of a right, the
supposed right becomes a link between two sets of rules: the rules
about the acquisition of the right and the rules referring to the
existence of the right." This function is very important. "Its
significance can hardly be overrated; how a legal system could be
constructed without the connecting function of 'rights' is difficult
to understand" (Olivecrona 1971, 199).

This theory created an unbridgeable gap between ordinary beliefs
of the lawyers and legal philosophy. A lawyer was thereby encouraged
to use such concepts as "valid law" and "rights", because this was
deemed to be socially beneficial. As a legal philosopher, meanwhile,

he maintained that their use was objectionable. This gap may easily
cause professional frustration, leading to a retardation of legal
dogmatics. "A right man cannot be a man and feel himself a trickster
or a charlatan" (Llewellyn 1960, 4).
Paradoxically, Olivecrona provided a masterly analysis of the use
of these concepts within the framework of the legal system. Among
other things, his analysis of informative function of a right (see
above) comes close to some insights which inspired the next
generation of philosophers to abandon Legal Realism. For example,
Ingemar Hedenius defended the concept of a right by pointing out the
following link between ownership and reality: If A has a factual
disposition over the property, then there is a prima-facie
assumption that he is the owner; whoever says the opposite, has the
burden of argument (cf. Hedenius 1975, 37 ff.). One may compare this
with Olivecrona's insight: if A is recognised as the owner, then
there is an assumption that he has a factual disposition; whoever
wants to justify the opposite view, must use additional data.

5.5.3. Tore Strömberg's Conventionalism

Tore Strömberg has elaborated a theory of law, based on Olivecrona's
ideas but also including some original points.
Strömberg has pointed out that the most important legal orders are
connected with states, each having its own territory. The existence
of a nation is based on a common belief that, e.g., a part of the
earth's surface is Swedish, and the people there living, mostly are
Suedes. Strömberg has concluded that the concept of Swedish legal
order, valid Swedish law, is conventional. If one tries to verify,
e.g., the proposition that the Real Property Act of 1970 is a valid
Swedish statute, one finds ultimately no ground for this proposition
but the common belief that so is the case. Strömberg has called this
belief a social convention (cf. Strömberg 1980, 39 ff.).
The causes of the convention are complex. Strömberg has emphasised
a historically given ideology of power and authority, expressed in
the constitution, on which other laws are based.
Legal rules are thus regarded as valid at a certain territory.
According to Strömberg, the belief in their "binding force" is
metaphysical, not corresponding to anything extant, yet it
constitutes a condition for efficacy of the law, its capability to
direct the conduct of people.
The content of legal rules according to Strömberg partly
corresponds to the facts, that is, human actions and situations,
partly does not. The non-real part of this content consists of
imaginary legal qualities and competences together with the idea of
legal validity (cf. Strömberg 1980, 63 ff.).
According to Strömberg, one can present the whole legal order as a
system of three kinds rules, i.e., rules of conduct, qualification
and competence (cf. section 5.5.3 infra). The legal order includes
also individual counterparts of the rules, determined in time and
space, that is, individual imperatives of conduct (e.g. an order to

pay), qualification acts (e.g. an appointment of a guardian) and competence acts (e.g. drawing an authorisation). A legal duty, quality or competence can be created only by a person who in his turn has a competence to do it. All legal competence is thus ultimately based on the assumed validity of the constitution. In this connection, Strömberg has accepted Alf Ross's idea (cf. section 5.5.4 infra), inspired by Kelsen, that the meaning of all rules of a national legal order constitutes a totality of interrelated parts. This totality rests ultimately on a social convention.

Strömberg thus claims that the concept "valid law" does not refer to anything extant. The reason is that valid legal rules would disappear had people not thought about legal rules. However, cannot one say the same about material things? The fact that one now and here sees a forest depends not only on the forest but also on the eyes and the mind of the observer. A bird perhaps notices only particular trees. An insect may see only separate branches, without integrating them into a tree. Without ability to interpret the data provided by one's senses, one would perhaps merely notice colours, noises, smells and other "sense data", not branches, trees or forests. Had people not interpreted the "data" as a forest, the forest would disappear, precisely as valid law. All concepts are conventional. Yet, it is absurd to claim that no concepts refer to anything extant. One cannot live a normal life nor perform everyday actions, if one regards other people, their houses etc. as one's dreams. Can one live a normal life then, regarding other persons' money, property, citizenship etc. as mere products of imagination?

5.5.4. Alf Ross's Predictionism

Alf Ross was the best known representative of Scandinavian Realism. He studied legal philosophy for Kelsen in Vienna and for Hägerström in Uppsala. Later, he accepted some ideas of the so-called Vienna Circle and the American Legal Realism. He thus showed a great ability to integrate different influences into a coherent theory.

I will discuss only a part of Ross's extensive scientific production, namely his predictionist theory of valid law.

1. Ross expressed the following opinion: The scientific assertion that a certain rule is valid is, according to its real content, a prediction that the rule will form an integral part of justification of future legal decisions (cf. Ross 1958, 44).

More precisely: "the real content of the [scientific - A.P.] assertion 'P (the Bill of Exchange Act, section 28) is valid law of Denmark at the present time' is a prediction to the effect that if a case in which the conditions given in the section are considered to exist is brought before the courts, and if in the meantime there have been no alterations in the circumstances which justify P, the directive to the judge contained in the section will form an integral part of justification of the judgment" (Ross 1966, 55. Translation here and infra according to Aarnio and Peczenik 1986).

In this connection, Ross made the distinction between scientific and unscientific statements about valid law, the former constituting a part of legal dogmatics, the latter uttered, e.g., by judges. The predictionist thesis concerns only the scientific statements.

2. The philosophical background of this theory is, what follows: Scientific propositions must have verifiable consequences concerning physical conduct and mental experiences of the persons who monopolise the use of physical force in the society. This conclusion follows from the following theses, expressed by Ross:

a) A proposition about reality must imply a certain procedure by means of which one can test the truth of the proposition. (Ross 1958, 39 and 1966, 52).

b) Every meaningful proposition must refer to to observational data concerning physical facts or mental experiences (cf. id.).

c) The law consists of rules for the monopolised exercise of physical force (cf. Ross 1958, 34 and 1966, 47).

Thesis a was influenced by Logical Empiricism (cf. Ross 1958, 40 n. 1)., thesis b by Hägerström, and thesis c by Kelsen. (Re influence of Kelsen and Hägerström, cf. Ross 1958, X).

3. All this sounds quite simple. However, for reasons explained later on, Ross was also forced to employ more obscure expressions. He claimed that the law is "a supraindividual, social phenomenon in the following sense: Legal patterns of action constitute a common ideology, operative in many persons. Consequently, an interpersonal complex of meaning and motivation is created... Legal norms constitute the abstract, normative content which, used as a scheme of interpretation, makes it possible for one to understand legal phenomena... and to predict law in action within certain limits" (Ross 1966, 41. The English translation, 1958, 29, is not correct).

Ross' theory is, however, open for objections.

1. Concerning the predictivist definition of valid law, one can give counter-examples. One can consider some laws to be valid even though no grounds exist for expecting them to be applied in the courts. In Sweden in 1940 (and in Finland even later) the Criminal Code still contained Ch. 7 on the breaking of the Sabbath. In England it is customarily said that while such obsolete rules are not applied by the courts, they are nevertheless valid (cf., e.g., Makkonen 1965, 65). One can also conceive a contrary situation. During the second world war the courts of a number of countries were compelled to apply rules which were forced on them by the occupying power. After the war, however, it was decreed that these rules were never valid, not even during the period in which they were applied.

2. What is to be predicted and how to predict? According to a "robust" predictivism, "valid law consists of a particular judicial (or other official) action predicted to occur in a particular case. Moreover, the lawyer who is predicting the outcome is to base his prediction not only on any relevant preexisting rules but also on such factors as past instances of judicial behaviour... the ideologies, personalities, and personal values of the judges, and their social backgrounds, and the like" (Summers 1982, 118). Robust predictivism is untenable (cf. Summers 1982, 121 ff.). If the predictions are not based on preexisting rules, they are not easy to

make. Neither is it easy to tell what valid law is if the prediction turns out to be an error and the judge decides differently.

3. There also exists a risk of a vicious circle. The real reason for the prediction that the rule will form an integral part of justification of future legal decisions is precisely the fact that it is a _valid_ rule. Let us suppose that a statute comes into force as of January 1, 1989. A legal scholar could then forecast on December 31, 1988 that the statute will be applied by the court during the year 1989. What grounds has he for this prediction? As a rule he does not carry on any detailed sociological investigations concerning the probability of the future implementation of the statute. He is not a "robust" predictivist but a "mild" one. His predictivism "is mild in two respects: the lawyer is not predicting some particular outcome, but a precept that is likely to prevail in the generality of cases, and the lawyer uses only preexisting law as the bases for his predictions" (Summers 1982, 118).

The main basis of the prediction that the statute will be applied, is thus the fact that it was published in the collection of valid statutes. The statute will be applied, since it is valid. How can one simultaneously say that it is valid because it will be applied?

4. The risk of a vicious circle explains also why Ross wrote about "a supraindividual, common ideology". The following quotation is crucial: "When the basis for the validity of the law is sought in the decisions of the courts, the chain of reasoning may appear to be working in a circle. For it may be adduced that the qualification of judge is not merely a factual quality but can only be assigned by reference to valid law, in particular to the rules of public law governing the organisation of courts and the appointment of judges. Before I can ascertain whether a certain rule of private law is valid law, therefore, I have to establish what is valid law in these other respects. And what is the criterion for this? The answer to this problem is, in principle, that one simultaneously verifies the legal system as a whole, as a meaningful complex of the rules of private and public law. One can understand the pattern of behaviour of persons who exercise force, as a result of an ideology that, at the same time, explains _that_ they act as 'judges', and _why_ they act as judges. There is no Archimedes's point for the verification, no part of the law which is verified before any other part" (Ross 1966, 49. Cf. Ross 1958, 36 where the reference to "ideology" is omitted).

The theory of valid law as a part of "supraindividual ideology" cannot be an empirical hypothesis fitting Ross's verificationist philosophy of science. It implies that many decisions will be understandable, if one explains them on the basis of the law as a whole. A sociologist influenced by Logical Empiricism and Hägerström has no means to verify what is and what is not "understandable as a whole". This holistic language, necessary for jurists, is far too vague for him (cf. Aarnio and Peczenik 1986 passim).

Ross failed to make legal dogmatics scientific in the assumed sense. His predictionism, devised for this purpose, is pointless.

5.5.5. Some Critical Remarks On Legal Realism

Olivecrona   and   Strömberg   consistently   accepted
Hägerström´s thesis that valid law merely was a product
of imagination, but they paid a high price for it: one
could not scientifically study valid law. Ross, too,
assumed this thesis and, consequently, proposed a new
definition of valid law. This, however, made his theory
open for both counter-examples and philosophical doubts.
   The reason for all these troubles lies in Hägerström´s
view   that   value   statements,   including   the   lawyers´
statements about valid law, are self-contradictory,
unless regarded as pure expression of feelings. But I
have claimed in sections 2.2 - 2.4 supra that value
statements   have   both   practical   meaning,   related   to
feelings etc., and theoretical meaning, related to
good-making facts. It is difficult to understand why
these two meaning components must contradict each other.

If any contradiction exists there, it is not worse than many other
contradictions, inherent in the commonsense picture of the world,
indispensable for a normal life. We all assume, e.g., that our
knowledge is true. Otherwise it would not be a knowledge. At the
same time, however, we recognise that we can be wrong; what we think
we know may be false. Generations of philosophers have tried to
resolve this apparent contradiction, but few claimed that we have no
knowledge at all. We all also assume that our will is free. I want x
but I could have preferred non-x. Yet, at the same time, we
recognise causal influence upon our will. This contradiction is by
no means easier to avoid. Yet very few people conceive themselves as
either entirely lacking free will, or as entirely free beings.

Legal Realism shows a sceptical attitude towards many
concepts used in the everyday life.   The ultimate
basis for this form of scepticism is another concept, the
concept of reality, composed of facts extant in time and
space. From this concept, the Legal Realists derive their
criticism of fundamental concepts of law. But what makes
the concept of reality better than the legal concepts?
There are many views of reality, each corresponding to a
different   ontological   or   metaphysical   system.   The
validity of any metaphysics is relative. A metaphysics
presupposes a background theory which defines the concept
"real" (cf. Quine 1969, 53 ff.) and states what to regard
as individual objects, their parts, their kinds etc. (cf.
Goodman 1978, 7 ff.). There may be many metaphysical
systems, "all such systems being wholly comprehensive and

mutually incompatible, but all equally valid descriptions
of one's reality" (Castaneda 1980, 19).

If one studies Legal Realism looking for advice how to
define valid law, the result is fatal. Either one accepts
a predictionist definition or one concludes that no
definition is possible. The predictionist definition,
apparently very precise, promises to create a high degree
of fixity of the law. But the promise is an illusion. At
the theoretical level, one is forced to use obscure terms
such as "supraindividual common ideology". At the
practical level, one must accept as valid law whatever
the courts are likely to say. It may easily happen that
judges, especially if regarding the law as something
philosophically suspicious, would create a lesser degree
of fixity than the traditional doctrine of the sources of
the law would make possible. The second choice, not to
define the valid law at all, would be obviously worthless
for the purpose of creating fixity of law. It would,
instead, create a gap between ordinary beliefs of the
lawyers and legal philosophy. A lawyer, even if
encouraged to use such concepts as "valid law" and
"rights", would have no means to submit them to rational
scrutiny. A legislator would be encouraged to regard his
power as a mere tool for achieving any political goals
whatever. All this is obviously incompatible with the
postulate of coherent and rational thinking about
practical matters. Neither is it certain at all whether
such a situation would promote fixity of the law. By
chance or not, the Swedish law-givers usually change the
law very rapidly, and did so especially often at the time
of the greatest influence of the Realism.

5.5.6. The Three Worlds

To analyse the concept "valid law", I must make some more
liberal assumptions concerning reality. I thus assume a
certain interpretation of <u>Karl Popper's</u> ontology (cf.
Popper 1972, 73 ff.). According to his theory, there
exist three different "worlds".

1. World 1 is physical. It includes mountains, animals,
cars etc., existing in time and space.

2. World 2 includes conscious experiences of people,
e.g., a lawyer's thoughts of valid law. Such mental
processes exist in time but do not have any spacial

dimension in the literal sense of "spacial". One cannot tell how long or how wide a thought is. A mental process has, however, an indirect connection with space, since it exists in consciousness of a person extant in space.

3. World 3 consists of logical contents of thoughts, books, libraries, computer memories etc. It contains concepts, propositions, properties, sets, numbers, problems, solutions etc. They have no time dimension. Neither can one locate them in space. The number "five" is one and the same, everywhere and always. To deny world 3 would be both unproductive and strange. It would thus be difficult to abstain from using such expression as "there is an answer to this question", "there exist prime numbers greater that one million" and so on. It would be strange to deny that thoughts of different persons can be the same. John and Peter can have the same views of Charlie's book. It does not matter that John's mental experiences must differ from Peter's, since the former exist in John's consciousness, the latter in Peter's. Neither does it matter that John reads one copy of the book and Peter another. The book is one and the same, printed in many copies. A computer can automatically elaborate a table of logarithms; one can store it in a library where nobody reads it. Yet it has a content.

Although Popper invented the terms "world 1", "world 2" and "world 3", the distinction of various levels of existence is old, known, e.g., to some medieval scholars. Among modern philosophers, one must mention Nicolai Hartmann. Not even Hägerström definitively denied existence of problems, concepts, etc.; cf. section 5.5.1 supra.

To avoid misunderstandings, one can distinguish between different senses of such words as "there is", "exists" etc. Physical objects $exist_1$, in physical sense. Mental experiences $exist_2$, in mental sense. Concepts, theories etc. $exist_3$, in ideal sense (cf. Peczenik 1984, 97 ff.).

In this context, one may inquire in which sense do institutional facts, such as chess, money and valid law (cf. section 5.3.3 supra) exist. An institution is a complex of interrelated components, such as people, their consciousness and their products, some belonging to world 3, e.g., the content of the law. Some properties of the components are independent from the complex, e.g., height, weight, strength etc. of a human being. Other properties are emergent, that is, depending on the membership of the component in the complex. Such

properties of a person as citizenship or profession are
thinkable only in a society. I regard legal validity as
an emergent property some norms have because of their
membership in a complex system, in which the norms are
related to some actions, values and other norms.

5.5.7. Components of Valid Law

I am going to develop the following theses.

Valid law is a complex (a "tuple") of interrelated
components. Two kinds of components occupy a central
position in this comples: 1) some norms; and 2) some
actions (cf. Klami 1980, 12; cf. Peczenik 1984, 97 ff.).

There are also some secondary components, that is, 1a)
legal values, justifying and explaining the norms; and
2a) mental processes, connected with the actions.

Of course, norms, values, actions and mental processes
appear not only within valid law but also in other
normative orders. In valid law, they have, however,
special properties which will be described below.

The "formalist" legal theories emphasise the norms
(cf., e.g., section 5.3.1 supra), the so-called "realist"
ones emphasise action (cf., e.g., section 5.5.4 supra),
but one must pay attention to both components.

These components jointly constitute the socially
established law. This is an institutional fact, cf.
section 5.3.3. supra. But the concept "valid law" is
ambiguous and also designates something else, the
interpreted law (cf. Peczenik 1984, 97 ff.).

The process of interpretation involves mental processes
and actions connected in an intricate manner with the
socially established law. Its result, the interpreted
law, has a modified content, but its structure is the
same as the socially established law: it is a complex of
norms and actions, together with values and mental
processes attached to these.

Since interpretation of law is permeated by moral
evaluations, a theory emphasising the relation of legal
validity to interpretation, expresses the moral view of
valid law. The complete analysis of the concept "valid
law" must also pay attention to this aspect (cf. section
5.4 supra).

This theory is an attempt to reorganise some results achieved in Polish legal theory, in which one traditionally distinguishes between three "planes" of the law: human behaviour, mental processes and norms (cf. Lande 1959, 913 ff., written 1953/54, and a hint at pp. 149 ff., written 1925). The fourth, axiological, plane is often added, and the planes are understood ontologically, epistemologically and/or methodologically. Cf. Lang, Wróblewski and Zawadzki 1979, 31; cf. Opalek and Wróblewski 1969, 983-995 and Wróblewski 1969, 996-1006. Ziembinski 1980, 76 has reduced the planes to two aspects: formal and real.

Similar views have been formulated in many traditions. Let me give some examples. Radbruch 1950, 123 (the theory first published in 1914) has claimed that "<u>Recht ist die Wirklichkeit, die den Sinn hat, dem Rechtswerte, der Rechtsidee zu dienen</u>": the law is the part of reality whose meaning is to realise the idea or value of the law. Reale 1962, 343 ff. and Recaséns Siches 1959, 159 (cf. Laakso 1980, 291 and 299) interpret the law as composed of fact, value and norm. Hall 1947, 313 and 1973, 54-77 (cf. Laakso 1980, 303) has written about the totality composed of value, fact and idea (form). Sethna 1962, X (cf. Laakso 1980, 306 n. 122) has claimed that the law can be studied historically, philosophically, comparatively, analytically, sociologically and teleologically.

The whole complex is legally valid. Particular norms have also the property of legal validity. Legal validity of the norms is an "emergent" property, that is a property they have because of their membership in the complex.

Let P be a property of a certain component of a system, X. Then P is a resultant property if, and only if, P is a property that the component of X possesses independently from its membership in X. Otherwise P is an emergent property. Cf. Bunge 1977, 97 ff. and 1981, 26 ff. Cf. Oppenheim and Putnam 1958, 15.

Lang 1962, 25 ff. and 59 ff., claims that the law has a complex ontological structure "in a semantical sense": One cannot identify any of its "planes" (that is, behaviour, mental processes and norms, cf. supra) as legal without paying attention to other planes.

The property of legal validity is relative (normative, derivative) in the sense explained in section 5.1.3 supra. The expression "Norm N is legally valid" implies that N ought to be observed. To speak about valid norm, one must thus imagine <u>two</u> norms, the valid one and another, determining its validity. As regards <u>legal</u> validity, the validity-determining norm may have various character. It can be legal or not. If not, it is not a member of the complex called "valid law" but a member of another complex, such as morality, culture, ideology, language or (rational) discourse. Using a term invented by <u>Hector-Neri Castaneda</u>, one may call these additional the entourage of the law.

5.6. NORMS AS A COMPONENT OF VALID LAW

5.6.1. Introductory Remarks On Legal Norms

The first component of valid law consists of norms. One often distinguishes between a norm-expressive statement and a norm. A norm-expressive statement is a linguistic unit, expressing a norm.

A norm-expressive statement is a complex (a tuple) of the following components:

1) World 1 entities, existing$_1$: an inscription or an utterance in a physical sense, that is, printed characters, voice etc.

2) World 3 entities, existing$_3$: the normative meaning of this inscription or utterance; cf. section 2.2 - 2.4 supra.

While a norm-expressive statement is a linguistic unit, it is not easy to tell what a <u>norm</u> is. <u>Inter alia</u>, the following interpretations of the concept are reasonable.

1) A norm is the same as a norm-expressive statement, that is, an inscription or an utterance, having a normative meaning; see above about its mode of existence.

2) A norm is the same as the normative meaning content of an inscription or an utterance. The meaning is a world 3 entity, existing$_3$. One may make a distinction between two modes of such existence:

a) A norm as a meaning content exists$_3$ (ideally) if at least one inscription or utterance exists$_1$ (physically) which has the normative meaning in question.

b) A norm as a meaning content exists$_3$ (ideally) in the language, if this language has resources necessary to formulate it (cf. Castaneda 1975, 179 ff.). That is, an inscription or utterance <u>can</u> exist$_1$ (physically) which would have the normative meaning in question.

3) A norm is the same as the normative meaning content of thoughts of an individual. The meaning is a world 3 entity, existing$_3$, if at least one individual experiences corresponding thoughts; these exist$_2$ (mentally).

This view about norms is particularly controversial, as the following argument amply shows: One can ask whether "an expression with which actually nobody's thoughts are being associated, can be said to constitute the reality of the norm. The question is to be answered in the affirmative... because in the case of associating thoughts with this expression these thoughts would be just of the particular (normative, directive) type" (Opalek 1970, 298).

4) A norm is the same as an inscription or an utterance, or a complex of inscriptions and utterances, strongly supporting a conclusion which possesses a normative meaning; cf. sections 2.7.5 and 3.2.4 on the concept "strong support". These inscriptions or utterances exist$_1$ (physically). The normative meaning they support exists$_3$ (ideally), that is, as a meaning content.

5) A norm is the same as a complex of human actions or dispositions to act, provided that the theoretical proposition, which states precisely that these actions or dispositions exist, strongly supports a conclusion which possesses a normative meaning. These actions are complex entities, including various components, among other things some physical behavior of certain individuals which exists$_1$ (physically). The normative meaning they support exists$_3$ (ideally), that is, as a meaning content.

Among dispositions of this kind, one may mention a disposition to argue that a given way of acting is prescribed, forbidden and so on; a disposition to act according to these prescriptions, permissions, prohibitions, etc.; and a disposition to criticise people violating them; etc.

6) A norm is the same as a combination of a norm-statement and such a complex of human actions or dispositions to act (cf. Sundby 1974, 17).

In this section and in sections 5.6.4 - 5.6.5 infra, I am going to discuss some classifications of norms, but one can say the same about norm-expressive statements.

Norms are either individual, regulating a particular case (e.g., Peter shall Pay John 100 kronor), or general, regulating a set of cases having a given property, e.g., "whoever kills another person should be sentenced to prison".

An individual norm is either conditional, formulating some conditions of its application, or categorical, that is, unconditional.

A general norm, grammatically categorical, can always be translated to a conditional one. One can thus reformulate the moral norm "One ought not to kill people", as follows: "If x is a human being and y another human being, then x ought not to kill y". Most general norms are also conditional in another sense, that is, they admit some exceptions. The last remark is, *inter alia*, applicable to almost all *legal* norms.

When considering *legal* norms, one must make a distinction between (1) a legal norm as the meaning of a certain legal (norm-expressive) statement, e.g. a statutory provision; and (2) a legal norm as a *complete* legal unit, as completely as possible stating (a) what is prescribed, prohibited, permitted etc., and (b) all conditions for the prescription, prohibition etc. One can construct a single complete norm by putting together several legal norm-expressive statements or their parts. Of course, the complete norm also contains (c) the conjunction "if... then" and the normative component, such as "should", "should not" or "may".

The provision "Whoever kills another person should be sentenced for *murder* to ten years in prison or to life imprisonment" (Ch. 3 Sec. 1 of Swedish Penal Code) thus does not express a complete norm in this sense. The complete norm is even more complex than "Whoever intentionally kills another person should be sentenced by the competent court for *murder* to ten years in prison or to life imprisonment, provided that he did not act in self-defence, under influence of insanity or under circumstances showing that the act is to be regarded as less grave" etc.

This is one of many possible views of a complete legal norm. The question is controversial. For instance, a complete legal norm is said to involve a pattern of behaviour or not, to involve a sanction (or even a complete chain of sanctions) or not; etc. Cf. Peczenik 1968b *passim*. See also Alchourrón and Bulygin 1971, 59.

5.6.2. Internal Validity of Legal Norms

Of course, not all norms are legal. Some other norms characterise morality, etiquette, fashion, various games, legal or illegal practices and organisations etc. The legal norms differ from other ones through their membership in the *legal system*. This relation between the concepts "legal norm" and "legal system" affects the theory of legal *validity*.

One must thus make a distinction between internal validity of particular norms and external validity of the system as a whole.

When stating that a certain norm is legally valid, one implies that it belongs to the valid legal system. This it may do because of its origin or content.

1) The doctrine of the sources of the law determines the relation between legal validity of particular norms of the socially established (prima-facie) law and their origin. This is a clear criterion of internal validity, highly fulfilling the demand of fixity of the law. The following points are important in this context.

a) First of all, such a norm is legally valid, if it was created in the legally correct manner, stipulated by higher legal norms (cf. Kelsen´s theory, section 5.3.1 supra). The legal system thus constitutes a "dynamic" hierarchy of norms. The constitution tells us, for instance, how to enact statutes, statutes tell us how to make judicial decisions and contracts, etc.

b) However, this idea merely constitutes the main theory to be completed with auxiliary theories explaining some deviations. Though some procedural norms on the higher level are decisive for legal validity of a "lower" norm, others are not. Legal validity of a rule depends also on its agreement with a number of other, non-procedural, rules of higher standing which place certain demands on the content of the rule in question. The distinction between higher rules thus affecting and not affecting validity of the lower ones seems to depend on a complex network of criteria (cf. Merkl 1968, 195 ff., Kelsen 1960, 271 ff. and Paulson 1980, 172 ff.) These, however, are seldom complete, vary from one legal system to another, and one can always reinterpret them.

c) Moreover, a norm can acquire or lose its validity because of circumstances about which the established higher norms are silent. One sometimes recognises validity of the so-called original laws (cf. Raz 1970, 60 ff. and 180). , enacted in an unconstitutional manner. This happened, e.g., with the Swedish Press Freedom Act of 1812. On the other hand, a rule created in a legally correct way can lose its validity by desuetudo, cf. section 1.2.7 supra.

d) Finally, some norms, originating from precedents, legislative history, juristic literature etc., although not binding, are acceptable premises of legal reasoning and posses a kind of authority. Cf. section 6.2 infra about must-, should, and may-sources of the law.

2) As regards the <u>content</u>-oriented test of validity,
what matters is the relation of the law to <u>morality</u>. Some
norms, mainly principles, are thus legally valid if
constituting conclusions of a set of premises including
both correctly created legal norms and moral norms. This
is obvious as regards the all-things-considered
(interpreted) law, but it applies also to some
<u>prima-facie</u> legal norms. In other words, needs a
content-oriented test in order to establish their
<u>prima-facie</u> legal validity (cf. Dworkin´s theory, section
5.9 infra). Since the moral premises are not so fixed as
the legal ones, one may doubt whether the
content-oriented test of validity is acceptable. Yet, its
advantages weigh more than the decreased fixity.
Admitting contentually identifiable principles as a part
of valid law, one greatly increases the set of premises
supporting a legal conclusion. In this way, one increases
coherence of legal reasoning.

<u>Robert S. Summers</u> (1985, 76 ff.) has made the distinction between
the following types of validity-tests: (a) source-oriented (which I
would rather call "origin-oriented"), (b) content-oriented, (c)
process-oriented, (d) acceptance-oriented and (e)
effectiveness-oriented. As regards the "process-oriented" test, one
may claim that valid law must possess some qualities, necessary to
make the <u>process</u> of their application <u>morally</u> justifiable. "Thus...
a statute may not be counted as law because not sufficiently
intelligible to be administered in a law-like manner, or... because
improperly retroactive" (Summers 1985, 76). Since insufficient
intelligibility and retroactivity are properties of the <u>content</u> of
the law, these examples of the "process-oriented" test of law seem
to be a special case of the content-oriented test b.
  One may also claim that legal validity in some cases requires that
the putative law passes a test of actual acceptance and
effectiveness. This is, however, a matter of social facts, not the
content of norms. See section 5.7 infra.

**5.6.3. External Validity of Legal System. Criteria
Concerning the Content of Norms**

On the other hand, one needs criteria of external
validity when stating that the constitution is legally
valid, the doctrine of the sources of the law should be
followed, and the normative system as a whole is a
socially established <u>(prima-facie)</u> valid law. In this

section, I pay attention only to criteria concerning the content of the norms, not, e.g., their social results.
Valid law has usually the following content.

a) It constitutes a "dynamic" hierarchy of norms in which higher norms determine the proper method of creating lower norms (cf. section 5.3.1 supra).

The same circumstances that decide about internal validity of particular norms are thus relevant for external validity of the legal order as a totality. (A moral system has another structure. Validity of its norms depends solely on their content, not origin).

b) Valid law includes not only norms of conduct but also constitutive rules which enable us to speak about institutional facts, such as contracts, promises, marriage, citizenship etc. (cf. section 5.6.5 infra).

c) Valid law includes some norms claiming that the legal order possesses authority to regulate any type of behaviour (cf. Raz 1979, 116 ff.) and constitutes the supreme system of norms in the society (cf. Raz 1979, 118). Supremacy means that legal norm override all other norms, incompatible with the law.

Moral norms, too, claim overridingness, cf. section 2.5.2 supra about prescriptivity in Hare's sense. This is one of the reasons why the relation between the law and morality is difficult to describe.

Valid law includes also some norms claiming that the legal order has the sole right to authorise physical exercise of force in its territory (cf., e.g., Ross 1958, 34; Olivecrona 1971, 271). The sole right excludes illegal exercise of force. On the other hand, the Mafia also claims the right to authorise force but has nothing against the law doing the same.

When emphasising the relation of legal validity to the origin and content of legal norms, we express the formalist view of law (in the broad sense of "formalist"). This does not mean, however, that a formalist definition of valid law is sufficient. Factual efficacy of the legal system is also essential for its validity.

5.6.4. Regulative Norms

As stated above, valid law includes not only norms of conduct but also constitutive rules which enable us to speak about institutional facts. Let me discuss this distinction in a more elaborated way, starting from the norms of conduct.

Norms of conduct are a species of <u>regulative</u> norms. A regulative norm qualifies (1) an action or (2) a state of affairs as prescribed, permitted or prohibited. As regards states of affairs, cf. Peczenik 1967, 129 ff.; 1968, 117 ff. and 1969, 46 ff. (1970, 27 ff., 9 ff. and 60 ff). Cf. Olivecrona 1971, 219 ff.

In the first case, it is a norm of conduct, e.g. "Whoever finds a thing should without unreasonable delay report it to the police" (Sec. 1 of the Swedish Lost Property Act). In the second case, it is a goal norm, stipulating the prescribed, permitted or prohibited state of affairs, not the action that causes it.

Some moral norms are thus goal norms, e.g. "Everybody ought to have a guarantee of a decent standard of living". Regulative <u>legal</u> norms are, however, almost always norms of conduct. One can thus regard the important provision "Social aid ought to guarantee everybody a decent standard of living" (Sec.6 Par. 2 item 1 of the Swedish Social Service Act) as a part of the legal norm "The social welfare committee should grant aid, guaranteeing everybody a decent standard of living".

The conclusion that regulative legal norms are almost always norms of conduct follows from two premises, (1) the definition of a legal norm as a complete legal unit (see above) and (2) the fact that the law seldom formulates goals without stating precisely who should see to it that they are fulfilled. If one provision stipulates the goal and another decides who should fulfil it, the provisions jointly constitute a single legal norm; this is a norm of conduct, not a goal norm.

A norm of conduct can prescribe punishment or another sanction for a person who violates another norm. One can thus make a distinction between a sanctioned and a sanctioning norm. One may call the latter a sanction norm. The norm "One ought not to kill people" is thus sanctioned by the provision of Ch. 3 Sec. 1 of Swedish Penal Code, "Whoever kills another person should be sentenced for <u>murder</u> to ten years in prison or to life imprisonment". An additional sanction norm stipulates nearly always legal consequences of violating the first sanction norm. Ch. 20 Sec. 1 of Swedish Penal Code thus contains a sanction for abuse of public power, including an act of a judge violating the provision of Ch. 3 Sec. 1.

The chain of sanctions ends here. If the judge is not sentenced for the abuse of power, the same provision of Ch. 20 Sec. 1 provides the legal support for punishment of the other one who neglected to sentence him, and so on <u>ad infinitum</u>. The chain of sanctions can also end in other manners. I have no space to discuss this problem.

5.6.5. Constitutive Norms

Constitutive norms (cf. Searle 1969, 50 ff.), on the other hand, enable us to speak about institutional facts, such as organisations, the state, valid law, duties, rights, money, calender, contracts, promises, marriage, citizenship, various games etc. A chess move, e.g., is precisely what chess rules make a chess move. A constitutive norm is thus a condition of existence of an institutional fact. It may be a necessary, a sufficient or a necessary and sufficient condition (cf. Conte 1981, 14 ff.). It may also be a weaker condition. For instance, it may be a component of an alternative set of conditions; if none of the alternatives is fulfilled, the institutional fact in question does not take place.

Social groups, knowledge, science, culture, literature, life styles, religions, churches etc. are also institutional facts in some sense. Science is thus a complex of some people (researchers), types of action (research) and propositions (results of research). Some norms decide that one must perform research in a certain way. Only if they are observed, the result of research is scientific.

Legal qualification norms are a special case of constitutive norms, giving some actions, persons, states of affairs, things, complexes etc. a certain legal quality. They make an action a theft, two people a married couple, a person a Swedish citizen, a thing a pawn, a complex of actions a trial etc. Such a quality is institutional. A Swedish citizen is the person the norms make a Swedish citizen. Without such norms, nobody would be a Swedish citizen. (Cf. Strömberg 1980, 80 ff.; Sundby 1974, 77 ff.; Eckhoff and Sundby 1976, 84 ff.).

In some cases, an institutional fact occurs if (1) a certain constitutive norm is valid and (2) a certain event takes place. For example, one is born as a Swedish citizen; cf. Sec. 1 of the Swedish Citizenship Act. In other cases, an institutional fact occurs if the following conditions are fulfilled: (1) a certain constitutive norm is valid and (2) a certain action is performed. An alien who reached the age of eighteen can thus receive Swedish citizenship; the case is to be decided by the National Immigration and Naturalisation Board; cf. Sec. 6 of the same statute. Such as action is a performative act. It can be physical, e.g. moving a chess pawn, or linguistic, e.g. to grant a person citizenship. In the latter case, one utters a performative statement (cf. Austin 1962, 1 ff. and Olivecrona 1971, 217 ff.). Performative acts thus create institutional facts.

Legal competence is an ability to bring about intended legal effects. The law thus gives the National Immigration and Naturalisation Board capacity to convert an alien to a Swedish citizen. Cf. Ross 1968, 130: "Competence is the legally established ability to create legal norms (or legal effects) through and in accordance with enunciations to this effect. Competence is a special case of power. Power exists when a person is able to bring about, through his acts, desired legal effects".

The quality of being a Swedish citizen is institutional. The ability to create it is institutional, as well, not physical. A legal competence norm thus gives a person an ability to bring about an intended institutional quality. Such a norm is a qualification norm, or a part of it, expressed in a special manner. (However, Strömberg 1980, 86 ff. regards competence norms as a third kind of norms, besides norms of conduct and qualification).

Let me give an example. The norm "If the National Immigration and Naturalisation Board performs the action H, the alien A becomes a Swedish citizen" is a qualification norm. The norm "The Board can perform the action H and thus convert the alien A to a Swedish citizen" is, on the other hand, a competence norm. These norms differ from each other solely as regards their form. Their legal content is the same.

But the competence terminology is not applicable to qualification norms which make the institutional effect dependent on an event (instead of an action, see above). One is thus born as a Swedish citizen, without any legal competence involved in the process.

One must also remember that competence is a kind of a right (cf. sections 2.3.4 and 2.4.6 supra). Since a norm which creates a competence is a qualification norm, it is plausible to regard norms which create other rights as qualification norms, too, or at least as complexes of norms, each containing at least one qualification norm. Plausibility varies, however, depending on what kind of rights the norm in question creates.

A norm which creates A's liberty to do H is a kind of a norm of conduct rather than a qualification norm.

A norm which creates A's claim against B is a different matter. A claim-norm does not directly regulate a claim-holders conduct. Instead, it is related to another person's conduct. If a person, A, has a claim that another person, B, does H, then B has a duty to do H. The reverse implication is more complex. Sometimes a duty exists without a corresponding claim. But if a person, B, has a duty to do H, and a "claim-making" relation between B and another person, A, exists, then A has a prima-facie claim that B does H. I have mentioned two kinds of these relations, (1) the explicit or implicit content of the norm establishing both A's duty and B's claim; and (2) the fact that this norm is justifiable by B's claim. Nothing prevents regarding a claim-norm as a qualification norms, which qualifies A as a claim-holder.

Not only permissibility, claims and competences but also more complex entities, such as ownership, are called rights. These composed rights can be analysed as complexes of permissibility, claims and competences. One can certainly call such a complex right-norm a qualification norm.

The question whether a certain right-norm is a single norm or a complex of norm has a highly speculative flavour, and will be omitted here.

One can ask the question whether constitutive norms can be reduced ("translated") to norms of conduct. In this context, I will discuss two different attempts to make such a reduction.

1. One can regard constitutive norms as stipulative definitions and these as a kind of norms of conduct, thus stipulating that one should assume that a certain action or event creates an institutional fact, e.g., converts a person to a Swedish citizen. But what should one actually assume? What does it mean that one is a

Swedish citizen? Some advocates of the Uppsala school would say that
it only means that others regard him as a Swedish citizen. Whoever
talks about citizenship thus means that someone else thinks about
citizenship. But in such a case, the other person thinks that a
third one thinks that a fourth thinks... about what? At the end, one
must either label the thoughts as "empty" (cf. section 5.5.2 supra)
or state precisely the facts the last person in the chain thinks
about. If one assumes that the thoughts are empty, one shows a
radical scepticism concerning the ordinary language. If one assumes
that they are not empty, one needs constitutive norms to
characterise the phenomenon the thoughts concern. One wished to
"reduce" constitutive norms to norms of conduct, yet they came back.

2. Let me now discuss another attempt at reducing constitutive
norms to norms of conduct. What does it mean that A is an owner of a
property? "Ownership" is an "intermediate" concept. Its meaning is
related to two clusters of norms, the first determining conditions
of becoming an owner, the second prescribing legal consequences of
being an owner (cf. Ross 1958, 190 ff.). If A bought the property or
if he inherited it or if he received it as a gift, then he owns the
property. If he owns the property then he may use it and he can sell
it and he can start a legal action against a person interfering with
his use of it. Cannot one state the same through formulating a
number of norms of conduct? One can, e.g., say what follows: If A
bought this property or if he inherited it or if he received it as a
gift, then he is permitted to use it and he can sell it and he can
start a legal action against a person interfering with his use of
it. One may hope to thus obtain a norm whose structure is "If
conditions v_1-v_n are fulfilled, then x should (may, can etc.) do H".
For that reason, <u>Ross</u> interpreted "ownership" as a mere tool of
presentation, summarising "factual conditions" (to buy, to inherit,
etc.) and normative consequences.

As regards norms of competence, here interpreted as a kind of
qualification norms, Ross wrote the following: "Norms of competence
are logically reducible to norms of conduct in this way: norms of
competence make it obligatory to act according to the norms of
conduct which have been created according to the procedure laid down
in them" (Ross 1968, 118).

To be sure, Ross and other "reductionists" recognised the fact
that even if one could translate the whole legal order to norms of
conduct, in which no such words as "ownership" occurred, such a
translation would exceed all bounds. Constitutive norms, introducing
such concepts as "ownership", are thus useful tools of presentation,
enabling one to formulate the law in a much more concise manner.
Yet, they insisted that the translation is possible, albeit
inconvenient (cf., e.g., Ziembinski 1970, 30).

A more important objection is, however, this. The translation
makes it impossible for one to grasp the <u>point</u> of constitutive
norms. The institutions they create, such as ownership, have a more
extensive meaning, not reducible to the norms of conduct.

a) Ownership does not merely imply that the owner is permitted to
use the property but also that he can sell it. This means that he is
competent to see to it that the buyer becomes the owner of the
property. Moreover, the buyer is competent to sell to another buyer

and so on <u>ad infinitum</u>. Regardless of how long one continues the analysis, one cannot get rid of the concept of ownership.

Certainly, one can avoid this kind of infinite regress by means of a stipulative definition which disregards the consequences of ownership and identifies the concept with "factual conditions": The owner is then understood as the person who has bought, inherited etc. the thing. Yet, the situation is almost equally difficult, as regards the conditions of ownership. The person A became the owner of the property by buying it. To buy is to obtain the property from its former owner etc. To be sure, the legal order as a whole contains rules for cutting off this kind of regress. The first owner of the discussed chain has gained his position through occupation, acquisition in good faith, etc. (cf. Strömberg 1980, 112-113; cf. Wedberg 1951, 246 ff.). One can thus attempt to define "ownership" by recourse to the norms regulating the conditions of acquiring the original ownership. But again, occupation would not have created the first ownership, had the first owner known that somebody else owned the property; in this way the concept of ownership-by-occupation presupposes that nobody was the owner at the moment of occupation (cf. Eckhoff 1969, 63 ff.). Again, one cannot eliminate either ownership or the constitutive norms creating it.

b) Various ideas concerning ownership etc. are a part of a well established picture of the world, endorsed by many people. Such concepts as "owner", "citizen", "marriage" etc. are thus necessary not only when one describes the wording of the laws but also when one participates in a moral and political debate concerning the right interpretation of them. Among other things, the list of conditions and the list of consequences of ownership is vague and can be discussed in a reasonable manner. One can, e.g., claim that it is wrong to expose an owner of a real estate to a prolonged threat of expropriation combined with a building ban (cf. the famous case Sporrong and Lönnroth vs. Sweden, Publications of the European Court of Human Rights, Ser. A, Vol. 52). Such a discussion would be very difficult if the constitutive norms about ownership had disappeared.

Similar remarks apply to citizenship. The institutional quality of being a Swedish citizen, created by a constitutive norm, constitutes a condition for application of several other norms, both regulative and constitutive. For example, the provision "Only a Swedish citizen may be a judge..." (Ch. 11 Sec. 9 par. 3 of the Swedish Constitution, <u>Regeringsformen</u>) is a part of a qualification norm. Many other norms state precisely what a judge must, may or can do, cf. Ch. 4 Sec. 11 of the Constitution. Now, one can try to replace the institutional terms "Swedish citizen" and "judge" with a complicated description of conditions of becoming a Swedish citizen and a judge. Such a description must contain an information that the person in question was born of Swedish parents or naturalised in Sweden. One must also say that the parents themselves were born of Swedish parents etc., perhaps back to the Viking period.

Many people, however, have a disposition to discuss the question whether an alien resident of Sweden should in some respects be placed on an equality with Swedish citizens. The debate is possible because they have well grounded views on the role of citizenship in various contexts, such as the right to vote in general elections, to execute the judicial power etc. But one would not grasp the point of the discussion if various intricate descriptions suddenly replaced the constitutive norms stipulating the sense of such words as "citizen".

One may say the same about many other examples of legal qualification. No cluster of norms of conduct is a complete translation of constitutive norms stipulating who is a Swedish citizen, a judge, a husband or a wife, an owner of a real estate and suchlike. A cluster of norms containing a constitutive norm is the same as a number of norms of conduct together with an irreducible and controversial rest. This rest decides that constitutive norms are not merely efficient means to concisely formulate norms of conduct, but a logically distinct category of norms, indispensable in a moral, political and legal debate.

To be sure, the institutional concepts, such as "citizenship" or "ownership", are related to value judgments and, via their practical meaning, to one's feelings. Yet, these value judgments also have a theoretical meaning; see sections 2.2 - 2.4 supra.

One may also follow the Uppsala school and search for the origin of such ideas as "ownership" in ancient magic, metaphysics of the suum etc. But the origin is one thing and the present situation another.

When participating in such a debate, one must weigh and balance various principles, cf. section 2.4 supra. Such institutional facts as valid law, marriage, citizenship or ownership are conditions of applicability of some (not all!) principles. The principles are, however, not directly applicable to intricate descriptions, at any price avoiding such words as "ownership", "marriage" etc. Institutional facts, constitutive norms (inter alia, legal qualification norms) and moral principles thus hang together.

The following example elucidates the connection:

a) A constitutive norm stipulates some conditions of becoming an owner.

b) To be an owner is an institutional fact.

c) A principle stipulates that ownership ought to be protected.

d) Weighing and balancing of this principle and some others, concerning such values as equality and freedom, justifies introduction and interpretation of several norms of conduct.

If one attempts at reducing constitutive norms to norms of conduct, one must thus either cut off the link between the law and moral debate or reformulate many moral principles in a new way, no longer connected with institutional facts. Such a reform program is gigantic and it is not clear what its purpose would be.

5.7. MORE ABOUT EXTERNAL VALIDITY OF LEGAL SYSTEM. ACTION AS A COMPONENT OF VALID LAW

In section 5.6.3 supra, I discussed some "formal criteria" of external validity of a system of socially established (prima-facie) law, that is criteria concerning the content of the norm. Some criteria concern, however, other things. Not only norms but also some actions are components of valid law.

The system of valid law thus possesses a high degree of effectiveness. Efficacy is a matter of correspondence between legal norms and actions.

An action in itself is a complex of interrelated components, such as a) behaviour and b) intention; one acts to fulfil a goal.

In connection with valid law, one must consider the following kinds of action, (1) intentional creation of norms, e.g. legislation; and (2) another social practice, supporting the conclusion that some norms are valid law.

All social norms have a connection with some action. The action creating legal norms is, however, nearly always particularly complex. One may emphasise this complexity when proposing a definition of valid law.

As regards an intentionally created norm, one may make a distinction between the actions which create a norm and those which give it efficacy.

a) Acts of norm-creation. These are intricate complexes, including actions of many human beings. An act of legislation is thus a complex of various actions performed, e.g., by some parliament members. These act on the basis of knowledge of other complex actions, performed by members of the legislation committee, the responsible minister, the institutions giving opinions about the draft etc.

b) Actions determining efficacy are even more complex. A normative system is valid law if the most important norms of conduct belonging to it are almost always observed, and if other norms of this system are by and large observed.

Efficacy is most important when one discusses validity of the legal order as a whole, but one cannot disregard it even when determining validity of particular norms. Some efficacious norms are valid though not correctly created (cf. section 5.3.1 supra) while others, correctly enacted and not derogated are invalid because the courts do not apply them (cf. section 1.2.7 supra about desuetudo).

Efficacy means two things. First of all, if we consider a given territory we shall find that in this territory the majority of legal norms are observed by far more people and in a far greater number of situations than the norms of non-legal organisations. The legal system is "omnivorous"; it controls the society as a whole, in all of its aspects, at least indirectly (by sanctioning all societal norms); it creates a basic frame for everything that takes place in the society. Ordinary people must frequently apply legal norms to perform everyday actions like buying, selling, paying apartment rents, doing office work, applying for a bank credit, paying taxes, marrying, etc. (cf. Finnis 1980, 268 ff.).

Secondly, this type of efficacy of legal norms is supported by another one, that is by an effective, legally authorised force, exercised by means of complex actions of judges, prosecutors, police, execution officers etc. In brief, some people, possessing official positions, apply legal norms, inter alia sanction norms, to affect actions of others. The legal system thus governs the work of the paramount force-exercising organisation in a given territory (cf. Olivecrona, e.g., 1971, 271 ff.).

Efficacy is often, though not always, a result of acceptance (cf. Summers 1985, 76). In general, the law causes people to develop special attitudes toward it, inter alia to recognise its authority, legitimacy, binding force and so on (cf. Ross 1946, 89-90 and Olivecrona 1971, 70-71). Ultimately, efficacy presupposes coordinated conscious experiences of various individuals. In other words, there must exist an "supraindividual common ideology" in Ross's sense (cf. section 5.5.4 supra).

However, one cannot be certain whether efficacy is enough to make a distinction between valid law and other normative orders, inter alia governing practice of such illegal organisations as the Mafia or the international terrorist network. One needs perhaps some additional criteria. These have various character. The common denominator is a relatively public character of the law and a relatively high degree of its institutionalisation (cf. Ross 1958, 62). One may mention, e.g., open and public activity of the law-applying persons. Moreover, the boundary between states is thus openly delimited, legal norms are published, various public agencies carry signs indicating what they are, trials are public, members of the military and police force wear uniforms, and so on. The judiciary, the police etc. are engaged

full-time in compelling people to observe the legal
system. The law is taught in a systematical manner and
frequently interpreted by professionals (the lawyers),
using established, noticeably technical and advanced
methods and doctrines; etc., etc. (cf. Peczenik 1968c,
260 ff).

When emphasising the relation of legal validity to
efficacy, institutionalisation etc., we express the
so-called _realist_ view of law. This does not mean,
however, that a "realist" definition of valid law is
sufficient. The content of the system of legal norms is
also essential for its validity; cf. section 5.6 supra.

5.8. FACTS AND VALUES IN THE LAW

5.8.1. More About External Validity of Legal System: Law-Making Facts

In sections 5.6 and 5.7 supra, I have discussed
components of valid law and their usual properties. At
present, I will derive some general conclusions.

There exists an established list of criteria of
external validity which determine the fact that a
normative system as a whole is a system of socially
established _(prima-facie)_ valid law. In other words, a
"value-free" analysis of the legal language, thus not
affected by the feelings of the person who performs it,
shows that one may proffer some facts as meaningful
reasons for the conclusion that a normative system is
valid law. Allowing the word "fact" to refer to any
possible combination of "simple" facts, regardless its
complexity, one may thus claim that the following thesis
is a plausible explications of an analytic relations :

(1.1)   There exists at least one consistent
          description of a (law-making) fact, such that the
          following holds good: if this fact takes place, then
          the normative system S is _prima-facie_ valid law.

Let now the symbols $F_1 LAW(S)$ - $F_n LAW(S)$ stand for all
facts which are included in the complete list of
established criteria of law. This list of law-making
facts contains, _inter alia_, the fact that a legal system
has a hierarchical structure, that is consists of various
levels in _Kelsen's_ sense, or of primary and secondary

rules in Hart´s sense. Moreover, it contains not only
rules of conduct but also constitutive rules. It claims
supremacy, completeness and monopoly of force. It must
possess a certain degree of efficacy, etc.

Now, one may claim that the following theses are
plausible explications of analytic relations between
practical statements and, on the other hand, good- and
ought-making facts:

(1.2)   If at least one established law-making fact
          $\{(F_1 LAW(S)$ or $F_2 LAW(S)$ or, ... or $F_n LAW(S)\}$ takes
          place, then the normative system S is prima-facie
          valid law, in the weak sense of "prima-facie"

and

(1.3 If at least one law-making fact $\{(F_1 LAW(S)$ or
     $F_2 LAW(S)$ or, ... or $F_n LAW(S)\}$ takes place, then it
     is reasonable that the normative system S is
     prima-facie valid law, in the strong sense of
     "prima-facie".

The weak sense of prima-facie implies in this context
that it is not linguistically strange to consider these
facts as criteria of law. The strong sense of prima-facie
implies more, that is, that the culture in question
compels one to consider them within the act of weighing
which determines what is the all-things-considered law.

The thesis 1.3 admits, inter alia, a reasonable
interpretation implying that if F is a fact which the
language does not make strange to consider in an act of
weighing concerning the question whether S is, all things
considered, valid law, then the hypothesis is reasonable
that all normal people within the corresponding culture
take for granted, at least implicitly, that F should be
thus considered.

The following theses are also plausible explications of
an analytic relations concerning the established list of
the criteria of law:

(2.1)   There exists at least one consistent
          description of a (law-making) fact, such that the
          following holds good: if this fact takes place, then
          it is reasonable that the normative system S is, all
          things considered, valid law

and

(2.2)   If   all   the   <u>established</u>   law-making   facts
{F_1LAW(S) and F_2LAW(S) and, ... and F_nLAW(S)} take
place, then it is reasonable that the normative
system S is, all things considered, valid law.

More precisely, one may state that the following facts,
<u>inter alia</u>, constitute such criteria of law.

1. Some facts concern the content of the norms.

F_1) A legal system consists of several levels; a
certain norm is valid if it was created in accordance
with a norm of a higher level.

F_2) A legal system includes not only norms of conduct
but also constitutive rules which enable us to speak
about institutional facts, such as contracts, promises,
marriage, citizenship etc.

F_3) A legal system includes some norms claiming, what
follows: the law is the supreme system of norms in the
society; it has the sole right to authorise exercise of
physical force in its territory; it has authority to
regulate any type of behaviour.

2. Other facts concern various kinds of action.

F_4) A legal system includes certain norms intentionally
created by a complex of various actions jointly
constituting the legislation process.

F_5) A legal system is efficacious in the following
sense. The most important norms of conduct belonging to
it are always or nearly always observed in the practice
of ordinary people, performing everyday actions like
buying, paying taxes, marrying, etc.; other norms of
conduct included in this system are by and large thus
observed; most of them are at least not systematically
violated.

F_6) A legal system is also efficacious another sense.
Some important norms of conduct belonging to it are
always or nearly always observed in the practice of
officials, thus applying them to affect actions of
others. Some of the officials, e.g. judges, prosecutors,
police, execution officers etc., participate in the
exercise of a legally authorised force.

F_7) The law is often published and applied openly; it
is also frequently interpreted by professional lawyers,
using established and noticeably advanced methods and
doctrines.

5.8.2. Ought-Making Facts As Law-Making Facts

Moreover, it is plausible to assume that a system of valid law may not be too immoral, since it is morally better for a society to allow an individual to decide all cases according to his moral judgment than to establish a normative order that too often leads to morally wrong decisions. The extreme immorality of such "law" as some parts of Hitler´s or Pol Pot´s legislation makes it impossible for a lawyer to use the legal method in order to reduce injustice of legal practice. In a normal situation, a person who applies the socially established law may weigh and balance its literal content against other prima-facie moral reasons. But when a provision of the socially established "law" is extremely immoral, there is a gap in the interpreted, all-things-considered law (cf. section 5.4.6 supra). Weighing and balancing does not lead to any correct result at all, because no norm-statement is conceivable which would simultaneously fulfil two necessary conditions of legal interpretation, that is, would have 1) strong support of socially established legal norms and 2) sufficient support of prima-facie moral norms. As soon one pays attention to the established law, one must disregard morality and vice versa. There is no all-things-considered law which such provisions strongly support.

Assume now, that the "legal" system in question contains very many extremely immoral provisions. It is extremely immoral on average, "im grossen und ganzen" (cf. Kriele 1979, especially 177; Dreier 1982, 41 ff.). A significant part of its provisions cannot strongly support any all-things-considered law. It is plausible to assume that this "legal" system is not even a prima-facie valid law. "Lex iniustissima non est lex".

This thesis may be compared with the "central tradition of natural law" which "has affirmed that unjust laws are not law... Lex iniusta non est lex"... implies (i) that some normative meaning-content has for some community the status... of law, (ii) that that law is unjust..., and (iii) that compliance with that law is... not justified" (Finnis 1980, 364-5). But "(t)hat gives bad laws too short a shrift... We must therefore say... that lex iniustissima non est lex" (Lucas 1980, 123).

In brief, a normative system is a socially established (prima-facie) law, only if it does not contain or generate too many grossly immoral norms and practices. Moral reasoning decides what is grossly immoral and how much is "too many".

Since the democratic legislation process is not perfect, unjust laws can be enacted not only in a totalitarian state but also in a democratic society. One may criticise them, even if approving of the legal system as such. Legal systems of such countries as South Africa or Cuba deserve a more comprehensive criticism, but one must recognise their character of valid law. Only _extreme_ immorality of a normative system as a whole supports the conclusion that the system is no valid law.

The assumption that an extremely immoral "law" is not valid law is controversial because the expression "valid law" is ambiguous. One may interpret it either in accordance with this assumption, or in a strictly positivistic manner, excluding evaluative criteria of valid law. The latter interpretation is quite natural within a legal discourse of a civilised country. In such a discourse, there is no reason to doubt legal validity of the established system of norms which highly fulfils the descriptive criteria, discussed above. But within a general meta-theory of law, one must also discuss less civilised societies, such as Pol Pot´s. In such a society, legal discourse loses its point. One must be engaged in a broader moral discourse, in which one may and ought to doubt legal validity of the system.

The following facts, _inter alia_, constitute reasons _against_ considering a normative system as extremely immoral (cf. section 2.3 supra).

F_8) The normative system in question is not such that its implementation causes extreme suffering.

F_9) The normative system in question is not such that its implementation to an extreme degree contradicts important preferences of a significant number of people.

F_{10}) The normative system in question is not such that its implementation to an extreme degree prevents fulfilment of human talents.

F_{11}) The normative system in question is not such that its implementation clearly contradicts the goals characterising important social practices.

F_{12}) The normative system in question is not such that its implementation is extremely unjust, since it to an extreme degree contradicts the principle "like people should be treated alike".

F_{13}) The normative system in question is not such that its implementation is extremely unjust, since it to an extreme degree contradicts the principle that weak members of the society should be protected.

F_{14}) The normative system in question is not such that its implementation is extremely unjust, since it to an extreme degree contradicts the principle that individuals may decide about the products of their own work.

To be sure, admitting moral circumstances as criteria of valid law may make the legal system less fixed, because the test of extreme immorality is vague. However, fixity of the recognition procedure of the law decreases significantly only in rare borderline cases, when the normative system in question is such that one must consider whether it is extremely immoral. In civilised societies, the problem simply does not occur.

Moreover, the decrease of fixity of the procedure of recognition may also result in an increase of fixity of the law itself! Namely, the morally-laden, less fixed, recognition procedure excludes legal validity of very unfixed systems. Since the recognition procedure rules out lex inuistissima, one is not forced to accept as valid law some systems based on limitless arbitrariness of power-holders. Extreme immorality is often a result of contempt of the demand of universalisability. The power-holders treat the subjects differently without any universal principles justifying the discrimination. In such a system, a gang of terrorists can exercise power through entirely unpredictable terror. An extremely immoral law would not be fixed enough. Neither would it be very coherent. An important criterion of coherence consists in universalisability which, at the same time, constitutes the core requirement of morality.

5.8.3. Evaluative Openness of Valid Law

There can exist reasons to expand this list of the criteria of law. The following hypothesis is thus reasonable, that is, neither falsified not arbitrary: If one had more information about the attitudes of officials, jurists and laymen, more knowledge of their use of language and a better insight into interconnections of one´s own moral judgments, one would be able to objectively (without influence of one´s own feelings) elaborate a more extensive list of criteria

that may serve as meaningful reasons for the conclusion
that a normative system is valid law.

Can one objectively (freely from emotional bias)
formulate the _sufficient_ condition for the conclusion
that a normative system is _all things considered_, (not
only _prima facie_) valid law?

Such a sufficient condition would consist of (1) the
complete list of _prima-facie_ law-making facts, and (2)
the complete list of statements determining the relative
weight of these facts in the context of the normative
system to be evaluated as "valid law". (1) and (2) would
jointly imply a subset of law-making facts which are
sufficient for the all-things-considered legal validity
of a normative system.

Such a subset can, e.g., include the above-mentioned facts F_1, F_3,
F_5, F_7-F_{10} and another fact, F_{15}, so far not stated precisely, that
turns out to be relevant for the concept of valid law. Another
subset of this kind can include other facts, e.g. F_1, F_4-F_6, F_{11},
F_{12}-F_{14} and an additional fact, F_{16}, that turns out to be relevant,
and so on.

However, one cannot precisely and objectively determine
such sufficient combinations of all-things-considered
criteria for legal validity. One can only give some
prima-facie reasons, neither sufficient nor necessary,
both for and against a given choice of a combination of
criteria. Weighing and balancing of those reasons decides
about the final selection of facts one considers as
sufficient and/or necessary for legal validity. It
decides, e.g., about the character and intensity of the
properties a normative system must have to be valid law.
This act of weighing thus decides how perfect the
hierarchical structure (F_1) of a legal system worth the
name must be; how far-reaching claims to supremacy,
completeness and monopoly of force (F_3) it must make; how
high a degree of efficacy the system must possess (F_5-F_6)
etc. The same act of weighing and balancing decides how
much suffering a normative system may cause, how unjust
it may be etc. (F_8-F_{14}) before one denies its character
of valid law. When performing such weighing and
balancing, one can, e.g., "compensate" the system's moral
deficiencies with its great efficacy. One can e.g. say
that Hitler's fairly efficacious system of 1942 was valid
law in spite of such atrocities as extermination of Jews.
In 1945, however, the efficacy of the system decreased

and its injustice increased so much that one could doubt
its legal validity.

In brief, one must perform an act of weighing and
balancing, and thus decide about the final selection of
facts one considers as sufficient and/or necessary for
legal validity. The following thesis is then a plausible
explication of an analytic relation:

(2.3)   If   the   most   important   law-making   fact,
       F_w LAW(S), takes place, then the normative system S
       is, all things considered, valid law.

Of course, the most important law-making fact is not
simple. It is rather an immense complex of facts. To
identify it, one must perform an act of weighing and
balancing of the competing criteria of law. Moreover,
some particular criteria to be balanced are value-laden;
to apply such a value-laden criterion one must rely upon
weighing and balancing. To be sure, the "formalist"
criteria F_1 - F_3 may be formulated in a weighing-free
manner: A legal system consists of several levels; it
includes constitutive rules; and it includes some norms
claiming its supremacy, monopoly of physical force and
authority to regulate any type of behaviour. The same may
be said about some "realist" criteria: Some legal norms
are   enacted   by   legislation   (F_4),   published,   applied
openly and interpreted by professional lawyers, using
established methods (F_7). But other "realist" criteria,
F_5 and - F_6, assume weighing: The <u>most important</u> norms
belonging to the legal system are always or nearly always
observed in the practice of ordinary people or officials;
other norms included in this system are <u>by and large</u> thus
observed; <u>most of them</u> are at least not <u>systematically</u>
violated. Finally, the moral criteria F_8 - F_{14} are
obviously value-laden, for example (F_8), the normative
system in question is not such that its implementation
causes <u>extreme</u> suffering.

Ultimately, each of these acts of weighing and
balancing involves one´s feelings. The concept of valid
law is value-open. It has some theoretical meaning, that
is, there exist some established criteria of law. At the
same time, it has a practical meaning, related to
feelings, will and reasons of action. When calling a
normative system "valid law", one states that a kind of
approval - let it be weak - of the system is justifiable.
This hangs together with the normative character of the
concept "valid law" (section 5.1.3 supra). Legal validity
of a norm implies that it ought to be observed, either in

the light of some established legal, moral or linguistic
rules, or in the judgment of the person using the
concept.

The concept of valid law is _vague_, yet one can proffer
non-arbitrary, _inter alia moral, reasons_ for and against
the conclusion that a certain normative system is valid
law and thus ought to be observed. When expressing this
thesis, one denies strong natural-law doctrines,
according to which one can state _precisely_ the moral
content of the concept "valid law". One also denies
strong "realist" theories, showing scepticism as regards
the reasonable character of the concept "valid law".
Finally, one denies strong positivist theories, according
to which knowledge of valid law is entirely independent
of moral reasoning.

Vagueness should, however, not be misunderstood as
uncertainty. To be sure, there exists a "big crowd" of
criteria of law, neither sufficient nor necessary. Yet,
the criteria are numerous. Moreover, most legal systems
fulfil most of them. In effect, the certain core of the
vague concept of "valid law" is quite extensive, while
its "penumbra" is small. Only when dealing with Pol Pot´s
creations and suchlike, one is in doubt whether a system
in question is or is not valid law. In spite of
vagueness, the procedure of recognition of valid law is
quite fixed.

Each criterion of the law, involved in the recognition
procedure, is intended to apply to almost all legal
systems. In consequence, the criteria are so chosen that
they indicate the most fixed parts and aspects of the
legal system. A legal system consists of several levels;
a certain norm is valid if it was created in accordance
with a norm of a higher level. The levels are usually
very stable: a constitution level, a legislation level
and an administrative-judicial level. It is not likely
that the number of levels will significantly change. A
legal system includes not only norms of conduct but also
constitutive rules which enable us to speak about
institutional facts, such as contracts, promises,
marriage, citizenship etc. Again, the institutions thus
created are relatively stable. To be sure, one may
dramatically change some provisions of the law of
contracts or marriage but it is not likely that one
entirely gives up the principle _pacta sunt servanda_ or
monogamy. A legal system includes some norms claiming,
what follows: the law is the supreme system of norms in
the society; it has the sole right to authorise exercise
of physical force in its territory; it has authority to

regulate any type of behaviour. This is a minimum of centralised power, very unlikely to be given up in the modern society. The most important norms of conduct belonging to the law are always or nearly always observed in the practice of ordinary people, performing everyday actions like buying, paying taxes, marrying, etc. To give up the totality of such norms is very unlikely. It would be the same as giving up our form of life. Some important norms of conduct belonging to the law are always or nearly always observed in the practice of officials, thus applying them to affect actions of others. Even this fact is unlikely to change, since this would create chaos nobody would accept. The law is frequently interpreted by professional lawyers, using established and noticeably advanced methods and doctrines. This fact is very stable, indeed. Generations of law theorists tried to change it, with no success at all. One may give more examples.

At the same time, the theory of law, presented here, assigns a great role to rationality and coherence in the law. This is, among other things, a result of the fact that it admits some moral principles as a part of the law. I have already stated that such principles, being universalisable, fulfil an important criterion of coherence. Moreover, the fact that the law, according to this theory, includes not only socially established but also interpreted norms makes the legal system very rich, thus composed of enacted statutes, established precedents, other authority-sources and moral principles. This fact makes the number of accessible premises of legal reasoning very great, and thus makes it possible to reason in a highly coherent manner.

In brief, the theory seems to fit both the postulate of fixity of the law and coherence of legal reasoning.

5.8.4. The Basic Norm For the Law

From the psychological point of view, there is no doubt that the lawyers spontaneously, without reasoning, recognise a normative system as a system of socially established law. One may thus enumerate legal statutes, precedents, etc. of a given country, without recourse to any general definition of law. This information is, however, more bibliographical than theoretical (cf. Wedberg 1951, 254). One gains the information through entering a certain socially established practice. The law

students often begin their studies by acquiring a general
view of this "bibliography". Among other things, they
learn a list of the sources of the law, such as statutes,
precedents etc., to which one must, should or may pay
attention. The lawyers learn in their practice, too, how
to perform legal reasoning. They thus master the use of
the concept of valid law.

Once having done this, they enter the way of thinking
which can be coherently understood only if one
presupposes the <u>Grundnorm</u> in Kelsen´s sense. They thus
think that the constitution is valid law. If one
seriously claims that the constitution is valid law, one
thereby means that it ought to be observed. The <u>Grundnorm</u>
says precisely the same, that the constitution ought to
be observed; cf. section 5.3.1 supra.

From a normative point of view (in the context of
justification) one can, nevertheless, ask the lawyer, <u>Why</u>
is this constitution valid law?, and, Why ought it to be
observed? One can thus demand rational reconstruction of
the spontaneous process of cognition of valid law.

The lawyer is not prepared for such questions. But had
he the required analytical skill, he would answer,
-Because such facts as F_1, F_3, F_5, F_6, F_8 and F_9 exist,
and the normative system thus corresponds to the criteria
of law. This answer presupposes the following reasoning.

Premise 1:   This normative system consists of several levels;
the facts   a certain norm is valid if it was created in
F_1, F_3,   accordance with a norm of a higher level.
F_5, F_6,   This system includes some norms claiming, what
F_8 and F_9 follows: the law is the supreme system of norms in
                    the society; it has the sole right to authorise
                    exercise of physical force in its territory; it
                    has authority to regulate any type of behaviour.
                    The most important norms of conduct belonging to
                    this system are always or nearly always observed
                    in the practice of ordinary people, performing
                    everyday actions like buying, paying taxes,
                    marrying, etc.; other norms of conduct included in
                    this system are by and large thus observed; most
                    of them are at least not systematically violated.
                    Some important norms of conduct belonging to this
                    system are always or nearly always observed in the
                    practice of officials, thus applying them to
                    affect actions of others. Some of the officials,
                    e.g. judges, prosecutors, police, execution
                    officers etc., participate in the exercise of a
                    legally authorised force.
                    The normative system in question is not such that
                    its implementation causes extreme suffering.
                    Neither is it that its implementation to an
                    extreme degree contradicts important preferences
                    of a significant number of people.

Conclusions: One ought to observe the constitution of this normative system. Consequently, one ought to observe other norms, belonging to it. In other words, this normative system is valid law.

Depending on the context, one gives various emphasis to each one these three conclusions. I am disregarding this problem.

The conclusions do not follow logically from the proffered premise. The step from the premise to the conclusions is thus a jump.

As stated above, the lawyer performs this jump spontaneously, without considering the questions, Why is this system valid law?, and, Why ought it to be observed? He has a capacity to directly cognise the norms that are valid law and thus ought to be observed. He registers some simple facts but "sees" valid law. In a certain sense, he spontaneously derives the conclusions concerning valid law from a number of premises neither mentioning nor expressing valid law. One may call this spontaneous inference the jump into the law.

The problem of this jump is merely theoretical. Practically oriented lawyers have no need to consider criteria for legal validity of the legal system as a whole. They simply assume that it is legally valid.

In this manner, the legal mind transforms knowledge of some simpler facts into cognition of valid law. Metaphorically speaking, it transforms these facts into valid law. One can call this mental transformation the transformation into the law (cf., e.g., Aarnio, Alexy and Peczenik 1981, 142; Peczenik 1983, 12).

Borrowing the terminology of Uppsala school, one can therefore ask the question whether valid law is not a product of imagination. But the same kind of doubts can occur as regards physical facts. The fact that one sees a forest depends not only on the forest but also on the mind of the observer. A bird sees perhaps only particular trees, an insect particular branches, without interpreting them as a forest. In other words, human brain transforms the sense data about colours, sounds etc. into one's knowledge of branches, trees and forests. It would be, however, strange to call the forest a product of imagination. One could not live a normal life when regarding forests etc. as one's own dreams. But neither could one live a normal life when regarding valid law as a product of imagination; cf. section 5.5.3 supra.

The step from a description of non-legal facts to the conclusion that the normative system is valid law and thus ought to be observed etc. is a jump, but one can convert it to a logical deduction by adding a premise. The following inference is thus logically correct:

Premise 1:
the facts
F_1, F_3,
F_6, F_7,
F_8 and F_9

This normative system consists of several levels; a certain norm is valid if it was created in accordance with a norm of a higher level. This system includes some norms claiming, what follows: the law is the supreme system of norms in the society; it has the sole right to authorise exercise of physical force in its territory; it has authority to regulate any type of behaviour. The most important norms of conduct belonging to this system are always or nearly always observed in the practice of ordinary people, performing everyday actions like buying, paying taxes, marrying, etc.; other norms of conduct included in this system are by and large thus observed; most of them are at least not systematically violated. Some important norms of conduct belonging to this system are always or nearly always observed in the practice of officials, thus applying them to affect actions of others. Some of the officials, e.g. judges, prosecutors, police, execution officers etc., participate in the exercise of a legally authorised force. The normative system in question is not such that its implementation causes extreme suffering. Neither is it that its implementation to an extreme degree contradicts important preferences of a significant number of people.

The added
premise 2

If the following facts occur:
-This normative system consists of several levels; a certain norm is valid if it was created in accordance with a norm of a higher level.
-This system includes some norms claiming, what follows: the law is the supreme system of norms in the society; it has the sole right to authorise exercise of physical force in its territory; it has authority to regulate any type of behaviour.
-The most important norms of conduct belonging to this system are always or nearly always observed in the practice of ordinary people, performing everyday actions like buying, paying taxes, marrying, etc.; other norms of conduct included in this system are by and large thus observed; most of them are at least not systematically violated.
-Some important norms of conduct belonging to this system are always or nearly always observed in the practice of officials, thus applying them to affect actions of others. Some of the officials, e.g. judges, prosecutors, police, execution officers etc., participate in the exercise of a legally authorised force.
-The normative system in question is not such that its implementation causes extreme suffering. Neither is it that its implementation to an extreme degree contradicts important preferences of a significant number of people;
-Then one ought to observe the constitution of this normative system. Consequently, one ought to

> observe other norms, belonging to it. In other words, this normative system is valid law.

Conclusions: One ought to observe the constitution of this normative system. Consequently, one ought to observe other norms, belonging to it. In other words, this normative system is valid law.

The added premise 2 connects some facts with the conclusions concerning legal validity of the normative system and hence with the obligation to observe the norms belonging to the system. One can also say that the original premise strongly supports these conclusions in the sense developed in sections 2.7 and 3.2 supra.

Premise 2 is a concretisation of the following schematic statement:

If a sufficiently great number of facts exist, belonging to the set F_1-F_n, then the normative system N is valid law, i.e., one ought to observe the constitution of N and, consequently, other norms belonging to it.

Many such concretisations are possible. The facts F_1, F_3, F_5, F_6, F_8 and F_9 are not the only criteria of valid law. One may, e.g., also proffer such criteria as F_7 (The law is often published and applied openly; it is also frequently interpreted by professional lawyers, using established and noticeably advanced methods and doctrines) etc.

Within the legal paradigm (section 3.3.3 supra), one presupposes several premises of this kind. Transcending the legal paradigm, one can, nevertheless, argue for them. Premise 2 thus has support of various moral reasons, such as the following one: A morally objectionable chaos would occur in a modern society, if it no longer possessed a hierarchical, efficacious etc. normative system. Such a moral justification of the law can also receive a further support of certain, presupposed, proved and otherwise reasonable statements (cf. section 2.7, 3.2 and 3.3 supra).

The choice between various possible concretisations of the schematic statement, binding the facts F_1-F_n with the conclusion that the normative system N ought to be observed etc., depends both on the legal paradigm and on moral considerations. One may thus regard the concretisations as moral norms a law theorist creates when discussing the problem of legal validity.

As stated before, the addition of premise 2 eliminates a
jump. The jump from the original premise (about some
facts) to the conclusions concerning valid law is thus
converted into a logically correct inference. Since
premise 2 itself is justifiable by certain, presupposed,
proved and otherwise reasonable statements, the jump is
reasonable, cf. sections 2.7 and 3.2 supra.

One can regard both the schematic statement "If a
sufficiently great number of facts exist, belonging to
the set F_1-F_n, then the normative system N is valid law,
i.e., one ought to observe the constitution of N..." etc.
and its various concretisations, such as premise 2 supra,
as versions of the basic norm for the law, the Grundnorm
(cf. Peczenik 1981 and 1982 passim).

Let me point out some differences between this
Grundnorm and Kelsens Grundnorm ("one ought to observe
the constitution"; cf. section 5.3.1 supra). Our
Grundnorm is conditional, thus including the clause "if a
sufficiently great number of facts exists, belonging to
the set F_1-F_n...". To be sure, Kelsen's Grundnorm,
although formulated in an unconditional way, also
presupposes some conditions, namely that the legal order,
whose constitution ought to be observed, is fairly
efficacious, related to the exercise of force and
consisting of several levels, higher norms deciding how
the lower are to be created. But our list of conditions
is both more extensive and openly related to moral
reasoning.

I am disregarding the fact, here not important, that Kelsen
emphasises the obligation to obey the constitution, while the
schematic statement, developed above, also deals with the obligation
to obey other norms etc.

One can also regard both the schematic statement "If a
sufficiently great number of facts exists, belonging to the set
F_1-F_n, then the normative system N is valid law etc." and its
various concretisations as material inference rules in Toulmin's
sense. Although not logically true, they are presupposed in the
everyday life.

Legal validity of the normative system N, or legal
validity of its constitution, is validity relative to two
things:

1) the existence of another socially established norm,
namely the inference norm "If a sufficiently great number
of facts exists, belonging to the set F_1-F_n, then the
normative system N is valid law etc."; and

2) the _existence_ of a sufficiently great number of facts, belonging to the set F_1-F_n.

One can regard this theory as a paraphrase of von Wright's theory of validity (cf. section 5.1.3 supra), according to which the validity of the constitution is not validity relative to the _validity_ of another norm but it is validity relative to the _existence_ of another norm. At the same time, one must remember that the condition "a sufficiently great number of facts exists, belonging to the set F_1-F_n" is not value-free. In order to ascertain whether the condition is fulfilled or not, one needs not only the factual data about F_1-F_n but also an act of weighing and balancing, determining whether a _sufficiently_ great number of such facts exist. Moreover, some particular criteria of law to be balanced are value-laden; to apply such a value-laden criterion one must rely upon weighing and balancing. For example, the _most important_ norms belonging to the legal system are always or nearly always observed in the practice of ordinary people or officials; other norms included in this system are _by and large_ thus observed; _most of them_ are at least not _systematically_ violated; the normative system in question is not such that its implementation causes _extreme_ suffering; etc.

In brief, legal validity is relative to _existence_ of a socially established norm but this norm requires weighing and balancing of many factual criteria.

5.8.5. A Classification of Jumps and Transformations in Legal Reasoning

All these problems result from the great role of _value judgments_ in legal reasoning. Value judgments occur in three places:

1. In order to establish the content of some legal norms, one must perform an evaluative interpretation of such sources of the law as statutes, precedents, legislative history etc.

2. Value judgments are indispensable when one discusses such questions as, How great authority do various sources of the law have?, What is the _prima-facie_ priority order between them?, and so on.

3. Value judgments are also necessary when one deals with the question whether the whole normative system under consideration is valid law.

Various justificatory jumps correspond to these kinds
of value judgments. One may also say that jumps result in
transforming our knowledge of the law, and perhaps also
the law itself.

The term "transformation" is appropriate to emphasise the fact that
some of the added premises, converting the jump into a deductive
inference, may be adopted without any "certain" justification. For
example, one must in some cases rely on an ultimate act of weighing
and balancing, depending on one's will and feelings; cf. section
2.4.5 supra.

Let me comment upon the legal jumps in the reverse order,
to start with the question of legal validity of the
normative order as a whole.
    A. The most difficult problems concern the jump into
the law, from the criteria of law to legal validity. In
the preceding section, I have already described how one
through a jump derives the conclusions concerning valid
law from a number of premises neither mentioning nor
expressing valid law.
    The jump results in the transformation into the law.
The legal mind transforms knowledge of some simpler facts
into cognition of valid law. Metaphorically speaking, it
transforms these facts into valid law.
    B. A jump inside the law occurs, on the other hand,
when one through a jump derives conclusions concerning
valid law from a set of premises containing at least one
statement mentioning or expressing valid law. Such a jump
results in a transformation inside the law (cf. Aarnio,
Alexy and Peczenik 1981, 149-150 and Peczenik 1983, 33
ff.). In this context, let me make a distinction between
legal source-establishing jumps and legal interpretative
jumps.
    B1. A legal source-establishing jump occurs, when one
through a jump derives conclusions concerning some
sources of the law, e.g., legislative preparatory
materials, from a set of premises containing a statement
about another source of the law, e.g., a statute.
    One thus needs a jump when implementing some precedents
as premises for a conclusion concerning the appropriate
role of legislative preparatory materials in the
statutory interpretation. First of all, one must then
interpret the precedents themselves, for instance to
establish a general norm, implicitly based on them. To
perform such an interpretation of precedents one must,

inter alia, supplement them with some established norms of legal reasoning.

These norms are related to the concept of legal reasoning. It would be strange to *simultaneously* refute a significant part of the set of such norms and still try to perform a *legal* reasoning; cf. section 3.3.3 supra and chapters 6 and 7 infra.

But the established reasoning norms do not unambiguously determine the interpretative conclusion. One also needs some moral premises, first of all moral principles. One must often weigh and balance various precedents, reasoning norms and moral principles, thus ultimately relying on one´s will and feelings, cf. sections 2.4.5 supra.

Such jumps result in legal *source-establishing transformations*. The lawyer transforms knowledge of some sources of the law into knowledge of other such sources.

B2. *A legal interpretative jump* occurs, when one through a jump derives conclusions concerning interpretation of a norm from a set of premises containing a statement about the wording of a source of the law, e.g., a statute or a precedent.

One thus needs a jump, e.g., when implementing some provisions of the law of torts as premises for a conclusion concerning liability in cases of remoteness of damage. To perform such an interpretation of a statute, one also needs some additional premises, among other things both some established reasoning norms (see above) and moral principles. One must often weigh and balance various reasons, *inter alia* the wording of statutes, precedents, reasoning norms and moral principles, again ultimately relying on one´s will and feelings.

Such jumps result in legal *interpretative transformations*. The lawyer transforms knowledge of the wording of the sources of the law into knowledge of interpreted law.

5.9. ONE RIGHT ANSWER TO ALL LEGAL QUESTIONS?

5.9.1. Introductory Remarks

In Chapters 2, 3 and 4, I have described three demands of
rationality, Logical, Supportive and Discursive. Assume
now that an example of legal reasoning is L-rational and
fulfils the demands of S- and D-rationality to a maximal
possible degree. Must such a reasoning always lead to a
single right conclusion? The question is highly
controversial because it involves, among other things,
basic problems of moral theory, analysis of the concept
of valid law, and the prima-facie moral duty to obey
valid law (cf. sections 5.4 - 5.8 supra). I will now
critically discuss Ronald Dworkin´s answer to it.

Dworkin's theory includes three parts, 1) law and morality, 2) the
rights thesis, and 3) the right-answer thesis. Let me discuss them
in this order.
   Concerning the relation between law and morality, Dworkin points
out that in addition to legal rules, there are legal principles. I
have already discussed the contentual difference between rules and
principles, cf. section 2.4 supra.
   Dworkin own formulation is, what follows: "Rules are applicable in
an all-or-nothing fashion. If the facts a rule stipulates are given,
then either the rule is valid, in which case the answer it supplies
must be accepted, or it is not, in which case it contributes nothing
to the decision... A principle... states a reason that argues in one
direction, but does not necessitate a particular decision."
   In addition to it, rules and principles have, according to
Dworkin, different basis of validity. "(Legal rules) are valid
because some competent institution enacted them". Legal principles,
on the other hand, must to a high degree simultaneously fulfil two
demands. They must conform to "a sense of appropriateness developed
in the profession and the public over time". At the same time, they
must fit statutes, judicial decisions and their "institutional
history" (Dworkin 1977, 40 and 340).
   As regards various views on the role of principles in the legal
order, cf., e.g., Alexy 1985, 71 ff.; Esser 1964, 39 ff.; Jörgensen
1970, 96 ff.; Ekelöf 1956, 207 ff.
   The relation between these two demands is this. "(N)o principle
can count as a justification of institutional history unless it
provides a certain threshold adequacy of fit, though amongst those
principles that meet this test of adequacy the morally soundest must
be preferred" (Dworkin 1977, 342). An American court was thus able
to discover (not to create!) the validity of the principle that
nobody should profit from his own wrong, though this principle had
not been formulated in any previous statute or decision (the case
Riggs v. Palmer, 115 N.Y. 506, 22 N.E. 188, 1889).

5.9.2. The Rights Thesis

This leads Dworkin to the "rights thesis". Morally justifiable
principles, not "policies", typically justify judicial decisions in
"hard" cases. These principles "are propositions that describe
rights" (Dworkin 1977, 90). The task of the court is to discover
pre-existing rights of the parties. To be sure, counter-examples
demonstrating that judges often base decisions in "hard" cases on
policy grounds instead on rights and principles abound.
   The Swedish Supreme Administrative Court, e.g., often relies on
policy considerations, cf., e.g., the cases concerning municipal
competence, quoted in the semi-official Swedish Statute Book in
connection with sec. 4 of the Local Government Act.
   But Dworkin replies that "(t)he difference between an argument of
principle and an argument of policy... is a difference between two
kinds of questions that a political institution might put to itself,
not a difference in the kinds of facts that can figure in an answer.
If an argument is intended to answer the question whether or not
some party has a right to a political act or decision, then the
argument is an argument of principle, even though the argument is
thoroughly consequentialist in its detail" (Dworkin 1977, 297).
   Obviously, this "rights thesis" does not exclude the fact that a
judge - when establishing the rights of the parties in hard cases -
must rely upon weighing and balancing of various considerations.
   On the other hand, the role of weighing and balancing within
Dworkin's theory is restricted by his thesis that rights are
"trumps" of an individual, in the sense of always having priority
before policies. The latter, often concerning collective goods, are,
in Dworkin's view, not to be weighed and balanced against rights.
   The "rights thesis" is, however, open to criticism. In this
context, let me briefly discuss three theses, (1) rights are
"trumps", (2) rights occupy a special position in the law, as
compared with morality and (3) rights are pre-existent.
   1. Only all-things-considered rights are "trumps" which cannot be
balanced against anything else. So is the case not because they are
rights but simply because they are have the all-things-considered
quality. On the other hand, prima-facie rights, like all prima-facie
norms, are to be weighed against other reasons (cf. Alexy 1986).
   Moreover, the reasons which one thus must weigh and balance
against rights include collective values, e.g., environment, order,
culture and progress. The latter are not reducible to the individual
rights. To justify this thesis, let me merely report Alexy's
argument: The best way to enforce collective goods is by collective
processes, and this shows that collective goods are not a simple sum
of individual rights. Cf. Alexy 1986. (To be sure, Alexy admits a
prima-facie priority of individual rights in the cases of doubt.).
   At the same time, I agree with Alexy that individual rights cannot
be satisfactorily justified by collective values only. Such a purely
collectivist justification would mean that in all cases in which an
individual right collides with the collective value constituting its
justification, the later must prevail. But this unrestricted
priority of collective values is possible only in a system in which

an individual is not treated seriously, and such a system is unjustifiable (cf. Alexy 1986).

Briefly speaking, in moral weighing and balancing in general, the position of rights and collective goods is the same: all of them must be considered, no general priority relation is justifiable.

2. On the other hand, one must admit that rights occupy a special position within the law.

First of all, a right (precisely speaking, a claim) occupies a special position as a reason supporting a legal duty of another person; this makes the following thesis plausible:

> If the prima-facie law explicitly contains, implies or at least strongly supports the conclusion that B ought to do H, then such a claim-making relation exists between B and another person, A, that the law also supports A's prima-facie claim that B do H.

Given a legal duty, one may thus always find the underlying claim, often constituting a part of a right to a holding.

Second, one can think that although a judge never may ignore the actual rights, he may in some cases ignore collective goods and deal only with rights.

But even if this is so, the role of weighing and balancing in the law remains great because, as pointed out above, the prima-facie rights must be weighed and balanced against each other.

3. Dworkin has also pointed out that the rights the judge states are "pre-existent", regardless of whether or not any statute or precedent already established them. But this theory also is open to criticism. As stated before, when the judge interprets valid law, he is confronted with many questions, some concerning rights. But not even when dealing with rights, is he always concerned with the question what rights the parties already have. No doubt, the judge must pay attention to the sources of law, to socially established moral norms, to customary legal reasoning-norms and to other pre-existing factors. But he also must reconcile (harmonise) these factors. He must thus perform an act of weighing and balancing.

Is this act of weighing an appropriate means to cognitively establish pre-existing rights, duties, etc.? Or can the right etc. in question, in some cases, come to existence in the moment of interpretation, not before? I will return to this question later on.

Another problem indicated by Dworkin's theory is this. The theory implies that one cannot meaningfully deny what the people participating in a legal process assume. They claim that certain rights, and the judicial obligation to enforce these, had existed already before the judicial decision recognising their existence was made. Therefore, they did exist already before the decision.

In my opinion, on the other hand, all participants of a judicial process, provided that they understand the sense of the words "the court", "litigation" etc., must take for granted that the task of the process is to answer the question who is right. But "to be right" is not the same as "to have a right". "To be right" means in this connection to rightly interpret the relevant legal norms. Some of the norms stipulate rights, some do not. Some are principles, other are rules. Some are norms of conduct, other are qualification norms, e.g. giving one a power or competence to perform a certain legal act. Some are pre-existent, some continually created.

Neither is it certain that a law theorist had to share the opinion of the participants of a judicial process, even if they had assumed that the point of litigation always is to establish pre-existent rights. To be sure, it is difficult to refute what everybody claims when participating in a definite practice, such as a legal process; cf. section 4.4.6 supra on the form of life. But such claims can contradict some other common assumptions, made within our Weltaschauung and concerning the question what the word "pre-exist" means. Since our Weltaschauung is dominated by scientific thinking, we do not tend to acknowledge existence of so elusive entities as rights which nobody has so far formulated. Such assumptions can force one to revise the naive belief in pre-existing rights.

5.9.3. The Right Answer Thesis

Another important thesis in Dworkin's theory is that the question, what is the law on this issue, always or almost always has only one right answer.

Dworkin starts from the following thesis. In his opinion, a judge should apply the "constructive model"; that is, he must accept precedents "as specifications for a principle that he must construct, out of a sense of responsibility for consistency with what has gone before" (Dworkin 1977, 161).

Dworkin thus "condemns the practice of making decisions that seem right in isolation, but cannot be brought within some comprehensive theory of general principles and policies that is consistent with other decisions also thought right" (p. 87). His theory of legal "integrity" (i.e., coherence) compares a lawyer with a writer, participating in writing a novel seriatim. Each lawyer intends to make his additions fit both the material he has been given and his substantive value judgments (cf. Dworkin 1986, 176 ff. and 225 ff.).

Let me call this view a coherence thesis, and emphatically declare my unconditional agreement with it.

However, Dworkin also believes that such a method would, in theory if not in practice, almost or almost always result in the one right answer. Only Hercules could accomplish so much but every judge can and should try to get as close to this result as he can.

Let me mention at once two factors explaining, inter alia, why I do not believe that this is the case. First, legal language is vague. Second, legal reasoning includes value judgments.

Dworkin, however, does not admit that these reasons justify the anti-Herculean conclusion. He must admit vagueness of the legal language but he would insist that a combination of enacted law with moral judgments always or almost always generates the one right answer to difficult legal questions. Dworkin admits that vagueness of the enacted law may force a judge to use his value judgment when applying the law. He also admits that a judge has the last word;

nobody may change the results he thus reached. However, he rejects "strong" judicial discretion which would exist, if the judge had not been bound by standards set by the enacted law. At the same time, he says that Hercules J., thus bound by the enacted law, can interpret it in the light of legal principles together with his moral judgment, and thus find the one right answer to all legal questions. Now, the fact that this value-laden interpretation leads to the one right answer means that the enactment together with the principles give the judge a precise directive. The enactment must thus be precise in the context of the principles. In other words, Dworkin claims that almost all legal norms are contextually precise, though they may be lexically vague.

Before going further, let me reconstruct an important part of Dworkin's reasoning, as follows.

a. All participants of a judicial process, provided that they understand the sense of the words "the court", "litigation" etc., must take for granted that the task of the process is to answer the question who is right.

Therefore:

b. In any judicial process, one party is right.

Therefore:

c. In any judicial process, the disputed question has the one and only one right answer.

Therefore:

d. All or almost all legal questions have the one and only one right answer.

But one can replace this reasoning by a more cautious one:

a. All participants of a judicial process, provided that they understand the sense of the words "the court", "litigation" etc., must take for granted that the task of the process is to answer the question who is right.

Therefore:

b'. In any judicial process, one <u>asks the question</u> which party is right.

Therefore:

c'. In any judicial process, one can answer the disputed question in one of the following ways:

c1. Statutes, precedents and other sources of the law constitute a sufficient ground for concluding which party is right.

Or:

c2. Statutes, precedents and other sources of the law together with such reasonable premises as the traditional legal reasoning-norms, justifiable moral judgments etc. constitute a sufficient ground for concluding which party is right.

Or:

c3. Not even so expanded set of premises does constitute a sufficient ground for concluding which party is right.

Therefore:

d. Although some legal questions have the one right answer, other have many competing right answers. In the latter case (cf. item c3), the judge must make a discretionary choice.

Dworkin, however, refutes the idea of judicial discretion. He says that the probability of "a tie" - a situation in which the reasons

are perfectly balanced, thereby making a single best answer
theoretically impossible - is so low that it can be ignored (cf.
Dworkin 1977, 286).

To this objection, one can provide the following reply. Dworkin
counts only with three possibilities:
1) the reasons for a conclusions weigh more than the
counter-arguments;
2) the counter-arguments weigh more;
3) the reasons and the counter-arguments weigh precisely equally.
He overlooks the fourth possibility, that is,
4) the reasons and the counter-arguments are incommensurable.

5.9.4. The Incommensurability Thesis

A "single scale of measurable values" for legal reasoning
is unavailable. One needs weighing and balancing which
"involves multiple criteria", so that "neither of the
opposing cases is stronger than the other, and yet they
are not finely balanced" (cf. Mackie 1977b, 9).

Let me now proffer some reasons in favour of the
incommensurability thesis. First of all, legal language
is not absolutely precise. To be sure, Dworkin must know
this, but he would insist that a combination of enacted
law with moral judgments always or almost always
generates the one right answer to difficult legal
questions. In other words, Dworkin would claim that
almost all legal norms are contextually precise, though
they may be lexically vague.

However, and this is the point, legal reasoning
includes value judgments and these have not only
theoretical but also practical (volitional, emotive,
conative) meaning. In my opinion, this practical meaning
prevents even a Hercules from discovering the only right
answer to difficult legal questions. The ultimate
reasons, shaping weighing and balancing of other reasons,
must be incommensurable and the act of weighing cannot
establish anything pre-existent. To show this, let me
argue that the act of weighing must be ultimately
dependent not only on one´s moral or legal knowledge but
also on one´s will and feelings. This view is intuitively
convincing. Weighing and balancing can depend, e.g., on
the assumed political ideology, the chosen method of
statutory construction etc. In other words, the set of
premises, from which a judicial decision of a hard case
follows, contains reasonable but not proved premises. Can

one <u>prove</u>, e.g., that the economic reasons for a tax reduction weigh more than equality reasons against it?

A more detailed argumentation consists of three steps.

1. First of all, all reasoning must have an end. As soon as one claims that a certain reason weighs more than another, one faces the question "Why?". The answer can be supported by further reasons. These, too, can be weighed and balanced against thinkable counter-arguments. One can thus assume that the objectively best weighing takes into consideration <u>all</u> relevant reasons for the conclusion in question and <u>all</u> relevant counter-arguments (that is, reasons for the opposite conclusion). However, if one does not wish to be engaged in a circular reasoning, one must take the "last", ultimate reason for granted, without further reasons; see section 2.4.5 supra.

2. The second step involves the following question, How can one know that a moral conclusion which thus rests on an unsupported assumption is right? In other words, how can one know that all important reasons for and against a given action have been taken into consideration? How can one know that no unknown counter-arguments weigh more? In theory, there exist the following possibilities.

a. The ultimate assumption is <u>obvious</u>, that is, so convincing that one can by Reason alone, objectively, freely from emotions, gain knowledge that it is right.

b. The reasoning is so <u>coherent</u> that one can objectively (freely from emotional bias) gain knowledge that it is right.

c. The reasoning is accepted spontaneously, under influence of one´s <u>will, feelings and emotions</u>.

Although I do not exclude that some practical statements may be obviously right, I insist that they are too few to bear the edifice of practical reasoning. One also needs a combination of the second and the third possibility. Moral reasoning involves both will, feelings and emotions but a reasonable person has a disposition to emotionally accept as coherent reasonings as possible.

3. The third step begins with the insight that, of course, one can still find some philosophical grounds for insisting that, at the final point of weighing, there always is an ultimate assumption, so obvious that one can by Reason alone, objectively, freely from emotional bias, gain knowledge that it is right. But this kind of foundationalism is incompatible with the following metaphysical assumptions.

a. The list of all-things-considered reasons for action <u>cannot</u> be determined by objective criteria only. A human being is free in this sense: In the last resort, he can by his fiat decide which reasons of action are compelling and which are not.

b. We all assume that there is only one world, common for everybody. In spite of difficulties concerning the correspondence theory of truth, one can assume that something in the world makes theoretical propositions true or false. In this respect, there is no space for a fiat. On the other hand, we do not expect the same objectivity in the practical sphere. An action can be good from the point of view of some persons and evil from the point of view of others. Not even a person who denies that one ought not to kill is so insane as an individual who thinks that he lives in another world than others.

See also Mackie 1977, 15-49.

However, I do not think that this implies "an error theory, admitting that a belief in objective values is built into ordinary moral thought and language, but holding that this ingrained belief is false" (id. 48-49). I would rather say the following: A belief in justifiable values is built into the moral thought. This belief is true, provided that "justifiable" means "included in a highly coherent theory". But since incompatible moral statements can be simultaneously included in highly coherent theories, holding this belief does not imply that there is only one right answer to all moral questions.

If these assumptions are right, then unshakeable foundations, if any, are not enough to ultimately justify practical conclusions. In particular, they are not enough to establish all-things-considered rights.

Yet, let me finish with a caveat. The metaphysical assumptions, asserted above, constitute a component of one of many possible systems of metaphysics, cf. section 5.5.5 supra. As such, there are contestable. But can one think in a profound manner without a metaphysics?

5.9.5. Existence of All-Things-Considered Law

These assumptions made, all-things-considered rights cannot be pre-existent. On the contrary, they come to existence with the act of weighing. Yet, the latter is not entirely arbitrary. One needs the idea of ultimately free weighing in combination with the idea of coherence.

When the judge interprets valid law, he is confronted with many questions, <u>some</u> concerning rights. But not even when dealing with rights, he is always concerned with the question what rights the parties already have. In some cases, the right in question comes to existence in the moment of interpretation, not before. No doubt, the judge must pay attention to the sources of the law, the socially established moral norms, the customary legal reasoning-norms and other pre-existing factors. But he also must reconcile (harmonise) these factors. He must thus perform an act of weighing and balancing, ultimately dependent not only on his legal knowledge but also on his will and feelings.

The point of legal decision-making is thus either to establish and enforce the rights of the parties or at least to decide, by weighing and balancing various factors, to what degree their interests should be protected. The latter decision involves weighing and balancing of various considerations. Collective goods and policies may be taken into account in the process of weighing but never to such a degree that the rights are entirely ignored.

A consequence of this view is this. When the interpreter uses value judgments to establish valid law, he expects that others will endorse the interpretation. He thus assumes that the interpreted law is the same for everybody. The expectation is sometimes satisfied, sometimes not. We have thus to do with three different things:

1) the socially established law;

2) the interpreted law, the same for everybody; and

3) a cluster of various proposals, each recommending a different interpretation of law.

The interpreted law <u>can</u> be the same for everybody because the interpreters are fairly similar to each other. They share the same legal paradigm. In other words, they use similar concepts and believe in similar rationality ideals; they assume that interpretation should aim at establishing valid law; they have a similar view on the sources of the law, legal method, legal certainty and justice; cf. section 3.3.3 supra.

In some cases, however, proposals of interpretation may differ, albeit all are aiming at rationality. Such a situation can occur because similarity of interpreters is limited. Their opinions of legal concepts, rationality, legal method, etc. are similar but not identical.

Consequently, the interpreted law comes to existence in the moment of interpretation, not before. The

interpretatory statement thus cannot be true in the
literal sense, since it creates, not describes the
interpreted law.

All this may be said about all kinds of rights, moral
and legal and, generally, about all kinds of moral and
legal conclusions. However, there also exist situations
in which there is a single right answer to a certain
moral question, yet no right answer at all to the
corresponding legal question. This conclusion follows
from the fact that the all-things-considered law is a
result of weighing and balancing of two different sets of
prima-facie reasons, the socially established legal norms
and moral considerations. These two sets may be
incompatible. I have thus stated in section 5.4.6 supra
that when the immoral law is very clear, weighing and
balancing of it against moral considerations does not
lead to any result at all. It is then impossible to
formulate a norm-statement which simultaneously would
have 1) a strong support of socially established legal
norms and, 2) a sufficient support of prima-facie moral
norms. In such a case, an all-things-considered legal
norm simply does not exist. There is a gap in the
interpreted, all-things-considered law.

5.9.6. Some Remarks on "External Scepticism"

Dworkin finds this kind of "external scepticism" (cf. Dworkin 1986,
78 ff. and 266 ff.) is untenable, for the following reason. No
important difference exists between the statements (1) "slavery is
wrong" and (2) "there is only one right answer to the question of
slavery, namely that slavery is wrong". If one thus agrees that
slavery is wrong, one must accept that there is only one right
answer to such moral questions.

Yet, Dworkin overlooks an important difference between the moral
statement 1 and the philosophical statement 2. To be sure, both
statements have a certain theoretical meaning. But only the first,
not the second also has a practical meaning, that is, expresses
emotional rejection of slavery and constitutes a reason for fighting
it. It follows, that a person who seriously claims that slavery is
wrong can admit that another sane person can share the emotions of
most ancient Greeks and Romans and deny that slavery is wrong. One
admits that the opponents judgment is ultimately is based on
different feelings. On the other hand, one cannot seriously utter
the philosophical thesis 2 that there is only one right answer...
etc., and simultaneously show this kind of tolerance against people
who say that no such answer exists. For either a theoretical
proposition is true, or it is false. Tertium non datur.

This difference is even clearer as regards negation statements. Dworkin's reasoning implies what follows. The statement (3) "there is no single right answer to any moral question" implies the statement (4) "there is no single right answer to the moral question of slavery", and this implies that (5) "slavery is not wrong". In other words, a person like myself must think that slavery is not wrong. But this devastating conclusion does not follow at all, due to the following important difference between the moral statement 5 "slavery is not wrong" and the philosophical statement 4. Only the moral statement 5 declares that the speaker has no bad feelings against slavery. The philosophical statements 4 does not imply anything at all as regards feelings. Consequently, it cannot imply the statement 5 either.

5.9.7. Alexy on the Right Answer

This discussion makes it easy to accept Alexy's answer to the problem of the single right answer to all legal questions. According to Alexy, the rationality rules applicable to all kinds of practical discourse "offer no guarantees that an agreement can be achieved in respect to every practical issue, nor that an agreement which has in fact been attained is final and unalterable. There are several reasons for this: first, some discourse rules can only be imperfectly fulfilled; second, not all the steps in the argumentation are tied to the rules; and third, any discourse must start from the existing normative convictions of its participants" (Aarnio, Alexy and Peczenik 1981, 272). This fact creates "the necessity of a legal order", that is, "the necessity of three... procedures: (i) the procedure of establishing positive legal norms..., (ii) the procedure of legal argumentation; and (iii) the procedure of legal court proceedings" (Aarnio, Alexy and Peczenik 1981, 274). The procedure of legal argumentation is thus a special case of practical discourse. The consequence is this. "Ordinary practical decisions simply claim to be rationally justifiable. Legal decisions, however, raise a more limited claim: that of being rationally justifiable within the framework of the valid legal order" (id., 275). The existence of positive legal norms and the procedure of legal argumentation reduce the space of discursive possibilities considerably but not to the point where the outcome is certain (id. 274).

CHAPTER 6
THE DOCTRINE OF THE SOURCES OF THE LAW

6.1. SUBSTANTIVE REASONS AND AUTHORITY REASONS. THE SOURCES OF THE LAW

6.1.1. Introductory Remarks

It follows from the preceding chapters that legal practice should simultaneously fit two postulates: rationality of legal reasoning and fixity of the law. The remaining part of the book deals with the question, how these postulates affect the sources of law and legal method. An extensive study of this topic would require a comparison between many different legal orders. It would also require several distinctions, _inter alia_ between constitutional law, statute law, case law etc. However, such a comprehensive study would exceed the limits of the present work. I must thus restrict the discussion to one country and one form of interpretation, that is, to Swedish customary norms, concerning the sources of the law and the method of statutory interpretation.

6.1.2. Substantive Reasons and Rationality

At the beginning, let me introduce the concepts "substantive reason", "goal reason", "rightness reason", "authority reason" and "source of the law". A great part of our discussion of the first four concepts follows Robert Summers´s well-known theory (1978, 707 ff.).

Substantive reasons are statements whose content can support a legal conclusion. The support depends solely upon the content, not on other circumstances, such as who proffers the reasons. Substantive reasons are moral, economic, political, institutional etc. Some are theoretical propositions, e.g., about the facts of the case, other are practical statements. The latter are always supported by some moral statements, since

economic, institutional and other practical reasons in
the law must be morally acceptable.

Such practical statements may but must not consider
some goals. One proffers a goal reason when stating that
a certain decision ought to be made because it can be
predicted to have good effect; this effect constitutes
the goal. Legislation introducing speed limits, e.g.,
serves the goal to reduce the number of car accidents.

One proffers a rightness reason when stating that a
certain decision ought to be made because it is right or
good, regardless any causal connection with a goal. It is
thus a (prima facie) good thing to help people etc.; cf.
sections 2.3.1 and 2.3.2 supra on moral criteria.

In the case NJA 1973 p. 628, a contract between a Swedish charterer
and a foreign shipping company contained a clause, according to
which disputes between the parties should be decided by Greek
courts. When a Greek court made such a decision, the question
occurred whether it may be executed in Sweden, in spite of some
objections of the ordre-public character. The Swedish Supreme Court
decided the question in the affirmative. The main reason was the
following. The opposite decision would make it possible for a party
to demand that the dispute should be decided by a Greek court and,
at the same time, that such a decision should not be executed in
Sweden. Provided that all his assets were in Sweden, this would
leave the other party without access to justice. The decision thus
followed from a set of premises, including (a) the norm that one
shall have access to justice; (b) the description of possible
objections of a party; and (c) the description of his possible
economic situations (all the assets in Sweden).

No doubt, one may say that the assumed goal was not to leave a
party without access to justice. But this is a consequence of what
the assumed norm demands. Such a demand can be always presented as a
goal. On the other hand, the connection between the statement of
this goal and the decision did not involve any causal statements.

One can support both rightness reasons and goal reasons
by further reasons. Any reason can thus follow from a set
of premises, containing further rightness and/or goal
reasons. One may thus support, e.g., the value statement
that a given effect constitutes a goal to be pursued.

Such terms as "consequentialist reasoning", "consequence-oriented
decision-making" (cf., e.g., Rottleuthner 1980 passim and 1981, 211;
Koch and Rüssman 1982, 227 ff.), "goal reasoning", "teleological
reasoning", and so on, are ambiguous. In ordinary legal parlance,
they refer to the situation where one judges a decision according to
whether or not its causal results correspond to assumed goals.

Sometimes, however, they also include evaluation of <u>logical</u>
consequences. <u>Neil MacCormick</u> (1978 pp. 105-6, 108-119, 128, 129-151
etc.) thus maintains that the consequentialist character of legal
reasoning consists of the fact that one evaluates both logical
implications and causal outcomes of rival possible rulings.

The preceding chapters support the following theses about
substantive reasons in the law. Most interpreters of law
actually have a disposition to endorse coherent systems
and to act as if they had intended to approximate a
perfectly rational discourse. If one intends to correctly
think about practical matters, one should have this
disposition. One should also have it, if one intends to
create stable consensus concerning practical matters. A
stable consensus facilitates achievement of such goals as
efficient organisation, minimisation of violence and,
ultimately, survival of the species.

6.1.3. Authority Reasons and Fixity

One proffers an <u>authority reason</u> when stating that a
certain legislative, judicial or other decision ought to
be made because of other circumstances than its content.
For example, the following sentence is an authority
reason: "Future cases of this kind should be decided in a
way resembling a certain case, $\underline{C}$, because this case
constitutes a precedent." One thus argues for a certain
decision by reference to the authority of a precedent,
not by recourse to the view that its content is right.
The conclusion thus follows from a set of premises which
contains a statement of authority, that is, a statement
that a certain authority-creating fact exists. Authority
may be ascribed to a certain individual person, A; one
should do H because this person claims that one should do
H. The statement which ascribes an individual person
authority needs, however, a further justification; it
must be supported by a general statement of authority.
The latter may be either an authority reason (e.g., one
should do what A claims because A has a certain position,
such as being a judge), or a substantive reason (e.g.,
one should do it because A has some moral qualities). In
the law, the former situation is more important.

According to <u>Jacob Sundberg</u> (1978, 24 ff.), authority of the
legislator justifies authority of statutes; similar relations exist
between legislative committees etc. and legislative preparatory
materials, between judges and precedents, between the people and
customary law, and between legal scholars and legal "doctrine".

When authority is ascribed to an official position, it
requires often that the person or persons, occupying this
position, followed a certain procedure, such as the
legislative or judicial process etc. For example, an
authority reason may be based upon the fact that a court
previously settled a dispute in the way one now argues
for; one ascribes authority to the judge or judges,
provided that they have followed the court procedure.

As stated in the preceding chapters, the great role of
authority reasons in the law results from the following
facts. People expect in general that legal decisions are
highly predictable and, at the same time, highly
acceptable from the point of view of other moral
considerations. Predictability is more important in legal
reasoning than in a purely moral reasoning. To assure
predictability, the law itself must be relatively fixed.
At the same time, if legal reasoning had not fulfilled
the demands of coherence and discursive rationality, its
results would be unacceptable from the moral point of
view; in particular, they would be unpredictable.

The relation between substantive reasons and authority
reasons is complex. <u>Robert Summers</u> (1978, 730 ff.) has
claimed "the primacy of substantive reasons" and stated
that they, "more than authority reasons, determine which
decisions and justifications are the best". In my
opinion, however, this theory is too simple. The
following distinctions should be made.

1) Substantive reasons are logically indispensable in
profound justification of legal reasoning. It is always
logically possible to support authority reasons with
substantive reasons. For example, a lawyer often bases
his reasoning on a precedent. But why ought one to follow
precedents? To answer this question, one may refer to
another authority, e.g. a statute, but this may also be
questioned. At the end, perhaps first in the realm of
profound (deep, not merely legal) justification of legal
reasoning, one needs a substantive reason, such as this:
When following precedents, the decision-maker increases
morally valuable predictability of legal decisions.

2) However, such "underpinning" substantive reasons are
often <u>tacitly</u> taken for granted in the contextually

sufficient legal justification, i.e., in legal research and practice. Some substantive reasons thus support the Grundnorm that the constitution ought to be observed, but the lawyers assume this norm without reasoning.

3) To be sure, other substantive reasons enter also the contextually sufficient legal justification. Though they are omitted in easy cases, they are indispensable in "hard" cases, in which a person, performing legal reasoning, must rely upon value judgments; cf. section 5.8.5 supra. They thus are indispensable in three contexts: (a) One must use substantive reasons in order to perform an evaluative interpretation of the content of such sources of the law as statutes, precedents, etc.

As regards precedents, Summers claims the following: "A judge cannot apply a precedent wisely without determining which proposed application is most consistent with the substantive reasons behind the precedent" (Summers 1978, 730). And, "(a)lthough precedents may provide answers, these answers may be wrong" (p. 733).

(b) Substantive reasons are also necessary when one discusses such questions as, How great authority do various sources of the law have?, What is the prima-facie priority order between them?, etc. (c) Finally, substantive reasons are necessary in those rare cases in which a lawyer deals with the question whether the whole normative system under consideration is valid law.

4) Yet, this leaves the question of "primacy" unsolved. Both authority reasons and substantive reasons are necessary for legal thinking. Inter alia, the following theses are plausible: Had a certain kind of reasoning practice solely relied upon substantive reasons, without referring to or at least presupposing authority, then, by definition, this reasoning would not have been legal (cf. section 3.3.5 supra). Had a certain kind of reasoning practice as a whole solely relied upon authority, without reference to substantive reasons, then it would not have been legal, either, but servile with regard to the power-holders (cf. sections 5.4.1 - 2 supra).

6.1.4. Sources of Law

All legal reasons are sources of the law in the broadest
sense. All texts, practices etc. a lawyer must, should or
may proffer as authority reasons are sources of the law
in a narrower sense, adopted in this work.

I do not discuss other senses of the ambiguous term "a source of the
law"; (cf., e.g., Ross 1929, 291 and Raz 1979, 45 ff.). Inter alia,
the following senses are conceivable.
  1. The term "a source of the law" can refer to causes of the fact
that a legal norm has a certain content. For example, political
views of a minister responsible for drafting a statute are a source
of the law in this sense. This conception, however, leads to
unacceptable conclusions. There are, of course, many things which
causally influence some judges, e.g. prejudices concerning political
enemies, good or bad health, the judge's family and personal
situation etc. Are all of them sources of the law?
  2. Moreover, the term "a source of the law" can refer to a source
of knowledge concerning the content of legal norms. But there are
many sources of knowledge, e.g. newspapers, private conversations
etc. Again, are all of them sources of the law?
  3. The term "a source of the law" can also refer to a "source of
validity" of legal norms. Here it is a matter of the last factor
which transforms a completed project into valid law. With regard to
statutes, promulgation is a source of the law in this sense, since
it converts a draft into a statute.
  Stig Strömholm (1988, 297) regards the expression "texts which a
lawyer must, should or may proffer" as less adequate than "texts
which a lawyer must, should or may pay attention to". Certainly, the
former has a formalistic flavour. Many sociologists would certainly
find it more important that a certain factor affects the
decision-making than that it is cited. Yet, the concept "source of
the law" is not a sociological but a normative one, adapted to the
context of justification. In this context, one can hardly imagine a
justificatory norm which tells a judge: "You may allow this text to
affect your decision-making but you may never cite it". Such a norm
would promote dishonesty. Whatever may actually affect the
decision-making, may also be cited.

6.2. MUST-SOURCES, SHOULD-SOURCES AND MAY-SOURCES OF THE LAW

6.2.1. Why Three Categories of Sources of Law?

The division of the sources of the law into three categories that one must, should or may proffer as authority reasons is applicable to many legal orders. It reflects the following distinctions.

1. Some texts, practices etc. are sources of the law, other are not. One cannot imagine a legal system without authority reasons, that is, without sources of the law.

To be sure, one can imagine a _society_ without authority. All reasoning would then solely rely on substantive reasons. But within this reasoning, one could not regard legal norms as binding or valid. Since the concept of valid law has a certain normative content (cf. section 4.7.2.), a valid legal norm, by definition, possesses an authority: One ought _prima facie_ to obey it, not because of its content but because it is a legal norm.

It follows that one can make the distinction between some texts etc. that are and some that are not authority reasons. One _may_ proffer the former, not the latter, as such reasons. Legal textbooks, e.g., though not binding, may be proffered in this manner, newspapers etc. may not.

2. Some sources of the law are _binding_. In Sweden, the binding law consists mainly of statutes; Cf. Ch. 1 Sec.1 para. 3 of the Swedish Constitution _(Regeringsformen)_: "Public power ought to be exercised under the law". It follows that one can make the distinction between some sources of the law (or authority reasons) that are and some that are not binding. Only the former _must_ be proffered as authority reasons, while the latter _may_ be thus proffered.

To be sure, one can imagine a legal system in which only one category of the sources of the law exists. For example, it may consist solely of binding statutes. But it would be unreasonable to forbid lawyers to quote precedents or legal literature. Consequently, the latter materials would sooner or later gain some authority, albeit they are not binding. But in a democratic society, it would not be acceptable to make legal literature as binding as the statutes. In other words, one needs two categories of legal sources, mandatory and permissive (cf., e.g., Hart 1961, 247 and Bodenheimer 1969, 393-4).

3. Some sources of the law, though not binding, have a particular authority, not much lesser than statutes. They are guiding the legal practice. Precedents, legislative preparatory materials and some other sources play precisely this role in Sweden. It follows that one can make the distinction between binding, guiding and permitted sources of the law. One must proffer the first category, should proffer the second and may proffer the third as authority reasons.

To be sure, one can imagine a legal system in which only two categories of the sources of law exist, e.g., binding statutes and permitted materials. The latter category would include, _inter alia_, both precedents and juristic literature. But many reasons tell for a further differentiation of the sources of law. It is, e.g., quite reasonable to assign precedents a higher authority than legal textbooks. Thus, one needs at least three classes of legal sources: binding, guiding and permitted.

6.2.2. Concepts of Must-, Should- and May-Source

The discussed distinction is an idealisation. One can elaborate more complex classifications of the sources of law. Moreover, only vague definitions of the "must-sources", "should-sources" and "may-sources" of the law are universally acceptable. Precise interpretation of these concepts varies from one legal order to another, from one part of a legal order to another and from one time to another. Different people can suggest different precise interpretations, serving different purposes etc.

Consider, e.g., the differences between the Common Law systems and the continental European systems. In new legal systems, the doctrine of the sources of law is often unclear. In the European Community, controversies occur concerning, _inter alia_, the role of the Community directives, not "transformed" by the internal legislation. These have been considered as binding in England, cf. Yvonne von Duyn case, Eur. Court Rept. 1974 p. 13-37, but not in France, cf. Cohn-Bendit case, Conseil d'Etat 12 Dec. 1978, Rev. trim. dir. Eur. 1979 p. 157.

Consequently, a list of materials which must, should or may be taken into account also varies. In Sweden, for example, the list contained in the international private

law differs from that found in the rest of the legal
order; the list fitting private law may be questioned in
the taxation law, etc.

The following comments elucidate the complex meaning of
"must", "should" and "may".

1. The "must-sources" are more important than the
"should-sources" which are more important than the
"may-sources".

One way to make this hierarchy of importance precise
is, what follows.

a) The more important sources are stronger reasons than
the less important ones.

b) Reasons strong enough to justify disregarding a less
important source may be weaker than those required to
justify disregarding a more important one.

c) If a more important source is incompatible with a
less important one, e.g. if a statute is incompatible
with a view expressed in legislative preparatory
materials, the former has a prima facie priority. One
thus ought to apply the more important source, not the
less important one, unless sufficiently strong reasons
support the opposite conclusion.

d) Many cumulated weak reasons often take priority over
fewer strong ones.

e) Whoever wishes to reverse the priority order, has a
burden of reasoning.

2. If one only considers judicial reasoning, one may
add, what follows. The courts have a strong duty to apply
the "must-sources". They have a weak duty to apply the
"should-sources".

This distinction is, however, difficult to state
precisely. One way is to point out that the consequences
of disregarding the "should-sources" are usually milder.

In Swedish law as of 1974, an official's failure to take into
account must-sources was a ground of criminal prosecution; his
failure to use should-sources, however, had no criminal
consequences. In Swedish law as of 1987, the criminal charge applies
only to the intentional and grossly negligent disregard of a
must-source (cf. Ch. 20 Sec. 1 of the Criminal Code). Ordinary
negligence is not criminal. The legal consequence of disregarding
should-sources consists mainly of the risk of cancellation of the
decision. In Sweden, the state may also be liable in torts, should
its agent negligently disregard a should-source.

6.3. NORMS CONCERNING THE SOURCES OF THE LAW

6.3.1. The Character of Source-Norms

I will now discuss some norms concerning the sources of the law, in brief source-norms. Let me describe their character, function, mode of existence, degree of justifiability and legal position.

A. The _Prima-facie_ Character of the Source-Norms

The source-norms have only a _prima-facie_ character. In a concrete situation, one may disregard each such norm, if sufficiently strong reasons justify it.

B. The Functions of the Source-Norms

1. The source—norms determine the position various sources of the law have in the legal system.
2. They help to convert some argumentative jumps into logically correct inferences.

One thus needs a jump, e.g., when implementing some precedents as premises for a conclusion concerning the appropriate role of legislative preparatory materials in the statutory interpretation. One must then interpret the precedents themselves. To do this, one must, _inter alia_, supplement them with some source-norms. The conclusion follows logically, that is, without a jump, from an expanded set of premises containing the precedents, the source-norms and some other reasonable statements.

3. The source-norms make the practice of legal reasoning more stable and the interpreted legal norms more fixed.

C. The Existence of the Source-Norms

The judges and other lawyers perform reasonings in the way suggesting that they - consciously or not - follow the source-norms. The norms constitute an important part of the legal paradigm, cf. section 3.3.3 supra.

Paraphrasing von Wright´s theory of validity (cf. section 5.1.3 supra), one may say that the legal position of the sources of the law (as such which must, should or may be proffered) is relative to the _existence_ of source-norms. Existence of these norms has an empirical and an analytic dimension.

1. Their empirical existence is the same as the existence of a complex of human actions or dispositions to act whose description strongly supports them; cf. section 5.6.1 supra. One may mention here a disposition to argue that it is correct to follow these norms, a disposition to criticise people violating them; etc.

In this context, one may discuss the empirical question whether a certain-source norm exists or not. When reading such domestic and foreign sources as, inter alia, writings in legal dogmatics, and perhaps participating in the legal practice, one discovers some information about these norms. Thus inspired, one may elaborate a relatively coherent hypothesis about their content. The hypothesis must be tested through studies of legal reasoning, inter alia, studies of arguments contained in justification of judicial decisions. One may accept the hypothesis until such studies show that the authorities, judges and other lawyers do not follow the source-norms.

Stig Strömholm claims, that source—norms are a second order source of law (cf. Strömholm 1988, 298). This is understandable, since he defines the sources of law as "factors" to which the lawyers actually pay attention. He thus claims that they actually pay attention to (a) statutes, precedents etc., and (b) norms, according to which they should pay attention to statutes, precedents etc.

2. But the source-norms have also an analytic dimension: They are related to the concept of legal reasoning. Though one may disregard each such norm, it would be strange to simultaneously refute a significant part of the set of such norms and still try to perform a legal reasoning; cf. section 3.3.3 supra. Moreover, if one thus were unable to perform legal reasoning, our form of life would change, cf. section 4.4.6.

D. The Justifiability of the Source-Norms

1. One may inquire whether such a source—norm is justifiable. This question presupposes some normative standards, other than the discussed source-norm itself.

2. In the realm of profound justification, such standards are easy to think about; e.g., some source-norms are more just or more democratic than others.

3. In the contextually sufficient legal justification, the problem is more difficult. What _legal_ standards determine the legal position of standards which determine the legal position of statutes, precedents etc.?

Yet, the question is meaningful. One may certainly use some source—norms as a basis for reasoning, justifying theses about other source-norms. The former convert the latter into a kind of second order customary law, or second order sources of law. The second order customary law is _valid_. Its validity is relative to the _existence_ of the other source-norms, used to justify it.

4. Ultimately, one aims, and ought to aim, at _coherence_ of the doctrine of the sources of law. Such coherence is always a result of an act of weighing, aimed at an optimal balance of numerous source norms and numerous criteria of coherence.

5. Since order is _prima-facie_ better than chaos, a source norm which actually exists is, _ceteris paribus_, better than another, proposed but so far not followed. On the other hand, when considering several competing and not falsified hypotheses about the content of actually existing source-norms, one ought to prefer the content which has support of most coherent moral reasons.

E. The Position of the Source-Norms in the Hierarchy of Legal Norms

Assuming that the normative question of justifiability of the source—norms is meaningful, and that they can be regarded as second order customary law (cf. item D3 supra), one may discuss the position of the source-norms in the hierarchy of legal norms.

1. From the logical point of view, the source-norms are meta-norms, determining the legal status of other norms.

2. The source-norms can be altered as a result of the amendment of a statute. A statute can, e.g., prohibit the courts to quote precedents. They can also be altered in consequence of the change of other sources of the law, such as precedents, legislative preparatory materials etc. In this respect, the source-norms are thus ranked lower than many other sources of the law.

3. On the other hand, one uses the source-norms in order to justify validity and hierarchical position of other legal sources, such as precedents, legislative preparatory materials etc. One may also use them when arguing about validity and invalidity of the statutes.

No doubt, the conclusion that one should obey statutes follows from the Constitution (in Sweden, cf. Ch. 1 Sec. 1 para. 3). But one can use some source-norms to support the conclusion that a statute is obsolete or even invalid (as a result of desuetudo), even though it came to existence in a manner consonant with the Constitution. One may also proffer the source-norms to support the conclusion that some statutes (the "original laws") are valid, despite their having come into existence in a way conflicting with the Constitution.

From this point of view, the source-norms are ranked higher than statutes.

4. Validity of the Constitution itself is stipulated by the Grundnorm, presupposed within the legal paradigm (cf. sections 3.3.3, 5.3.1 and 5.8.4 supra). One may regard the Grundnorm as a source-norm, supported both by legal concepts and legal custom. Apparently, this source-norm is ranked even higher than the Constitution. Yet, it is doubtful whether it is possible not only to presuppose the Grundnorm within the legal paradigm but also justify it within this paradigm. It is more natural to claim that any justification of the Grundnorm transcends the limits of the legal paradigm. If this is the true, one can accept Kelsen´s view that the Grundnorm is not a valid legal norm. Then, the question of its position within the hierarchy of legal norms does not occur at all.

6.3.2. Complexity of the Swedish Doctrine of the Sources of Law

The Swedish doctrine of the sources of the law is very flexible and complicated. It thus differs from the view, e.g. defended by the French exegetical school of 19th Century, that all legal questions are to be answered by recourse to statutes.

The most important source-norms in Sweden have the following content.

S1) When performing legal reasoning, one must use statutes and other regulations as authority reasons, if any are applicable.

All courts and authorities must thus use applicable statutes and other regulations in the justification of their decisions.

The expression "other regulations" refers to general norms issued by the Government, subordinate authorities and municipalities.

The Government can issue regulations
a) on the basis of authorisation, given by the Parliament (cf. Ch. 8 Sec. 6-12 of the Constitution);
b) as regards enforcement of a statute (cf. Ch. 8 Sec. 13 para. 1 item 1 of the Constitution);
c) as regards matters that, according to the Constitution, should not be regulated by the Parliament; this is the "rest-competence" of the Government (Ch. 8 Sec. 13 para. 1 item 2 of the Constitution).

Subordinate authorities can issue regulations on the basis of authorisation, given by a statute or the Government (Ch. 8 Sec. 13 para. 3 of the Constitution). The National Tax Board has thus a statutory authorisation to issue some norms that <u>must</u> be used as authority reasons; cf., e.g., Sec. 32 para. 3 item 2 of the Municipal Tax Act.

The power of the municipalities to issue regulations is based on Ch. 1 Sec. 7, and Ch. 8 Sec. 5, 9 and 11 of the Constitution).

Source-norm S1 does not exclude the fact that the courts and authorities may regard some statutes or regulations as obsolete or even invalid on the basis of <u>desuetuto derogatoria</u>, cf. section 1.2.7 supra.

The duty to use statutes and other regulations in the justification of judicial decisions does not necessarily imply that a court must explicitly quote them. But it must be at least implicitly clear what the statutory framework of the decision is. If a statute disregards some problems such as, e.g., the question of remoteness of damage (cf. section 3.1.2 supra), a court would often neglect to cite a specific provision of a statute. But if a statutory regulation is directly applicable, it would be a grave mistake not to follow it.

A statute or another regulation can decide that some other sources of law <u>must</u> be applied within legal reasoning.

a) Some forms of custom, e.g., commercial custom, must be thus applied.

Cf. Sec.1 and 10 para. 2 of the Contracts Act; Sec. 1 of the Sale of Goods Act; Sec. 1 of the Commission Business Act; Ch. 5 Sec. 12 of the Marriage Code; etc. A body organised within the Chamber of Commerce publishes the content of commercial custom.

Cf. sections 6.4 and 6.5 infra, concerning the status of custom and precedent as the sources of the law.

b) Contracts must be also thus applied, cf. Sec. 1 of the Contracts Act. Standard contracts play a particularly great role, comparable to small legal orders <u>per se</u>.

Further, collective agreements are important, especially for the practice of the Labour Court; cf. Sec. 1 of the statute, regulating the procedure in labour disputes.

S2) When performing legal reasoning, one should use precedents and legislative preparatory materials as authority reasons, if any are applicable. One should also use international conventions, underlying the applicable national legislation, together with preparatory materials and other interpretatory data concerning these conventions (cf. Pålsson 1986, 19 ff.).

Cf. the "Tsesis-case" (NJA 1983 p. 3), concerning interpretation of a statute imposing liability for oil damage at the sea.

In the case NJA 1984 p. 903, the Supreme Court proffered the Europe- and UN-conventions concerning human rights to justify a refusal of extradition for a crime, although no Swedish statute supported the decision.

One also should use some customs, well established in the society, expressing general principles or accepted by previous decisions of the courts or authorities. Finally, one should use applicable "general recommendations" (cf. Sec. 1 of the regulation concerning the statute-book), issued by various authorities and public institutions.

Let me mention National Tax Board, Bookkeeping Board, Consumer Authority, Bank Inspection Authority, etc. (cf. Bernitz et al. 1985, 142 ff.).

This fact reflects a highly organised character of the Swedish society, where several public or semi-public organisations demand and often receive high respect.

S3) When performing legal reasoning, one may use, inter alia the following material.

a) Some custom (so far it does not constitute a must- or should-source of the law, see S1 and S2).

b) Some quasi-legal norms, issued by various private or semi-private institutions.

One may mention the Press Ombudsman, the Press Opinion Council, the Radio Council, the Trade and Industry Stock Exchange Committee, Sweden's Bar Association, etc.

c) Professional legal literature (e.g., handbooks, monographs etc.).

d) Precedents and legislative preparatory materials which do not directly touch upon the interpreted legal text but which give information on evaluations in adjacent areas of law.

e) Judicial and administrative decisions which are not reported in the leading law reports, NJA (and therefore do not have the same standing as the precedents published in NJA).

f) Draft statutes.

g) Repealed statutes, provided that they give information about still actual evaluations.

h) Foreign law, unless it is incompatible with some overriding reasons, such as the so-called ordre public.

i) Other materials, constituting evidence of well-established evaluations, e.g. private pronouncements by members of various legislation draft committees, members of Parliament, ministers etc.

Established evaluations are (may-) sources of the law, because their justificatory relevance depends not only on their content but also on the fact that they are established. They thus are proffered as authority reasons, not as substantive reasons. Cf. section 6.3.5 infra on the character of the latter.

It is difficult to make a list of materials that one may not use in legal reasoning. Certainly, within justification of judicial decisions, one may not use political opinions expressed by the parties or interest groups, such as trade unions or employers organisations. This fact reflects a demand of objectivity the courts and authorities are expected to fulfil. This demand of objectivity is, however, difficult to state precisely (cf. Eckhoff 1987, 308 ff.). One certainly may use materials showing that a given group, say consumers, deserve special protection.

Within legal dogmatics, the demand of objectivity has a partly different character. For the sake of space, I must leave this problem aside.

As far I know, the growing complexity of the doctrine of the sources of law is an international phenomenon, by no means restricted to Sweden. A plausible explanation of this trend is this. Modern society is more and more complex and dynamic. This fact results in increasing complexity and rapid change of legislation. At the same time, citizens demand that the law is highly fixed and acceptable at the same time. Legislation alone cannot fulfil these postulates. A very free interpretation of

statutes could perhaps fulfil the demand of acceptability
but hardly the requirement of fixity. One needs an
extensive set of authority reasons and, at the same time,
a relative freedom to organise them into a coherent
whole. The should- and may-sources of the law create such
an extensive set, yet permit the interpreter to
relatively freely insert morally required modification.

6.3.3. Are Substantive Reasons Sources of the Law?

The discussed list of may-sources is apparently strange
because it does not contain substantive reasons. No
doubt, one may proffer various substantive reasons,
including moral judgments one endorses. Among various
substantive reasons, one certainly may consider
historical knowledge of conditions the statute was
intended to remedy, history of the language and concepts,
the so-called "nature of things" subject to the statute
etc. For that reason, e.g., Aulis Aarnio (e.g., 1987, 87
and 92) regards substantive reasons as a kind may-source
of the law. Indeed, all legal reasons, substantive or
not, are sources of the law in the broadest sense.
  Yet, substantive reasons are qualitatively different
from authority reasons. They are by definition no sources
of law in the narrower sense, adopted in this work. This
definition covers only texts, practices etc. a lawyer
must, should or may proffer as authority reasons.
  One "underpinning" reason in favour of this definition
is the fact that it reflects the fairly established
language which makes often a distinction between the
authoritative sources of the law and other, substantive,
reasons (cf., e.g., Raz 1979, 53 ff.)
  Moreover, substantive reasons are difficult to place in
the classification of must-, should- and may-sources.
Consider, e.g., the following view of Hughes (1968, 430):
"Does (the argument from injustice - A.P.) stand on any
different footing from the argument that a court should
adopt a certain interpretation because there are earlier
authoritative decisions which hold that way? It would not
suffice to say that the latter is a legal argument
because courts must be persuaded by it while the argument
from injustice is only one that they may listen to, for
courts have frequently brushed aside precedent and
declared openly that for reasons of justice they will
create a new rule." Neither can one say that precedents

are <u>prima-facie</u> prior to substantive reasons. This would mean that precedents have priority over considerations of injustice, unless some additional reasons exist which justify the reverse order. But what are these additional reasons? If they are substantive reasons, as it is plausible to assume, then the whole combination of substantive reasons is generally prior to precedents! It is difficult to make sense of the reverse priority order, <u>prima-facie</u> or not. Finally, it would not suffice to regard the argument from justice and other substantive reasons as must-sources, since the latter are <u>binding</u> in a sense in which substantive reasons are not. The best solution is thus to regard substantive reasons as qualitatively different, located <u>outside</u> of the hierarchy of legal sources.

One must weigh and balance substantive reasons and authority reasons. The weight of the latter is <u>prima-facie</u> determined by the must-, should- and may-hierarchy. The weight of the former is independent from this hierarchy.

6.4. CUSTOM

The postulate that custom must be followed is the most ancient means to increase fixity of practical conclusions. Substantive reasons may fail to give a single right answer to a practical question. This might cause social conflicts. To avoid problems, one can always do the same others do.

A complication results from the fact that no reason exists for an individual to do <u>everything</u> his neighbours do. Though all my neighbours prefer whisky, I am perfectly free to rather drink vodka. On the other hand, I am not so free to drink much more then they do. The following distinctions must thus be taken into account in connection with custom.

A1. Custom in the broader sense can be defined as any kind of factual regularities in human behaviour.

A2. Custom in the narrower sense covers only such regularities in human behaviour as are connected with endorsement of a norm stating that one should behave in this manner.

We are interested only in the second kind of custom.

The role of custom in the law is also affected by the fact that the law is intimately connected with practice of the courts and authorities. One must thus make the following distinction.

B1. Customary law in the primary sense is defined as custom of the people (connected with a norm-endorsement, cf. A2), which __must__ or __should__ be regarded as a legal authority reason. In this sense customary law arises among the people, and courts should adapt themselves to this customary law.

B2. Customary law in a secondary sense is defined as an established practice of the courts and authorities. It is created by this practice, not by the people.

To be sure, one may perhaps ignore what one's neighbours expect but it is not so easy for persons affected to ignore judicial decisions. This fact together with the influence of Legal Positivism and Legal Realism explains this strange identification of customary law with judicial practice. However, contrary to suggestions made by some Legal Realists (e.g., Strömberg 1980, 50 ff.), I do not adopt this terminology. It is better to call the judicial practice "judicial practice", not "customary law" (cf., e.g., Strömholm 1988, 216). It is also important not to adopt a terminology which encourages one to ignore the spontaneous norm-creating activity of people. Only weak moral reasons support the conclusion that the courts and authorities should have monopoly of creation of legally binding norms. One may thus argue that judicial and administrative practice create relatively fixed norms which have a democratic legitimacy. This is true but it does not imply that fixity of the spontaneous custom is lower and its legitimacy inferior. Much stronger reasons support the contrary conclusion. Firstly, the custom of people may be relatively fixed, perhaps more so than the practice of the authorities. Secondly, an indirect democratic legitimacy of judicial and administrative practice is hardly superior to the direct democratic legitimacy of popular consensus. Finally, the hypothesis is plausible that people tend to live together in a morally acceptable way. The hypothesis is also plausible that authorities can make mistakes. In consequence, such a spontaneous custom may easily have an even more coherent support of moral reasons than the norms created by legislation and judicial practice.

A more important complication results from the fact that one may regard the very source-norms, determining the legal status of __all__ the sources of the law, as a kind of custom. Existence of the source-norms involves complex of human actions or dispositions to act whose description __strongly__ supports them; cf. section 5.6.1 supra. Among dispositions of this kind, one may mention a disposition to argue that it is correct to follow these norms, a disposition to criticise people violating them; etc. These dispositions can certainly be called "custom". This custom determines legal validity of all legal norms, including, _inter alia_, norms of customary law.

In Swedish law, the legal status of customary law is not uniform. Some custom must, some should, some may and some may not be regarded as a legal authority reason.

The following kinds of custom, _inter alia_, must or should be regarded as authority reasons (cf., e.g., Eckhoff 1987, 229 ff.).

a) Custom which is both reasonable and well established, e.g., in some professions or some parts of the country (cf., e.g., Sundberg 1978, 172). This demand reflects the postulates of rationality and fixity.

b) Custom which expresses some general principles of law. This requirement corresponds to generality as a criterion of coherence, cf. section 4.1.4 supra.

c) Custom of the people which the courts and authorities recognise as a legal authority reason.

These three kinds of custom are, of course, not independent from each other. A well-established custom often both expresses some general principles and is recognised by the authorities.

An institutionally recognised custom (item c supra) receives an additional authority. A special case of an institutional recognition occurs when a body of experts writes down some kinds of customs. Responsa of the Swedish Chamber of Commerce provides a good example (cf. Bernitz et al. 1985, 144 ff.). A particularly strong "amplification" of the authority of custom may result from the fact that some statutes confirm the duty to obey customary law and stipulate some conditions of it. For example, the condition of reasonableness is formulated in the Finish Code of Procedure, Ch. 1 Sec. 11 (cf. Klami 1984, 16 ff. and 43 ff.; cf. Aarnio 1987, 80).

The normative questions, such as Why ought one to obey customary law in general?, Why ought one, in particular, to obey customary law possessing the above-mentioned properties?, etc. usually exceed the framework of the legal paradigm. When engaged in the deep justification of the legal reasoning one may, however, give a moral answer to them, e.g., emphasising the fact that people expect relatively fixed and reasonable custom to be respected.

6.5. PRECEDENT

6.5.1. Introductory Remarks

A precedent is a decision of a concrete case which becomes an authoritative pattern for future decisions. The point of following precedents is, of course, to make the law fixed and judicial decisions predictable.

Swedish courts regularly follow precedents, perhaps in ever increasing dependence. The following source-norm is acceptable in legal reasoning concerning Swedish law (cf. Bernitz et al. 1985, 109 ff.):

S4. a) Decisions rendered by the Supreme Court, the Supreme Administrative Court and the highest special courts such as, for instance, Labour Court, Housing Court, Market Court and High Insurance Court, should be taken into account in legal reasoning in relevantly similar cases, both in practice and in legal dogmatics.

b) Decisions rendered by such courts as courts of appeal, administrative courts of appeal, lower insurance courts etc. may be taken into account in legal reasoning in relevantly similar cases. They also should be taken into account in relevantly similar cases before the court that has made the precedent decision, in legal dogmatics, and perhaps also before lower and regionally parallel instances with similar competence. Finally, they should be taken into account in legal dogmatics,

This norm is open: one might use the term "precedent" in a broader sense, to include decisions of other higher courts and even authorities. It is, however, not easy to tell, how great the authority of some instances is. Cf. section 7.6.2 infra (collision-norm C9) about various factors, influencing authority of precedents.

6.5.2. Ratio Decidendi and Rationality

How is it possible for a legal system based on constant copying of old decisions to change?

Of course, the law can change through legislation, but it also evolves without a change of statutes. A decision rendered in pleno can also change a precedent (the Code of Procedure, Ch.3 Sec.5), but a change may take place without involving plenum.

The answer is that only in similar cases do precedents become patterns for later decisions. One may always find differences between the precedent and the case to be decided.

An example. In the case NJA 1937 p. 1, the Supreme Court pronounced that debts in dollars can be paid according to their nominal value despite the decline in the value of the dollar, but in the case NJA 1952 p. 382, the Court refused to recognise this principle as regards Polish zlotys. By the way of reason, the court stated that zloty notes cannot, according to Polish statutes, be imported into Poland. The deeper reason must have been that zloty notes, as a result of this prohibition, are difficult to sell abroad according to their nominal value. The situation of dollars is different.

Is it then possible to avoid following any precedent whatever? No. A precedent must be followed only in such cases as essentially resemble the precedent case.

The essential elements of the precedent case, used as guidelines for the subsequent case, are the ratio decidendi; other elements are obiter dicta. The ratio is a necessary condition of the decision which thus would have been different if the ratio had been different. Every use of a precedent as a pattern for future decisions is actually a generalisation of the precedent into a precedent-rule, stating that one must decide all cases with the same ratio in the same way.

What elements should one regard as essential, i.e., as the ratio decidendi? It depends on a complex reasoning in the concrete case, involving weighing and balancing of two kinds of reasons. First, one may consider reasons adduced by the court in the precedent decision with the aim of justifying the decision and with the belief that they were necessary to justify it. Second, one may consider the reasons estimated as necessary to justify the decision, even if not adduced in the decision (constructed ratio decidendi; cf. Eckhoff 1987, 143).

A good method to establish the constructed ratio decidendi is to consider a set of precedents, at best extended in time.

In interpretation of precedents use is made of a number of arguments which in part resemble conclusion by analogy in statutory interpretation. Practice as a source of the law resembles a markedly casuistic statute, the application of which calls for conclusion by analogy on a large scale. But here, I disregard such problems.

The "reflective equilibrium", resulting from weighing of such reasons, varies between different persons, places and times, depending on moral evaluations, procedural rules etc. The accepted technique in Sweden is to re-explain and re-justify the ratio. No simple criteria of ratio are thus established. Neither do they exist in other countries (cf., e.g., Simpson 1961, 148 ff. and 1973, 77 ff.). Following the established evaluations by determining what cases are essentially similar, only helps us to some extent to distinguish between ratio and dicta. Though a few guiding principles assist deciders, the step from the "given" premises (such as the description of the case together with the established criteria of ratio) to the conclusion concerning the ratio constitutes a jump. To establish the ratio, one must mix "reason and fiat" (Fuller 1946, 376 ff.). However, this jump is reasonable, if the conclusion follows from these "given" premises together with some additional reasonable statements; cf. sections 2.7 and 3.2 supra. As stated in chapter 4 supra, the additional premises are thus reasonable, if they highly fulfil criteria of coherence and discursive rationality. "(T)he rules applied to the decision of individual controversies cannot simply be isolated exercises of judicial wisdom. They must be brought into, and maintained in, some systematic interrelationships; they must display some coherent internal structure" (Fuller 1968, 134). In brief, whereas the point of following precedents is to make the law highly fixed, the method of so doing is connected to the ideas of coherence and D-rationality.

6.5.3. Why and To What Extent Ought One to Follow Precedents?

The following substantive reasons support the conclusion that precedents should be followed by subsequent judicial practice.

1. Precedents should be followed because this will promote the uniformity of practice, and thereby justice and legal certainty. This corresponds to generality as a criterion of coherence, cf. section 4.1.4 supra.

2. By following precedents the court can avoid the evaluation afresh of similar cases, which would be unjustifiable from the viewpoint of economy (c. NJA 1972,

253). Of course, various coherent considerations support
the requirement of economy as such.

Further arguments exist for the following precedents of
<u>higher</u> courts.

3. The judges of superior courts are better qualified
and more experienced, and their decisions should
therefore be a model for lower courts.

4. Anyway, they are likely to reverse the lower court
on appeal, if this court does not pay attention to
precedents.

On the other hand, some substantive reasons tell
against a very extensive use of precedents in order to
create general norms.

1. The primary task of the courts is to decide
<u>individual</u> cases, while the legislator is empowered to
enact general norms. A high degree of faithfulness to
precedents may disturb this division of powers.

2. Since the judges are appointed, not elected in a
democratic manner, the increased power of the high courts
is contestable from the point of view of democracy. (Yet,
the democratically elected parliament can always change
the statutory law and thus affect the judicial practice.)

One may, however, doubt whether these reasons,
connected with the opinion that the courts should not be
made too strong, are applicable to a country like Sweden,
where the parliament and the administration are in many
respects stronger than the courts.

3. A clear statutory norm provides a better support for
predictions of future decisions, and thus for the fixity
of law and legal certainty, than a precedent decision of
an individual case.

This reason provokes some doubt, too, since such a
clear and, at the same time, just statutory norm may be
impossible to design.

It is thus plausible to conclude that on balance, the
reasons for following precedents weigh, **ceteris paribus**,
more than the reasons against.

6.5.4. Methods of Justifying Judicial Decisions

The value of precedents depends on weighing and balancing
of those pro- and counter-arguments. One must, however,
also consider the quality of the justification of the
precedent decision. The following methods of justifying
judicial decisions can be distinguished, depending on how

general and extensive (and thus coherent) the reasoning
is. (See also a similar but not identical classification
elaborated by Tore Strömberg, 1980, 146 ff.).

1) A pseudo-justification is neither general nor
extensive. In some older cases, the courts gave extremely
brief reasons for the decisions, in other the reasons
were quite unclear. In the decision it was written, e.g.,
that the plaintiff or the respondent had or had not a
certain right, without stating any exact ground for this
statement. Often it was not possible to know at all which
general rule the court had followed.

The method dominated in Sweden in the first half of
20th Century. To some extent, it still is applied, e.g.,
in Finland and Denmark.

As an example one may cite NJA 1947 p. 299. An association was held
responsible for damage negligently caused by the supervisor of a
shooting range owned by the association. The Supreme Court majority
expressed itself so obscurely that it was not clear whether it
considered the association liable because the supervisor's position
was considered to be equivalent to one of management; or because his
position was judged as connected with particular risk; or because a
contract-like relation was considered to exist between the
association or the injured person.

A decision might also be justified with the use of unclear
expressions of the type "must be assumed" etc. For example, in the
case NJA 1954 p. 268 a person having a significant connection with
Bulgaria made an application to collect an amount which had been
deposited in Sweden for his account. The Bulgarian state contested
his right to collect the amount personally and stated that the
payment should take place through a Swedish-Bulgarian clearing
account and be made to him in Bulgaria. The Supreme Court majority
recognised the Bulgarian state's right to plead in the case but
without giving any reason other than that the members of the
majority "found no hindrance to exist to the consideration of the
Bulgarian state's plea", after which the case was decided in a way
favourable to that state.

This method makes coherence of the decisions very low.
For this reason, it is, at least prima-facie or
ceteris-paribus, not acceptable.

2) The simple subsumption method is general but
insufficiently extensive. The court presents the decision
as a logical consequence of a general rule and some
facts. It does this even in hard cases, in which the
general rule is not contained in a statute but
constitutes a result of an evaluative interpretation,
based on additional premises which are not reported.

The method dominated in Sweden at the end of 19th
Century. It still is applied, e.g., in France.

In many cases, the court forced the whole reasoning into one
sentence with many subordinate clauses and the decision as a
consequence ("since... and since... inasmuch as..., then" etc.).
Stig Strömholm cites the following examples: NJA 1875 p. 489, 1876
p. 458, 1877 p. 487 and 1877 p. 334.

The method is prima-facie, or ceteris-paribus, not
acceptable. To be sure, it fulfils one criterion of
coherence, that is, the requirement of generality but it
totally sets aside another criterion, demanding numerous
and long chains of justification, cf. section 4.1.3
supra. Coherence and hence acceptability results from
weighing and balancing of all criteria of coherence. The
act of weighing may result in a total elimination of one
of them only if its fulfilment would very significantly
decrease the degree of fulfilment of the other.

3) The fact-stating method is extensive but
insufficiently general. In the decision there are
statements concerning facts, but neither value judgments
nor norms. The interpreter must himself guess which
statutory rules, norms for statutory construction, moral
value judgments and other premises together with the
proffered facts logically imply the conclusion.

In Sweden, the method is often used in lower courts and
even in the courts of appeal, albeit there to a
decreasing extent. Cf. also NJA 1952 p. 184 (the Supreme
Court). The High Insurance Court uses this method
frequently; cf., e.g., the cases 1086/75:1, 872/79:8,
1498/81:3 and 1516/82:4.

This method is prima-facie, or ceteris-paribus, not
acceptable, either. To be sure, it fulfils the criterion
of coherence demanding numerous and long chains of
justification but it totally sets aside another
criterion, generality.

The following two methods are both extensive and
general.

4) The dialogue method. The court proffers clearly both
the reasons for and against the decision, including
facts, norms and - often general - value judgments; then
it concludes that the former weigh more in the case at
bar; cf. section 3.2.1 supra.

The method, influenced by the Common Law jurisdiction,
is frequently used also in Norway (cf., e.g., the case RB

1978 38:78). It occurs also in Sweden; cf. NJA 1984 p. 693, where the Supreme Court performed weighing and balancing of reasons for and against the principle that security transfer according to foreign law should have an effect against the transferor´s creditors in Sweden.

In Sweden, the method is frequently used, e.g., by the Housing Court. Cf., e.g. , the case RB 1978 38:78 where the court completed an extensive reasoning with the following statement: "A reasonable weighing of the reasons proffered above leads, according to the Housing Court, to the result that the tenancy-relation ought to expire, unless particular reasons tell against this conclusion."

5) The sophisticated subsumption method (or "scientific" method). The court proffers clearly both the reasons for and against the decision, including facts, norms and value judgments; then it modifies these reasons in such a way that the decision becomes a logical conclusion of them (cf. section 3.2.2 supra). The proffered norms and value judgments are often general. Inter alia, one aims at formulating a clear precedent-norm.

The method, influenced by the German practice, occurs also in Sweden, especially in some courts of appeals; cf. also NJA 1983 p. 487.

The dialogue method and the sophisticated subsumption method often involve formulating general principles, even if these are controversial.

The majority of the Supreme Court in the case NJA 1977 p. 176 thus expressed the following, both important and highly controversial, general principle of evidence. "In torts, there is often a controversy about what caused the actual damage or injury... Many courses of events.., independently of one another, can constitute a possible cause... In such cases, full evidence .. can scarcely be given... If thus, in the light of all the circumstances of the case, it is clearly more probable that the actual course of events was that which the plaintiff has pointed out than that ... pointed out by the defendant, the statement of the plaintiff should form the basis for the decision".

In the case NJA 1976 p. 458, a bicycle pump was changed so that it could be used for shooting a cork. The owner of the pump, A, a 9-year-old, permitted B, a 6-year-old, to play with it. The cork got stuck. B asked D, a 9-year-old, to withdraw the cork. D tried to do it, accidentally "shot" with the pump, and the cork hit B's eye. All instances ruled against B's claim for compensation from A. The majority of the Supreme Court denied A's negligence, since the risk of injury had been minimal. Justice Nordenson dissented and made several subtle conceptual distinctions, in a way unthinkable in the

older Swedish practice, <u>inter alia</u> between the problems of
negligence, remoteness of damage and the purpose of protection given
by the law of torts. He also expressed a series of general
principles.
     Cf. NJA 1981 p. 622. Concerning the Supreme Administrative Court
(Regeringsrätten), cf., e.g., the case RÅ 1978 1:19.
     In the case Rt 1975 p. 290, the Norwegian Supreme Court formulated
a general norm that a patient has a right to read his case record.

In future, the Swedish high courts are perhaps going to
more frequently formulate general principles.
     <u>Ceteris paribus</u>, only a highly general and extensive
justification of a decision is acceptable.
     However, one must not overrate the results of the
justification. In hard cases, it must contain a jump. Not
even the most extensive and general justification can
show that the decision is the only right one; cf. section
5.9 supra. Not even such a justification can show that
the decision follows from a highly coherent set of
premises, solely consisting of certain statements and
statements presupposed within a particular practice,
belonging to in the culture under consideration.
     No doubt, the decision may follow from a highly
coherent but <u>contestable</u> set of premises. The decision
may also follow from a set of certain and presupposed
statements together with an additional premise, neither
falsified nor arbitrary. Since the added premise is not
arbitrary, the hypothesis is not highly corroborated that
it does not logically follow from a highly coherent set
of certain and presupposed statements (cf. section 3.3.7
supra). Yet, though one cannot exclude the possibility of
this logical connection, one cannot demonstrate the
connection either. Neither can one show that the decision
follows from a <u>more</u> coherent set of premises than any
other possible decision.

6.5.5. Coherence of Judicial Decisions

I have stated above that that a judicial decision fulfils
criteria of coherence only if it is, <u>ceteris paribus</u>,
both extensive and general. One may thus ask the question
whether all judicial decisions should be accompanied by a
both extensive and general justification. The answer must
be, <u>ceteris paribus</u>, affirmative. That is, it must be
affirmative in an ideal situation, in which all

conditions of a perfect judicial decision-making are fulfilled. The judge has thus unlimited time, knowledge, intelligence, resources etc. In the real life, however, a less extensive and less general justification of a decision is not always wrong. Sometimes, it provides the best solution, because of the following circumstances.

1. A judicial decision is, <u>ceteris paribus</u>, morally right only if <u>someone</u>, not necessarily the judges themselves, can justify it on the basis of an extensive set of general premises. One is a good judge, if one can adjudicate correctly, that is, in the manner <u>someone</u> can justify in a highly coherent manner on the basis of both the law and morality. The judge himself may thus rightly <u>feel</u> that the decision is morally justifiable, but at the same time be unable to formulate a satisfactory justification. He may thus rely more on his decision than on highly general and otherwise coherent reasons he can put behind it. This situation is psychologically quite natural, since a great part of human decision making is dictated by unconscious mechanisms. To be a good judge, one need not be an equally good legal philosopher: One may, <u>inter alia</u>, be unable to make it clear, which general value judgment and reasoning norms would in combination with the statutory provision and the facts of the case logically imply the decision.

2. A judge deciding the precedent case can be <u>unable to predict</u> all the cases the precedent is going to cover. Not even the best justification entirely prevents undesired applicability of the precedent to cases that, for various reasons, often concerning their surprising consequences, ought to be decided differently.

3. The courts may regard as their primary task to decide <u>individual</u> cases; and consider only the legislator as empowered to enact general norms.

4. When a number of judges jointly decide the case, they often must find an acceptable <u>compromise</u>. In some cases, only a less extensive and less general justification can satisfy this demand. When <u>unanimously</u> accepted, it can be a stronger precedent than an extensive and general majority opinion, accompanied by a dissenting opinion. One may thus proffer highly coherent reasons for the conclusion that a less coherent justification accompanied by consensus of the judges is superior to a more coherent one without consensus.

5. In many cases, finally, the judge has no <u>time</u> to prepare general and extensive justification.

On the other hand, several reasons support the conclusion that the courts themselves ought to justify

their decisions in a highly extensive and general manner.
The following reasons of this kind have been listed by
<u>Gunnar Bergholtz</u> (1987, 352 ff.).

1. The modern society is no longer oriented towards
obeying judgments merely supported by an uncontroversial
authority, perhaps felt as reflecting God´s or the king´s
will. The parties rather wish to have immediate access to
general and extensive reasons, answering the question <u>why</u>
the court has decided in a certain way.

2. Democracy requires that the courts sufficiently
respect the statutes, enacted by the representatives of
the people. In hard cases, an extensive and general
justification is a necessary condition for making it
clear that the court has actually fulfilled this
requirement; cf. section 1.4.2 supra.

3. An extensively and generally justified decision
directly fulfils the demand of intersubjective
testability and thus an important principle of rational
practical discourse (cf. section 4.3.3 supra). In other
words, one knows on which grounds one may criticise it.
Testability promotes objectivity of the decision, and
thus legal certainty.

4. A decision gains a strong position as a precedent,
if it is justified in an extensive manner, facilitating
its criticism and yet not proved wrong (cf. section 3.3.2
supra on Popper´s falsificationist theory of science). At
the same time, a highly general character of the
justification makes the precedent widely applicable. This
fact promotes uniformity and thus coherence of the system
of law in action. It thus promotes predictability of
judicial decisions and fixity of the law.

5. An extensive and general justification helps the
parties to decide whether to appeal against the decision.
It also increases their chance to obtain a change of the
decision, if such is justifiable.

But general and extensive justification can, at the
same time, be cautious. Assume, e.g., that the court has
to make a choice between two ways to justify the
decision, one implying an important but contestable
material principle, the other merely stating a
non-controversial rule of procedure. A cautious court may
then prefer the latter.

In some cases, one may have doubts. In the case NJA 1975 p. 92, the
Supreme Court thus avoided the question whether the action of the
accused person constituted a crime or not, and merely stated that

this "crime" had not been satisfactorily proved. (A critic asked the question, Can a non-crime be "not satisfactorily proved"?).

In torts, the courts often avoid difficult problems of choice between the demands of necessary and sufficient causation, and simply apportion the damages.

Cautiousness is sometimes forced by procedural rules, e.g., the prohibition to decide a case, amenable to out-of-court settlement, on grounds of reasons not proffered by the parties (cf. Ch. 17 sec. 3 of the Code of Judicial Procedure).

6.5.6. The Role of Precedents in Swedish Law

Although not binding, precedents are regularly followed by Swedish courts. A lower court decides contrary to a precedent, established of a higher one, in principle only when wishing to give the latter a possibility to reconsider its practice, e.g. because the contested precedent conflicts with a statute, legislative preparatory materials or another precedent.

Using the terminology developed in section 6.2 supra, one can say that the Swedish courts have a _weak_ duty to follow precedents. They _should_ follows precedents, though it is not so that they _must_ do it.

The practice of following precedents has a long tradition. In Rome, the edicts of the praetor played a great role since 2nd Century B.C. (To be sure, the edicts contained general guidelines, not particular decisions, but the praetor was the highest judicial authority, without legislative power.) In canonical law, both the decisions of the Pope and established judiciary practice were binding. In the Swedish state in the 17th Century, precedents still played an important role.

Later, however, there set in a period of hostility to precedents. In Denmark, one stated that "precedent makes no law" (1672). The corresponding Swedish maxim was that judicial practice "should be based on written law, not on occasional judgments" (1803). In this connection, one can cite Prussian Landrecht of 1794, having forbidden the courts to take account of precedents.

In 20th Century, the role of precedents increased again. In the majority of European countries, the precedents are not binding. Yet, the courts _should_ follow them in the sense developed in section 6.2 supra.

In the Common Law countries, precedents are formally binding, although it is difficult to say whether the courts in these legal systems really follow precedents more frequently and more thoroughly than, e.g., in the case of Sweden. Indeed it might be maintained that the influence of precedents in Sweden is even greater than in England. In England there are some rules which state when a court is not bound by precedents. In Sweden, in absence of such rules, the precedents have a very strong influence.

In Finland, the role of precedents resembles that in Sweden. It also varies between different parts of the law, e.g., the precedents are more important in taxation law than in civil law. In Denmark and Norway, the situation is similar; cf. the Danish case U 1950 p. 413 Ö. The latest Norwegian case, in which a lower court intentionally disregarded a precedent of the Supreme Court is Rt 1910 p. 476.

The view that precedents are not binding has been officially expressed in Sweden, though perhaps in a somewhat exaggerated way. The Parliamentary Commissioner for the Judiciary (Justitieombudsman), in his annual report (1947), criticised a lower-court judge who had dealt with a legal question in conflict with a decision by the Supreme Court in pleno. In consequence of this, the Parliament's First Standing Committee on Legislation declared that the lower instance is not bound by precedents and that "only the weight of the reasons referred to by the Supreme Court in justification of its judgments should be determinative for the influence of the Supreme Court on the application of law in the lower instances." This pronouncement provoked a lively discussion, in which Folke Schmidt (1955, 109) expressed the following opinion: "The Swedish judge follows precedents precisely because they derive from the Supreme Court. He does this even where he believes that a different decision would in itself have been more suitable. Only if there are strong reasons indicating that he ought to adjudicate in the matter in a way different from that indicated by the precedent does the question arise of examining the weight of the reasons invoked by the Supreme Court."

The actual role of precedents in the Swedish law is significant. One thus does not know at all many important segments of such parts of the law as torts, if one ignores the precedents.

In connection with the importance of precedents in Swedish legal practice it is necessary also to take into account the amendments of 1971 to the procedural law, and the corresponding rules of administrative law. According to Ch. 54 Sec. 10 of the Code of Judicial Procedure, and Sec. 36 of the Code of Administrative Procedure, in principle the Supreme Court and the Supreme Administrative Court are only to act in cases in which (a) it is important that a general ruling be given by way of precedent for judicial practice or (b) special reasons exist, such as a grave mistake made by the lower court. The legislative preparatory materials to these provisions support the conclusion that the law-givers intended to strengthen the role of these courts in creating precedents (cf. Govt. Bill 1971 no. 45 for amendment of the Code of Judicial Procedure etc., especially p. 88).

It is not certain whether the amendments caused the increase of the role of precedents (cf. Strömholm 1988, 338), or vice versa. The most reasonable hypothesis is that of a causal feedback: the increased role of precedents caused the amendments, and then the latter amplified the former (cf. Bergholtz 1987, 429 ff.).

In this connection, one may also take into account Ch. 3 Sec. 5 of the Code of Judicial Procedure, and Sec. 5 of the Administrative Courts' Act, according to which the Supreme Court and the Supreme

Administrative Court may decide a case at a plenary sitting, if any
of the divisions of the Court, when deliberating a decision,
expresses an opinion diverging from a legal principle or statutory
construction which has formerly been adopted by this Court.

It is not possible to read into these provisions a strong duty on
the part of these courts to follow their earlier decisions. But
those decisions that have been rendered in pleno have an
exceptionally large influence.

6.6. LEGISLATIVE PREPARATORY MATERIALS

6.6.1. Introductory Remarks

A draft of a statute is often accompanied by legislative
preparatory materials (travaux préparatoires), explaining
its meaning, reasons and purposes.

In Sweden, one elaborates the travaux préparatoires at the following
stages of the legislation process (cf. Bernitz et al. 1985, 87 ff.).

1) The Government or the Parliament takes the legislative
initiative; the latter may demand that the Government appoints a
legislation committee.

2) The Government appoints the legislation committee or, in some
cases, an individual investigator. The responsible minister issues a
pronouncement, containing directives for the committee or the
investigator, prepared by the staff of the ministry. The directives
are published in the series "Committee Directives" and in the
Parliamentary Reports (riksdagstrycket).

3) The committee or the investigator prepares a report, published
in the series "Official Investigations of the State" (Statens
offentliga utredningar, SOU).

The Government can instead let a ministry or a central
administrative agency perform the investigation; the ministry
publishes the resulting memorandum in a special series. The
Government can also appoint a governmental committee.

4) The ministry staff discusses the report.

5) Several persons and bodies are invited to present comments.

6) The report is again discussed within the ministry.

7) The Council on Legislation (lagrådet) may be asked to issue a
pronouncement about the report, especially if it regards important
matters.

8) The ministry prepares a Government Bill. It consists of a draft
of the statute; a general justification; a special justification,
section by section; and a summary of the previously elaborated
material. The Bill is published and included into the Parliamentary
Reports.

9) The relevant parliamentary commission discusses the Bill. The
result is published in the Parliamentary Reports.

10) The Parliament <u>in pleno</u> discusses the Bill.
11) The Parliament enacts the statute; the statute is promulgated and published in the official statute-book, <u>Svensk författningssamling</u>.
<u>Nytt juridiskt arkiv (NJA)</u>, part II, contains a survey of important preparatory materials.

6.6.2. Ratio Legis

Why are preparatory materials valuable? The answer to this question within the legal paradigm (that is, within the contextually sufficient legal justification) is "because they constitute a result of legislative work and we usually take them into account". The answer within the <u>deep</u> justification is, on the other hand, "because they constitute the evidence of the purpose of the statute (<u>ratio legis</u>)". The idea of <u>ratio legis</u> is complex (cf., e.g., Klami 1980, 17 and Aarnio 1987, 99 and 125). One must pay attention to the following facts.

1) One may argue that what the legislator intended to say is more important than what he actually said in the statute. The literal text of the law may have been unfortunately phrased. For that reason, one recommends the so-called <u>subjective construction of statutes</u>, following the <u>ratio legis</u>.

2) The <u>travaux préparatoires</u> constitute the evidence of what the individuals who participated in the legislative process, such as members of the legislative committee, the persons invited to present comments, the minister, the members of the Parliament etc. thought and wished. This evidence is regarded as a data basis of the subjective construction of statutes.

3) Though often called "the will of the legislator", the <u>ratio legis</u> is, however, not the same thing as the personal views of the individuals who participated in the legislative process. It is rather the most coherent system of value-statements and norm-statement, consistent with everything they said, or at least with the most important opinions they expressed.

The idea that the main purpose of statutory construction is to discover the legislator´s will was expressed in the year 1750 by <u>C.H. Eckhardus</u> (1750, 2): "To interpret is nothing else as to derive the author´s opinion from his words and reason" (<u>interpretari nihil aliud esse, quam sensum auctoris ex eius verbis et</u>

<u>ratione declarere</u>). In the first half of the 18th century
this idea was expressed by Thibaut and Savigny, among
other authors, in the second half, for example, by
Windscheid, at the beginning of the present century,
among others, by Bierling (cf. Wróblewski 1959, 160-1 n.
26). The subjective construction of statutes were,
however, often based on other premises than the <u>travaux</u>
<u>préparatoires</u>. Until the World War I, the role of the
latter was rather insignificant.

6.6.3. Is Subjective Interpretation of Statutes Possible?

When commenting upon the role of the so-called subjective
interpretation of statutes, one must, however, answer
some well-known objections.

1. We cannot see into the mind of another human being. Consequently,
some critics pointed out that we cannot <u>know</u>, but merely guess, what
the persons participating in the legislation actually wanted.
   However, this objection disregards the fact that one may have
quite good reasons to justify one's guesses about other people's
thoughts. The main argument is analogy. If I am pale, shout abuse
and hit out at everybody who gets in my way, then I am angry. <u>A</u>
resembles me in many ways. At present A is pale, is shouting abuse
and hitting out at everybody who gets his way. Conclusion: <u>A</u> is
angry at the present time.
   R. Tuomela (1977, 39 ff.) has developed a more sophisticated idea
(introduced by Sellars) that mental "acts" of thinking can be
analysed by analogy to speech acts. Cf. Chisholm 1966, 62 ff.

2. The concept "legislator´s will" can be criticised in
another way as well, and this has in fact been done by,
<u>inter alia</u>, Hägerström (1953, 17 ff. and 354 ff.),
Lundstedt, Olivecrona (71 ff. and 73 ff.) and other
representatives of the Uppsala School. They have pointed
out that one could not consistently understand this
concept to mean that the legislator is an individual
person who with his will embraces at one and the same
time the entire legal system; cf. section 5.5.2 supra.
   However, subjective construction of statutes does not
need to rely on such fictions. To be sure, one proposes
as a correct constructional method one which derives the
interpretation of the statute from a set of premises
including the information of its <u>ratio</u>. It is also true

that one supports the ratio with propositions about the
will of the persons that participated in the process of
legislation. But neither the ratio nor the proposed
construction of statutes follow logically from the
description of this will alone. Neither they follow from
a set solely containing these propositions together with
some certain premises and premises taken for granted
within the legal paradigm.

The step from the travaux préparatoires to the
conclusion concerning psychological will of the persons
participating in the legislation is a jump. The step from
the information about this will to the ratio legis is
another jump. The step from the ratio to the proposed
construction of the statute is a third jump. All three
jumps can be reasonable, if derivable from a set of
reasonable premises.

To put it more exactly, the "subjective" interpretatory
conclusion can be derivable from a complex set of
premises including some which are reasonable, although
neither certain nor presupposed. The conclusion thus can
follow from a set of reasonable premises containing

a) some pronouncements in the travaux préparatoires;

b) some source-norms telling one in what a way one
should let the travaux préparatoires affect statutory
construction; among other things, how one should
establish a priority order between pronouncements of
different persons and thus eliminate contradictions;

c) the hypothesis that these pronouncements often
express various (neither permanent nor unitary)
intentions held by various (not always the same) persons
who participated in the legislative process; and, finally

d) some more profound reasons, inter alia general
principles, supporting both these pronouncements and
their use in a concrete piece of statutory construction.

3. Another objection to subjective statutory
construction is based on the fact that in some
exceptional cases evidence may show that a pronouncement
in the preparatory materials is not in accord with the
actual intention of the person who pronounced it.

However, the travaux préparatoires should be taken into
account in the statutory construction because they as a
rule correspond to such intentions. The practice of
subjective construction of statutes reflects this normal
situation. The demand of fixity of the law, and thus
predictability of the statutory construction is a reason,
perhaps sufficient, for the conclusion that one always
should pay attention to the travaux préparatoires, even
at the expense of sometimes making a mistake as regards

the real intentions. But even if someone thinks that such mistakes are never to be accepted, the following norm is reasonable: Whoever holds that the pronouncements in the preparatory materials do not correspond to the actual intention, has the burden of argument.

4. The last objection that I intend to discuss here is the following one. The legislative power in Sweden belongs, first of all, to the Parliament. Thus the "legislator´s will" ought to be sought above all in the Riksdag. Despite this, in judicial practice ratio legis is as a rule extracted from the statements of legislation committees, statements of the responsible minister, the opinion of the Council of Legislation etc. One pays much less regard to speeches made in the parliamentary debates on the matter. In other words, it seems that the "legislator´s will" lies in statements by the legislator´s assistants, not in statements by the "legislator" himself. How does this fit the idea that in subjective construction of statutes one discovers the legislator´s will? (cf. Strömholm 1966, 216).

This objection can be answered by repeating that the subjective construction of statutes is based on the ratio legis, not on the personal views of the individuals who participated in the legislative process. As stated above, the ratio legis is the most coherent system of value-statements and norm-statement, consistent with everything they said, or at least with the most important opinions they expressed. Both the problem and the solution have been well-known since a long time. Cf. Thibaut 1802, 103: "Die Raison des Gesetzes" is "durch eine Art juristische Fiktion als besonderer Wille des Gesetzgebers zu betrachten."

6.6.4. Is Ratio Legis Compatible with Democracy?

One must, however, consider the following objection. Democracy requires that the Parliament has the legislative power. This power is exercised by real people who have real intentions. Is it compatible with democracy to replace this reality with the ideal construction of the ratio? One can answer this objection in the following way. The power of the Parliament is not the same as the possibility of any parliamentary majority to immediately fulfil all its intentions. The transformation of these to the statutes is regulated by legal norms

whose justifiable <u>ratio</u> is to impose <u>rational limitations</u>
upon the intentions.

This fact creates some analytical problems. Whereas the law is
construed according to the "legislator's" will, the "legislator" is
constructed according to the law. This is, however, <u>not</u> a vicious
circle but rather a "spiral". A vague idea about the content of the
law helps one to identify the legislator and his authority. The
relation to this authority is a reason for a more precise
interpretation of the content of the law.

In this connection, one must pay attention to two
concepts, 1) democracy and 2) rationality.
   1. The main idea of democracy, the power of the people,
is not the same thing as an unrestricted power of the
majority. The majority rule is a mere <u>approximation</u> of
the democratic decision-making. The latter is a mere
approximation of the moral decision-making. One can,
e.g., say that the majority rule approximates the
calculus of human preferences. To decide what actions are
morally good, one must thus pay attention not only to the
number of people having certain preferences but also to
the strength of the preferences.

Consequently, the concept of democracy is not the same as
"unrestricted majority rule". It is a much more complex and
sophisticated notion, more or less intimately related, <u>inter alia</u>,
to the following criteria of democracy: 1) political representation
of the interests of the citizens, 2) majority rule, 3) participation
of citizens in politics, 4) freedom of opinion, 5) some other human
and political rights, 6) legal certainty, 7) division of power and
8) responsibility of those in power. One needs moral considerations
in order to state the criteria more precisely and apply them to
concrete states and social orders; cf. section 1.4.2 supra.

This idea of democracy thus does not imply the
possibility of any temporal parliamentary majority
whatsoever to immediately fulfil all its intentions.
   2. A legal view, <u>inter alia</u>, concerning statutory
construction is correct if it is as rational as possible.
This idea of rationality is very complex. It implies that
a correct legal view is supported by an as <u>coherent</u> as
possible set of certain, presupposed or otherwise
reasonable premises. Coherence demands, among other
things, that the conclusion is supported by such a set of

premises, and so on. In this way, a great number of statements hangs together. "Certain" premises are taken for granted by all people or at least all normal people belonging to the culture under consideration. "Presupposed" premises are taken for granted within a particular practice belonging to the culture under consideration, e.g. within the legal paradigm; cf. section 3.3.5 supra. The relation to "culture under consideration" and "legal paradigm", makes the law more fixed as a pure morality. This relation also elucidates the role of consensus in legal reasoning. Correctness depends on both coherence and consensus. Paying attention to the relationship between consensus and rational discourse (section 4.3 supra), one may conclude that a legal view is correct, if it is as rational as possible in view of an act of weighing and balancing, which pays attention to the postulate of fixity of the law and to various coherence criteria and discursive rationality. In brief, it is correct if it unanimously would be accepted by lawyers who think as coherently as possible and participate in a perfect discourse.

Democracy provides the best institutional framework for legal reasoning thus highly fulfilling the criteria of coherence and discursive rationality. But, of course, democracy is not a sufficient condition of correctness of such a reasoning.

6.6.5. Should One Pay Attention to Preparatory Materials?

The following reasons, inter alia, tell for the technique of legislation keeping the text of statutes short and leaving the details to the travaux préparatoires.

1) Provided that the preparatory materials fulfil high standards of quality, this technique brings more information into the legal system. Different persons whose pronouncements the preparatory materials contain, formulated different reasons. One can conceive the preparatory materials as a kind of dialogue (cf. section 3.2.1 supra). The person who performs the statutory construction thus gains access to a many-sided "store" of reasons to weigh and balance. On the other hand, if the legislator were forced to put all the authoritative information to the very text of the statute, he could not report both arguments and counter-arguments. He would be

forced to make a choice. The information given to the
interpreter would be less extensive. This would decrease
coherence of legal reasoning. The greater the number of
statements the interpreters may pay attention to, the
greater the coherence of statutory interpretation; cf.
section 4.1.3 supra.

2) By keeping the text of statutes short and leaving
the details to the travaux préparatoires, the legislator
also brings morally justifiable elasticity to the legal
system. General rules can be too rigid to be just. It may
be morally better to guide judges by means of a dialogue
of the kind described above.

Provided that extensive preparatory materials exist,
the following are some reasons for taking legislative
preparatory materials into account within legal reasoning
in general and statutory construction in particular.

1) A rational interpretation uses as many reasons as
possible, cf. section 4.1.3 supra on coherence. Ceteris
paribus, one thus should make use in the statutory
construction of all the aids which are available,
including preparatory materials.

2) When interpreting statutes, one should pay attention
to their ratio, and this is connected with the travaux
préparatoires.

3) The travaux préparatoires should be taken into
account because they form a part of a democratic
legislative procedure, (cf. above and, e.g., Eckhoff
1987, 64).

4) Regard for justice legal certainty and generality as
a criterion of coherence requires that statutes shall be
interpreted uniformly. Uniformity is promoted if all
interpreters take into account the same preparatory
materials, provided that these contain more information
than the statute itself (cf., e.g., Eckhoff 1987, 64;
Strömholm 1966, 214 and 1988, 328).

5) If the authors of the travaux préparatoires were
outstanding experts and used much time to prepare the
pronouncements, one may expect that their opinions are
well-founded.

6) The persons participating in the legislative process
expect travaux préparatoires to be taken into account. In
this context, one may state the following.

a) The statute is often formulated in a brief, abstract
and vague manner, since the legislators expect that
provisions which are found to be insufficiently clear
will have been commented upon in the travaux
préparatoires (cf. Eckhoff 1987, 64-5).

b) Were the courts to show indifference toward preparatory materials, they would run the risk that "those who have passed the statute would have some reason to feel disappointed" (Thornstedt 1960, 243) and might restrict the court´s competence in the field of statutory construction.

On the other hand, the following arguments are among those adduced against taking legislative preparatory materials into account within statutory construction.

1) _Ceteris paribus_, a statute, containing a consistent system of rules, must be more fixed than a dialogue, that is, a set of pro- and counter-arguments, contained in the preparatory materials. For that reason, a restriction of the system of the sources of law to statutes, without preparatory materials, would increase fixity of law.

2) It is also an empirical fact that _travaux préparatoires_ are sometimes less clear than the statute itself.

Cf., e.g., a minority report of Herlitz and J.W. Pettersson, _Kommunallagskommittéens betänkande_ I, SOU 1947:53, 163; cf. Schmidt 1957, 172.

The purposes of the legislation are often stated only partially in the legislative materials. Many problems of interpretation are disregarded there. From this it follows that the help they give one to predict legal decisions might be very limited.

3) The statute itself is more concise and often easier to read than the _travaux préparatoires_. This is another reason for the conclusion that predictability of legal decisions might decrease if the courts base their practice on the preparatory materials, instead of the text of the statute.

4) The fact that the interpreter pays great attention to the _travaux préparatoires_ may possibly have the effect that the legislator does not take much care with the drafting of the text, since he expects to clear up obscurities in the preparatory materials (cf., e.g., Eckhoff 1987, 65). But the materials are less accessible than the statute itself.

"It is quite strange to tell (the citizen) that instead of reading the statute books he should try to find his way through the labyrinth of the Parliamentary Report"; cf., e.g., a minority report of Herlitz and J.W. Pettersson, o.c. 163; cf. Schmidt 1957, 172.

Fixity of the law, predictability of legal decisions and
hence legal certainty might decrease if the courts rely
upon the parliamentary publications containing the
legislative materials, instead of the statute book.

5) It is not clear which precedents, and how many, are
to be considered sufficient to set aside contrary views
in the legislative materials. This fact might also
negatively affect predictability of judicial practice
relying on the travaux préparatoires.

6) To bind the courts to the travaux préparatoires is
to disturb the commonly accepted division of powers in
the community.

a) The preparatory materials restrict the number of
possible choices the courts have when construing a
statute. They may also gain priority before precedents.
In this manner, the power of the courts is unduly
restricted and the power of the legislator is dangerously
increased (cf. Ekelöf 1951, 28).

b) The travaux préparatoires are not subjected to the
same parliamentary debate as the statutory draft itself.
In the travaux préparatoires senior civil servants and
politicians might express ideas which would not be
accepted by the Parliament. In this way the increased
importance of the preparatory materials also upsets the
balance of power between the Riksdag and, on the other
hand, the Government and higher civil service.

7) The preparatory materials cannot be amended
afterwards. If one desires to alter legal practice
resulting from the preparatory materials, one must amend
the text of the statute itself even though the only error
is in the travaux préparatoires (cf. Ekelöf 1958, 94-5).

In abstracto, it is difficult to weigh and balance the
discussed arguments for and against the conclusion that
legislative preparatory materials should be used in legal
reasoning, particularly in a judicial construction of
statutes. But in the actual situation in Sweden, the
materials should be taken into account. The following are
some reasons therefor.

1) The high speed of legislation makes it impossible
for the law-givers to create a consistent, precise and
complete system of rules. They must make an
insufficiently fixed law. The only way for them to make
their intentions clear is to also elaborate extensive
preparatory materials. This is possible, since the
demands of consistency, preciseness and completeness are

less applicable when one writes in a dialogue-form then when one enacts rules.

2) The high speed of legislation does not leave jurists sufficient time to elaborate commentaries, handbooks and other auxiliary means for statutory construction. At the same time, the confidence in legal dogmatics decreased, as a result of both its decreased possibility to do good work (see above) and the severe - albeit often mistaken - criticism it received from the Uppsala school. When legal dogmatics cannot make the law fixed enough, the interpreter needs all help the travaux préparatoires might give him.

3) The rapid changes of the society also diminish the confidence of lawyers in the customary law. This fact decreases the fixity of the law and thus increases the need of help from the preparatory materials.

4) The political stability, typical for Sweden, justifies a rather high degree of confidence in the civil servants and politicians who elaborate the legislative materials. They may be less competent as one would expect but, as a rule, they do not use the preparatory materials to promote particular interests or for other morally objectionable purposes.

6.6.6. The Role of Preparatory Materials in Swedish Law. General Remarks

Although not binding, preparatory materials are regularly followed by Swedish courts. Using the terminology developed in section 6.2 supra, it can be said that the Swedish courts have a weak duty to follow the travaux préparatoires. They should follow these materials, although one cannot say that they must do it.

In some states an explicit statutory rule requires that the lawgiver's intention shall be sought in construing the statute: cf. Ch. 1 Sec. 12 in the Italian Civil Code and Sec. 6 in the Austrian ABGB. In these countries, however, there is often an inclination to find the legislator's intention above all in the text of the statute and not in the travaux préparatoires. In French legal writing, too, it is considered that the legislator's will should be sought above all in the text of the statute, the travaux préparatoires being considered of less importance. According to a traditional view among English legal writers, travaux préparatoires should not be used at all in statutory interpretation. It may be that this view is not so strongly held as before, but nevertheless the importance of travaux préparatoires in England is still small. In the United Stated, the tradition resembles the English one, yet the importance of the preparatory materials is greater.

In the Nordic countries, the legislative preparatory materials have as a rule greater importance than in other states. The rather concise Norwegian travaux préparatoires succeed often to grasp the essential goals of the statute. In most (though not all) cases, they are also highly respected. Eckhoff (1987, 74 ff.) thus quoted some cases (Rt 1921 p. 406 and 1916 p. 648) giving evidence that the courts dare to judge in conflict with both the preparatory materials and the wording of the statutes, and other cases (Rt 1982 p. 745 and 1961 p. 98) showing that this only happens in exceptional situations. In Finland, the legislative preparatory materials are often less exhaustive, yet very important. The role of legislative materials in Denmark is probably lesser than in the other Nordic countries.

Even compared with the Nordic neighbours, Swedish courts estimate the importance of the legislative materials to an extraordinarily high degree (cf. Sundberg 1978, 232 ff. re the historical background). Until ca. 1980, Swedish legislative materials were also as a rule more exhaustive than in other Nordic states.

The idea that the Swedish preparatory materials occupy a position as important as precedent was formulated by Folke Schmidt (1955, 103 ff., = 1957, 172 ff.). Schmidt influenced the subsequent development of the Swedish doctrine of the sources of the law. In a later work (1976, 262), Schmidt expressed his opinion even more clearly: "The text of the statute received more and more a function of a headline to remember when one searches for what has been wished in detail. The pronouncement of the responsible minister states the main purposes, what alternative solutions have been refuted and what can be the more precise content of the draft..., all this to to govern the administration of justice."

Jan Hellner (1988, 66) summarised the situation, as follows: "The travaux préparatoires are often the most important aid, used in the statutory construction. One can find numerous examples of an interpretation explicitly supported by the preparatory material, but one can also find examples of judicial decisions contradicting the preparatory materials".

Hellner quoted the following case as an example. In NJA 1985 p. 659, the majority of the Supreme Court used preparatory materials as the reason for placing site leaseholdership on an equality with ownership, in spite of the fact that the interpreted statute had not explicitly supported this conclusion. The minority pointed out that other statutes always contain explicit provisions, if such a conclusion is intended.

In NJA 1981 p. 920, the Supreme Court unanimously affirmed the decision of the court of appeal which has followed clearly conflicting with the literal wording of the statute. The reason was that the final text of the statute was a result of the fact that the legislature had made a clumsy change in the text proposed to it. Though the change was not intended to affect the problem under consideration, the resulting wording contradicted this intention. It must be noted that one member of the court of appeal dissented and that a view had been expressed in the literature that, because of the clear wording, the statute must be interpreted in a way which contradicts the intention (cf. Hellner 1988, 69).

In RÅ 1974 Fi 850 the Supreme Administrative Court followed the travaux préparatoires instead of the wording of the statute. Justice Reuterswärd claimed that a literal interpretation would be both strange and irrational.

In some cases, however, the Supreme Court decided to disregard preparatory materials conflicting with the wording of the statute; cf., e.g., NJA 1978 p. 581. In the case NJA 1972 p. 296, the Supreme Court dissociated itself from a series of statements by the responsible minister in the travaux préparatoires of the Liability for Damages Act. Cf. NJA 1977 p. 273; 1976 p. 483 and 1952 p. 195.

In this context, let me mention NJA 1976 p. 483. The Real Property Code, Ch. 4 Sec. 7 stipulates what follows: "Purchase according to which a separate owner acquires some area within a real estate is valid only if a creation of a (new) real estate takes place according to this purchase through an official proceeding for which one applies latest six months after the purchase contract was drawn up and, if the proceeding is not finished within this time, it shall be executed in accordance with the purchase." In the case under consideration, the seller applied for a creation of the new real estate and later sold the corresponding area. The proceeding was not finished within six months after the purchase. The buyer applied for an entry in the land register. The court registrar refused, since the contract was to be considered invalid, on the basis of clear preparatory materials to the quoted statute. The Supreme Court, however, refuted the preparatory materials and remanded the case to the court registrar. The reasons were both the literal text of the statute and its purpose. The purpose was thus to avoid indefinitely prolonged uncertainty concerning validity of purchase. This purpose was not actual in the case under consideration, since no uncertainty would remain as soon as the proceeding is finished.

The importance of the travaux préparatoires varies from one part of the law to another. The greatest is it in the tax law. Their role in private law is also significant. Criminal jurisdiction is less affected by the preparatory materials. This is a consequence of the so-called legality principle, "nulla poena sine lege", implying high respect for the literal wording of the statutory text. Yet, the travaux préparatoires may be important in criminal cases, too. In, e.g., NJA 1980 p. 94, the decision of the Supreme Court supported itself on the preparatory materials to the statute (1976:56), amending the provision of Ch. 11 Sec. 4 of the Criminal Code.

6.6.7. The Role of Preparatory Materials in Swedish Law. Some Source-Norms

The most important source-norms in Sweden concerning legislative preparatory materials have the following content.

S5) The following texts constitute the travaux préparatoires that should be considered in legal reasoning: The legislation committee reports, memoranda prepared by a ministry or a central administrative agency; statements by persons and bodies invited to present comments; pronouncements of the responsible minister; pronouncements of the Council on Legislation (lagrådet); bills of the members of the Parliament and opinions of the relevant parliamentary commission (cf. Bernitz et al. 1985, 87 ff.).

Besides, one may consider the directives for the legislation committee and what is said during plenary debates in the Parliament.

The latter material is as a rule not respected very much, because it may contain things said for political advantage, and thus less coherent.

S6) Old preparatory materials may be taken into account.

The age thus weakens the position of the travaux préparatoires (cf., e.g., Schmidt 1957, 196 and Thornstedt 1960, 243). It is no longer so that one should pay attention to them.

Sometimes preparatory materials age rapidly. In Govt. Bill 1932:106 containing proposals for inter alia an act on mortgages on farming stock, the responsible minister made the following pronouncement: "Only such property as belongs to the debtor is covered by the preference right in mortgaging. This right can thus not be applied to effects which have been purchased on instalments." (NJA 1932 II p. 223). Twenty years later (NJA 1952 p. 195), however, the Supreme Court extended the preference right in mortgaging to effects which have been purchased on instalments.

S7) Consideration should be given, as a rule, only to materials which have been published in printed form.

S8) Pronouncements in the preparatory materials relating to questions outside the scope of the legislation under consideration should, as a rule, not be taken into account (cf. Schmidt 1957, 174).

However, the following exceptions must be noticed.

a) A body undertaking inquires concerning a number of statutes may in connection with one draft statute express its opinion about another draft dealt with earlier (cf. Schmidt 1957, 175). Such a pronouncement should be considered as of equal value with other travaux préparatoires.

b) In the interpretation of an earlier statute one should pay attention to preparatory materials of new statutes which regulate an adjacent area.

The antiquated but still valid provision in Ch. 1 Sec. 5 of the Commercial Code of 1734 ("If one sells goods to two persons one shall pay damages and the person who bought first shall keep the goods") has for example been commented upon with the support of an inquiry of 1965 (SOU 1965:14, p. 37 ff.)

S9) Pronouncements in the preparatory materials should not be taken into account if they introduce entirely new norms, for which no support exists in the text of the statute.

In spite of this norm, a phenomenon occurs, sometimes called "legislation through preparatory materials". This takes place when 1) the travaux préparatoires claim priority before the wording of the statute; 2) they are relatively precise while the statute is very vague; or 3) they contain norms not supported at all by any statutory provision. Let me discuss some examples.

1) Sec. 3 of the MBL (the statute stipulating a comprehensive right of the employee representatives to be consulted in connection with the employer's policy) stipulates, what follows: If a statute or a norm enacted on the basis of statutory authorisation contains a special provision contrary to this statute, the provision is valid. The Stock Corporation Act, Ch. 8, Sec. 11, contains a clear provision of this kind. Yet, the minister wrote in the travaux préparatoires to the MBL (Government Bill 1975/76:105, appendix 1) that, as regards collective agreements, the MBL should have priority before this provision. To assure that this pronouncement does not overrule the statutory provision itself, the non-socialist majority of the Parliament, elected 1976, had to complete the MBL with a new Sec. 32, confirming that Sec. 3 still is in force, even in the case of collective agreements (cf. Ailinpieti 1980).

2) Sec. 36 of the Contracts Act gives the courts possibility to modify or set aside a contractual stipulation, "if it is undue (unreasonable) with regard to the content of the contract, circumstances of its origin, subsequent circumstances and other circumstances"; one must also pay particular attention to the need of protecting the person who, "as a consumer or otherwise occupies an inferior position in the contractual relation". The pronouncement of the responsible minister in the preparatory materials completed this general clause with more precise guidelines: One should set aside a contractual stipulation giving a party unilateral right to decide, especially if this stipulation is included in a standard contract elaborated by the clearly stronger party. One should also set aside a contractual stipulation incompatible with good business custom within a given branch. On the other hand, one need not accept a stipulation corresponding to what a given branch considers to be good business custom; etc. (Government Bill 1975/76:81, p. 118 ff.). Cf. section 1.2.2 supra, re NJA 1979 p. 666.

3) The statute of 1915 concerning installment purchase received 1953 an amendment stipulating invalidity of a reservation making the buyer's right to the goods dependent on his fulfilling another obligation. The statute was then replaced by Consumer Credit Act (1977:981) and Commercial Installment Purchase Act (1978:599). Neither contains a corresponding provision. Sec. 15 para. 2, concerning another question is, however, accompanied by the travaux préparatoires stating precisely that such a reservation is invalid (Hellner 1982, 231 ff.).

4) Ch. 4 sec. 19 of the Real Property Code deals with seller's liability for defects in the sold real property. Nothing in the statute indicates that the buyer cannot base his claim on a defect which he had noticed had he performed a careful inspection. Yet, this is the view the Supreme Court expressed in several cases, cf., e.g., NJA 1978 p. 301, no doubt under influence of the clear travaux préparatoires (cf. Hellner 1988, 70).

The legislation by preparatory materials may be explained as resulting from insuperable difficulties the legislator must face when attempting to create a fixed, consistent, precise and complete system or rules; cf. above.

S10) Pronouncements in the preparatory materials intending to change established practice based on an earlier statutory provision should be taken into account in exceptional cases only (cf. Schmidt 1957, 177).

But what is an exceptional case? Sec. 42 para. 1 of the MBL stipulates that neither the employer nor the employer organisations may support an illegal labour conflict. The provision was received unchanged from Sec. 4 of the previously valid Collective Agreements Act. In this connection, rigorous rules evolved in practice; both the legislation committee and the responsible minister "derogated" these in the travaux préparatoires to the MBL (Govt. Bill 1975/76:105 p. 277).

S11) Wholly obscure preparatory materials should not be taken into account (cf. Strömholm 1966, 175 ff.).

Concerning the source-norms about collisions between various kinds of travaux préparatoires and between these and other sources of the law, cf. section 7.6.2 infra.

Ulf Bernitz (1984, 17) has pointed out that the recent development as regards the travaux préparatoires might jeopardise their position as a source of the law. About 1978, one thus began to abstain from elaborating a systematic presentation of statements by persons and bodies invited to present comments. Instead, one attached a chaotic appendix, in some cases only obtainable as a mimeograph. A couple of years later, one introduced a practice of merely attaching a very brief and rather uninteresting summary of such statements.

Cf., e.g. the Govt. Bill 1981/82:40 on home sale and the Govt. Bill 1983/84:16 on broker business.

At the same time, the quality standard of committee reports decreased, inter alia in consequence of growing practice to omit the customary presentation of foreign law, references to the professional literature and any deeper justification whatsoever.

One may explain this development by the fact that complexity and speed of change of the society has already become so high that not only the statutes themselves but also preparatory materials are too difficult to elaborate. Perhaps the law-givers do as much they can, but cannot do much. Or have they already lost the hope of doing a good work?

This development causes the following risks.

1) An important reason to consider the travaux préparatoires consists in the fact that they constitute a kind of a dialogue, in which the legislation committee, the persons and bodies invited to present comments, the responsible minister, the Council on Legislation and others pronounce reasons for and against a certain solution. These reasons constitute a basis of a rational weighing and balancing to be performed in various cases by the courts, authorities and legal scholars. The value of this basis depends on its extensiveness and completeness, now more and more questionable.

2) One may use fragmentary pronouncements, published in the travaux préparatoires, not knowing that they received a severe criticism of the persons and bodies invited to present comments.

3) The responsible minister has now gained an opportunity to conceal this criticism, e.g. for political reasons.

At the same time, the role of the travaux préparatoires has increased, as a result of the increased speed and decreased standard of legislation combined with the growing disposition of the courts to use all available means for justification of their decisions.

The situation is thus unstable. One cannot expect a peaceful coexistence of the growing rationality of judicial practice (cf. section 6.5 supra), the decreasing rationality of the travaux préparatoires, and the high degree of confidence of the courts in the legislative materials.

Perhaps some new ideas are needed, how to optimise the postulate of fixity of law and coherence of legal reasoning.

6.7. PROFESSIONAL JURISTIC LITERATURE

The so-called doctrine is of significant importance for legal reasoning. The word "doctrine" refers first of all to the professional legal writing in legal dogmatics, whose task is to systematise and interpret valid law (cf. section 1.1 supra).

The word "doctrine" may also refer, in some contexts, to other types of legal writing, such as history of law, sociology of law, law and economics, philosophy of law etc.

In legal reasoning performed within legal research, importance of previous research is obvious. The author of a legal writing must, of course, pay attention to existing literature concerning the discussed matter. But the doctrine also influences legal reasoning in judicial and administrative practice. The mandatory literature affects all students of law, including future judges and officials. The outstanding legal researchers, appointed as high judges or members of a legislative committee, continue to pay attention to the professional literature which have been a necessary tool of their profession.

The doctrine plays an important role because it aims at rationality. The main point of systematising and interpreting valid law in the legal dogmatics is to present the law as a highly coherent system, supported by general reasons (cf. sections 3.2 and 4.1 supra). To deny the role of the doctrine as an auxiliary tool of legal reasoning would be the same as to refute rationality.

The doctrine constitutes also an important source of the law. In other words, one pays attention to theses developed in legal writing not only because of the quality of reasons there proffered but also due to the

authoritative position legal writers occupy. It is a
well-known phenomenon that a doctoral dissertation gains
more authority as soon as the author becomes a professor
or law. This is, of course, a result of the expectation
of fixity of the law. When the law-givers and the courts
fail to make the law sufficiently fixed, one looks for
other fixed sources of the law. Books are fixed enough,
especially when some parts of the law are monopolised by
a single writer, as it must happen in a small country.

As a rule, the Swedish courts merely refer to the
common scholarly opinion, without stating precisely the
author or the title of his work. But explicit quotations
occur in some cases, as well. An efficient method is to
include an expert opinion as a part of justification of
the decision, cf., e.g., NJA 1966 p. 210. In this manner,
the court may quote even some controversial juristic
views, as containing reasons to be weighed and balanced
against other considerations.

Doctrine has been of varying importance in the history of law. In
Rome Augustus gave to certain prominent jurists the right to answer
questions of law by authority of the Emperor, ius publicae
respondendi ex auctoritate principis. Other emperors, too, gave a
similar right to certain jurists. The courts regarded the views of
these jurists as valid law. Certain statutes of 4th and 5th
centuries A.D. regulated the order in which these jurists should be
cited, if their views were incompatible. The so-called
citation-statute from A.D. 426 accorded binding force to books of
Papinian, Paulus, Ulpian, Gaius and Modestinus, and regulated in
detail the relative authority of these jurists.
In Medieval Europe the legal communis opinio doctorum, based on
Roman sources and embraced by the majority of celebrated legal
writers, mostly French or Italian, had a dominating influence.
Opinions of the "doctors" were often used in the canonical process.
In Swedish law the position of doctrine was at its peak in the
17th and 18th centuries (cf. Sundberg 1978, 86 ff.). Not
infrequently, the courts made explicit reference to the works of
Loccenius, Rålamb, Kloot and others. References to the leading works
of foreign legal writers were common. Some famous foreign scholars
became also in various ways attached to the Swedish state. Pufendorf
become thus a professor in Lund, Grotius received a Swedish
diplomatic position.
The authority of doctrine underwent a decline in centralised
monarchies, more and more emphasising the role of legislation; e.g.
a draft of the Prussian Landrecht of 1794 thus prohibited writing
any comments to this code. Also some ideas of the division of power
preserved lawmaking as an exclusive domain of the lawmaker. Later,
however, one noticed that all laws need interpretation. In Germany,
one also needed the gemeines Recht, common to the plurality of small
centralised states. Doctrine thus made a comeback in the 19th

century. Great scholars, such as C. F. von Savigny, influenced the German legal development of this period. The German Pandektenwissenschaft, based on sophistication of Roman law, achieved a uniquely high level, influenced the final codification of civil law (BGB of 1896) and was highly influential even outside the boundaries of Germany.

At the end of 19th century, the standing of doctrine in Sweden was strong (cf. Sundberg 1978, 177-186.) A professor even stated that lawmaking in judicial practice is nothing but applied doctrine (id., 185). No doubt, this statement was highly exaggerated, yet it was significant that such a view could be seriously considered at all.

In the present-day Sweden, some jurists are afraid of the risk of a significant decrease of the role of doctrine (cf. Sundberg 1978, 262 ff.). However, one must pay attention to differences between various parts of the law. Legal writing has, e.g., a great influence in international private law. In public international law, it also has a clear position as a recognised source of the law, cf. Sec. 38 of the statute of the International Court of Justice.

The following factors increase probability of a high position of doctrine.

1) The greater respect the decision-makers have for rational reasoning, the greater is the role of doctrine.

2) The lower the speed of legislative change, the greater is the chance that jurists have sufficient time to elaborate commentaries, handbooks and other auxiliary means for statutory construction.

3) The more numerous statutory provisions, precedents, pronouncements in travaux préparatoires and other sources of the law are, the greater is the need of their systematisation and interpretation in legal writing.

4) The lower the degree of fixity and coherence of other sources of the law, the greater the need to look for help in the literature.

Taking some risk of exaggeration, one may state, what follows. There is a tension of two incompatible trends.

1. The respect the contemporary Swedish decision-makers have for rational reasoning is not particularly great. Some politicians often think that manipulating emotions is a more efficient means of influencing people than rational reasoning. There is also a tendency to rely less on scholarly views of an individual author than upon "teamwork", i.e. statutory construction proposed by legislation committees, various organisations and governmental bodies etc. This may be due to the fact that various teams have greater working resources at their command than has the individual scholar. But it may also be due to the fact that there is less confidence than there once was in the ability of legal researchers to

find reasonable answers to hard legal questions. This
would explain the tendency to rather rely on the economic
and political power concentrated in the state and in the
organisations.

Confidence in legal writing may have decreased as a result of -
often mistaken - criticism it received from the Uppsala School, cf.
section 5.5 supra. Jacob W. F. Sundberg called this phenomenon "the
suicide of legal research" (cf. Sundberg 1978, 266.). Many Swedish
scholars, inter alia Knut Rodhe, attempted at studying the law in a
value-free manner (cf., e.g., his brief but influential remarks in
1944, 4 and 1971, 179), thus merely developing alternative solutions
of legal problems; the final choice between these was left for
"unscientifically" thinking legal politicians. (The distinction
between value-free legal science and evaluative legal politics was,
by the way, quite popular in the first half of the present century.
Inter alia, Leon Petrazycki (e.g., 1892 passim), Hans Kelsen (cf.
section 5.3.1 supra) and Alf Ross (cf. section 5.5.4 supra) argued
for this idea.) One can, nevertheless, doubt whether such a
borderline can be precise. To be sure, both Rodhe's main works,
Obligationsrätt (1956) and Sakrätt (1985) exert a significant
influence; the same was true about works in judicial procedure by
Karl Olivecrona, the greatest Swedish disciple of Axel Hägerström.
It is, however, not certain whether these works really fulfil the
demand of value-freedom. Moreover, another outstanding disciple of
Hägerström, Per Olof Ekelöf, has openly advocated a certain
teleological method of statutory construction; the method is
normative, by no means value-free, cf. section 7.5 infra. Anyway,
the high level of the Uppsala school together with its anti-juristic
edge caused a certain shift of emphasis in works of some legal
scholars who either preferred legal sociology to legal dogmatics or
exercised the latter in a casuistic, overcautious manner. But of
course, Swedish legal dogmatics also produced some great works by,
inter alia, Ekelöf, Rodhe, Jan Hellner and Folke Schmidt.

At the same time, the speed of legislative change in
Sweden is high indeed, and this makes the task of the
doctrine excessively difficult.
    2. Yet, the hypothesis is plausible that the role of
doctrine will increase once again and thus satisfy the
growing demand of ordinary people for rationality. Some
hopeful signs are already here: Our system of the sources
of the law is so extensive that the doctrine can always
find interesting research topics, given time. Moreover,
the fact that other institutions fail to make the law
sufficiently fixed and rational makes the doctrine
particularly important and encourages scholars to think
creatively. The increasing size of justification of
judicial decisions creates a need of judges to gain

access to an extensive list of reasons they can employ.
The recently increasing honesty of our political debate
makes it probable that the politicians, too, will more
frequently look for rational reasons and perhaps find
some of them in the legal literature. The new interest of
legal philosophy in problems of rational justification
may help the doctrine to increase its professional level.

6.8. FOREIGN LAW

Foreign law may, of course, give some inspiration for
Swedish legal thinking. A conceptual distinction made in
a foreign statute, a question asked in a foreign case
etc. may be interesting for a Swedish lawyer who, e.g.,
can ask himself whether to pay attention to them when
commenting upon the domestic law. In this manner, foreign
law may be also valuable in legal education, thus
providing examples of interesting cases etc.

Passing from the question of inspiration (in other
words, the so-called context of discovery) to the
question of justification, one may at first make the
obvious remark that the substantive reasons proffered in
foreign decisions, doctrine etc. are applicable also in
Sweden. This is obvious, as regards empirical reasons,
e.g., concerning the nature of causation. Causality in
Sweden cannot differ from causality in other countries.
Although the matter of substantive practical reasons is
more complex, one certainly may find moral reasoning
performed by a foreign court right, just, highly
plausible etc. Ultimately, this is, as always, a matter
of weighing and balancing, guided by various criteria and
principles of coherence and discursive rationality.

One may, however, regard foreign law also as a kind of
authority reason. As all authority reasons, foreign law
thus regarded is apt to increase fixity of the domestic
law.

First of all, foreign law may gain authority in
consequence of special circumstances, such as the
following.

1. Some domestic norms of the so-called international
private law, international criminal law etc. authorise an
application of foreign norms in cases which in various
manners have relationship to foreign countries.

2. Domestic norms may also be based on international
law. As regards interpretation of rules based on

international conventions, much importance is attached to foreign law which may have influenced the convention.

NJA 1983 p. 3 concerns the application of a Swedish statute on oil pollution, based on an international convention of 1969. The Court found that the rule under consideration had been introduced at the proposal of the British delegation to the conference at which the convention was adopted. Consequently, the Court interpreted the convention in accordance with the English interpretation rules, especially the principle "ejusdem generis". The Court thus surveyed English cases starting with Sandiman v. Breach (1827)- cf. Hellner 1988, 54.

3. International legislative cooperation can lead to uniform legislation. The same statutory rules are then valid in several countries. Such uniform statutory rules may be construed uniformly in these countries. In Sweden this kind of situation arises in particular in connection with Nordic cooperation (cf. Korte 1984, 700 ff.).

On a large scale, a similar development takes place in EEC countries (cf. Sec. 100-102 of the Treaty of Rome).

4. Harmonisation can take place even if legislation is not uniform. At the beginning of 1970th, particularly in Sweden, some influential politicians opposed the uniform legislation, since it slowed down their attempts to perform radical reforms. In 1974, Nordic Council issued a recommendation, according to which, even if uniform legislation is not possible in some branches of the law, efforts should be made to adapt statutes in the Nordic countries to one another. Ministers of justice of the Nordic countries established a net of relationships which promotes harmonisation of the law (cf. Korte 1984, 712 ff.). It is not my intention to comment upon the obvious political aspects of this development. From a philosophical point of view, the most important is the eternal tension between the value of uniformity and the value of flexible adjustment of the law to particular situations.

Harmonisation measures may lead to attempts to seek a mutual adjustment of the statutory interpretation in the countries concerned. The interpretation of uniform Scandinavian laws thus tends to be quite similar in particular countries (cf. Eckhoff 1987, 256). A common

Scandinavian case law, however, did not evolve, except the maritime law (cf. Sundberg 1978, 188).

Reception constitutes an extreme case of authority of foreign law. Foreign statutes can be adopted as valid law in another country. Thus late Roman statutes and other Roman sources of the law exerted great influence in many European states. It is sufficient to recall how the codification performed by the Emperor Justinianus in the 6th century affected the work of the glossators and postglossators in the 12th, 13th and 14th centuries as well as the work of the German pandectists as recently as in the 19th century. The Roman law have been thus adopted in Germany, Austria and the Netherlands, among other countries. Later, German and Swiss statutes have been adopted in, e.g., Japan, China and Turkey. English Common Law has been adopted on a large scale in the United States, Canada, Australia and even partly in India, East Africa etc.; French civil law has been adopted in a number of countries, inter alia in part of Poland, etc. It is clear that an interpretation of these statutes in the country of origin may influence their interpretation in the countries which have adopted the statutes.

I will, however, omit such special problems and concentrate attention upon the role of foreign law in interpretation of "average" domestic law. The existence of harmonisation of statutory rules etc. is not necessary for foreign statutes and their interpretation to gain some influence as authority reasons. For example, a foreign decision may deserve attention not only because it has been well justified but also because it has been made by a respected court. In particular, statutory construction chosen in a foreign context may be proffered as a kind of support for a similar construction of a corresponding domestic statute.

Thus French and German civil codes and their interpretation affected a number of European countries which did not adopt these statutes as valid law. In Sweden, both the making and the interpreting of statutes have been influenced with varying intensity by foreign statutes and foreign legal writing, at least from the 17th century to our own days. It is sufficient to refer to great Swedish jurists from the 17th and 18th centuries (Loccenius, Rålamb, and others), as a result of whose writing foreign law come to influence lawmaking and judicial practice in Sweden. Richert's celebrated legislative proposals of 1826 and 1832 (cf. section 6.9 infra), as well as a large proportion of subsequent Swedish legislation, are also patterned in part on foreign - chiefly French and later German and Anglo-Saxon originals.

When considering foreign law as an authority reason in
the domestic legal context, one must, however, pay
attention to the difference between legal research and
legal practice. For a legal researcher, it is quite
natural to seek support in foreign law. A judge, on the
other hand, must be more aware of the difference between
the domestic law he has a duty to apply and foreign law.
Moreover, a judge has much less time to perform a
profound study of foreign law (cf. Hellner 1988, 89).

Differences between various parts of the legal order
are also relevant. For example, the role of foreign law
is continually growing as regards some branches of the
law, particularly sensible to international cooperation,
such as maritime law etc.

One must also pay attention to differences between
various legal orders. In Sweden, it is most plausible to
recognise authority of some Scandinavian statutes and
decisions. These are, of course, not binding in Sweden,
but one may attach some weight to the fact that a
respected Danish, Finish, Islandic or Norwegian court
made a certain decision.

The case NJA 1966 p. 210 concerned the right to damages of the owner
of a factory when a cable bringing electric current to the factory
was cut off. The majority of the Supreme Court pronounced a
principle which was word by word identical with a decision by the
Norwegian Supreme Court (cf. Hellner 1988, 90).

As regards, e.g., German cases, the problem is a little
more difficult, due to some differences between legal
systems in question. The Common Law of England, United
States etc. is even less applicable in this context,
since the conceptual apparatus of it is vastly different
from the one known to the Swedish lawyers. Without
advanced studies in comparative law, it is thus not easy
to grant these legal systems any authority in legal
reasoning performed on the basis of the Swedish law.

Yet, there are some exceptions. Jan Hellner thus gave the following
example. The case NJA 1987 p. 692 concerns the liability of an
appraiser who had negligently valued real property at a much higher
price than it was worth. The Supreme Court was probably influenced
by the English decision in the Hedley Byrne case (1964) A. C. 465,
discussed in a book which appeared shortly before the Swedish
decision was made.

6.9. DRAFT STATUTES AND FORMERLY VALID LAW

In legal reasoning one may pay attention to draft statutes. Even draft legislation which never became valid law is sometimes of considerable importance. In Sweden, Richert´s proposals of 1826 for a general civil code and of 1832 for a general criminal code have for generations exerted influence on Swedish judicial practice and legislation (Hafström 1969, 207 ff.).

The more technical points in the proposals influenced statutory interpretation almost from the beginning, whereas changes involving matters of principle naturally had to wait for new legislation, which in some cases did not come until more than a hundred years later. The idea expressed in the proposal for a civil code that even proceedings before the superior courts and the Supreme Court should be public and in part also oral was first put into effect in the Act of May 29, 1936, on the amendment of certain provisions in the Code of Judicial Procedure (Hafström 1969, 221.).

The following facts explain this role of draft statutes.

1) One may, of course, pay attention to the substantive reasons supporting draft statutes. As all such reasons, they are valuable if they make the reasoning more coherent.

2) A draft statute may also possess some authority based on such circumstances as high reputation of its authors etc.

3) Any draft statute expected to become valid law has an immediate authority derived from this expectation.

4) If clearer or more detailed, a draft statute may increase fixity of the law; one thus receives in advance clear rules to follow.

5) The like should be treated alike. It can be unjust to treat similar cases differently merely because one occurred immediately before and another immediately after a statutory change.

One faces here an objection that such a demand of like treatment would preclude any change of practice. However, the point is that a slow piecemeal change of practice is less unjust than a rapid legislative change, from one day to another. But of course, one must weigh and balance this point against others, supporting the different treatment of cases occurring before and after the legislative change.

Even a repealed statute can have an impact on legal reasoning, e.g., on the interpretation of its modern counterpart. In exceptional cases, even a foreign and repealed statute exerts such influence. The best example is to be found in the late Roman codification which was carried out by the Emperor Justinianus in the 6th century and which indirectly exercised immense influence in Europe long after the breakup of the Roman empire; cf. section 6.8 supra.

The following example elucidates the use of a repealed domestic statute. In Ch. 10 Sec. 26 of the old Code of Judicial Procedure a principle was expressed for distinguishing between a judicial and an administrative process: Administrative authorities thus had exclusive competence to decide cases concerning economics of the state, public offices etc. The principle implied that no appeal was possible in such cases to a general court, though, in some of them, one could appeal to an administrative court. The old Code of Judicial Procedure, including this provision, has been repealed, but in the travaux préparatoires of the promulgation act of the new Code, Sec. 5, it is stated that the principle must not be disturbed. The repealed provision of Ch. 10 Sec. 26 of the repealed Code of Judicial Procedure has therefore been regarded as a valid reason, supporting, e.g., conclusions concerning construction of statutes (cf. Westerberg 1973, 156 ff.).

As an another example, one may mention the prolonged use of the repealed provision stipulating invalidity of a reservation making the buyer's right to the goods dependent on his fulfilling another obligation, cf. section 6.6.7 supra.

This use of repealed statutes is often based on authority of other sources of the law, in the example quoted above the travaux préparatoires.

Justification of the use of repealed statutes is partly similar to that of the use of drafts. One may pay attention to the substantive reasons supporting them. If it was clearer or more detailed, a draft statute may increase fixity of the law; one thus follows the old rule if the new one is unclear. And again, it can be unjust to treat similar cases differently merely because one occurred immediately before and another immediately after a statutory change.

A repealed domestic statute can, however, also support a conclusion e contrario. The following example is theoretically interesting, albeit it lost its practical relevance, due to a further legislative change. "The

Business Names Act contains... in contrast to the (previously valid) Trade Marks Act of 1884 no provision which states what importance the registration may have for the creation of the right, and from this it may be concluded that the registration in this case lacks constitutive significance" (Ljungman 1971, 70).

The central problem in this connection concerns, of course, the choice between analogy and argumentum e contrario. I shall return to this problem.

A question may occur whether the use of repealed statutes creates a logical contradiction. To be sure, the act of derogation implies a norm stipulating that the repealed statute is invalid and thus not to be used. But a closer analysis shows that derogation merely means that the statute is no longer to be regarded as a must-source of the law. It says nothing about its position as a may-source.

CHAPTER 7
THE METHODS OF LEGAL REASONING

7.1. REASONING NORMS

7.1.1. Construction of Statutes in Hard Cases

In section 1.2.1 supra, I made the preliminary distinction between easy and hard cases. In easy cases, the decision follows from a set of premises solely consisting of a legal rule, a description of the facts of the case, and perhaps also some other premises that are <u>easy to prove</u>.

These "other premises" are either certain, or presupposed within a practice belonging to the considered culture, or easy to prove in the sense developed in section 3.3.5 supra.

In hard cases, the decision does not follow from a legal rule and a description of the facts of the case (either alone or together with easily proved premises). However, the decision follows from an expanded set of premises, containing a value statement, a norm or another statement the decision-maker assumes but cannot easily prove.

The decision-maker thus may endorse some value judgments, <u>inter alia</u> in order to perform a subsumption; to interpret a statute or another source of the law; to establish and fill up gaps in the law; to establish facts of the case; to perform legal qualification; to choose a legal consequence or to answer the question whether a statute is obsolete.
  The step from the legal rule and the description of the hard case to the decision is a jump, if and only if at least one of the premises which one must add to make the step logically correct is neither certain, nor presupposed, nor proved, cf. section 3.2 supra. If all these premises are certain, presupposed or proved, there is no jump, but the case still is hard, if a premise is <u>difficult</u> to prove.
  In the contextually sufficient legal justification, (cf. section 1.5.3 supra), in other words, within the legal paradigm (cf. section 3.3.3 supra), one may either explicitly spell out all these additional premises of the hard case or omit some of them. But since the case is hard, a lawyer would consider it natural, not strange, to mention them. On the other hand if, e.g., a philosopher of law

alone would think it natural to mention such premises, then they are
juristicaly trivial, perhaps presupposed within the legal paradigm,
perhaps easily provable within it. The case is then easy, not hard.

I shall now discuss construction of statutes in hard
cases. If a case is hard as a result of a constructional
problem, the construction of the statute is creative, not
merely clarificatory.

Clarificatory construction (interpretatio secundum
legem) establishes the meaning of the statutory provision
in the light of its wording. It does not improve or
change the wording. Where no other basis of clarification
exists, it ends with pinpointing the obscurity of the
statute.

Creative construction of statutes is either
supplementary or corrective.

Supplementary construction (interpretatio praeter
legem) involves a choice between possible interpretations
of a vague or ambiguous statutory provision but it does
not conflict with the wording of the statute.

When a construction of a statute so conflicts, it is
not supplementary but corrective (contra legem).

Section 4 of the old Swedish Constitution (Regeringsformen),
derogated as late as 1969, thus stipulated that "the King has the
right to govern the realm alone". The actually applied norm was,
instead, "The Government, responsible to the Parliament, has the
executive power"; cf. section 1.5.3 supra.

Corrective interpretation may result in a so-called
reduction, if the statutory provision receives a new,
more restricted sense, or even elimination, that is, a
total withdrawal of the norm in question from the legal
order. It may also result in creation of a more general
new norm. A special case occurs when legal norms collide
with each other, e.g., statutory provisions are logically
incompatible. One needs then a solution of the collision,
either by reinterpreting these norms, or by arranging a
priority order between them.

The Swedish Supreme Court normally construes statutes with caution
and depends heavily on the legislative material. Some remarkable
cases of creative interpretation, however, have occurred, as the
following examples show (criticised by Hult, 1952, 579 ff.).

NJA 1935 p. 157 and 1938 p. 35. The Court acknowledged an oral contract for the purchase of real estate to have a certain effect notwithstanding that the statute requires a written form if such a purchase is to be valid. Cf. the provision of Ch.1 Sec. 2 of the Real Property Code then in force.

NJA 1949 p. 82. In accordance with Ch. 3 Sec. 2 of the Act concerning international aspects of marriage, then in force, aliens might only obtain a divorce or separation in Sweden were a reason for this step to be found under both the national law of the spouses and Swedish law. In this case, however, the Court adjudicated a divorce case between two Baltic refugees exclusively in accordance with Swedish, not Soviet, law.

NJA 1949 p. 195. A person was injured by an electric vehicle undergoing repair inadvertently set in motion by a mechanic. The court of appeal declared that this situation comes under the statute concerning injuries caused by "drivers" and which have "arisen in consequence of traffic" with a vehicle. (Cf. NJA 1962 p. 172).

NJA 1951 p. 265. The Court applied the statutory rule concerning the father's contribution to the mother's maintenance in connection with the birth of an illegitimate child to a man who had impregnated the woman, even though the pregnancy had been terminated.

In the case NJA 1966 p. 210, the Supreme Court deviated from general tort principles concerning damage to a third party because the development of the contents of law of torts "in a number of central respects - such as negligence, cause, remoteness of damage, unlawfulness, and what is meant by damage..., must to a large extent fall to the courts."

Construction of statutes in hard cases is supported by various types of premises. Some of these imply that one uses a certain interpretative reason, such as analogy, argumentum e contrario or suchlike. Others reveal an application of more comprehensive procedures, or methods of statutory construction. For instance, one usually distinguishes between linguistic (often called grammatical), logical, historical, systematic (cf. Savigny 1840 § 33), comparative, and teleological construction of statutes. Different methods imply that one pays attention to different contexts. When performing a systematic construction of a statutory provision, one thus takes into account its connections with such interpretatory data as other statutory norms, the structure of the statute, theories elaborated by legal dogmatics, etc. A historical construction supports itself on opinions and other facts that influenced the legislation. When performing a comparative construction of a domestic statute, one pays attention to foreign law. A teleological construction pays attention to data elucidating the purpose of the statute; etc.

7.1.2. Reasoning Norms

Some norms regulate legal reasoning, in particular they indicate how one should construe statutes. These reasoning norms have character, function, mode of existence and degree of justifiability resembling the source norms, cf. section 6.3.1 supra. Character. The reasoning norms have a prima-facie character: in a concrete situation, one may disregard each reasoning norm, if strong reasons justify it. Existence. The lawyers actually perform reasonings in the way suggesting that they - consciously or not - follow these norms. When reading, inter alia, writings in legal dogmatics, and perhaps participating in the legal practice, one may elaborate a relatively coherent hypothesis about their content. The hypothesis must be tested and may be accepted until studies of legal reasoning show that the authorities, judges and other lawyers do not follow these norms. The reasoning norms are also related to the concept of legal reasoning. It would be strange to simultaneously refute a significant part of the set of such norms and still try to perform a legal reasoning; cf. section 3.3.3 supra. Moreover, if one thus were unable to perform legal reasoning, our form of life would change, cf. section 4.4.6. Justifiability. One may use some reasoning norms as a basis for justification of other reasoning norms. Ultimately, one aims, and ought to aim, at coherence of the system of reasoning norms. Such coherence is always a result of an act of weighing, aimed at an optimal balance of numerous reasoning norms and numerous criteria of coherence. Function. One uses these norms often as presupposed premises of legal reasoning. They help to convert some argumentative jumps into logically correct inferences.

Consider again the following case, constituting a simplified version of the Swedish decision NJA 1950 p. 650; cf. section 1.2.2 supra. A person injured by a car lost his working capacity and, in consequence of it, a part of his income. A little later, it was discovered that he had suffered from a gastric ulcer that would have made him incapable to work, even if he had not been injured. The Supreme Court did not hold the driver liable for the part of the loss for which the ulcer alone had been a sufficient cause. The reason for this decision was that the car accident had not been a necessary cause of the loss. The decision can be seen as a choice between the following two analogies (cf. Hellner 1972b, 166).

   Analogy No. 1. Assume that we have two competing sufficient causes of a loss of working capacity, a traffic accident and a normal circumstance such as old age. Compensation would comprise only the difference between the victim's actual income and what he would have earned, if he had been a man of the same age etc. not injured in any accident. Consequently, in the case under consideration, only a similar difference should be compensated: between the actual income and a hypothetical income of an _ill_ employee, not injured in any accident.

Analogy No. 2. Assume instead that we have to deal with a different pair of competing sufficient causes, a traffic accident and another person's intentional or negligent action, such as poisoning the victim. The person responsible for the accident would then have to pay full compensation, regardless responsibility of the other tortfeasor. Consequently, in the case under consideration, full compensation is justified, despite the illness of the victim.

The Supreme Court chose Analogy No. 1. Adding some premises, one can convert the reasoning of the Court to the following, logically correct, inference.

(1) A non-controversial legal norm, cf. now Ch. 2 Sec.1 of the Tortious Liability Act, Sec. 18 of the Car Traffic Liability Act etc.

A person who caused damage in consequence of traffic with an engine-driven vehicle should compensate the damage if, and only if there exists a legal ground therefor.

(2) A non-controversial premise: the customary adequacy-rule

A legal ground for the conclusion that the tortfeasor should compensate the damage exists, if the causal connection between his action and the damage was adequate.

(3) A non-controversial premise: a description of facts

B, injured by a car driven by A, lost his working capacity and, in consequence of it lost a part of his income. A little later, it was discovered that he had suffered from a gastric ulcer that would have made him incapable to work, even if he had not been injured.

(4) An added and reasonable premise: a description of law in force

No other legal ground exists for the conclusion that A should compensate B's loss in consequence of working incapacity.

(5) An additional premise implied by the decision of the Court: a general and established norm of civil law

If someone suffers a loss as a consequence of another person's action but would have suffered the same loss as a result of such a normal circumstance as

(6) An additional premise:
implied by the decision
of the Court: an estimate
of relevance of an
analogy

his reaching the retirement age,
the causal connection between
this action and the loss is not
adequate.

A relevant resemblance exists
between the actual case (in
which B, injured by a car driven
by A, lost a part of his income
but would have suffered the same
loss as a result of a gastric
ulcer) and the situation in
which one suffers a loss as a
consequence of another person's
action but would have suffered
the same loss as a result of
such a normal circumstance as
his reaching the retirement age.

(7) An additional premise:
a reasoning norm

An established norm of civil law
should be applied by analogy to
cases relevantly resembling
those it explicitly covers.

Conclusion

A should not compensate B's loss
in consequence of working
incapacity.

This inference is correct because one has added, inter alia, premise
7, that is, a reasoning norm.

Reasoning norms thus support legal conclusions. A legal
conclusion follows from a set consisting of a reasoning
norm together with some other reasonable premises. This
enables one to test a legal reasoning another person
performs. More precisely, one can reconstruct the reasons
supporting the conclusion he presents. Moreover, this
makes it possible for one to weigh and balance these
reasons against some other ones, deserving attention. In
particular, one may in a clear manner adapt the construed
statute to other sources of the law and to the
requirements of morality. The reasoning norms thus
increase rationality of legal conclusions. In brief, the
reasoning norms make the practice of legal reasoning more
stable and the interpreted legal norms more fixed.

But such norms are vague. More precisely, they are
value-open; their sphere of application depends on value
judgments endorsed by the interpreter. In consequence,

one constantly changes emphasis given to different
reasoning norms. For that reason, one often mixes
together many methods of statutory construction. This is
the only way to assure reasonableness of one´s practice
of statutory construction in hard cases. The
interpretatory practice based on a single method leads
often to unreasonable results.

Of course, reasoning norms are partly the same partly
different in different legal orders, due to diversity of
reasoning tradition, legislative technique, accessibility
of statutes, precedents and legislative materials, etc.
Moreover, reasoning norms vary from one part of the legal
system to another. In the Swedish criminal law, the
legality principle <u>nullum crimen, nulla poena sine lege</u>
thus restraints an application of statutes by analogy.
The taxation law is also interpreted fairly literally,
although the relatively recently introduced general
clause (Sec. 3 of the Tax Evasion Act) makes the picture
somewhat complicated. The Swedish civil law, on the other
hand, is quite open for extensive interpretation and the
use of analogy. This reflects a more general problem,
namely, that the statute does not play the central role
in all cases in civil law; cf. the above-mentioned
problem of remoteness of damage in torts. Some statutory
provisions are also very vague; cf. the general clause of
Sec. 36 of the Contract Acts, according to which a court
may ignore or modify udue contractual provisions. In
public law, one meets two phenomena, so to say acting in
the opposite directions. The interpretation tends to be
very loyal to the intentions of the authors of the
statute. On the other hand, the statutes are often so
vague, and the preparatory materials so fragmentary, that
the interpreter must relatively freely guess these
intentions. In the procedural law, the situation is much
better from this point of view: difficulties to establish
the purpose of the statute exist but are not <u>so</u> great.

In general, many reasoning norms are principles, not
rules. When they collide with each other, one needs
weighing and balancing. To be sure, the necessity to
weigh may be postponed when one successfully formulates
<u>second order reasoning norms</u>, indicating which of the
colliding reasoning norms, methods and reasons one should
apply in a given class of situations (cf. Wróblewski
1959, 143 ff. and 399 ff.). Yet, the second order norms
may also collide. At the end, weighing is inevitable.

All those circumstances make it difficult for a sociologist of law to use the reasoning norms to predict the judicial decisions. But this fact does not matter for a jurist whose task is not to predict but to recommend a reasonable decision. The recommendation is always based on value judgments, but these are much more rational if supported by extensive sets of premises, inter alia containing the legal reasoning norms.

7.2. LOGICAL, LITERAL AND SYSTEMATIC INTERPRETATION

7.2.1. Logical and Quasi-Logical Interpretation

Let me now briefly discuss logical, literal and systematic interpretation of statutes.

Some remarks on historical, teleological and comparative interpretation have already been made in section 6.6 (on legislative materials) and 6.8 (on the role of foreign law). Teleological interpretation will be discussed in detail in section 7.5 infra.

The term "logical interpretation of statutes" suggests that one draws logical conclusions from the considered statute. Among other things, one checks whether the statute is logically consistent. Consistency is the most fundamental demand or rationality (cf. sections 2.2.4, 3.2 and 4.4.1 - 2 supra) and a precondition of coherence.
  Since the statute often is vague, it can be consistent in one interpretation, inconsistent in another. If it is inconsistent, one may remove inconsistency, inter alia using collision norms. I will discuss these in section 7.6.2 infra.
  The term "logical interpretation of statutes" also covers questions of subsumption, cf. sections 1.2.1 supra. The following reasoning norm emphasises importance of subsumption:
  I1) Every judicial decision of an individual case, and every juristic recommendation of such a decision, must be logically derivable from a general norm, along with further reasonable premises.
  Such a general norm may be stated in a statute, based on a precedent or supported by another source of the law.
  This norm expresses the requirement of generality, that is, a criterion of coherence, cf. section 4.1.4 supra.

At the same time, it also promotes predictability of
judicial decision, which is a typical result of the fact
that decisions are made on the basis of general norms.
    Cf. Alexy´s rationality rules (J.2.2.), (J.6.), (J.8.),
(J.10.) and (J.18.); section 4.3.4 supra.
    One may also mention some quasi-logical maxims. Their
vagueness makes it possible for one to interpret them as
norms of customary law, moral norms or logical
propositions. Let me mention three of them.
    I2) No one has a duty to do what is impossible.

This maxim has been cited in for example, the following connection.
Sec. 21 para. 1 of the Sale of Goods Act reads: Where goods have not
been delivered at the proper time, and this is not due to the buyer
or an event for which he bears the risk, it is free to him to decide
whether he will demand the delivery of the goods or cancel the
purchase." Jan Hellner made the following comment: "The Sale of
Goods Act does not make any exception to the buyer's right to demand
fulfilment of the contract even for the case where the purchase
related to certain specific goods and these were already destroyed
at the time of the contract or were destroyed later. If this is
established, however, the buyer cannot obtain a judicial decision
for the fulfilment of the purchase; this is usually justified by
reference to the maxim 'impossibilium nulla est obligatio' (no one
has a duty to do what is impossible)" - Hellner 1967, 82.

If one interprets the word "duty" as "a duty explicitly
imposed by a statute", the maxim does not express any
logical necessity. A statute can exist, demanding of one
to do the impossible. But if the word "duty" means
"morally justifiable duty", one can argue that a "duty"
to do the impossible cannot be a (moral) duty at all; in
the same manner as a "bachelor" cannot be "married".
    I3) Nobody can transfer more rights than he himself
has.
    Interpreted most naturally, this maxim is a norm, not a
logical proposition.

Let me consider the following situation: A person, A, is the owner
of a real-estate property which is encumbered by the fact that the
right of use has been given over to B. A sells the property to C and
manages to do this in such a way that B loses the right of use
without receiving any compensation. In this way C has got more than
A had, namely a right of ownership not encumbered by a right of use.
There is no logical impossibility in this situation. Only the clear
legal norm seeks to prevent it (cf. Ch. 7 sec. 11-15 of the Real
Property Code).

One may also regard the maxim I3 as a <u>moral</u> norm, justifiable by B´s claim to legal certainty.

Yet, interpreted in a particular manner, perhaps lacking practical importance, the maxim expresses a kind of logical necessity. The word "to transfer" presupposes that nobody can transfer what he does not possesses. Analogously, nobody can pour a quart of water from a jug which only contains a pint.

I4) A statute cannot have effect in the past.

Not even this maxim, interpreted in the most natural way, expresses any logical necessity. If a statute has been enacted today it can be used tomorrow in order to judge actions which were concluded yesterday. In this sense, the statute has effect in the past. There is no logical inconsistency in such a retroactive norm. A retroactive norm is, however, immoral, since it can cause a person unpredictable loss. Only when interpreted in a superficial manner, unduly influenced by the literal sense of the words "to have effect in the past", the maxim expresses logical necessity, since not even a Swedish statute can literally change the past.

Regarded as norms, the discussed maxims provide a moral support for statutory interpretation which thus helps the law to avoid injustice connected with retroactive norms, norms demanding the impossible etc. To regard the maxims as analytical propositions is less plausible but one can argue that the very possibility of it indicates that it would be unreasonable to refute them.

7.2.2. Literal Interpretation

Literal interpretation is a clarificatory description of the content of the statute in accordance with the ordinary, general or legal, linguistic usage. Literal interpretation is not corrective, not even supplementary. It merely establishes the meaning of the statutory provision in the light of its wording. The chief contribution of literal interpretation is to assure fixity of the law. One can discover the linguistic content of a statutory text by studying the following data:

- legal definitions and other explanations contained in the text itself, regarding the meaning of words and expressions which occur in the text;
- dictionaries, results of linguistic research etc.;

- the ways in which words and expressions occurring in
the text have been used in other connections, i.e. in
other legal sources, in technical legal usage, in
everyday speech, etc.;
- stylistic qualities and peculiarities in the
statutory text or even in other texts which have been
written by people who have exerted great influence on the
legislative work.

Literal interpretation thus does not improve or change
the literal content of the statute. However, one often
supplements it with a recourse to some reasoning norms,
justifiable by recourse to the idea that the statute
should be as perfect means of affecting people as
possible. These norms thus express the so-called
goal-rationality which is a principle of rational
practical discourse (cf. section 4.3.3 supra). Inter
alia, the following norms belong to this category:

I5) One must not interpret the same words or
expressions occurring in different parts of the same
statute in different ways unless strong reasons for such
an interpretation exist (cf. Wróblewski 1959, 247 ff.).

Cf. Alexy´s rationality rule 1.4. (in section 4.3.2
supra).

If the statute is a perfect means of affecting people,
it does not contain words whose interpretation shifts
from one part of it to another. Moreover, such an
interpretation would be ceteris-paribus incompatible with
generality (which is a criterion of coherence, cf.
section 4.1.4 supra).

This idea of uniform interpretation was expressed, e.g., in the
pronouncement of the Council on Legislation on the concept "business
activities" in the Liability for Damages Act (cf. Govt. Bill 1972:5,
p. 635).

Sometimes, however, strong reasons justify a shifting
interpretation. The penal-law term "resistance", e.g.,
was not construed uniformly even in the same statute.

But the lawmaker found the shifting interpretation to be
unsatisfactory. This fact affected the new formulation of Ch. 8 sec.
5 of the Swedish Criminal Code.

In any case, it is doubtful whether a more radical
reasoning norm is justifiable, demanding that one must

not interpret differently the same words or expressions occurring in <u>different</u> statutes. Such a requirement is surely <u>not</u> justifiable if the statutes belong to different parts of the legal system. In this case, generality must yield to other criteria of coherence, and perhaps to other reasons. For example, the Swedish word "tomt" ("plot of land") has one meaning in real-estate law and another in penal law. Even purely descriptive words without any conventional or technical content may be interpreted in penal law in another way than i private law; the Swedish word "samlag" ("sexual intercourse") is construed in penal law in a way which differs from the construction in the Code on Parents and Children.

I6) If different words or expressions are used in the same statute, one should assume that they relate to different situations, unless strong reasons for assuming the opposite exist (cf. Wróblewski 1959, 247 ff. n. 119).

If the statute is a perfect means of affecting people, it is not formulated in a misleading manner.

In fact, however, some statutes are <u>not</u> perfect. In secs. 6 and 45 of the Insurance Contracts Act we find the words "the occurrence of the insurance case or the extent of damage", whereas in a similar context in sec. 121 of the same statute we find the words "the occurrence or extent of the insurance case". There are strong reasons for assuming that this divergence is not relevant.

I7) One must not interpret a statutory provision in such a way that some parts of the provision prove to be unnecessary (cf. Wróblewski 1959, 248).

If the statute is a means perfectly fitting the goal of affecting people, it contains only words actually contributing to fulfilment of this goal.

I8) One must not interpret words and expressions occurring in the statute in conflict with ordinary linguistic usage unless strong reasons for such an interpretation exist.

I9) If, however, it has previously been established that a word or an expression has a technical meaning incompatible with everyday language, one should interpret that word or expression as having such a special meaning, without reference to everyday language (cf. Wróblewski 1959, 245-6).

If the statute is a perfect means of affecting people, it must be intelligible. One thus must pay attention to the everyday language. But strong reasons may exist,

justifying introduction of technical terms, thus making
the language more precise.

7.2.3. Systematic Interpretation

Systematic interpretation of statutes includes <u>inter alia</u>
the following arguments:

1) the use of a statutory provision for interpreting
another such provision;

2) interpretation influenced by the systematic of the
statute;

3) interpretation influenced by another type of
conceptual analysis;

4) interpretation influenced by other legal-dogmatic
theories.

I10) When interpreting a statutory provision one must
pay attention to other provisions which

a) are necessary in order to make the answer to the
considered legal question more complete;

b) deal with cases relevantly resembling those the
interpreted provision regulates;

c) in any other way contribute to understanding of the
interpreted provision.

The following examples elucidate this reasoning norm:

a) In order to be able to apply a penal provision one
must also pay regard to other statutory norms which
answer the question how criminal responsibility is
affected by, e.g., mental illness or other grounds for
diminished responsibility.

b) Frequently an old statute is interpreted in a way
adapted to new enactments which regulate similar
questions. In this manner the remaining rules in the
Commercial Code of 1734 can by means of interpretation be
adapted to Contracts Act, Sale of Goods Act, end so on.

c) Various expressions in statutes often form a kind of
hierarchy. Cf., e.g., the following expressions from the
Sale of Goods Act: "immediately" (secs. 27, 32, 52), "as
soon as it can be done" (sec.6), "without unreasonable
delay" (secs. 26, 27, 31, 32, 40, 52, 60), and "within a
reasonable time" (secs. 26 and 31). Owing to the fact
that these expressions are construed in connection with
one another, we see, e.g., that the expression "within a
reasonable time" refers to a longer period than "without
unreasonable delay" (cf. Hellner 1969, 136-7).

The so-called "corresponding application of law" is another example. A certain statutory provision, e.g. Ch. 8 sec. 13 of the Criminal Code, is applicable to certain cases (e.g. theft, larceny etc.). Another statutory provision, e.g. Ch. 9 sec. 12 of the Criminal Code, states, however, that the first provision is also to be applied to other cases (e.g. deception, blackmail, etc.). In this way the first provision, in addition to its ordinary area of application, acquires another, secondary area. In some cases, such an extension requires a modification. Cf., e.g., Sec. 1 para 2. of the Sale of Goods Act which reads as follows: "The provisions of this act concerning purchase shall where applicable also regulate barter." The "inapplicable" parts of this statute contain, for example, rules on the fixing of the purchase price (secs. 5-8).

When paying attention to the relation of the considered provision to other ones, the interpreter obviously utilises the latter as premises. Already this fact makes the interpretation more coherent than it would be had one merely considered one provision; cf. section 4.1.3 supra as regards the number of premises as a criterion of coherence. Moreover, such an interpretation avoids violation of the other provisions. As always, obedience to rules promotes predictability of decisions. Finally, the interpretation assures that coherent reasons which probably support the other provisions are not ignored.

Ill) When interpreting a statutory provision one may pay attention to
a) the title of the statute and
b) the membership of the interpreted provision in a certain part of the legal system, a certain statute and a particular part of that statute.

Ch. 3 sec. 9 of the Criminal Code reads as follows: "If anyone from gross carelessness exposes another person to mortal danger or danger of severe bodily injury or serious illness, he shall be sentenced for causing danger to another person to a fine or to imprisonment for not more than two years." In connection with this provision there arose the question whether for the arising of responsibility it must be required that a concrete, specified person or group of persons was exposed to danger. The question could be supposed to have been answered in the affirmative since in the Criminal Code the offence has been placed among offences against individuals. A number of authors have, however, rejected this interpretation, proffering both substantial reasons and analogies with other provisions.

This kind of interpretation assumes that the established
classification and distribution of legal norms into
different subsets reflects essential differences between
them. This is perhaps analogous to the criterion of
coherence requiring a distribution of the totality of
human knowledge into different fields, each characterised
by some premises with a special status; cf. sections
2.7.5, 3.2.4 and 4.1.3 supra.

I12) When interpreting a statutory provision one may
pay attention to conceptual analysis, inter alia to
logical relations between concepts and to their role in
theories, normative systems and the life in general.

Cf., e.g., section 4.4.6 supra on the role of concepts, and the
example given in section of 3.1.3 supra, concerning analysis of the
concept of adequate causation in torts. See also the remarks made
above about a hierarchy of concepts in the Sale of Goods Act and,
finally the complex case in torts, NJA 1976 p. 458. To be sure, in
the latter case the majority of the Supreme Court included distinct
circumstances, relevant for liability, into an unanalysed evaluation
of negligence. But Justice Nordenson performed an extensive and
subtle analysis, making sophisticated distinctions between
negligence, adequate causation and purpose of protection.

Logical consistency is, as stated above, a precondition
of coherence. Properties of concepts affect also
coherence of theories, cf. section 4.1.4 supra.

I13) When interpreting a statutory provision one may
pay attention to theories formulated in legal dogmatics.

Since value of these theories depends on coherence,
this reasoning norm demands in effect that the
interpretation is as coherent as possible.

The following example, elaborated by Aulis Aarnio,
elucidates the role of such theories. Under a long
period, legal dogmatics utilised a theory, T1, which
regarded ownership as a resembling a substance. At a
certain moment, all the aspects of ownership could belong
to one and only one physical or juridical person. Even if
several persons were co-owners of the same thing, each
had all the aspects of ownership, albeit with regard to a
part of the thing only, identified either physically or
ideally, e.g. in percent. A sale thus resulted in a
instantaneous transfer of ownership as a totality: first
the seller and then the buyer was a full owner. The only
problem to discuss was the precise determination of the
moment of this instantaneous and total transfer. This
theory determined interpretation of all statutory

provisions of transfer of ownership, including some provisions of inheritance law (cf. Ch. 18 of the Swedish Decedents´ Estate Code). On the other hand, according to a newer Scandinavian theory of ownership, T2, to be owner of a thing is the same as to be legally protected against certain other persons. Many kinds of protection exist. It is thus possible to be owner in some respects but not in others. This fact makes it possible for the newer theory to contemplate new cases, unthinkable in the light of the old one. One can now interpret transfer of ownership as a process, extended in time, in which one person successively acquires more and more aspects of ownership. At a certain moment, a buyer or an heir can thus already be owners in one respect, while other aspects of ownership still are ascribed to the seller or the death estate. One may consider the new theory, T2, as better than the old one, T1, because its vocabulary permits more distinctions (cf. Aarnio 1984, 46 ff.) and the new distinctions which it introduces reflect distinct evaluation of cases, provided that this evaluation is supported by highly coherent reasons.

Different kinds of systematic interpretation of statutes affect each other. Construction of a statutory provision depends at the same time on interpretation of other such provisions, systematic of the statute, conceptual analysis and theories formulated in legal dogmatics. A preliminary and vague understanding of connections between various provisions and their place in the legal system together with some conceptual analysis may thus influence theories of ownership. These affect a deeper understanding of the place of the interpreted provision in the legal system and a deeper analysis of the relevant concepts. One can, e.g., argue in favour of a thesis concerning the connections between various provisions by showing that this thesis is supported by (coherent with) some theory formulated in legal dogmatics. On the other hand, one can argue in favour of the theory by showing that it is supported by the thesis concerning the connections. If there is no satisfactory coherence, one can modify each of the components. One may thus modify and mutually adapt various forms of systematic interpretation in order to achieve a balance, resembling the "reflective equilibrium". In this connection, one may also speak about the so-called hermeneutical circle (cf. section 3.2.1 supra). Cf. section 4.1.3 supra on reciprocal relationships as a criterion of coherence.

All this hangs together, interpretation of statutory provisions, systematic of the statute, conceptual analysis and theories formulated in legal dogmatics. Various juristic theses support each other. Legal reasoning - and the legal system itself - thus gains coherence and hence rationality. Besides, the systematic interpretation generates concepts enabling one to treat relevantly similar cases alike. In this way, one fulfils another criterion of coherence, that is, generality.

7.3.   REDUCTION,   RESTRICTIVE   INTERPRETATION, EXTENSIVE INTERPRETATION AND CREATION OF NEW NORMS

The area of application of a legal norm, established as a result of legal reasoning, often differs from the area established by most natural linguistic, non-juristic reading of the norm. One can thus say, what follows:

Both reduction and restrictive interpretation result in the fact that the definitive area of application of a rule, established with the use of different interpretatory methods, is narrower that the area established with the use of literal interpretation alone.

Both creation of a more general new norm (inter alia through statutory analogy) and extensive interpretation result in the fact that the definitive area of application of a rule, established with the use of different interpretatory methods, is wider that the area established with the use of literal interpretation.

To exemplify these terms, let me invent the following rule: "All chess players are qualified for membership in the club". One may then state, what follows:

1. By literal interpretation one would construe the rule to include all persons who sometimes play chess and no others.

2. By restrictive interpretation of this rule, one might, e.g., eliminate people who sometimes play chess but have no official rating, granted by the national chess association and indicating their strength as chess players. Restrictive interpretation thus restricts the area of application of the rule to its linguistically uncontroversial core, that is, to cases certainly covered by the rule. It eliminates all cases which perhaps belong perhaps do not belong to the area of application of the rule, and thus constitute a "periphery" in relation to this area. Such a restrictivity may appear somewhat

strange, since a person sometimes playing chess with his
friends would not be called a chess player. But it is
linguistically possible to perform this interpretation
and preserve the term "chess player" only for officially
recognised players.

3. A reduction, however, would be more radical and
perhaps eliminate everybody but grand masters. Reduction
thus eliminates not only the "periphery" but also a part
of the linguistically uncontroversial core of the area of
application of the rule. Such a radical restrictivity
contradicts the ordinary language. It is linguistically
unthinkable to hold that the term "chess player" means
the same as "grand master". Reasons for the reduction are
not linguistic but concern, e.g., the extremely high
ambition of the club.

Reduction eliminates a part of the core of the
application-area of the norm. It thus replaces the norm
in question with another one having a smaller area of
application. This new norm is contentually similar to and
argumentatively connected with the old one.

4. By extensive interpretation one would probably
construe the discussed rule to include all persons
knowing chess rules, regardless whether they have played
even a single chess game. Extensive interpretation thus
embraces not only the core but also all "periphery" of
the area of application of the rule. Such a generosity is
perhaps somewhat strange but it is linguistically
possible to regard all persons knowing chess rules as
chess players.

5. Finally, one may create a new norm, perhaps
admitting bridge players, as well. The area of
application of the discussed rule is thus extended beyond
its linguistically possible "periphery". It is
linguistically impossible to call bridge "chess". The
most frequent method to create a more general norm is a
conclusion by analogy, cf. section 7.4 infra.

In some cases one goes beyond the reduction and
eliminates the whole rule, cf. section 1.2.7 supra on
desuetudo. A chess club can, e.g., successively change
its character. At first, one admits bridge players, too.
Then one eliminates everybody but very good players,
regardless whether they play chess or bridge. Finally,
all the chess players leave the club which thus becomes a
high-level bridge club. Someone perhaps remembers the
rule "All chess players are qualified for membership in
the club" but nobody takes it seriously. One can then
create a new norm, but this new norm is not

argumentatively connected with the old one. Neither must it resemble the old one.

The distinctions between reduction, restrictive interpretation, literal interpretation, extensive interpretation and creation of a more general new norm are based on the result of interpretation, that is, depend on how extensive the final area of application of the rule is. It is not relevant what methods are applied to obtain the result. The following picture elucidates the distinctions:

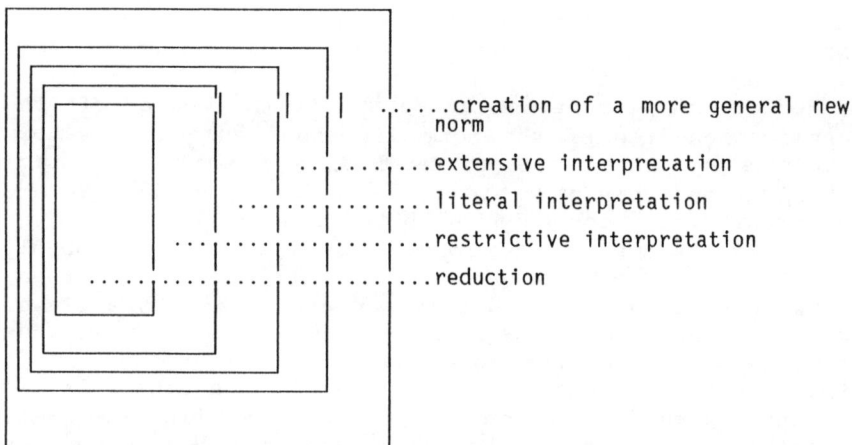

```
 _____
|  _____  |
| |  _____  | |    ......creation of a more general new
| | |  _____  | | |          norm
| | | |                            | | | |
| | | |                            | | | |    ............extensive interpretation
| | | |                            | | | |
| | | |                            | | | |    ...............literal interpretation
| | | |                            | | | |
| | | |                            | | | |    ..................restrictive interpretation
| | | |                            | | | |
| | | |                            | | | |    .....................reduction
| | | |_____| | | |
| | |_____| | |
| |_____| |
|_____|
```

One can regard literal, extensive and restrictive construction as three kinds of <u>precise interpretation</u> of the statutory provision. Reduction and creation of a more general norm are, on the other hand, kinds of <u>corrective</u> interpretation; cf. section 7.1.1 supra.

Creation of a more general new norm (<u>inter alia</u> through statutory analogy), unlike extensive interpretation, exceeds the linguistically acceptable periphery of the area of application of the norm in question. Some writers (e.g., Ross 1958, 149) reject this distinction. In judicial practice and in legal writing, however, one can find several examples of creating new norms by analogy which is generally considered to be more radical than mere extensive interpretation. Moreover, in penal law, e.g., courts may reason from analogy to a much lesser extent than by extensive interpretation. Should a court disregard the difference between them, it may unjustifiably begin to use analogy in cases where extensive interpretation is allowed (cf. Peczenik 1971, 334 ff.).

Besides, <u>all</u> the discussed distinctions are vague. Strictly speaking, one must distinguish between 1) what everybody in all situations recognises as the core of the area of application of the norm; 2) what at least some people sometimes recognise as the core and sometimes as a part of the periphery; 3) what everybody in all situations recognises as a part of the periphery; 4) what at least some people sometimes recognise as a part of the periphery and sometimes as belonging to the "outside area"; and 5) what everybody in all situations recognises as a part of the "outside area".

Reduction thus eliminates not only the "periphery" but also a part of the linguistically uncontroversial core of the area of application of the rule. Restrictive interpretation covers whole core, eliminates whole periphery and covers an indeterminate part of the area which perhaps belongs to the core perhaps to the periphery. Literal interpretation covers whole core and an indeterminate part of the periphery. Extensive interpretation embraces whole core, whole uncontroversial periphery and an indeterminate part of the area which perhaps belongs to the periphery perhaps to the outside area. Finally, a creation of a more general new norm results in an application-area which covers all this and, in addition to it, certainly extends beyond the periphery.

Of course, these distinctions are vague, too. One cannot state precisely, e.g., what certainly belongs to the periphery and what perhaps belong to the periphery perhaps to the core.

The picture may be further complicated. For instance, an interpretation may be restrictive in one extent and simultaneously extensive in another. One may even combine a reduction with a creation of a new more general norm by analogy. The rule "All chess players are qualified for membership in the club" may thus be applied to grand masters in chess and outstanding bridge players, while less successful chess players are eliminated. The elimination of the latter is a reduction, while the inclusion of the bridge masters is a creation of a more general new norm.

Whereas literal interpretation mostly promotes fixity of the law and thus predictability of legal reasoning, all the other forms of interpretation promote, first of all, coherence and discursive rationality.

The choice between the discussed forms of interpretation depends on weighing and balancing of various substantive reasons and authority reasons. Such a choice presupposes jumps and leads to a transformation of the law, cf. sections 2.7, 3.2, 5.9.5 and 7.1.2 supra. Yet, it can fulfil the rationality demands, discussed in chapters 3 and 4 supra.

7.4. CONCLUSION BY ANALOGY

7.4.1. Introductory Remarks on Statutory Analogy

By "statutory analogy" I mean that one applies a statutory rule to a case which, viewed from the ordinary linguistic angle, is included in neither the core nor the periphery of the application area of the statute in question, but resembles the cases covered by this statute in essential respects.

This definition is based both on the result of interpretation, that is, a radical extension of the area of application of the rule, and the method applied to obtain the result, namely proffering essential similarity of cases. A use of similarity argument which does <u>not</u> extend the linguistically possible area of application of a statute (<u>analogia intra legem</u>, cf., e.g., Nowacki 1966, 45 ff., Heller 1961, 87 ff.).

Consequently, the relation of statutory analogy is not reflexive, since the set of cases regulated by a norm is not analogous to itself. Neither is it transitive: a case, C_1, can be analogous to those regulated by the norm in question, another case, C_2, analogous to C_1, and yet C_2 need not be analogous to the regulated cases. Finally, the relation of analogy can be symmetrical or not: when C_1 is analogous to C_2, the latter can but need not be analogous to the former (cf. Frändberg 1973, 150-1, though the author writes about analogy of norms, not cases).

Let me give some examples of statutory analogy. In the case NJA 1981 p. 1050, a businessman left account material to a person who promised to take care of his bookkeeping. The Supreme Court stated that this person has no right of lien on this material, that is, no right to keep it as security for his fee. The Court pointed out, what follows: "A creditor has a right of lien in many cases... Since a long time, a craftsman has possessed such a right... In the juristic literature, one expressed the view that this right can by analogy be granted to a lessee, a commission-agent, a freight-conveyor or another person who on the basis of a contract obtained a possession of another person's property... (But on the other hand,) if a businessman has left his account material to an accountant or another person, he can obviously have a very strong need to get it back soon... Social reasons also support the conclusion that a businessman should freely use his account material... Consequently, a right of lien on account material seems to be inappropriate and one should not consider to introduce it by analogy to the above-mentioned rules..."

Another example is this. Chapter 7 of the Code on Parents and Children contains some rules on maintenance allowance for children. The general invalidity conditions, formulated in chapter 3 of the Contracts Act, are applicable only to the law of property and do not directly concern family law. In the case NJA 1936 p. 598, however, "the grounds for" (that is, analogy to) sec. 29 of Contracts Act were proffered as the reason to invalidate a contract concerning maintenance allowance for children.

The following example is more complex. Section 1 of the Cooperative Apartments Act defines the right to a cooperative apartment as concerning "house or a part of house". In practice, however, this right is extended to cover not only a one-family house but also the attached plot of land. A reason for this is analogy to Ch. 12 sec. 1 Real Estate Code, stipulating that a <u>tenancy</u> agreement can also cover a plot of land (Bernitz <u>et al.</u> 1985, 84).

The following, logically correct, inference is thus a part of the legal argument <u>ex analogia</u>:

Premise 1:   If the fact F or another fact, relevantly
                  similar to F, occurs, then obtaining of G is
                  obligatory

Premise 2:   H is relevantly similar to F

Conclusion: If H occurs, then obtaining of G is obligatory

Since this inference assumes <u>relevance</u>, it differs from Alexy's rationality rule J.16 (section 4.3.4 supra). An estimation of relevant resemblance often implies weighing and balancing of various reasons and counter-arguments; cf. sections 2.4.3 and 5.4.3 supra.

7.4.2. The Origin and Justification of Statutory Analogy

An estimation of relevant resemblance can include many different things. In some cases, it involves three steps. The first step is to establish that persons, things, documents, rights, duties, circumstances concerning space and time, etc., which occur in case C bear a resemblance to the circumstances in the cases regulated by statutory provision L. The second step is a prediction, based on these similarities, that an application of provision L to case C will produce relevantly similar social effects to those produced in cases which are regulated by this provision. The third step is to conclude that case C thus should be treated similarly to cases regulated by L.

The use of statutory analogy depends on weighing and balancing of various substantive reasons and authority

CHAPTER 7

reasons. Such a weighing presupposes jumps and leads to a transformation of the law, cf. sections 2.7, 3.2, 5.8.5 and 7.1.2 supra. Yet, it can fulfil the rationality demands, discussed in chapter 3 supra.

The traditional origin of statutory analogy is that a so-called gap occurs in the statute; cf. section 1.2.3 supra. If the gap can be discovered in a value-free manner, then the law is not sufficiently fixed. If an evaluative reasoning shows that there is a gap in the statute, then the statute is not satisfactorily rational.

In both cases, statutory analogy can be justified by the principle "like should be treated alike" and thus by considerations of justice and universalisability; the latter is a criterion of coherence, cf. section 4.1.4 supra.

7.4.3. Law-Analogy and Legal Induction

One should not confuse statutory analogy and another mode of reasoning called "law-analogy" or "legal induction". (Slightly oversimplifying the matter, let me regard the two latter terms as synonymous.) Law-analogy requires fulfilment of the following conditions:

1) A general norm, G, is justifiable on the basis of the resemblance between a number of established rules, $r_1 - r_n$, thus regarded as special cases of G.

2) A case, C, lies outside of the linguistically natural area of application of these rules, $r_1 - r_n$.

3) On the other hand, the general norm, G, covers C; in other words, C shows relevant similarities to cases regulated by the less general rules, $r_1 - r_n$.

4) One adjudicates case C in accordance with G.

Let me give an example. The so-called Scandinavian doctrine of wrongfulness (literally "unlawfulness"; cf. Hellner 1985, 48) formulated the following general norm: One should not be criminally responsible nor liable in torts, or one's responsibility should at least be restricted, if one's action was not wrongful, that is, if its positive results were more important than the risks it caused. This general norm is justifiable on the basis of such defences, restricting or eliminating liability, as duty, emergency, authorisation, contributory negligence of the victim, consent of the victim, the fact that the victim takes particular risks etc. These defences are merely special cases of the lack of wrongfulness. Assume, e.g., that A violently turned B out of the meeting he

disturbed. The court found that B's provocative behaviour justified
the conclusion that A should not be criminally responsible (cf. NJA
1915 p. 511). One may add that A's action caused more good than
harm. One may also say that circumstances of the action to some
extent resemble duty or emergency etc. In other words, one can
support elimination of responsibility either with the general norm
of wrongfulness, or with a series of statutory analogies.
    Cf. NJA 1962 p. 31. A credit report agency gave some clients a
false information that a person, B, had been involved in illegal
business. B demanded compensation for libel. The agency claimed
that, in order to fulfil its useful function, it must be permitted
to make mistakes. The Supreme Court, however, found the agency
liable. (As a consequence of a subsequent legislation, cf. sec. 20
of the Credit Report Act, the case has only an academic importance.)

Law-analogy can be justified in the same way as statutory
analogy, i.e., by the principle "like should be treated
alike" and thus by considerations of justice and
universalisability; the latter is a criterion of
coherence.

7.4.4. Argumentum e contrario

When deciding to reason by analogy, one can follow
another legal mode of reasoning, the so-called argumentum
e contrario. One must make a distinction between a weak
and a strong argumentum e contrario.
    Assume that a statutory provision or another legal
norm, L, regulates some cases in a certain way. By virtue
of weak argumentum e contrario, N is not a sufficient
reason to conclude that a similar case, C, covered by
neither the core nor periphery of the linguistically
acceptable application-area of this norm, should be
treated in this way. The following example elucidates
this situation:

Premise: rule N	All chess players are qualified for membership in the club
Conclusion	N is no sufficient reason to conclude whether or not bridge players are qualified for membership in the club

By virtue of strong argumentum e contrario, (similar)
cases covered by neither the core nor periphery of the

linguistically acceptable application-area of this norm, should <u>not</u> be treated in the way stipulated by the norm. <u>Qui dicit de uno negat de altero</u>. The following example elucidates this mode of reasoning:

Premise: rule N	All chess players are qualified for membership in the club
Conclusion	Bridge players are not qualified for membership in the club

The following, logically correct, inference is a part of the strong <u>argumentum e contrario</u> (cf. Alexy´s rationality rule (J.15), in section 4.3.4 supra):

Premise:	Obtaining of the situation G is obligatory only if the fact C takes place
Conclusion:	If the fact C does not occur, obtaining of G is not obligatory

The evaluative part of the reasoning concerns the question whether or not the premise should contain the word "only".

As stated before, the use of analogy can be justified by principle "like should be treated alike". <u>Argumentum e contrario</u>, on the other hand, is justifiable the demand that the law should be respected. Since this demand is further supported by the value of fixity of the law and predictability of legal decisions, one may say that the choice between the use of analogy and <u>argumentum e contrario</u> is to be determined by weighing and balancing of two aspects of <u>legal certainty</u> (cf. section 1.4.1), that is, predictability and other moral considerations.

7.4.5. The Choice Between Analogy and Argumentum e contrario

The fact that one must make a <u>choice</u> between the use of analogy and <u>argumentum e contrario</u>, apparently supports the following objection: These "maxims of interpretation are not actual rules, but implements of a technique which - within certain limits - enables the judge to reach the conclusion he finds desirable in the circumstances, and at the same time to uphold the fiction that he is only adhering to the statute and objective principles of interpretation" (Ross 1958, 154).

The word "fiction" indicates that the judge has hidden "real" reasons the "fiction" is supposed to conceal. However, the crucial question is "whether the reasons given do or do not provide a well-founded and legally valid justification of the decision... Thus, if the reasons given are well-founded and valid it does not matter whether they are judge´s ´real´ reasons. If, again, the reasons are not well-founded or not legally valid it equally does not matter whether they are judge´s ´real´ reasons. In either case, the reasons actually given will be judged on their own merits" (Bergholtz 1987, 441; cf. 421 ff.).

To answer the question whether statutory analogy and argumentum e contrario are well-founded reasons, I would like to emphasise the words "within limits" and the word "only", and endorse Schmidt´s opinion (1957, 195) that "(t)he old technique relies upon the principle that the judge should never create norms which are altogether new but should seek his guidance in rules which have already been recognised for other situations." More precisely: Statutory analogy and argumentum e contrario are no rules but argument forms, each supported by a different set of reasoning norms and other principles which a judge has to weigh and balance. They enable the judge to reach the conclusion which is justifiable in the circumstances.

The following reasoning norms help one to make a choice between the use of analogy and argumentum e contrario:

A1) If an action is not explicitly forbidden by a statute or another established source of law, one should consider it as permitted by the interpreted valid law, unless strong reasons for assuming the opposite exist.

In other words, one should, as a rule, interpret prohibitions e contrario, not by analogy. This is a liberal norm. It states that only a relatively fixed law may contain justifiable prohibitions.

The well-known maxim "everything which is not forbidden is permitted" is vague, inter alia because one must make a distinction between weak and strong permission. A weak permission of an action is the same as the fact that no legal norm exists which states that it is forbidden. A strong permission of an action, on the other hand, is the same as the fact that there exists a legal norm which states that it is permitted. If the mentioned maxim refers to weak

permission, it is a logical tautology merely stating "If an action
is not forbidden, it is not forbidden". If it refers to a strong
permission, one should not interpret it, e.g., as follows: If an
action is not explicitly forbidden by a statute, it is explicitly
permitted by it. This statement is simply a false theoretical
proposition. A reasonable interpretation of the maxim must thus be
more complex. The reasoning norm A1 is one of such reasonable
interpretations.

A2) Only relevant similarities between cases constitute a
sufficient reason for conclusion by analogy.

A3) One should not construe provisions establishing
time limits by analogy. Neither should one construe them
extensively, unless particularly strong reasons for
assuming the opposite exist.

When, e.g., Ch. 9 sec. 1 of the Parents and Children
Code says that "a person under eighteen years of age...
is a minor" this means - without the least doubt - that
people older than this are of full age. In this context
it would be strange to reason extensively or analogically
and to draw the conclusion that some eighteen-year-old
people   are   minors   because   they   resemble
seventeen-year-olds (cf. Ross 1958, 150).

The following considerations may justify this norm.
Ratio legis of the time limits is to assure fixity of the
law, whereas analogy and extensive interpretation tend to
lower fixity.

A4) One should not construe provisions establishing
sufficient conditions for not following a general norm
extensively or by analogy, unless strong reasons for
assuming the opposite exist.

Sec. 32 of the Contracts Act reads, as follows: "A person who had
made a declaration of will which, owing to an error in writing or
some other mistake on his part, has been given another content than
that intended, shall not be bound by the contents of the declaration
of will where the person to whom the declaration is addressed
realised or ought to have realised the mistake." One must interpret
this enactment with the use of argumentum e contrario (not
analogically); it would be strange to conclude that the person
making the declaration of will is bound by its contents if the other
party neither realised nor ought to have realised the mistake.
(According to a pronouncement in the travaux préparatoires of the
Act, 1914 p. 140, the latter interpretation is possible but only in
special cases; cf. Schmidt 1960, 184).

One can argue similarly in the following example. In the Real
Estate Code, Ch. 4 sec. 3 it is laid down that a provision not
included in the purchase document is invalid if it implies that (1)

completion or existence of the acquisition is subject to conditions, (2) the vendor shall not carry such responsibility as is referred to in sec. 21, (3) the buyer's right to transfer the real-estate property or to apply for a mortgage or to transfer a right in the property will be restricted. Here, too, it seems strange to have recourse to analogy and to draw the conclusion that such a provision concerning the purchase of real-estate property will be invalid even if it does not fulfil the conditions stated in 1 - 3 (cf. Hessler 1970, 24). The example elucidates also the following reasoning norm:

A5) Only very strong reasons can justify a use of analogy leading to the conclusion that an error exists in the text of the statute.

A6) One should not construe provisions constituting exceptions from a general norm extensively or by analogy, unless strong reasons for assuming the opposite exist.

This well-known norm, **exceptiones non sunt extendendae**, more general than A4, is subject to some controversies in the juristic literature (cf., e.g., Engisch 1968, 147 ff.).

One expects the law to be fixed. Full freedom to consider it erroneous would diminish fixity.

A7) Not all reasons justifying extensive interpretation of a statute are strong enough to also justify reasoning by analogy.

A8) One should construe provisions imposing burdens or restrictions on a person restrictively, unless very strong reasons for assuming the opposite exist (**odia sunt restringenda**).

Consequently, one should not construe such provisions extensively or by analogy.

This liberal norm states that only a relatively fixed law may justifiably impose burdens and restrictions.

Two special cases of A8 are of the greatest importance:

a) The so-called principle of legality in penal law demands that no action should be regarded as a crime without statutory support and no penalty may be imposed without a statutory provision (**nullum crimen sine lege, nulla poena sine lege**). This is a classical requirement of legal certainty, eliminating unforeseeable punishment (cf., e.g., Thornstedt 1960, 213 ff.).

Cf. Ch. 2 sec. 10 para. 1 of the Swedish constitution (**Regeringsformen**): No penalty or another penal sanction may be imposed for an action without a provision in a statute which was valid when the crime was committed.

According to Ch. 8 sec. 1 of the Criminal Code, a person should be sentenced for theft if he "takes what belongs to another". It is thus theft for one to come into possession of a valuable trade secret by unlawfully taking an already existing copy of a drawing. But to come into possession of the secret by copying the drawing, on the other hand, is no theft; copying is no "taking". One pays no regard to the fact that the difference between taking the existing copy, and the action of copying it, is not important from the victim's point of view (cf. Beckman et al. 1970, 280).

In some cases, however, the Swedish Supreme Court applied criminal sanctions analogically. In such cases, fixity and predictability had to yield for other moral reasons. The latter must, of course, be justifiable in a highly coherent manner.

The Tax Crime Act, Sec. 2, stipulates penalty for one who omits to declare his income and thus causes the fact that too low tax is imposed on him. In the case NJA 1978 p. 452, the Supreme Court applied this provision by analogy to convict a person who had omitted to declare his income with the consequence that no tax at all was imposed on him. The Court admitted that the decision contradicted the wording of the statute but corresponded to travaux préparatoires and the purpose of the statute.

In the case NJA 1959 p. 254, two men left a radioactive iridium isotope unguarded at their working site. They were sentenced for "causing general danger through spreading poison or... suchlike" (Ch. 19 sec. 7 of the Penal Code then in force, cf. now Ch. 13 sec. 7 of the Criminal Code). To leave the stuff unguarded was judged as analogous to spreading it.

In NJA 1956 C 187, a person threatened a cashier with a pistol that later turned out to be a toy and thus got some money. The Swedish Supreme Court decided that such an act constituted a robbery. The decision was based on analogy between a real danger and an action which the victim considers to constitute a danger.

In NJA 1954 p. 464, a man who made withdrawal from his account was sentenced for unlawful disposal, since he realised that the amount had been credited to the account by a mistake. This action was judged as analogous to unlawful disposal of what one has in one's possession (Ch. 22 sec. 4 of the Penal Code then in force, cf. now Ch. 10 sec. 4 of the Criminal Code). Literally, however, the defendant has never had the possession of the money.

The descriptions of offences in the Criminal Code are in general concerned with positive actions. They are also applied analogically to omission to act. According to Ch. 3 sec. 1 of the Criminal Code "a person who deprives another person of his life" shall be convicted of murder. This enactment would, however, be applied analogically to certain omission cases. If a person having the task of pumping air to a diver under water ceased pumping with intent to kill, and the diver was suffocated, he must be sentenced for murder.

b) In taxation law, the principle nullum tributum sine lege justifies the conclusion that one should apply analogy with restraint if it leads to increased taxation (cf. Welinder 1975, vol. 2, 242-3).

On the other hand, conclusion by analogy has priority before _argumentum e contrario_ in private law. Private law, connected with a sphere in which an individual may make relatively free decisions. In this sphere, only the limits of freedom, constituting the rules of the "game", must be highly fixed, even this causes some decrease of rationality. Other kind of legal rules must be, first of all, justifiable in a highly coherent manner.

A9) A statutory provision should be applied analogously to cases not covered by its literal content, if another provision states that they relevantly resemble those which are thus covered (cf. Hult 1952, 51).

According to Ch. 17 sec. 2 of the Decedent´s Estate Code, a descendant cannot in principle validly waive his right to his lawful inheritance portion. The provision is applicable by analogy to adoptive children as well, since the statute has otherwise in various respects equated them with descendants.

A10) One may utilise _argumentum e contrario_ only in exceptional cases, when interpreting rules based on precedents.

This reasoning norm has an indirect relevance in statutory interpretation, because the latter may be supported by a rule which itself is based on precedents.

The reasoning norm A10 is applicable to rules based on the the content of precedent decisions but it does not affect relatively rare cases in which statutory interpretation receives support from _argumentum e contrario_ based on a general rule, explicitly stated by the court which decided the precedent case.

A10 is supported by the following reasons. A rule based on a precedent has another character than a statutory rule. The latter contains general terms, _prima-facie_ establishing not only the sphere it covers but also the outer sphere it does not cover. On the other hand, the precedent decision does not establish any limit for the sphere of application of the rule it supports. The point of using a decision as a precedent is to obtain a pattern for analogous cases, and thus to facilitate creation of a general legal rule, not to settle the precise scope of the general rule. In spite of this, the practice of following precedents contributes not only to coherence of the legal system (since generality is a criterion of coherence) but also to fixity of the law. Though the rule, based on a precedent, has vague sphere of application, it gives the interpreter some information he would not have had he merely performed a pure moral reasoning. One thus knows at least two things: that the general rule in question covers the precedent case and that it is to be extended to analogous cases.

The case in question may from one point of view resemble
cases which are regulated by a statutory rule and at the
same time, from another point of view, resemble other
cases which are regulated by another statutory rule. If
statutory analogy is acceptable, i.e. _argumentum e
contrario_ is not, one thus encounters the problem of
which analogy one should choose.

Consider again NJA 1950 p. 650, section 7.1.2 supra, where the
decision has been regarded as a choice between analogies.
    Another example (made obsolete by a statute in force since 1988)
concerns the question who owns property which has been acquired
during the cohabitation resembling marriage (cf. Bengtsson 1969). If
one does not find it right to regard the parties separately, with
the consequence that the partner who has bought an object will be
owner of it, one can make a choice between the following analogies:
    a) One can treat the case as analogous to corresponding cases in
marriage and decide it according to rules in the Marriage Code.
    b) One can also treat this case as resembling purchases made for a
commercial partnership; the purchase would be considered to have
been made for the account of both parties and the right of
co-ownership would therefore exist.

When making choice between different analogies one takes
into account considerations similar to those obtaining in
the choice between analogy and _argumentum e contrario_.
    The reasoning norms A1-A10 make the choice between the
use of analogy and _argumentum e contrario_ relatively
fixed and thus _ceteris-paribus_ restrict arbitrariness of
the choice. They thus provide some support for the acts
of weighing and balancing between coherence (which
implies _inter alia_ generality and thus contributes to
justice) and, on the other hand, fixity of the law and
predictability of legal decisions. This support makes the
choice more _rational_.

7.4.6. _Argumentum a fortiori_

The following reasoning norms express two form of
argumentum a fortiori:
    A11) If the statute allows one to do more, then it also
permits one to do less (_argumentum a maiori ad minus_).

A12) If the statute forbids one to do less, then it also forbids one to do more (<u>argumentum a minori ad maius</u>).

<u>Argumentum a fortiori</u> is an amplified reasoning by analogy. One concludes that a case should be treated similarly to another one. The reason is not only that the cases are similar but also that the latter deserves this treatment in a still higher degree then the former.

Sometimes one derives the conclusion concerning the relation "more-less" from "value-free" premises, analytical or empirical. A deaf and dumb person, e.g., is more handicapped than a dumb (and not deaf) one.

The classical example is this. Premise: it is forbidden for two persons to ride one the same bicycle. Conclusion: it is forbidden for three persons to ride one the same bicycle (cf., e.g., Koch and Rüssmann 1982, 259).

Cf. the Polish case SN IV CR 1079/55. From the premise that deaf and dumb persons may carry out a legal act before a notary public, the Polish Supreme Court drew the conclusion that a dumb (and not deaf) person was even more entitled to do so (Peczenik 1962, 143).

Usually, however, the relation "more-less" is based on a value judgment, either expressed in some sources of the law or "free". For example, a decision having come into force is "more" than a decision not yet have done so.

The Polish case SN III CR 458/57 constitutes another example. From the premise that, after a decision has come into force, a person declared incapacitated in that decision may himself - not only through a guardian - in certain circumstances apply for the decision to be revoked, the Polish Supreme Court drew the conclusion that the person declared incapacitated is even more entitled to apply for the revocation before the decision has come into force (Peczenik 1962, 144).

In such cases, the interpreter formulates a <u>principle</u> and concludes that the case to be decided fulfils it to a higher degree than the ones covered by the statute.

<u>Argumentum a fortiori</u> may lead to questionable results. One can regard publishing of secret information as "something more" than the revealing it to friends. But in Sweden, as a consequence of the Freedom of the Press Act (cf. Ch. 7 sec. 3), an official publishing in some circumstances secret information in print is not criminally responsible; the same official, however, would

be prosecuted for revealing the information to his
friends (cf. Ch. 20 sec. 3 para. 2 of the Criminal Code).

The principle deciding what is "more" and what "less"
thus competes with other principles, that is, other value
judgments. When weighing and balancing them, one takes
into account considerations similar to those relevant as
regards other types of reasoning by analogy.

Argumentum a fortiori thus contributes to coherence of
legal reasoning. This is even clearer than in other cases
of analogy. Everything which makes a reasoning by analogy
to contribute to coherence is applicable to the reasoning
a fortiori. Besides, the latter has its own merits
because, instead of statements of similarity between
cases, one uses stronger comparative statements ("more"
and "less"). The fact one does not apply a statutory rule
to relevantly similar cases collides with the requirement
of generality. The fact that one does not apply the rule
to cases which even more deserve the application collides
not only with this requirement but also with the
principle stating what is more and what is less. The
latter has its own coherent justification. When this is
ignored, the degree of coherence must prima-facie
decrease.

7.5. TELEOLOGICAL CONSTRUCTION OF STATUTES

7.5.1. The Basic Structure

Teleological construction of a statute is its
interpretation in view of its purpose. According to
Alexy, its basic structure is, the following (cf. J.5 in
section 4.3.4 supra; cf. Koch and Rüssmann 1982, 259):

Premise 1:   Obtaining of the situation Z is prescribed

Premise 2:   If one had not do H, then Z would not be
                obtained

Conclusion: One should do H

One may argue that the step from these two premises to
the conclusion is not purely logical. To assure the
logical character of the step, one needs the following
additional premise:

If
1) obtaining of the situation Z is prescribed; and
2) if one had not do H, then Z would not be obtained;
then one should do H.
The following inference is thus purely logical:

Premise 1:   Obtaining of the situation Z is prescribed
Premise 2:   If one had not do H, then Z would not be
                    obtained
Premise 3:   If
                    1) obtaining of the situation Z is prescribed;
                    and
                    2) if one had not do H, then Z would not be
                    obtained;
                    then one should do H

Conclusion: One should do H

If so, then premises 1 and 2 alone merely support the
conclusion but not logically entail it. The
goal-reasoning is then a special case of S-rationality.

On the other hand, one can also argue that the step
from premises 1 and 2 to the conclusion is purely
logical, at least if one follows von Wright's advice
(1963, 167) and enlarges the province of logic.

The latter view, implying that premise 3 is a logical
statement, is perhaps more intuitive, since the
goal-reasoning seems to be a formal one rather than
substantive.

Regardless which view one assumes, the goal-reasoning
does not constitute any separate kind of rationality (a
"goal-rationality"), side by side with Logical and
Supportive rationality. It is only a special case of the
former or of the latter. Still less justified is the view
that all rationality is the same as "goal-rationality".

See also Alexy's principle of goal rationality, section
4.3.3 supra.

7.5.2. Subjective and Objective Teleological Interpretation of Statutes

Sometimes - though not often - a statutory provision
states precisely that obtaining the situation Z is
prescribed. Usually, however, a statutory provision is
formulated in a non-teleological manner. It merely

<u>supports</u> the conclusion that Z is prescribed. The
conclusion does not follow from the provision alone but
from a set, including the provision together with some
other reasonable premises. Yet, one may state that the
provision is a means to fulfil the goal Z. One may thus
express the point of teleological construction of a
statutory provision, as follows.

Premise 1:   The provision, L, is a means to fulfil the
                 goal, Z
Premise 2:   If one had not interpreted L as containing the
                 rule R, then Z would not be obtained

Conclusion: One should interpret L as containing the rule R

It is natural to pay attention to the purpose of the
statute. The statute consists of norms and the point of a
norm is incomprehensible without a thought of a will or a
purpose it expresses, cf. section 2.2.1 supra.

As stated above, the purpose of the statute (<u>ratio
legis</u>) as regards <u>hard</u> cases differs from the will of the
persons that participated in the process of legislation.
Neither the <u>ratio</u> nor the proposed construction of
statutes follow logically from the description of this
will alone. The conclusion about the <u>ratio</u> is only
derivable from a complex set of premises including some
which are reasonable, although neither certain nor taken
for granted within the legal paradigm, cf. section 6.6.2
supra. In other words, the step from the text of the
statute and data concerning the will of its "authors" to
the <u>ratio legis</u> is a <u>jump</u>.

One may thus make a distinction between a subjective-
and an objective-teleological construction of statutes.
The former is based on the will of persons participating
in legislation, or on <u>travaux préparatoires</u>. The
subjective-teleological construction has thus the
following two forms:

I
Premise 1:   The "legislator" regards the provision, L, as a
                 means to fulfil the goal, Z
Premise 2:   If one had not interpreted L as containing the
                 rule R, then Z would not be obtained

Conclusion: One should interpret L as containing the rule R

II

Premise 1:   According to the <u>travaux préparatoires</u>, the
                    provision, L, is a means to fulfil the goal, Z

Premise 2:   If one had not interpreted L as containing the
                    rule R, then Z would not be obtained

Conclusion: One should interpret L as containing the rule R

One may express the objective-teleological construction
of statutes, as follows. (See also Alexy 1989, 198 ff.).

Premise 1:   According to an interpretation, supported by
                    various   juristic   substantive   and   authority
                    reasons, the provision, L, is a means to fulfil
                    the goal, Z

Premise 2:   If one had not interpreted L as containing the
                    rule R, then Z would not be obtained

Conclusion: One should interpret L as containing the rule R

7.5.3. Radical Teleological Interpretation of Statutes

In this connection, the following questions occur: 1) Do
any other construction methods have priority before
teleological construction of statutes?, and 2) What
interpretative problems should one solve with support of
teleological construction of statutes?
   The classical answer to the first question assumes that
teleological construction of statutes is a last resort.
It is to be applied after one failed to remove vagueness
of the interpreted provision, in spite of having used the
literal, logical, systematic and historical methods. The
<u>radical teleological</u> approach claims, on the other hand,
that the teleological method is applicable since the very
beginning of the interpretatory process.
   The classical answer to the second question assumes
that one should use the teleological construction of
statutes only when aiming at reduction or creation of a
more general new norm, not when performing a restrictive
or extensive interpretation. The <u>radical teleological</u>
approach claims, on the other hand, that the teleological
method is applicable to all kinds of interpretatory
problems.

The radically teleological construction of statutes is a product of the evolution of legal method at the end of 19th and the beginning of 20th century. According to <u>Rudolf von Ihering</u>, the content of the legal system reflects the individual and common interests of people. Statutory interpretation should be teleological, i.e. should pay regard to legally-protected interests, concerning not only material goods but also honour, love, liberty, education, religion, art and science. Ihering saw, however, limitations of the teleological method. He thus refused to use the term "purpose of law" in definitions of juridical concepts, in the systematic of the penal code and in categorisation of private-law rights.

According to <u>Francois Gény</u>, who created the "free scientific research" of the law, the text of the statute must be taken into account when it is clear. Otherwise the interpreter should with the support of other sources of the law try to establish the value judgments which formed the basis of the statute. Where these sources give no answer, the judge may make a free interpretation, influenced by an assessment of interests, by conceptions of justice, and by considerations of social utility.

<u>Eugen Ehrlich's</u> "free-law school" followed Gény. But Ehrlich's pupils, among them <u>Hermann Kantorowicz</u>, expressed the following, more radical views. On all questions where the answer does not clearly appear from the text of the statute, the judge has no reason to conform to such sources as the <u>travaux préparatoires</u>. He is free to reject the value judgments which formed the basis of the statute, and he may decide the case in accordance with his own evaluation of interests which are protected by the statute. The judge's freedom to thus follow his own judgments, feelings and even intuition is restricted only where it is a matter of construing various organisational and procedural rules.

The <u>Interessenjurisprudenz</u>, founded by <u>Philipp von Heck</u>, was more cautious than the free-law school. The interpreter should not rely upon his own will or feelings but on research concerning interests and their evaluation in accordance with the values on which the statute is based. Where different interpretatory alternatives lead to a protection of different interests, judges should rely on the legislator's ideology and values accepted by him, in so far as these can be read from the statute. Secondarily they should rely on their own analysis of different interests. It is not sufficient to take into account the purpose of the statute. It is true that the purpose of the statute was the protection of certain interests. These "winning" interests, however, collided with others which lost the battle for legal protection but could nevertheless influence the formation of the statute e.g. the question of the extent to which the "winning" interests obtained legal protection. Thus the interpreter should take into account the struggle occurring in the community between different interests. Only where scientific analysis of different interests is not sufficient to find an unambiguous interpretation may the judge rely on his intuition.

In the USA, a related theory has been developed by <u>Roscoe Pound</u>. The function of the legal order consists in social engineering, comprising an acknowledgment of certain individual, public and social interests; a determination of the limits within which these interests are to be recognised and protected by the law; and a protection of recognised interests within thus determined limits. In this connection, Pound has developed a number of rules of interpretation which should be used in private law. Rules on the ownership and the majority of commercial-law rules should be interpreted with the use of precise arguments based on the sources of the law, since such an interpretation will protect the rule of law which is an important social interest. On the other hand, indemnity rules should be construed freely according to the interpreter's evaluation of colliding interests.

7.5.4. Teleological Interpretation of Statutes According to Ekelöf. Introductory Remarks

The teleological construction of statutes in Sweden is associated above all with the name of **Per Olof Ekelöf**. A summary of his views is as follows. In ordinary cases, judges and jurists should follow the vague meaning the statute has according to the ordinary linguistic usage. In "special" (uncertain, untypical, hard) cases, the interpreter ought not to perform linguistic analysis of the statute, nor feel oneself to be bound by the travaux préparatoires.

At the same time, Ekelöf regards precedents as more important as the travaux préparatoires (cf., e.g., 1958, 87 and 93 ff.). For Ekelöf a precedent is a source of the law side by side with the statute; the travaux préparatoires, on the other hand, are not. But it is not entirely clear to me how it is possible to justify this priority order where Swedish law is concerned.

Instead, one should consider the purpose of the enactment in question. One must establish this purpose of the statute by reference to its effects (its "total result", "actual function", or "practical function") in ordinary cases (cf. Ekelöf 1958, 84 ff. and 105 ff.; 1951, 23 and 28-9). Ekelöf thus recommends the following chain.
   1) Statutory construction in ordinary cases takes place through linguistically natural interpretation.
   2) This statutory construction affects the outcome of ordinary cases.
   3) The outcome of these cases leads to certain effects in the community.

4) Some of the actual effects of the interpretation of the law in ordinary cases constitute the purpose of the statute, i.e. the effects the statute ought to have.

5) The purpose of the statute, in its turn, is determinative in the construction of the statute in "special" cases.

By the way, the method has an American counterpart. Cf. Hart and Sacks 1958, 1153: "an expectation that interpreters of the statute would resolve cases of doubtful application by an effort to discern the purpose behind the instances of clear applicability (and inapplicability) and to arrive at conclusions consistent both with this purpose and these instances". But when determining "the purpose behind the instances of clear applicability", Hart and Sacks assume a different priority order of reasons than Ekelöf: The linguistic sense of the statute is relevantly less important for them (although certainly not totally irrelevant).

Ekelöf gives the following example (1958, 110 ff.). Ch. 45 sec. 5 para. 1 of the Code of Judicial Procedure reads as follows: "An indictment once made may not be changed. The prosecutor may, however, extend the indictment against the same defendant to include another offence if the court, having regard to the police inquiry and other circumstances, finds this appropriate."

Let us now assume that several persons are being prosecuted for having jointly committed a number of burglaries. One of them is prosecuted only for participation in one burglary. However, immediately before the trial, the prosecutor alters the indictment in such a way that this person is no longer prosecuted for this burglary but instead for participation in one of the other burglaries. The accused confesses to the offence, and there is also other evidence of this. Is such a change in the indictment permissible? The literal formulation of the statute provides no support for this conclusion. It is permissible only to "extend", not to change the indictment. Ekelöf's method, however, leads to a different conclusion. He first asks to what effects the provision leads in ordinary cases. Somebody is prosecuted for one crime and later for another in addition. Both offences are dealt with in the same trial. Everybody involved saves the time, money and trouble which would ensue from two trials. Ekelöf finds that such a saving must be regarded as the purpose of the statute. Finally, he reverts to the "special" case mentioned above and states that even where a person is prosecuted in the

given circumstances for one crime <u>instead</u> of another,
this will also lead to the same saving. The conclusion is
that the change in the indictment must be regarded as
permissible in this case.

7.5.5. Teleological Interpretation of Statutes According to Ekelöf. The Problem of Preciseness

Ekelöf´s method has three advantages.
1) It pays attention to the purpose of the statute.
Indeed, "(a)ny judicial opinion... which finds a plain
meaning in a statute without consideration of its
purpose... is deserving nothing but contempt" (Hart and
Sacks 1958, 1157).
2) It results in similar treatment of ordinary and
"special" cases, thus promoting justice, generality and
hence coherence of reasoning. In this manner, a person
deciding an actual case must refer to a whole set of
hypothetical cases. This kind of considerations is
commonly recognised as very important within legal
reasoning.
3) It supports decisions in "special" cases with
sophisticated reasons. In consequence, it conforms to the
demand of <u>S</u>upportive rationality and thus coherence.
The method is reasonable and one ought to use it in
<u>some</u> cases. However, in consequence of the following
problems, it should merely supplement, <u>not supersede</u>,
other methods of statutory construction.
First of all, the method is <u>not more precise</u> than other
methods of statutory construction. In other words, it
does not to a higher degree assure the required
predictability of legal reasoning and fixity of the law.
Uncertainty thus occurs when one attempts to precisely
answer the questions, a) What cases are ordinary?, b)
What are the results of the method in the ordinary
cases?, and c) What is the purpose of the statute?
a) What cases are ordinary and what are "special"?
Special are not only such cases as fall outside of the
letter of the law but also cases which are clearly
covered by this "letter" but which seldom occur or are
connected with "such special circumstances that a
mechanical application of the statute can be regarded as
militating against its purpose" (Ekelöf 1958, 84).
Ordinary are, on the other hand, those cases which are of
great importance or are for some other reason so striking

that the drafters of the statute could not have avoided
taking note of them. Moreover, due to social change
occurring after the statute has been enacted, some cases
can become ordinary though the drafters never thought of
them. Consequently, when making the distinction between
ordinary and "special" cases, one must rely on an
evaluative weighing of various vague criteria.

Ross (1953, 171 n. 2) has thus held that it is not possible to
establish which cases are "certain" and which are "special" before
the purpose of the statute has been determined.
   This difficulty to make a precise distinction between ordinary and
"special" cases occurs, e.g., when one has to interpret general
clauses. For example, sec. 36 of the Contracts Act gives the courts
possibility to modify or set aside a contractual stipulation, "if it
is undue (unreasonable) with regard to the content of the contract,
circumstances of its origin, subsequent circumstances and other
circumstances". Assume now that a standard contract prepared by a
big company, dominating the market, contains a certain arbitration
clause. A rather unexperienced businessman signs the contract.
Later, he claims that the clause is to be set aside. The clause may
be considered to be unreasonable. But is the case ordinary or
"special"? The wording of the statute does not answer this question.
The answer requires a moral reasoning. Some guidelines for this are
included in the travaux préparatoires (Government Bill 1975/76:81,
118 ff., cf. section 6.6.7 supra). These guidelines helped the
courts to make a number of decisions, cf., e.g., NJA 1979 p. 666
(section 1.2.2 supra).

b) What are the effects of the use of Ekelöf´s method in
the ordinary cases? It may be supposed that such
knowledge could be obtained through a sociological
investigation, but this can be difficult to perform. Most
probably, Ekelöf sometimes relies on the actual,
sociologically established effects and sometimes on the
hypothetical, foreseen effects (cf. Thornstedt 1960, 229
ff.). But how can one test a hypothesis about the latter?
   c) But to establish the purpose of the statute is still
more difficult (cf. id.). Ekelöf considers only some of
the actual effects of the application of the statute in
ordinary cases to be identical with the effects that the
statute ought to have, i.e. its purpose. Let me analyse
an example. On Swedish roads certain speed limits are in
force. What are their effects? Well, the first is that
the number of traffic accidents in Sweden has diminished
somewhat. Another is that the number of drivers who obey
traffic rules has declined even more. A third is that
Swedish drivers venturing onto German Autobahn, where no

speed limit apply, often drive badly because they are unused to fast driving. The sole purpose of speed limits, however, is clearly to reduce the number of road accidents in Sweden. It follows that the purpose of the statute includes only effects which, according to the interpreter´s judgment attributed to the lawmaker, are good. Ekelöf has explicitly admitted that the interpreter must rely on his own "good judgment". But who can know for sure what effects of, e.g., a complex tax legislation are good and what bad?

The general clause in the sec. 2 of the Tax Evasion Act of 1980 (changed in 1983) stipulates what follows:
  "When making the tax assessment, one should not pay attention to a transaction performed by the taxpayer..., if
1. the transaction... is included in a procedure that gives the taxpayer a not irrelevant taxation advantage,
2. the advantage, in view of the circumstances, can be regarded as having been the main reason for the procedure and
3. the tax assessment based on this procedure would contradict the grounds of the legislation."
  But what does contradict the grounds of the legislation? Assume that A transferred a number of houses to a company he totally owned and then sold shares in this company to a third party. In this way, A obtained a taxation advantage in comparison with a hypothetical situation in which he directly sold the houses. This procedure was judged as not contradicting the grounds of the legislation (cf. the case RÅ 83 1:35). On the other hand, the Supreme Administrative Court found that the following procedure was contradicting these "grounds": A death estate was divided in such a way that the widow received a farm. Then she sold it to the heirs who in this manner obtained a taxation advantage (cf. the case RÅ 84 1:92). What support can the interpreter find for making such distinctions? He may pay attention to the travaux préparatoires, "general structure of statutes" and "their purpose" (Government Bill 1980/81:17, pp. 26 and 197; Government Bill 1982/83:84, p. 19.) The travaux préparatoires, however, not always give the required information. "General structure of statutes" and "their purpose" can be found with help of Ekelöf's method. But then, one must be able to judge whether or not this general clause causes the same effects in this case as in the ordinary cases. What are then "the same effects"? This expression refers probably to abstract and complex matters only an advanced law-and-economics study can describe, such as a certain relation of taxation to one's capacity to pay. To make Ekelöf's method applicable to the tax evasion clause, one must thus discuss complex and profound problems.

Different problems connected with teleological interpretation of statutes hang together and affect each other. Ekelöf´s method to establish the purpose of a statutory provision depends on the distinction between ordinary and "special" cases. At the same time, this distinction requires a recourse to the purpose of the provision. The interpreter reasons in a "spiral". Cf. the remark in section 7.3 supra on the so-called hermeneutical circle.

A preliminary and vague determination of ordinary cases thus influences the establishing of the purpose of the statutory provision. The latter affects a deeper understanding of the distinction between ordinary and "special" cases. This results in a deeper understanding of the purpose. One may thus modify and mutually adapt various premises of teleological interpretation in order to achieve a balance, resembling the "reflective equilibrium" (cf. section 3.2.1 supra). Such a balance occurs in many other interpretative contexts as well. It is nothing special for Ekelöf´s method.

In this connection, one must also consider our remarks on jumps in legal reasoning, cf. sections 2.7, 3.2 and 5.8.5 supra.

7.5.6. Teleological Interpretation of Statutes According to Ekelöf. Multiple Goals

Ekelöf´s method is particularly difficult to apply to provisions having many purposes, often conflicting with each other.

In private law, interests of the parties compete with each other; in torts, e.g., the interest of the victim to receive compensation competes with legal certainty of the alleged tortfeasor. In public law, too, a number of considerations of purpose pull in different directions. When interpreting provisions of taxation law one must weigh and balance financial interests of the state, legal certainty of taxpayers, public interest to protect efficiency of trade and industry, the interest of the authorities to make the law easy to apply, etc. Where penal provisions are concerned, regard should be paid, inter alia, to general deterrence, to preventing recidivism, to re-education of the offenders and to the ideal of just punishment. One may even find competing purposes in Ekelöf´s procedural example, quoted above. Ekelöf emphasises saving the time, money and trouble which would ensue from two trials. But this is not the sole purpose to be considered. If it were, <u>all</u> changes of indictment would be permissible. The competing purpose is, of course, legal certainty of the defendant, in particular protection from being harassed through unpredictable and prolonged changes of indictment.

One can also speak about direct and indirect purposes. A provision of the law of torts may thus directly intend to compensate a certain type of damage and indirectly aim at promoting economic efficiency. "Thus, we can usually attribute to any rule or other precept that directs behavior one or more ´immediate´ (lowest-level) goals, one or more ´intermediate´ goals, and one or more ´ultimate´ (higher-level) goals" (Summers 1982, 64; cf. Weinberger and Weinberger 1979, 142).

Moreover, one must make a distinction between 1) purposes of the considered provision; 2) purposes of other provisions connected with it; 3) purposes characteristic of the part of the law to which the provision belongs, e.g., penal law; and 4) purpose considerations common to the whole legal system; an example of such a consideration is the purpose of protecting legal certainty. In fact, all legal substantive and authority reasons can be presented as such purposes. Can all of them be derived in Ekelöf´s manner, that is, from results of literal interpretation of the statutory provision in ordinary cases? If one can thus derive only some of them, why should one ignore the other? To conclude, Ekelöf´s method is too simple.

7.5.7. Teleological Interpretation of Statutes According to Ekelöf. Restricted List of Interpretative Methods and Sources of Law

For the sake of simplicity, Ekelöf cuts down the sources of law and the legal methods to a minimum. One should, in principle, pay attention to the statute, its results and own judgments telling one which of those are good.

As stated above, Ekelöf also recommends paying attention to precedents which he regards as more important as the <u>travaux préparatoires</u>. But this thesis is quite independent from and incoherent with the main point of his theory.

Why should one not recognises that also the travaux préparatoires, the juristic literature and the traditionally established juristic norms of reasoning possess some (different) degrees of authority? Ekelöf hopes that such a simplification makes his method more objective, less dependent on value judgments made by the interpreter. This would make the law more fixed. But, as stated above, this hope is not realistic. Just the opposite, the method deprives the interpreter of valuable data which would restrict the necessity to follow own judgment. The hypothesis is thus plausible that the method does not increase fixity of the law. At the same time, it certainly decrease coherence of legal reasoning, since it makes its supportive structure much less sophisticated. In particular, it decreases the data basis of legal reasoning; this collides with a principle of coherence (cf. section 4.1.5 supra). It also cuts down the chains of justification; also this effect diminishes coherence (cf. section 4.1.3 supra).

One may perhaps interpret Ekelöf´s idea to cut down the legal sources and methods as an expression of the radical optimism, typical for the reformist debate of the 1930th. He claims in fact that the judgment of the interpreter is sufficiently good to establish the reasonable purpose of the statute, without any auxiliary means but the statute itself and a radically restricted list of the sources of the law. In other words, the decrease of coherence due to the diminished list of authority reasons would be compensated with the increase of coherence due to the greater role of substantive reasons. My view is more conservative. It is difficult both for the law-givers and the interpreters to compute what is good for the parties and the society. As social engineering is concerned, our century is the time of failure. One needs reliance on tradition even to approximate the best solution of conflicts between people, as well in general as in particular cases. The established legal method is an extremely important part of this tradition. One should beware of rejecting it.

Ekelöf seems to recognise this conclusion in an indirect way when regarding precedents - though not the travaux préparatoires - as sources of the law side by side with the statute; he thus does not dare to deprive the interpreter of all the auxiliary means. If there is a precedent concerning a "special" case, then Ekelöf would always follow that precedent, although perhaps he would have solved the problem in another way if he had strictly followed his method. But why does he thus surrender only

as regards precedents? While not to follow the <u>whole</u>
established doctrine of legal sources and methods? One
can perhaps explain Ekelöf´s restrictive approach in this
connection by pointing at his background, that is the
Uppsala School scepticism as regards legal reasoning.
The same background explains perhaps why the purpose of
a statutory provision according to Ekelöf is to be
established by a detour through studying results of
literal interpretation of the provision in ordinary
cases. He seems to rely more on sociological hypotheses
about these results, combined with "good judgment" of the
interpreter, than, e.g., on clear pronouncements in the
<u>travaux préparatoires</u>. This may reflect the Uppsala
school disposition to introduce some "scientific"
sociology to the legal method, often regardless the
price. But this detour is unnecessary, since the
traditional legal method is not less rational than
sociology.

7.5.8. Teleological Interpretation of Statutes According
to Ekelöf. Conclusions

One can regard Ekelöf´s method as a special case of
reasoning by analogy, that is, a statutory analogy based
upon relevant similarities of results.

Ekelöf claims, among other things, that his method should supersede
both extensive interpretation of statutes and creation of more
general new norms through statutory analogy. In consequence, he
denies the relevance of the distinction between these interpretatory
methods. But this kind of scepticism has some disadvantages, cf.
section 7.3 supra.
   Frändberg (1973, 143 ff.) has elaborated a theory of statutory
analogy founded on the concept of "legal basis" of a legal norm, n,
defined as "a desirable state of affairs, t, such that n is an
instrument of achieving t." (id. 172). Frändberg's "legal basis" is
clearly related to the purpose of the statute in Ekelöf's sense.

This emphasis upon the results represents an effort to
recommend consequentialist reasons while maintaining
loyalty to the authority of statute. By the way, one or
another form of consequentialism is another typical
property of Legal Realism, including the Uppsala School.

Because of their substantive character, consequentialist reasons are justifiable by recourse to various criteria of coherence. Authority of statute, on the other hand, is justifiable by recourse to fixity of the law. As all serious methods of statutory interpretation, Ekelöf´s method must pay attention to both these values.

But is Ekelöf´s method superior in these respects than the traditional practice of statutory interpretation? Despite Ekelöf´s contrary opinion, one can suspect that the traditional legal method as a whole gives a higher degree of legal certainty than Ekelöf´s radical simplification. I have thus argued above that exclusive application of Ekelöf´s method, instead of the traditional one, certainly decreases coherence of legal reasoning. This means that it decreases the degree of support the reasoning receives from the prima-facie law and morality. I have also argued that exclusive application of this method probably decreases predictability of reasoning and thus fixity of the law.

These results are by no means surprising. During centuries of continual legal discourse the traditional method underwent repeated testing precisely from the point of view of both predictability and coherence of legal reasoning. Can all this evolution really be worthless?

One should use Ekelöf´s method in some cases, provided that no reasons exist to rather use other interpretatory methods. But the method deserves no monopoly.

7.6. SOLUTION OF COLLISIONS BETWEEN LEGAL NORMS

7.6.1. Collisions of Rules and Principles

I have already discussed some examples of corrective construction of statutes, inter alia reduction, creation of a more general new norm through statutory analogy, and some types of teleological interpretation. The so-called solution of collision between legal norms is another type of corrective interpretation.

When discussing collisions between legal norms, one must consider the following distinctions.

A collision of rules occurs when the rules are logically, empirically or evaluatively incompatible. Logical incompatibility violates the demand of

L-rationality. Empirical incompatibility violates the demand of efficiency, that is, it is incompatible with the principle of goal-rationality; cf. section 4.3.3 supra. Evaluative incompatibility means that the simultaneous obeying of two norms logically implies violation of a third one, corresponding to an assumed moral or legal value.

Two rules are thus <u>logically</u> incompatible (cf., e.g., Weinberger and Weinberger 1979, 132) if:

a) one of them commands an action while the other forbids it (a contrary logical incompatibility); or

b) one of them forbids an action while the other permits it (a contradictory logical incompatibility).

A special form of logical incompatibility occurs in connection with qualification rules (see section 5.6.5 supra). Two such rules are logically incompatible if one of them states that a certain circumstance is necessary and another that it is not necessary for the validity of a certain legal action. Consider the following examples. A rule stipulates that A has a power to make judicial decisions, another one stipulates that he has not. Or, one rule demands written form for validity of a certain contract, whereas another admits validity of both written and oral contracts of this kind; etc.

If two rules are logically incompatible, one cannot observe (or apply) them simultaneously. I disregard here some problems concerning permissive rules.

Two rules are <u>empirically</u> incompatible if they are not logically incompatible but nevertheless one cannot simultaneously observe (or apply) them for another reason. Suppose two rules, one of which obliges A to work daily from 4 a.m. to 4 p.m., the other of which obliges him to work daily from 4 p.m. to 3 a.m. These two rules are empirically incompatible; A cannot, as a practical matter, work for 23 hours a day.

Two rules are <u>evaluatively</u> incompatible even if one can - logically and empirically - observe (or apply) them simultaneously, when their simultaneous observance (or application) would lead to legally or morally objectionable effects, whereas each norm separately does not lead to such negative consequences. Suppose, e.g., two rules, one of which obliges A to work daily from 8 a.m. to 4 p.m., the other of which obliges him to work daily from 4 p.m. to 11 p.m. A can work for 15 hours a day but the labour law forbids it.

The Norwegian case Rt 1953 p. 1469 constitutes a good example. A
fisherman who had shot a seal in the sea was prosecuted for not
having paid the appropriate fee under the Game Act. He did, however
pay another fee - in accordance with the Seal Fishing Act. It is
clear that there is no logical incompatibility between these two
statutes. Logically speaking, the fisherman could pay a fee twice.
He could also probably do this from the physical and economic points
of view. It would, however, be morally objectionable to demand a
double fee of him. Cf. Eckhoff 1987, 276.

Collisions of _principles_ (cf. Alexy 1985, 78 ff.) are
connected with several difficult problems.

1. A _total_ logical incompatibility of _rules_ may be
ascertained analytically and _in abstracto_, without
considering particularities of the case; one rule
prohibits exactly the same as another one permits or
orders. (Concerning the distinction between total and
partial incompatibility, cf. Ross 1958, 128 ff.). On the
other hand, collision of principles occurs only in
particular cases. For example, an increase of freedom
leads in some _but not all_ cases to a decrease of
equality.

Yet, following _Aarnio_, one must play down this
difference. A _partial_ incompatibility of _rules_ also
depends on particular circumstances. Assume, e.g., that a
rule stipulates that shops must be open on Saturdays and
another rule demands that they must be closed on
religious holidays. Incompatibility occurs when a holiday
is on a Saturday. But the question whether any holiday is
on a Saturday or not cannot be answered by an abstract
analysis of the rules alone. One must know circumstances
of a particular case, exactly as when the question
concerns incompatibility of principles.

2. Following one principle only seldom totally excludes
following another. One may rather speak about _weighing
and balancing_: An increased degree of following of one
principle results in a decreased degree of following of
the other. Assume, e.g., that one principle demands
justice and another economic efficiency. In some
situations, increased justice results in decreased
efficiency and _vice versa_.

Yet, one should not think that weighing and balancing
occurs only when principles collide, not when rules
collide. Whenever one discovers a collision of
prima-facie rules one should set it aside, either by
reinterpreting (and thus reconciling, harmonising) these
rules, or by arranging a priority order between them, cf.
section 7.6.2 infra. The natural way to assure a

reconciliatory interpretation is to perform weighing and balancing of various considerations.

3. Still, when following one of the colliding prima-facie rules in the case under adjudication, one very often (though not always, see above) does not follow the other one. Paying attention to one principle has seldom such a result. In some situations, e.g., increased freedom results in decreased equality and vice versa, but one ought not to make decisions entirely disregarding either freedom or equality of the persons involved.

Yet, Aarnio has correctly pointed out that, in some cases, one of the colliding principles is to be entirely eliminated in the sense that, all things considered, it ought not to affect the decision of the case. The principle pacta sunt servanda, e.g., may be eliminated in this sense when one considers a case of an unreasonable contract and decides that it ought not to be followed at all (cf. the Swedish Contracts Acts, Sec. 36).

7.6.2. Collision Norms

When a non-jurist, e.g. a linguist, considers that two statutory rules are incompatible (logically, physically or evaluatively), he can describe this incompatibility and perhaps criticise it, but he cannot set it aside. Legal interpretation, on the other hand, has as one of its main purposes that of setting aside the incompatibilities and thus transforming the legal system into a perfectly consistent, more coherent and more D-rational one.

The following collision norms help the jurists to set aside collisions between legal norms.

C1) Whenever one discovers a collision of legal norms one should set it aside, either by reinterpreting (and thus reconciling, harmonising) these norms, or by arranging a priority order between them.

As regards principles, reinterpreting and harmonising is easier than arranging a priority order. One may thus try to understand, e.g., the principles of justice and economic efficiency in a way making it possible to simultaneously fulfil both these principles to a high degree. On the other hand, it would be difficult to justify a priority order demanding, for instance, that justice always goes before efficiency, fiat iustitia pereat mundus.

C2) Whenever one reinterprets or ranks norms which are colliding with each other, one should do so in a manner which one can repeatedly use when confronted with similar collisions between other norms. Strong reasons are required to justify a reinterpretation or a priority order applied <u>ad hoc</u>, i.e., only in the considered case.

This collision norm expresses an important criterion of coherence, that is, generality; cf. section 4.1.4 supra and Alexy´s rule J.8, section 4.3.4 supra.

C3) One should interpret different sources of the law, if possible, so that they are compatible. Interpretation of statutes, precedents, legislative preparatory materials etc. should thus affect each other (Aarbakke 1966, 499 ff.).

A reconciliation is thus often more important than arranging of priority orders. This is a consequence of the <u>prima-facie</u> character of socially established legal norms (cf. section 5.4.1 supra). <u>Prima-facie</u> reasons must be weighed and balanced.

C4) If strong reasons militate against such a reconciliation, the must-sources of the law have <u>prima facie</u> priority before the should-sources and these before the may-sources. If one abandons this priority in an individual case, one should justify one´s departure with strong reasons (cf. Alexy´s rule J.14; section 4.3.4 supra).

One must thus proffer strong reasons for, e.g., giving precedents priority before a clear statute. No reasons, on the other hand, are required to assign the latter a priority before the former.

C5) When a higher norm is incompatible with a norm of a lower standing, one must apply the higher.

Cf. sections 5.3.1 and 5.6.2 supra on the hierarchy of legal norms. Consider, e.g., the following hierarchy of Swedish legal norms: a) constitution; b) statutes; c) "other regulations" issued by the Government (on the basis of a parliamentary authorisation, as regards enforcement of a statute or as regards matters that, according to the Constitution, should not be regulated by the Parliament); d) "other regulations" issued by subordinate authorities on the basis of authorisation, given by the Government or by a statute; e) "other regulations" issued by the municipalities; cf. section 6.3.2 supra. This enumeration omits individual norms, such as judicial decisions.

A particular legal order must answer such questions as, What is the precise hierarchy of legal norms? What is the status of the

lower norm which collides with a higher one? Is it invalid ipso
iure; or can it be declared invalid if a given procedure is
followed; or is it inapplicable to the particular case under
consideration? What is the status of a particular decision which
follows the lower norm, not the higher one? Who has the power to
decide about consequences of violation of the collision norm C5?

A special question concerns the courts' competence to declare that
statutes incompatible with the constitution are invalid. This right
to review the material constitutionality of legislation exists, for
instance, in the United States [cf. the important case Marbury v.
Madison, (1803), I Cranch, (US Supreme Court Reports) 137] and to
some extent Federal Republic of Germany (Art. 100, Abs. 1 S. 1
Grundgesetz) but not in England or France.

In Sweden, Ch. 11 sec. 14 of the Regeringsformen provides that no
court or authority may apply in a concrete case a regulation
incompatible with the constitution. But if the parliament or the
government had issued the regulation, the court or the authority may
refuse to apply it only when the incompatibility is "obvious".

In Norway the right to review the material constitutionality of
legislation has not only been recognised to a large extent but also
been exercised in a number of cases from 1890 onwards and has been
expressly confirmed by the Supreme Court, cf., e.g., the case Rt
1918 I p. 401. In Denmark the right of review is recognised in
principle but exercised with such caution that, e.g., Alf Ross
(1958, 132) put in question its practical importance.

C6) Where an earlier norm is incompatible with a later
one, one must apply the later.

C7) One may apply a more general norm only in cases not
covered by an incompatible less general norm.

A person making a false income tax return is thus responsible only
for a tax offence, according to secs. 2-4 of the Tax Penal Act, but
not for fraud despite the fact that his action also fits Ch. 9 sec.
1 of the Criminal Code (concerning fraud).

Which norm is more general and which is less general? The
statute can explicitly answer this question through the
use of such words as "although", "unless", "apart from",
"in accordance with what is stated below", "to a wider
extent than", and similar expressions.

Sometimes the answer is obvious, even though no express
term in a statute indicates this, above all in the cases
where the area of application of one statute falls
entirely within that of another.

In this way the provision of Ch. 3 sec. 3 of the Criminal Code, concerning "a woman who kills her child at birth", is an exception from Ch. 3 sec. 1 dealing more severely with "anyone who deprives another person of his life".

But many cases are uncertain and then one must rely on weighing and balancing of various reasons.

Assume than an employer has deducted an amount from his employees' wages in order to pay tax. Assume that the employer's bankruptcy is impending. If he pays the amount to the tax-collection authorities, he can be punished for partiality against creditors, Ch. 11 sec. 4 of the Criminal Code. If he does not pay, he can be punished in accordance with sec. 81 of Tax Collection Ordinance. If the provision of the Ordinance is a "less general norm" in comparison with the provision of the Code, then he should pay but there are also reasons in favour of the opposite view (cf. the case reported in Svensk Juristtidning 1958, rf. 63).

C8) If a later general norm is incompatible with an earlier but less general norm, one must apply the earlier and less general norm.

The Bills of Exchange Act of 1932 is thus less general in relation to the Promisory Notes Act of 1936, since a bill is a kind of a promisory note. The former statute must thus be regarded as an exception from the latter.

The collision norm C7 is in this manner more important than the C6. But some reasons may support a reverse priority order.
   C9) If it is not possible to reconcile different precedents, one should determine which are the most important. In so determining, the following circumstances are relevant:
   a) The decisions of the Supreme Court have greater authority than those of lower courts.
   b) Among the Supreme Court´s decisions the most important are those reached in a plenary sitting.
   c) Old precedents, not confirmed by new ones, have as a rule less authority than do new precedents.
   d) The value of a precedent is diminished if the bench was divided or if the precedent has been criticised.

e) The authority of a precedent is increased if a strong need exists for a legal regulation in an area, e.g., not covered by sufficiently clear legislation.

f) Published cases have more authority than such which are not reported.

g) Cases fully reported in the NJA have more authority than cases summarily reported.

h) An established practice, based on several decisions, has greater importance than a single precedent.

C10) If it is not possible to reconcile different pronouncements in the travaux préparatoires, one should apply the following priority order: a) reports of relevant parliamentary commissions; b) pronouncements of the responsible minister; c) other materials.

However, incompatibility results in a decrease of the authority of all the incompatible parts of the travaux préparatoires. A pronouncement in the preparatory materials has thus the relatively greatest authority if not questioned by other pronouncements.

C11) If possible, one must harmonise the results of the use of different interpretatory methods. Whenever the use of different methods of statutory construction in a given situation results in incompatibility, one should set it aside by reinterpreting the provision in question.

The collision norms have the same character as other reasoning norms. They do not entirely solve "hard" cases. The practice of their application differs from one part of the legal order to another. They have a prima-facie character: one can disregard them if important reasons for doing so exist. Yet they increase coherence and thus rationality of statutory interpretation. They thus constitute additional reasonable premises, necessary to convert juristic jumps to logically correct inferences. They also constitute a kind of customary law or at least express established moral judgments. Moreover, they are connected with the very meaning of such words as "legal reasoning"; if one refutes a great number of them, one´s reasoning is no longer "legal"; cf. sec. 7.1.2 supra. And, let me repeat, they help the interpreter to transform the legal system into a perfectly consistent, more coherent and more D-rational one.

Bibliography

including only works referred to by the author's name and the year

Aarbakke, M. 1966. Harmonisering av rettskilder. Tidskrift for Rettsvitenskap.

Aarnio, Aulis. 1977. On Legal Reasoning. Turku: University Press.

----- 1979. Denkweisen der Rechtswissenschaft. Wien - New York: Springer.

----- 1979b. Linguistic Philosophy and Legal Theory. Rechtstheorie Beiheft 1.

----- 1984. Paradigms in Legal Dogmatics. In: A. Peczenik, L. Lindahl and B. van Roermund (eds.), Theory of Legal Science. Dordrecht/ Boston/ Lancaster: Reidel.

----- 1987. The Rational as Reasonable. Dordrecht/ Boston/ Lancaster/ Tokyo: Reidel.

Aarnio, Alexy and Peczenik. 1981. The Foundation of Legal Reasoning. Rechtstheorie.

Aarnio and Peczenik. 1986. Beyond the Reality. A Criticism of Alf Ross' Reconstruction of Legal Dogmatics. In: A. Peczenik, ed., Meaning, Interpretation and the Law. Tampere: Tieto.

Alchourrón, Carlos and Bulygin, Eugenio. 1971. Normative Systems. Wien - New York: Springer.

----- 1981. The Expressive Conception of Norms. In: R. Hilpinen, ed., New Studies in Deontic Logic. Dordrecht: Reidel.

Agge, Ivar. 1969. Huvudpunkter av den allmänna rättsläran. Stockholm: Juridiska föreningens förlag.

Ailinpieti, Folke. 1980. Tio exempel på lagstiftning genom förarbeten. Lund (unpublished Master thesis).

Alexy, Robert. 1978. Theorie der juristischen Argumentation, Frankfurt a. M.: Suhrkamp.

----- 1980. Die logische Analyse juristischer Entscheidungen. ARSP Beiheft Neue Folge 14.

----- 1985. Theorie der Grundrechte. Baden-Baden: Nomos (Frankfurt/M. 1986: Suhrkamp).

----- 1985b. Rechtsregeln und Rechtsprinzipien. ARSP Beiheft 25.

----- 1986. Individuelle Rechte und Kollektive Güter, a lecture given at the Nordic seminar on individual rights, Frostavallen, August 1986.

----- 1987. Argumentation, Argumentationstheorie. In Ergänzbares Lexikon des Rechts. Neuwied: Luchterhand. 26-2/30.

----- 1988. Problems of Discourse Theory. Critica.

----- 1989. Theory of Legal Argumentation. Oxford: Clarendon Press. Translation of Alexy 1978.

---- and Peczenik, Aleksander. 1989. The Concept of Coherence and its Significance for Discursive Rationality. In press, Ratio Iuris.

426

Andersson, Jan and Furberg, Mats. 1984. Språk och påverkan. 8 ed. Lund: Doxa.

Anscombe, G.E.M. 1958. On Brute Facts. Analysis 18.

Apel, Karl-Otto. 1976. Der philosophische Wahrheitsbegriff. In: Transformation der Philosophie. Band 1. Sprachanalytik, Semiotik, Hermeneutik. Frankfurt a. M.: Suhrkamp.

----- 1976a. Sprache und Wahrheit. In id.

----- 1976b. Das Apriori Kommunikationsgemeinschaft und die Grundlagen der Ethik. In: Transformation der Philosophie. Band 2. Das Apriori der Kommunikationsgemeinschaft. Frankfurt a. M.: Suhrkamp.

----- 1986. Kann der postkantische Standpunkt der Moralität noch einmal in substantielle Sittlichkeit "aufgehoben" werden?. In W. Kuhlmann (ed.), Moralität und Sittlichkeit. Frankfurt a. M.: Suhrkamp.

Anckar, Dag. 1985. Demokrati och rättssäkerhet. In: T. Segerstedt, Rättssäkerhet och demokrati, Stockholm: Ratio.

Aristotle. 1891. The Nicomachean Ethics. Book II. Transl. by F. H. Peters. London: Kegan Paul.

Austin, J.L. 1962. How to do Things with Words. Oxford: Clarendon Press.

Bay, Christian. 1968. Når lov må brytes. Oslo: Pax.

Beckman, N., Holmberg, C., Hult, B. and Strahl, I. 1970. Kommentar till brottsbalken 1. 3 ed. Stockholm: Norstedts

Bengtsson, Bertil. 1969. Om äktenskapsliknande samliv. In: Festskrift till Arnholm. Oslo.

Bergholtz, Gunnar. 1987. Ratio et Auctoritas. Ett komparativrättsligt bidrag till frågan om domsmotiveringens betydelse främst i tvismetål. Lund: Juridiska föreningen.

Bernitz, Ulf. 1984. För korta utredningar. Affärsrätt 1.

Bernitz, U., Heuman, L., Löfmarck, M., Ragnemalm, H., Roos, C. M., Seipel, P. and Victorin, A. 1985. Finna rätt. Juristens källmaterial och arbetsmetoder. Stockholm: Juristförlaget.

Bjarup, Jes. 1980. Reason and Passion. A Basic Theme in Hägerström's Legal Philosophy. Rechtstheorie 11.

Black, Max. 1977. The Objectivity of science. Bulletin of the Atomic Scientists. February.

----- 1978. Lebensform and Sprachspiel in Wittgenstein's Later Works. In: Wittgenstein and His Impact on Contemporary Thought. Proceedings of the Second Wittgenstein Symposium. Vienna.

----- 1980. Language-games with "Language-game". Dialectica.

Bodenheimer, Edgar. 1969. A Neglected Theory of Legal Reasoning. Journal of Legal Education 21.

Braithwaite, Richard B. 1960. Scientific Explanation. New York: Harper.

Browne, D. E. 1976. The Contract Theory of Justice. Philosophical Papers 5.

Bunge, Mario. 1974. Treatise on Basic Philosophy. II: Semantics II: Interpretation and Truth. Dordrecht - Boston: Reidel.

----- 1977. Treatise on Basic Philosophy. III: Ontology I: The Furniture of the World. Dordrecht - Boston Reidel.

----- 1981. Scientific Materialism. Dordrecht - Boston - London: Reidel.

Burks, Arthur W. 1977. Chance, Cause, Reason. Chicago - London: University Press.

Calabresi, Guido. 1970. The Costs of Accidents. New Haven.

Castaneda, Hector-Neri. 1975. Thinking and Doing. Dordrecht - Boston: Reidel.

----- 1980. On Philosophical Method. Indianapolis: Nous Publications.

Chisholm, R.M. 1957. Perceiving. Ithaca.

------ 1966. Theory of Knowledge. Englewood Cliffs: Prentice-Hall.

Chomsky, Noam. 1967. Recent Contributions to the Theory of Innate Ideas. In: R.S. Cohen and M.W. Wartofsky (edd.), Boston Studies in the Philosophy of Science. Vol. 3. Dordrecht: Reidel.

----- 1970. Sprache und Geist. Frankfurt a. M.

Conte, Amadeo Giovanni. 1981. Konstitutive Regeln und Deontik. In: E. Morscher and R. Stranzinger, edd., Ethik. Grundlagen, Probleme und Anwendungen. Akten des 5. Internationalen Wittgenstein-Symposiums. Wien: Hölder - Pichler - Tempsky.

Dalberg-Larsen. Jörgen. 1977. Retsvidenskaben som samfundsvidenskab Copenhagen: Juristforbundets forlag.

Dias, R.W.M. 1976. Jurisprudence. 4th ed. London: Butterworths.

Dreier, Ralf. 1981. Recht und Moral. In: Recht - Moral - Ideologie. Frankfurt a. M.: Suhrkamp.

----- 1982. Bemerkungen zur Theorie der Grundnorm. In: Die Reine Rechtslehre in wissenschaftlicher Diskussion. Wien: Manz Verlag.

Dworkin, Ronald. 1977. Taking Rights Seriously. Cambridge, Mass.: Harvard University Press.

----- 1986. Laws' Empire. London: Fontana.

Eckhardus, Ch.H. 1750. Hermeneuticae juris libri duo.... Jena.

Eckhoff, Torstein. 1969. Litt om det juridiske rettighetsspråk. In: Festskrift til Alf Ross. Copenhagen.

----- 1971. Rettfaerdighet. Oslo - Bergen - Tromsö: Universitetsforlaget.

----- 1980. Retningslinjer og "tumregler", Tidskrift for Rettsvitenskap.

----- 1987. Rettskildelaere. 2 ed. Tano.

---- and Sundby, Nils Kristian. 1976. Rettssystemer. Oslo: Tanum-Norli.

Eikema Hommes, Hendrik van. 1982. Rechtsstaat und das Prinzip der Repräsentation, Rechtstheorie.

Ekelöf, Per Olof. 1951. Är den juridiska doktrinen en teknik eller en vetenskap. Lund.

----- 1952. Är termen rättighet ett syntaktiskt hjälpmedel utan mening? Svensk juristtidning.

----- 1956. Processuella grundbegrepp och allmänna processprinciper. Stockholm.

----- 1958. Teleological Construction of Statutes. Scandinavian Studies in Law 2.

----- 1982. Rättegång vol. 4. 5 ed. Stockholm: Norstedts

Encyclopedia of Philosophy. P. Edwards (ed.). 1967. New York: Macmillan.

Engisch, Karl. 1968. Einführung in das juristische Denken. 4th ed. Stuttgart - Berlin - Köln - Mainz: Kohlhammer Verlag.

Esser, Josef. 1964. Grundsatz und Norm in der richterlichen Fortbildung des Privatrechts. 2 ed. Tübingen.

----- 1972. Vorverständnis und Methodenwahl in der Rechtsfindung. 2 ed. Frankfurt a. M.

Evers, Jan. 1970. Argumentationsanalys för jurister. Lund. Gleerups.

Feigl, Herbert. 1962. Some Major Issues and Developments in the Philosophy of Science of Logical Empiricism. In: Minnesota Studies in the Philosophy of Science. Vol. 1. Minneapolis: University Press.

Feinberg, Joel. 1975. Rawls and Intuitionism. In: N. Daniels, ed. Reading Rawls. Oxford.

----- 1980. Rights, Justice and the Bounds of Liberty, Princeton: University Press.

Finnis, John. 1980. Natural Law and Natural Rights. Oxford: Clarendon Press.

Friedrich, C.J. 1963. Justice: The Just Political Act. Nomos 6. New York: Atherton.

Frändberg, Åke. 1973. Om analog användning av rättsnormer. Stockholm: Norstedts.

----- 1982. Some Reflections of Legal Security. In: Philosophical Essays Dedicated to Lennart Aqvist. Uppsala: Philos. Society.

----- 1984. Rättsregel och rättsval. Stockholm: Norstedts.

Fuller, Lon. 1946. Reason and Fiat in Case Law. Harvard Law Review.

----- 1968. Anatomy of the Law. Midlesex.

Gärdenfors, Peter. 1980. Teoretiska begrepp och deras funktion. In: B. Hansson (ed.), Metod eller anarki. Lund: Doxa.

Goodman, Nelson. 1967. The Epistemological Argument. In: R.S. Cohen and M.W. Wartofsky (edd.), Boston Studies in the Philosophy of Science. Vol. 3. Dordrecht: Reidel.

----- 1978. Ways of Worldmaking. Sussex: Harvester.

Habermas, Jürgen. 1973. Wahrheitstheorien. In: Wirklichkeit und Reflexion. Walter Schultz zum 60. Geburtstag, Pfullingen: Neske.

Hafström, Gerhard. 1969. De svenska rättskällornas historia. Lund: Juridiska föreningen.

Hägerström, Axel. 1908. Das Prinzip der Wissenschaft. Eine logisch-erkenntnistheoretische Untersuchung. I: Die Realität. Uppsala-Leipzig.

----- 1929. Selbstdarstellung. In: R. Schmidt (ed.), Die Philosophie der Gegenwart in Selbstdarstellungen. Vol. 7. Leipzig.

----- 1953. Inquiries into the Nature of Law and Morals. Stockholm: Almqvist & Wiksell.

----- 1964. Philosophy and Religion. London.

Hall, Jerome. 1947. Integrative Jurisprudence. In: Interpretation of Modern Legal Philosophies. Essays in Honour of Roscoe Pound. New York.

----- Foundations of Jurisprudence. Indianapolis.

Hare, R. M. 1952. The Language of Morals. Oxford: University Press.

----- 1972/73. Principles. Proceedings of the Aristotelian Society.

----- 1973. Ralws's Theory of Justice. Philosophical Quarterly 23.

----- 1981. Moral Thinking, Oxford: University Press.

Harris, J. W. 1979. Law and Legal Science. Oxford: Clarendon Press.

Hart, H. L. A. 1961. The Concept of Law. Oxford: Clarendon Press.

Hart, Henry M. Jr. and Sacks, Albert. 1958. The Legal Process. Tentative edition. Cambridge, Mass.

Hanson, Norwood R. 1958. Patterns of Discovery. Cambridge: University Press

Hayek, Friedrich A. 1944. The Road to Serfdom. Chicago: University Press.

Heckscher, Gunnar. 1982. Demokratins begrepp och innehåll. In: G. Bohman et el., Demokratins villkor, Stockholm: Svensk tidskrift förlags AB.

Hedenius, Ingemar. 1975. Analysen av äganderättsbegrepp. In: B. Belfrage and L. Stille, edd., Filosofi och rättsvetenskap. Lund: Doxa.

Hegel, Georg W. F. 1970. Phänomenologie des Geistes. Theorie Werkausgabe, Bd. 3. Frankfurt/M: Suhrkamp.

Heller, T. 1961. Logik und Axiologie der analogen Rechtsanswedung. Berlin.

Hellner, Jan. 1967. Köprätt. Stockholm.

----- 1969. Analys av lagtext med hjälp av datamaskin. In: Festskrift till Arnholm. Oslo.

----- 1972. Värderingar i skadeståndsrätten. In : Festskrift till Ekelöf. Stockholm: Norstedt.

----- 1972b. Skadeståndsrätt. 3 ed. Stockholm: Almqvist & Wiksell.

----- 1982. Speciell avtalsrätt I. Köprätt. Stockholm: Juristförlaget.

----- 1985. Skadeståndsrätt. 4th ed. Stockholm: Juristförlaget.

----- 1988. Rättsteori. Stockholm: Juristförlaget.

Hempel, Carl G. 1958. The Theoretician's Dilemma. In: Minnesota Studies in the Philosophy of Science. Vol. 2. Minneapolis: University Press.

---- 1962. Deductive-Nomological vs. Statistical Explanation. In: Minnesota Studies in the Philosophy of Science. Vol. 3. Minneapolis: University Press.

Hermerén, Göran. 1973. Kunskapens utveckling. Insikt och handling.

Hessler, N. 1970. Nya jordabalken (Kap 16 och 18. Uppsala.

Höffe, O. 1977. Zur Rolle der Entscheidungstheorie bei der Rechtfertigung von Gerechtigkeitsprinzipien - kritische Überlegungen im Anschluss an Rawls. Erkenntnis 11.

Hudson, W. D. 1984. The 'Is-Ought' Problem Resolved?. In: Edward Regis Jr. Gewirth's Ethical Rationalism, Critical Essays with a Reply of Alan Gewirth. Chicago.

Hughes, Graham. 1968. Rules, Policy and Decision Making. Yale Law Journal 77.

Hult, Phillips. 1952. Lagens bokstav och lagens andemening. Svensk juristtidning. Quoted from reprint in Studiematerial i allmän rättslära. Stockholm 1971: Juridiska föreningen.

Jareborg, Nils. 1975. Värderingar. Stockholm: Norstedts.

Jörgensen, Stig. 1970. Law and Society. Akademisk boghandel. Translation of: Ret og samfund. Copenhagen: Berlingske Leksikon Bibliotek.

Kant, Immanuel. 1983. Kritik der Reinen Vernunft. Darmstadt. Werke, Bd. 3: Wissenschaftliche Buchgesellschaft.

Katz, Jerrold J. 1966. The Philosophy of Language. New York - London: Harper & Row.

Kekes, J. 1979. The Centrality of Problem-Solving. Inquiry 22.

Kelsen, Hans. 1928. Die Philosophischen Grundlagen der Naturrechtslehre und des Rechtspositivismus. In: H. Klecatsky, R. Marcic, H. Schambeck, edd., Die Wiener rechtstheorietische Schule. Frankfurt - Zürich - Salzburg - München 1968: Europa Verlag, Universitätsverlag, Anton Pustet.

----- 1929. Vom Wesen und Wert der Demokratie, 2nd ed., Tübingen. Reprinted 1981. Aalen: Scientia Verlag.

----- 1934. Reine Rechtslehre. 1st ed. Wien.

----- 1945. The General Theory of Law and State: New York.

----- 1951. Was ist ein Rechtsakt?. In: Wiener...

----- 1958. Der Begriff der Rechtsordnung. In: Wiener...

----- 1960. Reine Rechtslehre. 2nd ed. Wien: Deuticke.

----- 1960b. Vom Geltung des Rechts. In: Wiener...

----- 1961. Naturrechtslehre und Rechtspositivismus. In: Wiener...

----- 1964. Die Funktion der Verfassung. In: Wiener...

----- 1979. Allgemeine Theorie der Normen. Wien: Manz.

Kemp, John. 1968. The Philosophy of Kant. Oxford: University Press. Paperback ed. 1979.

Kenny, Anthony. 1975. Wittgenstein. Harmondsworth: Penguin Books.

Klami, Hannu T. 1980. Anti-Legalism. Turku: Turun Yliopisto.

----- Gewohnheitsrecht als Rechtsquelle. Turku: Turun Yliopisto.

Koertge, Noretta. 1978: Towards a New Theory of Scientific Inquiry. In: G. Radnitzky and G. Andersson, edd., Progress and Rationality in Science. Dordrecht - London: Reidel.

Korte, Kai: 1984. Om nordiskt lagsamarbete. Svensk juristtidning.

Kriele, Martin. 1979. Recht und praktische Vernunft. Göttingen: Vandenhoeck & Ruprecht.

Kuhlmann, Wolfgang. 1985. Reflexive Letztbegründung. Untersuchungen zur Transzendentalpragmatik. Freiburg/ München.

Kuhn, Thomas S. 1970. The Structure of Scientific Revolutions. 2nd ed. Chicago: University Press.

----- 1979. The Essential Tension. Chicago: University Press.

Koch, Hans-Joachim. 1977. Über juristisch-dogmatischen Argumentieren im Staatsrecht. In: H.-J. Koch (ed.), Seminar: Die juristische Methode im Staatsrecht. Frankfurt a. M.

----- and Rüssmann, Helmut. 1982. Juristische Begründungslehre. München: C.H. Beck'sche Verlagsbuchhandlung.

Kutschera, Franz von. 1972. Wissenschaftstheorie. München: Wilhelm Fink Verlag.

Laakso, Seppo. 1980. Übe die Dreidimensionalität des Rechts und des juristischen Denkens. Tampere: Tampereen Yliopisto.

Lachmayer, Friedrich. 1977. Die Geltungsneutralität der Grundnorm. Österreichische Zeitschrift für öffentliches Recht und Völkerrecht 28.

Lakatos, Imre. 1970. Falsification and the Methodology of Scientific Research Programmes. In Criticism and the Growth of Knowledge. In I. Lakatos and A. Musgrave, edd. Cambridge: University Press.

Lande, Jerzy. 1959. Studia z filozofii prawa. Warsaw: PWN.

Lang, Wieslaw. 1962. Obowiazywanie prawa. Warsaw: PWN.

-----, Wróblewski, Jerzy and Zawadzki, Sylwester. 1979. Teoria panstwa i prawa. Warsaw: PWN.

Larenz, Karl. 1983. Methodenlehre der Rechtswissenschaft. 5 ed. Berlin - Heidelberg - New York - Tokyo: Springer.

Lehrer, Keith. 1974. Knowledge. Oxford: Clarendon Press.

Levin, M. 1984. Negative Liberty. Social Philosophy and Policy 2,I.

Lindahl, Lars. 1977. Position and Change, Dordrecht: Reidel.

Ljungman, S. 1971. Industriell rättsskydd. Stockholm.

Lorenz, Konrad. 1973. Die Rückseite des Spiegels. Versuch einer Naturgeschichte menschlichen Erkenntnis. Munich.

Lucas, J. R. 1980. On Justice. Oxford: Clarendon Press.

MacCormick, Neil. 1978. Legal Reasoning and Legal Theory. Oxford: Clarendon Law Series.

----- 1981. H.L.A. Hart. London: Edward Arnold.

----- 1984. Coherence in Legal Justification. In Theory of Legal Science. Ed. A. Peczenik, L. Lindahl and B. v. Roermund. Dordrecht/ Boston/ Lancaster: Reidel.

───── and Weinberger, Ota. 1985. Grundlagen des
  institutionalistischen Rechtspositivismus. Berlin: Duncker &
  Humblott.

───── and Weinberger, Ota. 1986. An Institutional Theory of Law.
  Dordrecht: Reidel.

MacIntyre, Alasdair. After Virtue. A Study in Moral Theory. London:
  Duckworth.

Mackie, John L. 1977. Ethics. Inventing Right and Wrong.
  Harmondsworth: Penguin.

───── 1977b. The Third Theory of Law, Phil. & Pub. Affairs 7.

Makkonen, Kaarle. 1965. Zur Problematik der juridischen
  Entscheidung. Turku: Turun Yliopisto.

Marantz, H. 1979. Can the Obligation People Have to Obey the Law be
  Justified? IVR World Congress. Basel. Paper No. 097.

Marc-Wogau, Konrad. 1968. Studier till Axel Hägerströms filosofi.
  Falköping: Prisma.

───── 1970. Filosofin genom tiderna. Stockholm: Bonniers.

Marcic, René. 1963. Das Naturrecht als Grundnorm der Verfassung.
  Zeitschrift für öffenliches Recht Neue Folge 13.

Martin, Rex. 1986. On the Justification of Rights. In: G. Flöistad
  (ed.), Contemporary Philosophy, vol. 3. Dordrecht - Boston -
  Lancaster: Reidel.

Mattsson, Mats. 1981. Staffan Westerlund och rättssäkerheten. Svensk
  Juristtidning.

───── 1983. The Rule of Law in Legal Reasoning. In: A. Peczenik, L.
  Lindahl and B. van Roermund (eds.), Theory of Legal Science.
  Dordrecht/ Boston/ Lancaster: Reidel.

Mautner, Thomas. 1979. Kant's Relation to the Natural Law Tradition.
  IVR World Congress. Basel.

Merkl, Adolf. 1968. Justizirrtum und Rechtswahrheit (1 ed. 1925).
  In: H. Klecatsky, R. Marcic, H. Schambeck, edd., Die Wiener
  rechtstheorietische Schule. Frankfurt - Zürich - Salzburg -
  München 1968: Europa Verlag, Universitätsverlag, Anton Pustet.

Moore, Georg Edward. 1959. Principia Ethica. Cambridge: University
  Press (1st publ. 1903)

Moore, M. 1981. The Semantics of Judging. Southern California Law
  Review.

Morawetz, Thomas. 1980. Philosophy of Law. New York - London:
  Macmillan.

Moritz, Manfred. Der praktische Syllogismus und das juristische
  Denken. Theoria XX.

───── 1970. Inledning i värdeteori. 2 ed. Lund:
  Studentlitteratur.

Mulligan, K., Simons, P. and Smith, B. Wahrmacher. In: L. B. Puntel
  (ed.) Der Wahrheitsbegriff. Darmstadt: Wissenschaftliche
  Buchgesellschaft.

Naess, Arne. 1981. Empirisk semantik. Uppsala: Esselte.

Nordin, Ingemar. 1980. Teknologi, vetenskap and ad-hoc hypotheser.
  In: B. Hansson (ed.), Metod eller anarki. Lund: Doxa.

Nowacki, Józef. 1966. Analogia legis. Warsaw: PWN.

Nowell-Smith, P.H. 1973. A Theory of Justice? Philosophy of the Social Sciences.

Nozick, Robert. 1974. Anarchy, State and Utopia. New York: Basic Books.

Oakeshott, Michael. 1983. The Rule of Law. In: On History. Oxford: Blackwell.

Ofstad, Harald. 1980. Ansvar og handling. Oslo - Bergen - Tromsö.

Olivecrona, Karl. 1939. Law ad Fact. 1st ed. Copenhagen: Munksgaard and London: Milford, Oxford University Press.

----- 1959. The Legal Theories of Axel Hägerström and Vilhelm Lundstedt. Scandinavian Studies in Law 3.

----- 1969. The Concept of Right According to Grotius and Pufendorf. In: Festschrift für Germann. Bern.

----- 1971. Law ad Fact. 2nd ed. London: Stevens.

----- 1973. Das Meinige nach der Naturrechtslehre. ARSP LIX.

----- 1977. Die zwei Schichten im Naturrechtlichen Denken. ARSP LXIII.

Opalek, Kazimierz. 1957. Prawo podmiotowe, Warsaw: PWN.

----- 1964. The Rule of Law and Natural Law. In: Festskrift till Olivecrona. Stockholm: Norstedts.

----- 1970. The Problem of the Existence of the Norm. In: Festschrift für Adolf J. Merkl. München - Salzburg.

----- 1973. Directives, Optatives and Value Statements. Logique et Analyse XIII, 49-50.

----- 1974. Z teorii dyrektyw i norm. Warsaw: PWN.

----- and Wróblewski, Jerzy. 1969. Zagadnienia teorii prawa. Warsaw: PWN.

----- and Zakrzewski. 1958. Z zagadnien praworzadnosci socjalistycznej. Warsaw: Wydawnictwo Prawnicze.

Openheim, Paul and Putnam, Hilary, Unity of Science as a Working Hypothesis. In: Minnesota Studies in the Philosophy of Science. Vol. 2. Minneapolis: University Press.

Pålsson, Lennart. 1986. Svensk rättspraxis i internationell familje- och arvsrätt. Stockholm: Norstedts.

Patzig, Günther. 1976. Immanuel Kant: Wie sind synthetische Urteile a priori möglich?. In: Joseph Speck (ed.), Grundprobleme der Grossen Philosophen der Neuzeit II. Göttingen.

----- 1980. Tatsachen, Normen, Sätze. Stuttgart: Reclam.

Paulson. Stanley. 1980. Material and Formal Authorization in Kelsen's Pure Theory. Cambridge Law Journal 39.

Peczenik, Aleksander. 1962. Wykladnia a fortiori. Zeszyty naukowe Uniwersytetu Jagiellonskiego. Prawo 9.

----- 1966. Wartosc naukowa dogmatyki prawa. Cracow: University Press.

----- 1967. Doctrinal Study of Law and Science. Österreichische Zeitschrift für öffentliches Recht 17.

----- 1968. Norms and Reality. Theoria.

----- 1968b. Struktura normy prawnej. Studia prawnicze.

----- 1968c. Juristic Definition of Law. Ethics 78.

----- 1969. Empirical Foundations of Legal Dogmatics. Logique et Analyse XII, 45.

----- 1969b. The Concept of Rights. Archivum Iuridicum Cracoviense II.

----- 1970. Essays in Legal Theory. Copenhagen: New Social Science Monographs.

----- 1971. Analogia legis. Analogy from Statutes in Continental Law. Proceedings of the World Congress for Legal and Social Philosophy. Brussels.

----- 1972. Om rättvisa. Tidskrift for Rettsvitenskap.

----- 1974. Juridikens metodproblem. Stockholm: Almqvist & Wiksell.

----- 1979. Causes and Damages. Lund: Juridiska föreningen.

----- 1981. On the Nature and Function of the Grundnorm. Rechtstheorie Beiheft 2. Berlin.

----- 1982. Two Sides of the Grundnorm. Die Reine Rechtslehre in wissenschaftlicher Diskussion. Wien: Manz Verlag.

----- 1983. The Basis of Legal Justification. Lund: University Press.

----- 1984. Legal Data. An Essay About the Ontology of Law. In: Theory of Legal Science. Ed. A. Peczenik, L. Lindahl and B. v. Roermund. Dordrecht/ Boston/ Lancaster: Reidel.

----- 1985. Moral and Ontological Justification of Legal Reasoning. Law and Philosophy Vol. 4 No. 2.

----- 1988. Rätten och förnuftet. 2nd ed. Stockholm: Norstedt.

----- 1988b. Legal Reasoning as a Special Case of Moral Reasoning. Ratio Juris.

---- and Spector, Horacio. 1987. A Theory of Moral Ought-Sentences, ARSP.

----- and Wróblewski, Jerzy. 1985. Fuzziness and Transformation. Towards Explaining Legal Reasoning. Theoria.

Petrazycki, Leon. 1892. Die Fruchtverteilung beim Wechsel der Nutzungsberechtigten. Berlin: Verlag H.W. Müller.

----- 1959-1960. Theoria prawa i panstwa w zwiazku z teoria moralnosci. Warsaw: PWN. The first Russian edition of the book appeared in 1909.

Pettit,Philip. Judging Justice. London, Boston and Henley: Routledge & Kegan Paul.

Popper, Karl R. 1959. The Logic of Scietific Discovery. New York: Basic Books.

----- 1966. The Open Society and Its Enemies. 5 ed. London: Routledge & Kegan Paul.

----- 1972. Objective Knowledge. Oxford: Clarendon Press.

Prawitz, Dag. 1978. Om moraliska och logiska satsers sanning. In: L. Bergström, H. Ofstad and D. Prawitz (edd.), En filosofibok tillägnadAnders Wedberg. Stockholm.

Puntel, L. Bruno. 1978. Wahrheitstheorien in der neueren Philosophie. Darmstadt: Wissenschaftliche Buchgesellschaft.

Putnam, Hilary. 1967. The 'Innateness Hypothesis' and Explanatory Models in Linguistics. In: R.S. Cohen and M.W. Wartofsky (edd.), Boston Studies in the Philosophy of Science. Vol. 3. Dordrecht: Reidel.

Quine, Willard Van Orman. 1953. From a Logical Point of View. Cambridge, Mass.: Harvard University Press.

----- 1960. Word and Object. Cambridge, Mass.: Technology Press of MIT and Wiley.

----- 1961. Methods of Logic. Revised ed. New York: Holt, Rinehart and Winston.

----- 1969. Ontological Relativity and Other Essays. New York: Columbia University Press.

Radbruch, Gustav. 1950. Rechtsphilosophie. Stuttgart: Koehler Verlag.

Rawls, John. 1971. A Theory of Justice. Oxford: University Press.

----- 1980. Kantian Constructivism in Moral Theory. Journal of Philosophy 67.

Raz, Joseph. 1970. The Concept of Legal System. Oxford: University Press.

----- 1974. Kelsen's Theory of the Basic Norm. American Journal of Jurisprudence 19.

----- 1979. The Authority of Law. Oxford: Clarendon Press.

----- 1982. The Problem About the Nature of Law. In: G. Flöistad (ed.), Contemporary Philosophy, vol. 3. Dordrecht - Boston - Lancaster: Reidel.

Reale, Miguel. 1962. Filosofia do Direito. Sao Paulo.

Recaséns Siches, L. 1959. Tratado General de Filosofia del Derecho. Mexico.

Reichenbach, Hans. 1940. On the Justification of Induction. Journal of Philosophy 37.

----- 1949. The Theory of Probability. Berkeley.

Rentto, Juha-Pekka. Prudentia Iuris. The Art of the Good and the Just. Turku: Turun Yliopisto.

Rescher, Nicholas. 1966. Distributive Justice. Indianapolis - New York - Kansas City: Bobbs-Merrill.

----- 1973. Coherence Theory of Truth. Oxford: University Press.

----- 1977. Methodological Pragmatism. Oxford: Blackwell.

----- 1985. Truth as Ideal Coherence, 38 Review of Metaphysics 38: 795-806. German translation: Wahrheit als Ideale Koharenz. In: L. B. Puntel (ed.) Der Wahrheitsbegriff. Darmstadt: Wissenschaftliche Buchgesellschaft.

Rodhe, Knut. 1944. Gränsbestämning och äganderättstvist. Lund.

----- 1971. Allmän privaträtt - avtalsrätt - obligationsrätt. Svensk Juristtidning.

Rödig, Jürgen. 1973. Die Theorie des gerichtlichen Erkenntnisverfahrens. Berlin - Heidelberg - New York: Springer.

Ross, Alf. 1929. Theorie der Rechtsquellen. Leipzig - Wien: Deuticke.

----- 1958. On Law and Justice, London: Stevens.

----- 1963. Varför demokrati?. Stockholm: Kronos.

----- 1966. Om ret og retfaerdighed. 2nd ed. Copenhagen.

----- 1968. Directives and Norms. London: Routledge & Kegan Paul.

Ross, W. D. 1930. The Right and the Good. Oxford: Clarendon Press.

Rottleuthner, Hubert. 1980. Zur Methode einer Folgenorientierten Rechtsanwendung. ARSP Beiheft Neue Folge 13.

----- 1981. Rechtstheorie und Rechtssoziologie. Freiburg - München: Alber.

Savigny, Friedrich Carl von. 1814. Vom Beruf unsrer Zeit für Gesetzgebung und Rechtswissenschaft. Heidelberg: Mohr und Zimmer.

----- System des heutigen römischen Rechts. Vol. 1. Berlin.

Schmidt, Folke. 1955. Domaren som lagtolkare. In: Festskrift till Herlitz. Quoted from reprint in Studiematerial i allmän rättslära. Stockholm 1971: Juridiska föreningen.

----- 1957. Construction of Statutes. Scandinavian Studies in Law 1.

----- 1960. Model, Intention, Fault. Three Canons for Interpretation of Contract. Scandinavian Studies in Law 4.

----- 1976. Facklig arbetsrätt. Stockholm: Norstedt.

Schweitzer, O. 1959. Freie richterliche Rechtsfindung als Methodenproblem. Basel.

Searle, J.R. 1969. Speech Acts. Cambridge.

Sethna, M.J. 1962. Nature, Scope and Fruits of Synthetic Jurisprudence. In: Sethna, M.J., ed. Contributions to Synthetic Jurisprudence. Bombay.

Simmonds, N. E. 1986. Central Issues in Jurisprudence. Justice, Law and Rights. London: Sweet & Maxwell.

Simpson, A.W.B. 1961. The Ratio Decidendi of a Case and the Doctrine of Binding Precedent. In: A.G. Guest, ed., Oxford Essays in Jurisprudence. Oxford: Clarendon Press.

----- 1977. The Common Law and Legal Theory. In: A.W.B. Simpson, ed., Oxford Essays in Jurisprudence. Second Series. Oxford: Clarendon Press.

Singer, Peter. 1974. Democracy and Disobedience, Oxford, New York and London: Oxford University Press.

Sintonen, Matti. 1986. Subjectivity and Theory Choice. Philosophy of Science Association 1.

Spranger, E. 1950. Lebensformen. 8 ed.

Stegmüller, Wolfgang. 1975. Der sogenannte Zirkel des Verstehens. Darmstadt: Wissenschaftliche Buchgesellschaft.

Stening, Anders. 1975. Bevisvärde. Uppsala.

Stevenson, Charles L. 1944. Ethics and Language. New Haven: Yale
   University Press.

Stone, Julius. 1965. Human Law and Human Justice. Sydney: Maitland.

Strawson, P. F. 1964. Truth. In: G. Pitcher (ed.), Truth, Englewood
   Cliffs.

---- 1966. The Bounds of Sence. London: Methuen.

Strömberg, Tore. 1980. Inledning till den allmänna rättsläran. 8th
   ed. Lund: Studentlitteratur.

----- 1981. Rättsfilosofins historia i huvuddrag. Lund:
   Studentlitteratur.

Strömholm, Stig. 1966. Legislative Material and Construction of
   Statutes. Scandinavian Studies in Law 10.

----- 1988. Rätt, rättskällor och rättstillämpning. 3 ed. Stockholm:
   Norstedts.

Summers. Robert S. 1978. Two Types of Substantive Reasons: The Core
   of a Theory of Common-Law Justification. Cornell Law Review 66.

----- 1982. Instrumentalism and American Legal Theory. Ithaca and
   London: Cornell University Press.

----- 1985. Toward a Better General Theory of Legal Validity.
   Rechtstheorie 16.

Sundby, Nils Kristian. 1974. Om normer. Oslo: Universitetsforlaget.

Sundberg, Jacob. W.F. 1978. Fr. Eddan t. Ekelöf. Repetitorium om
   rättskällor in Norden. Malmö: Studentlitteratur.

Tammelo, Ilmar. 1971. Survival and Surpassing. Melbourne: Hawthorn.

----- 1977. Theorie der Gerechtigkeit. Freiburg - München: Alber.

----- 1980. Ungerechtigkeit als Grenzsituation. Schopenhauer
   Jahrbuch 61.

Taxell, Lars Erik. 1987. Demokrati. Åbo: Academy Press.

Tay. Alice Erh-Soon. 1979. The Sense of Justice in the Common Law.
   In: E. Kamenka and A. Erh-Soon Tay, ed., Justice. London: Edward
   Arnold.

Thibaut, A.F.J. 1802. Theorie der logischen Auslegung des Römischen
   Rechts. 2 ed. Reprinted in: H.G. Gadamer and C. Boehm, edd.,
   Seminar: Philosophische Hermeneutik.

Thornstedt, Hans. 1960. Legality and Teleological Construction of
   Statutes in Criminal Law. Scandinavian Studies in Law 4.

Toulmin, Stephen. 1964. The Uses of Argument. Cambridge: University
   Press.

Tranöy, Knut Erik. 1976. The Foundations of Cognitive Activity.
   Inquiry.

----- 1980. Norms of Inquiry: Rationality, Consistency Requirements
   and Normative Conflict. In: R. Hilpinen, ed., Rationality of
   Science. Dordrecht: Reidel.

----- 1985. Civil Disobedience. In: Rechtstheorie Beiheft 8. Berlin.

Trigg, Robert. 1973: <u>Reason and Commitment</u>. Cambridge: University Press.

Tugendhat, E. 1979. Comments on Some Methodological Aspects of Rawls' "Theory of Justice". <u>Analyse und Kritik. Zeitschrift für Sozialwissenschaften</u> 1.

Tuomela, Raimo. 1977. <u>Human Action and Its Explanation</u>. Dordrecht - Boston: Reidel.

Vaihinger, H. 1922. <u>Die Philosophie der Als-Ob</u>. 7th ed. Leipzig.

Verdross, Alfred. 1930. Die Rechtstheorie Hans Kelsens. In: H. Klecatsky, R. Marcic, H. Schambeck, edd., <u>Die Wiener rechtstheorietische Schule</u>. Frankfurt - Zürich - Salzburg - München 1968: Europa Verlag, Universitätsverlag, Anton Pustet.

----- 1971. <u>Statisches und dynamisches Naturrecht</u>. Freiburg: Rombach.

Walter, Robert. 1968. Kelsens Rechtslehre im Spiegel rechtsphilosophischer Diskussion in Österreich. <u>Österreichische Zeitschrift für öffentliches Recht und Völkerrecht</u> 18.

Wedberg, Anders. 1951. Some Problems in the Logical Analysis of Legal Science. <u>Theoria</u>.

Weinberger, Ota. 1971. Die Pluralität der Normensysteme. <u>ARSP</u> LVII.

----- 1978. Theorie der Gerechtigkeit und De-lege-ferenda Argumentation. <u>Österreichische Zeitschrift für öffentliches Recht und Völkerrecht</u> 29.

----- 1979. Jenseits von Positivismus und Naturrecht. <u>ARSP</u> Supplementa - Vol.1, Part 1. IVR World Congress. Basel.

----- and Weinberger, Christa. 1979. <u>Logik, Semantik, Hermeneutik</u>. München: Beck.

Welinder, Carsten. 1974. <u>Skattepolitik</u>. Lund: Gleerups.

----- 1975. <u>Beskattning av inkomst och förmögenhet</u>. 4th ed. Lund: Studentlitteratur.

Westerberg, Ole. 1973. <u>Allmän förvaltningsrätt</u>. Stockholm: Nordiska bokhandeln.

Wild, Aart H. de. 1980. <u>De Rationaliteit van het rechterlijk Oordeel</u> Deventer: Kluwer.

Winch, P. 1958. <u>The Idea of Social Science and Its Relation to Philosophy</u>. London: Routledge & Kegan Paul.

Wittgenstein, Ludwig. 1922. <u>Tractatus Logico-Philosophicus</u>. London, Boston and Henley: Routledge & Kegan Paul.

----- 1953. <u>Philosophical Investigations</u>. Oxford: Blackwell.

----- 1979. <u>On Certainty</u>. Oxford: Blackwell.

Wolff. R. P. 1971. In: E. Kent (ed,), <u>Revolution and the Rule of Law</u>. Englewood Cliffs.

----- 1977. <u>Understanding Rawls</u>. A Reconstruction and Critique of A Theory of Justice. Princeton.

Wright, Georg Henrik von. 1957. Deontic Logic. In: <u>Logical Studies</u>. London: Routledge & Kegan Paul.

----- 1963. <u>The Variety of Goodness</u>. London: Routledge & Kegan Paul.

----- 1963b. <u>Norm and Action</u>. London: Routledge & Kegan Paul.

----- 1972. Wittgenstein on Certainty. In: v. Wright (ed.), Problems in the Theory of Knowledge. Den Haag.

Wróblewski. Jerzy. 1959. Zagadnienia teorii wykladni prawa ludowego Warsaw: PWN.

----- 1969. Prawo i plaszczyzny jego badania. Panstwo i Prawo.

----- 1972. Sadowe stosowanie prawa. Warsaw: PWN.

----- 1974. Legal Syllogism and Rationality of Judicial Decision. Rechtstheorie.

Ziembinski, Zygmunt. 1966. Logiczne podstawy prawoznawstwa. Warsaw: Wydawnictwo Prawnicze.

----- 1970. Norms of Competence as Norms of Conduct. Archivum Iuridicum Cracoviense 3.

----- 1980. Problemy podstawowe prawoznawstwa. Warsaw: PWN.

Zippelius, Reinhold. 1982 Rechtsphilosophie. München: Beck.

Zittelmann, E. 1903. Lücken im Recht. Leipzig.

441